D1399750

LEARNING THROUGH MOVEMENT
Teaching cognitive content through physical activities

To Carol

LEARNING THROUGH MOVEMENT
Teaching cognitive content through physical activities

PETER H. WERNER, P.E.D.

Associate Professor
University of South Carolina
Columbia, South Carolina

ELSIE C. BURTON, Ph.D.

Associate Professor
Florida State University
Tallahassee, Florida

with 503 illustrations

The C. V. Mosby Company

ST. LOUIS • TORONTO • LONDON   1979

Printed in the United States of America

The C. V. Mosby Company
11830 Westline Industrial Drive, St. Louis, Missouri 63141

Library of Congress Cataloging in Publication Data

Werner, Peter H
   Learning through movement.

   Bibliography: p.
   Includes index.
   1. Perceptual-motor learning. 2. Physical educa-
tion for children. 3. Concept learning. I. Burton,
Elsie Carter, joint author. II. Title.
LB1067.W46   372.8′6   78-11895
ISBN 0-8016-5415-7

GW/M/M 9 8 7 6 5 4 3 2 1   02/C/215

PREFACE

In the concept of teaching, the whole child is paramount in modern curricular planning. Educators claim they teach through the cognitive, affective, and psychomotor domains but often simply end up teaching a fragmented curriculum not in the best interest of the child.

It is our contention that learning is an active process. We also believe it is impossible to teach every child every fact there is to learn. The approach taken in this book will allow educators to teach major concepts to children and, at the same time, be provided with concrete evidence of the learning outcome and tangible evidence of a goal achieved.

One of the principal advantages of the action-oriented learning activities included herein is that they are multisensory in nature. Because children are physically active, they are *doing* as well as observing. They are receiving sensory input from their tactual and kinesthetic senses, as well as from the visual and auditory. Therefore this approach is an effective means of stimulating and motivating all children, including those who experience learning difficulties.

This book has been written for all adults who have the desire to make children's learning more meaningful and joyful. This includes classroom teachers, curriculum coordinators, parents, and physical education supervisors, as well as the teachers in specialized subjects such as physical education, art, music, and special education. The outline format at the beginning of each learning activity facilitates locating the desired concepts and preparing the learning materials. The description of the activities is clearly written and well illustrated so that those individuals without previous experience in conducting physical activities can readily select and conduct any of the lesson content.

The introductory section establishes the framework of the book and provides the rationale for action-oriented learning. The book is then divided into five parts, each dealing with an aspect of the elementary school curriculum. Part One is concerned with the language arts. It is divided into three chapters relating how listening and speaking, reading and writing, and nonverbal communication can be taught through physical activities. Part Two presents the concepts of mathematics. Lessons that have been developed are the whole numbers and the metric system; mathematical sentences, sets, and field properties; and quantitative ideas, measuring and graphing, and geometry. Part Three discusses the teaching of science. It covers stability, levers, Newton's laws of motion, factors affecting the human body and its movement, sound, and biological and earth sciences. Social studies concepts including living and working together, our home the earth, our country's heritage, and regional studies are presented in Part Four. Part Five concerns the related arts concepts. Coverage includes activities designed to teach the concepts of music, with activities exploring dynamics, tempo, pitch, mood, shape, phrasing, and rhythmic structure. The common concepts of art and movement are explored to include line, form, shape, space, color, and design and composition.

The Appendix contains descriptions of stunts that can be used in providing active learning experiences for elementary school children.

The preparation of a manuscript of this kind requires the acknowledgment of many people's efforts. We would like to thank our fellow teachers, our students, and the children in the public schools of Columbia, South Carolina, and Tallahassee, Florida, for their cooperation in the testing of these lessons. Special thanks are extended to Mickey Adair for the excellent photographs, to Peggy Higgins for the fine drawings, and to Susan Jenkins for the line art.

We are grateful to Connie Lane for her assistance and to her students from the Developmental Research School, Florida State University at Tallahassee, for serving as the photographic models. We extend our appreciation to David L. Gallahue and Lisa Rini for their careful review of the manuscript. We are also indebted to our typists—Mary Steffens, Midge Gill, Ruby Peebles, and Kathy Hendrix. Finally, we would like to thank our families for being so understanding during those long hours we were at work.

Peter H. Werner

Elsie C. Burton

CONTENTS

INTRODUCTION TO ACTIVE LEARNING

I hear and I forget
I see and I remember
I do and I understand

CHINESE PROVERB

Learning through movement is the oldest teaching method. Among primitive people, one's education consisted of learning how to physically survive. The educational process consisted of parents teaching their children the skills necessary to survive in their environment. In time the pendulum swung from a system that was entirely physical to one that was purely intellectual. Gradually educators have come to realize that intelligence permeates all human activity and that it is inseparably interrelated with emotions, social interaction, and physical activity. This realization fostered the development of teaching methods that combine mental and physical activity.

MULTISENSORY LEARNING

Utilizing physical activity as a learning medium is essential in modern education because the world of today's children is information rich and action poor (Coleman, 1972). Electronic media have made possible rapid and effective transmission of vast amounts of information, providing children with a wide variety of vicarious learning experiences. Children have for the most part responded by spending more and more time in this sedate environment of artificially induced experiences and less and less time in activities involving contact with the real world. These factors evidence the need for learning experiences that involve the full range of the human body's sensory mechanisms.

The messages of electronic media are received by the visual and auditory senses. If children are to develop as fully functioning human beings, they must be aware of the world as perceived through all their senses: they must develop multisensory perception. They must physically and sensorially as well as mentally interact with the subject matter.

Learning involves an interaction between the learner and the subject matter. Thus the learning process has three components:

Child → Interacting with → Subject matter

The nature and extent of the learning that takes place is dependent on the frequency, variety, and intensity of this interaction. *What* the child learns as well as *how much* he learns and *how long it is retained* is determined by the stimulus properties of the learning medium and the effect these have on the child. When physical activity is utilized as the learning medium, the interaction between the child and the subject matter is more complete because the whole child is actively involved. For a long time educators have talked about the desirability of teaching the whole child; yet many have failed to realize this occurs only when the child is physically as well as mentally active.

There are several reasons why physical activity is an effective learning medium.

1. Children more readily attend to the learning task. Children in the primary grades typically have short attention spans, and the attention of children in the intermediate grades is easily distracted. When children are physically active, they tend to be totally involved in the learning experience. This assists them in focusing on the relevant attributes of the learning task and helps prevent their attention from being distracted by extraneous factors.

2. The children are dealing with reality. The facts are tangible. An action-oriented learning task provides direct rather than vicarious experience. The children actually manipulate objects or situations. This enables them to see the facts applied and the principles in opera-

The whole child actively involved in learning.

tion. They do not just read about the content—they experience it.

3. It is a process approach in which development of the affective domain is a primary concern. Affective development is enhanced because the children must closely attend to the stimulus message and actively respond to it. The movement response is both natural and pleasurable and therefore acts as a positive reinforcer. This promotes development of positive attitudes toward the learning process and the particular content being learned.

4. Action-centered learning helps compensate for some of the sensory deficiencies inherent in sedentary activities in which only cognitive operations are employed. When children are physically active, they receive sensory input from their tactual and kinesthetic senses. This makes learning a multisensory experience in which they are feeling as well as observing.

5. It is results oriented. Each learning activity culminates in an observable goal having been attained. Thus the children experience immediate rather than delayed gratification.

6. It provides an incentive for self-directed

learning. The learning process is exciting and satisfying. This has a tendency to promote participation in learning activities that are self-initiated.

These six points evidence how combining mental and physical activities can enhance the child's interaction with the subject matter. The activities described in this book were designed to assist you in making learning a stimulating and exciting adventure. These methods and activities are not viewed as replacements for seat work, multimedia, crafts, or other activities you have found to be effective. Rather, they are designed to serve as alternative ways for children to learn. Nor is the content presented here considered all inclusive. Instead it is viewed as a place for you to begin. It is anticipated that as you become acquainted with this method, you and the children will create additional ways of using movement as a learning medium.

LEARNING ACTIVITIES

To facilitate your locating and selecting lesson content, a clearly defined format has been followed in this text. A part of the book has been devoted to each curricular area. The parts have then been divided into chapters by grouping related concepts. These concepts are stated at the beginning of each learning activity. The learning activities are presented in the following outline form:

- Concept
- Level
- Subconcepts
- Materials
- Activities

The concept is the lesson theme, the principal fact or idea being studied. For example, one of the concepts from mathematics is "Identity is one of the field properties of mathematics." A concept from social studies is "A community gradually grows and changes."

Level refers to the learning level of the subject matter. The learning levels are specified as beginning, intermediate, or advanced, depending on the complexity of the concept and the learning tasks. Learning levels are not synonymous with grade levels. Rather, learning levels are primarily dependent on the child's previous experiences.

Activities designated as being on the beginning level are those in which the concept is a single basic fact. In a sequential curriculum, these would ordinarily be introduced in the primary grades. However, in some instances a subject may not be introduced until the intermediate or upper elementary grades, in which case it would be necessary to start with the beginning level concepts. You would, however, modify the learning activities so that they would be challenging to the older children.

Intermediate level refers to concepts and activities requiring some previous acquaintance with the content. Most of the intermediate level concepts would ordinarily be covered in the curriculum of grades ranging from 2 through 4. That is, these concepts are appropriate for second-grade children who have previously become familiar with the beginning level concepts of that particular subject. They are also relevant to older children who have been introduced to the subject but who are not ready to deal with advanced concepts.

The advanced level includes more complex concepts and those evolving out of a basic knowledge of the subject. These activities challenge the children to recognize relationships between several components of a problem as well as between the different elements of the learning task.

Subconcepts are divisions of the main concept. Whenever possible, the principal concept has been broken down into its simplest form and stated as subconcepts. In some instances it is more meaningful to deal with the principal concept as a whole, and in these instances no subconcepts are stated.

The activities presented in this book utilize materials available in most schools. Emphasis has been placed on using the existing equipment, and when different kinds of materials are needed, suggestions are given concerning how these can be improvised. Whenever possible, it is suggested that the children be responsible for making the equipment because this is considered an essential learning experience. Useful ideas and instructions for making simple equipment are given in the books *Inexpensive Physi-*

cal Education Equipment for Children and *Perceptual-Motor Development Equipment: Inexpensive Ideas and Activities* (cited at the end of the Introduction). Involving the parents and the parent-teacher organization in obtaining and developing equipment is an excellent way of opening the lines of communication and enhancing public relations. One of the advantages of active learning is that it can and should continue outside the class situation. If this carry-over is to be fully implemented, the parents must be made aware of the need and the opportunity. It is therefore essential that they play an active role in the child's learning whenever possible.

In most instances several learning activities are suggested for each concept or subconcept. They are sequentially arranged in order of difficulty. Some of the descriptions include suggested verbal cues. These are given as examples to assist you in formulating your own teaching techniques.

The learning activities in this text reflect the movement education approach to teaching physical activities. The tenets of this approach follow:

- Physical activity is referred to as human movement.
- Basic movements are taught first and then used as the basis for development of more complex skills.
- Exploratory and creative activities are the principal learning medium.
- Emphasis is placed on development of self and body awareness and on the child understanding his movement potential.

Because this is a relatively new approach, some of the terms used to refer to various aspects of children's physical activities may be new to you. An attempt has been made throughout the text to explain these. If you desire further information relative to this approach, you will find a much more extensive coverage in the books *The New Physical Education for Elementary School Children* and *A Conceptual Approach to Moving and Learning*.

LEARNING ENVIRONMENT

Active learning requires a physical environment designed for this specific purpose. Both indoor and outdoor facilities should provide maximum learning opportunities. The physical environment should stimulate the children's curiosity and evoke a desire to explore and participate. The facilities should be readily available so that children can use them for independent study and recreational purposes as well as for group classwork.

The school grounds should include a hard surface area (either asphalt or concrete) and a large, smooth sod or dirt surface. These areas should be level and well drained. An area with a natural slope or mounds provides additional play and learning opportunities. The hard surface area should have colorful permanent markings that include outline maps of the state and the United States, geometric designs, a clock face, grids with numbers and letters, and any other designs you find useful in conducting

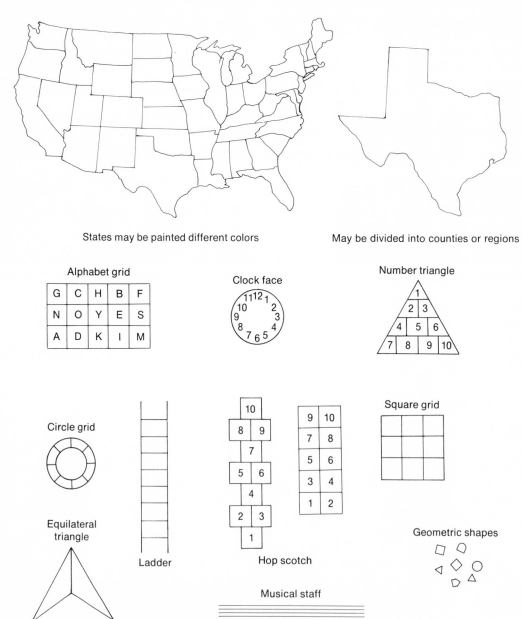

Examples of permanent playground markings on hard-surface areas.

games, contests, dances, or exploratory activities. A number of different permanent markings are shown in the accompanying illustrations. It is also helpful to have permanent markings on the sod surface, such as a goal line, starting line, and center line. Helpful suggestions for planning and constructing outdoor areas are given in the two articles "A Rebuilt Playground" and "An Experience Center for Elementary Physical Education."

A multipurpose room is preferable as an indoor teaching station, although a large classroom without furniture can be used. The primary consideration is that the children can move freely and safely. Again, it is convenient to have permanent markings such as lines and a center circle. These may be marked specific sizes and distances to facilitate working with math and music concepts. It may be helpful to mark the walls with the directional designations north, south, east, and west, the corners of the room being marked northwest, northeast, southwest, and southeast.

If these types of areas are not available in your school, improvise! Hallways, walkways, and a part of the parking lot can be used on a temporary basis. Then draw up a master plan and recruit the assistance of parents and other willing workers. The time spent in developing this type of learning environment is a worthwhile, long-range investment.

SELECTED REFERENCES

Burton, Elsie C.: The new physical education for elementary school children, Boston, 1977, Houghton Mifflin Co.

Coleman, James S.: The children have outgrown the schools, Psychology Today 5:72ff, Feb., 1972.

Cratty, Bryant J.: Active learning: games to enhance academic abilities, Englewood Cliffs, N.J., 1971, Prentice-Hall, Inc.

Cratty, Bryant J.: Intelligence in Action: Physical Activities for Enhancing Intellectual Abilities, Englewood Cliffs, N.J., 1973, Prentice-Hall, Inc.

Gallahue, David L., Werner, Peter H., and Luedke, George C.: A conceptual approach to moving and learning, New York, 1975, John Wiley & Sons, Inc.

Humphrey, James H.: Education of children through motor activity, Springfield, Ill., 1975, Charles C Thomas, Publisher.

Kidder, Worden: A rebuilt playground, Journal of Physical Education and Recreation 47:16-18, Sept., 1976.

Moore, Jane B., and Bond, Aletha W.: An experience center for elementary physical education, Journal of Physical Education and Recreation 46:21-23, Jan., 1975.

Werner, Peter, and Rini, Lisa: Perceptual-motor development equipment: inexpensive ideas and activities, New York, 1976, John Wiley & Sons, Inc.

Werner, Peter, and Simmons, Richard: Inexpensive physical education equipment for children, Minneapolis, 1976, Burgess Publishing Co.

PART ONE

Language arts

Forming letters and words with the body.

Language may be the most important tool children learn in the schools because it can help them deal effectively with all other information they process. The use of an appropriate language system helps children learn to communicate. They can learn to communicate well through a language arts program in the elementary school that includes the areas of listening, speaking, reading, and writing. Nonverbal language or communication through actions is also learned directly or indirectly by the use of various bodily gestures. It is similar to people not being able to hear the words because their actions give them away.

All facets of the language arts program are interrelated and can be divided into two general categories, receiving and interpreting messages and expressing messages. Receiving messages is sometimes called decoding and is the receptive phase of language development. Through this phase of development, a child learns to understand messages that come to him from an outside source. Effectively receiving visual, auditory, tactile, olfactory, and gustatory cues help a child interpret incoming messages to the brain. Auditory and visual cues become the primary way to decode messages in the development of a formal language system.

Children learn to decode auditory and visual messages by associating sounds and sights with different people and objects (listening). Initially the infant learns who "mama" is and what she does for him. Gradually concrete objects such as a rattle and ball are associated with word cues and sights or with word cues given to the objects. Later the child learns to associate abstract word cues such as right, left, in, on, and through with positions in his environment.

Refinement in the decoding process comes when the child is ready to visually decode the abstract symbols known as the alphabet into groups of letters known as words (reading). Initially children read pictures, as evidenced in the many illustrations in children's literature books. Gradually abstract symbols (TABLE), when arranged in a certain order, come to be interpreted as having the same meaning as a table. Children learn to attach meaning to words. Words are combined into phrases, sentences, and paragraphs as children gradually learn to decode written symbols from the left of the page to the right and from top to bottom.

The expressive phase of language development is sometimes called encoding. Through this phase of development, a child learns to respond to messages that he is receiving and interpreting. Responses are in the form of speaking (verbal expression) and writing and/or manual actions (motor expression). Children learn to make verbal responses to auditory and visual stimuli. Books, toys, pictures, television, conversations, stories, and games provide auditory and visual stimuli to encourage verbal responses. Auditory stimuli such as "Tell me what you did," "What do you like to do best?" and "Tell me the likenesses and differences of two different objects" provide specific cues to encourage a child's speaking abilities. Such cues are much better than those in which a child is allowed to make a one-word, yes or no, answer. Completing a story and telling stories are other auditory cues for verbal responses.

Motor expression progresses gradually from controlling the large muscle actions (grasping) to mastering the fine motor responses (writing). Children learn to express themselves motorically through pantomiming or imitating the actions of adults, other children, animals, or even toys. Manipulating materials such as blocks, dolls, toys, cans, dowels, and number rods are other ways in which children learn to express themselves. Dramatic play situations involving dress up materials, nursery rhymes, animal make-believe, fantasy, role playing, and adventure stories also provide opportunities for children to express themselves. Children learn to scribble, color, draw pictures, and construct geometric designs. Gradually they learn to put various straight, curved, or diagonal lines together to form letters of the alphabet. Children learn to write letters, words, sentences, and eventually their own stories.

As children learn to receive, interpret, and send messages, the concepts of association, closure, and sequential memory assist children in the development of their language skills. The concept of association enables children to interpret likenesses and differences in material presented through auditory or visual pathways. Children learn to classify or seriate objects according to color, size, shape, and texture. The concept of closure enables a child to complete a message he is receiving even though the message is incomplete. For example, if a child sees or hears the partial word *teleph,* he interprets the message to mean telephone. The important concept is to help each child use the incomplete information he has in an organized way to make an educated guess as to the correct response. Memory enables children to retain and interpret messages more effectively. Auditory and visual sequencing and processing of information in an orderly manner enables a child to recreate the order of events in a given situation in terms of time and/or space. Auditory and/or visual recall and the ability to reproduce a series of ordered number sequences, motor tasks, patterns, letters, or directions are examples of memory sequencing.

The different facets of language development are closely interrelated. Areas of study such as spelling, writing, listening, reading, speaking, and nonverbal communication should be considered as component parts of the broad area of communication. It was common practice to treat such areas of study as separate subjects in the past. Subjects became isolated and unrelated. Their full potential as mediums of expression have perhaps never been fully realized. Fortunately current approaches to language arts programs such as the Peabody REBUS Reading Program, the Sullivan Programmed Reading Series, the Science Research Associates Reading Program, Sesame Street, The Electric Company, and the language program resulting from the Illinois Test of Psycholinguistic Abilities relate the various language areas to particular areas of interest. Language arts textbook series also teach the development of a unified program rather than teaching each of the areas as separate entities. As a result, all facets of the language arts are used in the solution of problems in all curriculum areas.

Children who have difficulties in learning to communicate effectively with their environment are commonly referred to as being dyslexic, dysgraphic, slow learning disabled, or a variety of other labels. Various perceptual-motor problems such as body image, balance, laterality, directionality, spatial awareness, form perception, visual perception, and figure-ground perception prevent these children from learning to cope successfully with language development. Experiences in movement are often designed to aid such children in the development of readiness skills to prepare them for success in the communicative processes. However, since it is not the purpose of this book to develop a perceptual-motor program, Part One will be restricted to those physical education experiences that enhance the development of language arts skills.

Communication skills in the language arts should be developed in all areas of the curriculum in which physical education can be utilized to enhance the development of language skills. Sequential chapters will specifically outline how movement activities can be designed to reinforce listening and speaking abilities, reading and writing abilities, and nonverbal communication.

Chapter 1

LISTENING AND SPEAKING

Listening may be defined as the reception of familiar sound combinations to which a person brings meaning through his experience and from which he takes meaning as sources for reaction, interpretation, and knowing. As a result, any attempt to help children develop skills in listening must take into account the various levels of listening, purposes for listening, and factors that influence listening. During infancy there is little conscious listening on the part of the child. Because of his egocentricity during early childhood, he is easily distracted by people and objects and thus listens only when he is the center of attention. Half-listening occurs when the child is more interested in his ideas, waiting to break into the conversation. Passive listening follows when the child has little or no reaction to what is being said. Sporadic listening occurs when the child shows an interest in segments of the conversation that are related to his own experiences but "tunes out" when the conversation no longer relates to him. The highest levels of listening follow when the child shows reaction to what is being said through questions, comments, and emotional and/or intellectual response, resulting in a complete understanding of what is being said.

Just as there are different levels of listening, so are there different purposes for listening. One may listen to follow directions, for information, for enjoyment, to evaluate, to appreciate, to communicate, to discriminate sounds, and to solve problems. To achieve these purposes, listening experiences at the elementary level should include conversing, sharing experiences, discussing, interviewing, planning, evaluating, storytelling, dramatizing, improvising, reporting, and listening to music and poetry.

The factors that influence listening include a consideration of the physical environment and social, emotional, and psychological factors. With reference to the physical environment, it should contain no sound distractions that interfere with the primary sound source (figure-ground). A room or gymnasium with good acoustics is essential in this respect. Radios, vent fans, and air conditioning and heating systems should be controlled to prevent distractions to children. Outside, playgrounds should be located so that sound distractions are minimal from cars, trucks, and other people passing by. Teachers can control the social, emotional, and psychological factors that influence listening by providing for and reinforcing good listening habits in children.

Speech may be defined as the communication of thought and emotion by means of voice, language, and body action. Speaking is a refined method of stimulating thoughts, ideas, and concepts, for through speaking people share their experiences with others.

Just as in listening, children progress through several developmental levels as the speech process matures. A small infant in the random stage babbles sounds to communicate his needs and gain attention. The jargon stage follows as an infant takes pleasure in imitating the melodic patterns of those who talk to him (cooing). He gains skill in making chosen sounds at will. During the echolalic stage a small child makes his first attempts at native speech. Lip sounds (p, b, m, and w) used with the vowel sounds develop first. Sounds made with the tongue (t, d, n, k, and g) follow. Last to appear are the sound consonants (l, r, s, and z). By the time a child is 2 years of age he should be talking. Initially most words practiced are nouns. Later the child modifies nouns, uses verbs, and speaks in short phrases. By 3 years a child can speak in complete sentences. Structured awareness of the parts of speech and sentences and the creative use of speech follow from the child's elementary years through adulthood.

The objective purposes of speech at the elementary level include a desire to express ideas effectively, clearly, and accurately. The skill to use one's voice with articulation and inflection so that one can be heard, interpreted, and understood are further purposes of developmental speech. Speech activities to develop these objectives should include sharing experiences, conversing, telling news, making announcements, making introductions, telephoning, and giving directions, explanations, and instructions.

The physical environment as well as social, emotional, and psychological factors also affect the development of children's speech. Teachers should provide a positive environment where children are encouraged to interact with their peers and adults. The use of problem solving and discovery as teaching methods encourages children to have the freedom to interact and discuss in a group situation, rather than the teacher doing all the talking and decision making in the direct or command style of teaching. The resulting speech opportunities help the children become decision makers.

Although it is often taken for granted, the listening and speaking abilities of children can be greatly enhanced through experiences specifically oriented toward improvement in these areas. With attention focused on receiving and sending messages verbally, specific practice should be concentrated on (1) auditory directions with verbal responses, (2) verbal expressive abilities, (3) auditory association, (4) auditory closure, and (5) auditory memory. In each instance the child must first listen to the message before speaking and making his verbal response. Other exercises concentrate on auditory cues with motor responses and on visual cues with auditory and/or motor responses. Following are some movement experiences that develop the processes of listening and speaking.

Learning activities

Listening

CONCEPT: Listening to and making animal sounds helps develop language skills.

Level: Beginning.

Subconcept: Make-believe is a fun and exciting way to further a child's ability to make and distinguish various sounds (decoding).

Materials: None.

Activities: The children should be divided into small groups or partners. The objective of this experience is for the children to hear an animal sound, decide what animal has been described, and then make appropriate movements to interpret its particular characteristics. The game begins by having one of the children make an animal sound such as ''bow-wow,'' ''moo-moo.'' The children should then interpret the movements of that particular animal and discuss the characteristics of the animal orally.

CONCEPT: Responding to directions is an effective way to show you are listening.

Level: Beginning.

Subconcept: Learning about colors, parts of the body, balance, and listening skills may all be enhanced through a color grid movement experience.

Materials: A color grid is drawn on the floor (Fig. 1-2).

Activities: Depending on the size of the grid, 3 or 4 children should stand near the grid. One child should call out a color on the grid and a particular part of the body (head, right arm, left knee, etc.). Each participant should follow the directions by placing the appropriate body part on corresponding colors. The children may have to share squares. They must hold their body part on the square and add body parts on other colors until they are told to move a particular body part to a new position.

The game ends when the children either lose their balance or become so tangled they cannot move. The game should be repeated, allowing each child a chance to give directions.

Fig. 1-1. What animal are you?

Fig. 1-2. Color grid.

CONCEPT: A controlled physical environment will determine the extent to which one can speak and be heard effectively.

Level: Beginning.

Subconcept: Auditory figure-ground perception may be enhanced through movement experiences.

Materials: An audio cassette recorder.

Activities: This lesson is written to stress the importance of a good physical environment for speaking and listening effectively. To accomplish this, one may contrive learning situations with purposeful distractions to stress the need for a proper figure-ground relationship. Auditory distractions—and visual ones, for that matter—must be kept at a minimum for proper speaking and listening conditions. Some examples follow:

1. Tape record sound effects from records or from the child's environment, such as sirens, auto horns, toilets flushing, water running, and trains passing. Teach the children to recognize each of the sounds and move creatively to each.
2. Mask the sounds in no. 1 by placing distracting noises in the background. In addition to the sound effects, choose action words or give exercise commands and mask them with distracting noises (radio playing in the background). See if the child can distinguish the figure (primary message) from the background. Have the children move to the appropriate sound effect, action work, or verbal direction.
3. Record two or three sounds or words simultaneously or sequentially. Then play them as the child listens. Challenge him to identify all the sounds or words.
4. Play several similar sounds with variations of high or low pitch, loud or soft sounds, and harsh or mellow sounds. Have the child describe each sound that is made or compare two sounds that he hears. Then challenge him to make appropriate movements according to level, force, and flow.
5. Refer to the lessons on reasons why some sounds are not heard in Chapter 12.

CONCEPT: Listen to the story to comprehend its meaning and remember what happened.

Level: Beginning.

Subconcept: Creative storytelling and movement improvisation can be used as effective tools in teaching children the concept of auditory association.

Materials: None.

Activities: Choose a theme, focus, ethic, or moral, and fabricate a story to tell the children. Fabricate in the story ample opportunity for word association and creative movement possibilities.

EXAMPLES

- Why an elephant has a trunk
- If the moon is really made of green cheese
- Consequences of not eating well-rounded meals
- Why the tooth fairy rewards children
- The design and naming of the Volkswagen "bug"

Others are limited to your imagination. Here is a sample story.

Once upon a time there was a boy who was very hungry. So he went out in the woods to search for some food. While tracking in the woods, he stepped on some twigs that went "crack." Up jumped a rabbit. The rabbit ran and the boy chased. The faster the boy ran, the faster the rabbit fled. The rabbit ran into a cave. The boy entered the cave and began to search, but because he didn't have a light, he stumbled around. All of a sudden he touched something furry that growled. Can you guess what it was? Yes, a bear. The bear with its sharp teeth chased the boy out of the cave. The boy ran and ran up a hill, and then all of a sudden felt himself airborne. He had fallen off a cliff and was toppling until "splash!" He hit the water. He then decided he would catch some fish, but his hands were not quick enough, and he could not swim fast enough to catch the fish. The river he landed in was so swift that he was soon swept out to sea. All of a sudden he saw some fins circling. The fish's name begins with an *s*. Do you know what it was? Yes, a shark. Nearby he saw part of an old boat that had been wrecked. He climbed into it, and although it barely floated, he made his way to shore. Once on shore he entered the jungle to search for food. He saw animals whose names begin with *s, o, m, e, l, t.* Can you think of their names? Each time he tried to capture each animal he didn't succeed. The snake crawled too fast into a tree; the ostrich ran too fast; the monkey swung too fast from tree to tree; the elephant, lion, and tiger—well, they were just too mean, large, and ferocious for the boy to think he could capture them. So, very discouraged and ever so hungry, the boy walked out of the jungle and into a nearby village to search for something to eat. One of the villagers invited him to help with his chores. In return he fed the boy the greatest meal he could imagine. The villager was happy with the boy's work and the boy liked the food, so he decided to stay and help the villager with his work.

Morals or ethics. Humans may not be the fastest, largest, or most ferocious creatures on earth, but they can adapt their talents to use what they have to the best of their ability and be successful and happy. Be helpful around the house, do chores, contribute, and you will appreciate your meals, home, and love from your parents a little more.

CONCEPT: Listen to the beat of the music to develop rhythmical awareness.

Level: Beginning.

Subconcept: Experiences with rhythmical and temporal awareness help children develop auditory discrimination (decoding) and auditory sequential memory.

Materials: A record player and a record with 4/4 meter music such as ''Clap, snap, tap'' or ''And the Beatles Go On,'' both by Ambrose Brazelton.*

Activities: Activities to develop auditory discrimination and auditory sequential memory may be developed as follows:

1. Snap your fingers, clap your hands, and tap your knees in a specific sequence, such as snap, snap, tap, tap, clap, clap. Have the child repeat the sequence after you. Make up others.
2. Have the child close his eyes or turn around and perform this same activity. This time the child has to rely on auditory perception alone to interpret the sequence and then perform it.
3. Have the children work together in pairs to develop their own sequences. Play music and have them keep time to the music.
4. Give a sequence verbally to a child and have him perform it motorically without any practice.
5. Perform a sequence motorically and have the child verbally tell you what sequence was executed.

CONCEPT: Listening to the sounds of letters in words helps develop the skill of auditory decoding.

Level: Beginning.

Subconcepts: (1) The skill of auditory discrimination (decoding) can be enhanced through movement experiences. (2) Movement experiences can be used to develop auditory sequential memory.

Materials: Make a chart similar to Fig. 1-3 to aid children in learning respective body positions or poses for each of the letter sounds.

Activities: Go over the chart with the children and explain to them that you will verbally say words that begin (or end) with the letters in the chart.* When they hear a given sound, they should assume the body position or pose that corresponds to the sound. Practice several times with each of the sounds first so that the children can memorize the body positions for each in an effort to make the remainder of the lesson entirely verbal. When the children are ready, begin saying one word at a time, allowing a pause for the children to assume the correct body position. Use words whose letters sound similar. Begin by using words with first letters sounding alike, then switch to words in which the last letters sound alike. After the children have mastered one word, proceed to two-, three-, and four-word sequences. Then allow the children enough time to assume each of the body poses in order.

CONCEPT: Spelling lists are a source of opportunities for children to use their vocabulary and language skills.

Level: Beginning.

Subconcept: The auditory memory of the child and his ability to combine the individual letters into words are enhanced through movement experiences.

Materials: Tape or draw an alphabet grid on the floor or hard surface, using capital or small letters (Fig. 1-4).

Activities: Have the children work in pairs and design enough alphabet grids for each set

---

*Educational Activities, Inc., Freeport, N.Y.

---

*This lesson may also be used to help children learn to discriminate between long and short vowel sounds: ā, ă; bāle, băt.

Fig. 1-3. Decode the sound you hear.

of partners. Have one partner orally spell out a word, C-A-T. The other partner should sequentially hop or jump into each appropriate box, return to the outside of the grid, and vocally say the word that was spelled. Have the children take turns being the speller and mover. Spelling lists, word lists, dictionaries, etc. may be used for word sources. As a variation, the children may try to define the word spelled as they hop or jump out of the grid. They may also make up an oral sentence containing the word that was spelled.

CONCEPT: Verbalizing likenesses and differences of categories of objects helps children learn to express themselves.

Level: Beginning.

Subconcept: Letter and word association

Fig. 1-4. Spell a word.

can be used as stimulus ideas for movement experiences.

Materials: None.

Activities: Begin this lesson at a chalkboard by asking children words that they know which begin with various letters of the alphabet or which may be classified into categories (machines, animals, transportation). Then, within a list ask the children to make subclassifications. For example, in the O list, which words go together? Why? *(Orangutang, owl, and ostrich go together because they are animals.)* What are some other categories?

O

Orange	Ornery	Oak
Olympics	Owl	Oar
Orangutang	Open	Ostrich
Old		

Machines

Truck	Bicycle	Car
Motorcycle	Can opener	Wheelbarrow
Crane	Typewriter	Digger

In the machine list, which words go together? Why? *(The crane, truck, and digger are all used for road or construction work.)* What are some other categories? Encourage the children to verbalize their awareness of classification, seriation, and likenesses and differences. For

example, how are a can opener and a digger alike? How are a wheelbarrow and a truck alike? How are a bicycle and a motorcycle different? Show me by your movements.

Finally, encourage the children to make creative movement interpretations of the words they have been exploring. For example, what is the shape of an orange? *(Round, small, curved.)* Can you make your body assume that position and roll around the floor? Can you tell me the differences in movement of an orangutang, owl, and ostrich? What are they? Show me. Continue exploring each of the words on the board through movement. Help the children verbalize likenesses and differences of each category through association and movement.

CONCEPT: Beginning word sounds, vowel sounds, and prefixes may be used as cues for movement.

Level: Beginning.

Subconcept: The skills of auditory discrimination (decoding) and auditory closure can be enhanced through movement experiences.

Materials: A playing area laid out as shown in Fig. 16-20.

Activities: The object of this lesson is to play a game, traditionally called ''crows and cranes'' with the children for purposes of stressing auditory discrimination and auditory closure skills. Many variations should be encouraged. To outline the basics of the game, a few simple rules will be given. The group of children should be divided in half, with one team becoming the Crows and the other the Cranes. When the teacher or director says "Crows," the crows chase the cranes to their goal. When the teacher says "Cranes," the cranes chase the crows to their goal. Anyone caught before crossing the goal becomes a member of the other team. Distracter words should be used to keep children listening and in place without moving. Children who chase or flee when a distractor word is used become members of the other team. Variations may be played by using other words with the same beginning sound or letter, short or long vowel sounds, and prefixes.

EXAMPLES

	Word 1	Word 2	Distracter
Beginning sound	Crow	Crane	Cracker, crumpet, Christmas, cranberry, etc.
	School	Scare	Schedule, scarf, scamper, etc.
	Brook	Brick	Bracket, brad, bream, etc.
Beginning letter	Tap	Tape	Tool, ticket, tick, etc.
Vowel sounds	Main	Man	Mail, map, etc.
Prefixes	Important	Impress	Impotent, impact, immobile, etc.
Prefixes	Bicycle	Bicentenial	Bifocal, binoculars, etc.

CONCEPT: Discriminating the length and type of sounds being heard is an important aspect of listening.

Level: Intermediate.

Subconcept: Children can develop better auditory discrimination, auditory closure, and auditory sequential memory through listening to whistle cues.

Materials: Purchase some small toy whistles, yxlophones, or other toy musical instruments from a store.

Activities: Perform the following activities with a group of children to develop auditory discrimination and auditory sequential memory.

1. Stand behind the child and whistle or play a sequence. Use code signals such as long, short, long. Have the child repeat the sequence.
2. Use the whistle or instrument to develop a sequence. Give the child a pencil and paper and have him write it. For example, "—, –, –, —" is long, short, short, long.
3. Whistle or play a sequence of longs and shorts and have the child develop a motoric response such as hopping on one foot on the short cues and jumping on both feet on the long cues. Whistle or play the whole sequence first, then have the child interpret the sequence by jumping and hopping.
4. Whistle or play a sequence and have the child write it on paper, as in no. 2; then have the child interpret the written sequence by jumping and hopping.
5. Establish a playing pattern such as long, short, short, long. . . . Do not complete the sequence. Ask the child what cue follows.
6. Blow or play varying qualities of sound on the whistle or instrument, such as loud, soft, harsh, or mellow. Ask the child to discriminate between these sounds.
7. Develop an auditory tape based on the previous activities.

CONCEPT: Giving directions is an effective way to learn expressive language skills.

Level: Intermediate.

Subconcept: Movement experiences can be used to increase the child's ability to give oral directions and perform after receiving oral directions.

Materials: With tape or shoe polish, design a map on the floor made of names of streets going in different directions (Fig. 1-5).

Activities: The class should be divided so that each member has a partner. The object of this experience is for the student to try to orally explain to his partner how to get to a particular place by using the names of the streets and specific directions such as right, left, 1 block, 2 blocks. The child must first decide where he wants to take his partner. He then gives directions to the partner, who then follows the directions. After finding the appropriate place,

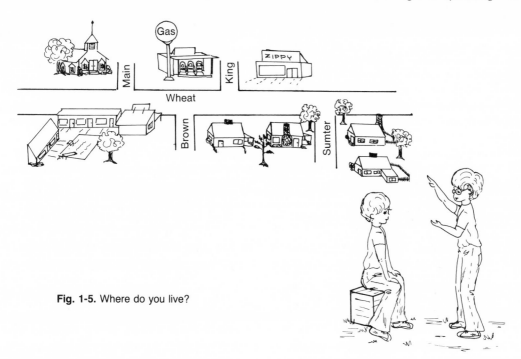

Fig. 1-5. Where do you live?

the partner should take a turn giving oral directions to the first child.

■　■　■

Level: Intermediate.

Subconcept: Auditory sequential memory and learning to give directions can be enhanced through movement experiences.

Materials: None.

Activities: Instruct the children in your group or class to find a partner. Have each set of partners find their own space in the room or gymnasium. Once they are in their own space, tell them that they will take turns being the direction giver and performer. The direction giver should choose action words for the partner to perform. Specific directions might be "Hop four times on the left foot, then three times on the right foot" or "Bounce the ball ten times at a low level with your right hand, then eight times at a medium level with your left hand." Encourage the children to be aware of level, direction, pathway, space, force, time, flow, and other movement qualities as they give directions. As the children become more accomplished, allow them to develop two-, three-, and four-part sequences to perform.

Speaking

CONCEPT: Creative movement expression can be stimulated by creative verbal expression.

Level: Intermediate.

Subconcept: Children can learn to make sounds and perform appropriate movements to accompany each sound.

Materials: None.

Activities: Teach the children that there are three ways to produce humming sounds—the letters *m, n,* and *g.* Have them practice each sound by varying pitch and loudness. Then have them combine their humming sounds with movement. What kind of movement does a humming sound suggest? *(Smooth, free, flowing.)* Have the children show you how they would move to a soft, low-pitched sound; a soft, high-pitched sound; a loud, low-pitched sound; and a loud, high-pitched sound. Change pitch and loudness and develop a humming sequence. What type of movement would be produced by a sound that started with a loud high pitch and finished with a soft low pitch? Next ask the children which letters of the alphabet, when repeated verbally, produce the sound of percussion. *(t, k, b, d.)* Can you think of others? What types of movement are suggested by the percussive sounds? *(Jerky, angular, sharp changes of direction, force, level, etc.)* Have the children practice their sound with accompanying movements. Remind them to change their pitch, loudness, and tempo and to vary their movements accordingly. Develop a sequence of percussive letter sounds with accompanying movements. Place an accent on one of the sounds and change level, direction, pathway, etc. accordingly.

What other sounds can the children make and move accordingly? To get you started, here are some suggestions.

Machine—how it starts, how it runs, how it stops or breaks down

Motorcycle—vroom or zoom; how it starts, runs, stops

Clock—tick, tock, bong, coo-koo

Waterfall—running, hitting, splashing on the rocks

Airplane—taking off, banking, making fancy loops, landing

Can you think of others?

CONCEPT: Telling stories or completing tales or familiar rhymes helps children develop better speaking abilities.

Level: Intermediate.

Subconcept: Auditory closure may be used as a stimulus for creative movement expression and speaking.

Materials: None.

Activities: Use the nursery rhymes (p. 56), fairy tales (p. 59), or stories and folk tales (p. 61) from the nonverbal communication and reading and writing chapters of this book as stimulus ideas in the following activity suggestions. As teacher you should begin a rhyme, tale, or story by saying the first word, line, or phrase. After listening to the beginning, the children should use their sense of closure to finish the rhyme, tale, or story. Then they should make up a movement sequence expression of the rhyme, tale, or story.

EXAMPLES

- Old Mother Hubbard . . . .
- Jack, be nimble . . . .
- Jack and Jill . . . .
- Mary, Mary, quite contrary . . . .
- Little Red Riding Hood walked through the woods taking a picnic basket to her grandmother, and on the way . . . .
- The three little pigs each built a house, and . . . .

CONCEPT: Develop a rhythmical sequence, then teach it to a partner or small group of children.

Level: Intermediate.

Fig. 1-6. What quality of movement does this sound suggest?

Subconcept: Lummi sticks or rhythm sticks can be used to help children develop auditory sequential memory, rhythmical awareness, and communication through speaking.

Materials: Obtain discarded mop handles or broom handles and cut into 12 to 18 inch sections, or purchase ⅜ × ⅓ inch dowel rods from a local hardware store and cut them into sections the same length. Each child should be provided with 2 sticks.

Activities: Have the children perform the following activities to develop their auditory perception skills:

1. Beat out a rhythm as the child watches you. For example, — — — - long, long, long, short or hard, hard, hard, soft. Then have the child beat out the same rhythm with his stick.
2. Perform the same activity while the child has his back turned so that all he can rely on is his auditory perception.
3. Have the child develop his own sequence of beats that he can repeat it or teach it to another child.
4. Play a record with 4/4 meter music, and have the child tap the head of one or two sticks (one or both hands at the same time) to the floor to the beat of the music.

Tell the children the following:

5. Tap the head of one or both sticks to the floor to the beat of the music.
6. While sitting on the floor with your legs spread apart, tap the sticks between your legs, both to the right and to the left, one on each side; or cross arms and tap one on each side.
7. Hit the sticks together in the air to the rhythm of the music while changing the position of the sticks in relation to your body.
8. Flip one or both sticks into the air and catch them to the rhythm of the music.
9. With a partner, tap your sticks to the rhythm of the music, using any of the previous patterns (nos. 4 to 8). Try to create a symmetrical sequence of 8, 16, or 24 beats that you can repeat.
10. Tap your sticks together with a partner to the rhythm of the music. Tap right to right, left to left; right to left, left to right; or cross the sticks and tap both at the same time.
11. With a partner, flip your sticks to each other to the rhythm of the music. Flip right to left, left to right, right to right, left to left, or both sticks at the same time.

Fig. 1-7. With a partner, beat the sticks together.

12. Make up a sequence with a partner, using the previous skills.
13. Using your communication skills of speaking and listening, teach your sequence or routine to another set of partners, and have them teach you theirs.

CONCEPT: Singing or chanting rhymes is an effective way to develop expressive language skills.

Level: Intermediate.

Subconcept: Jump rope activities may be used to help children develop listening and speaking abilities.

Materials: A short jump rope (approximately 8 feet) for each child and a long jump rope (approximately 16 feet) for every group of 3 to 5 children.

Activities: Have the children perform the following jump rope activities to develop their listening and speaking (chanting or singing) abilities:

1. Short jump rope
   a. Place the rope on the floor in a long line and walk along it in as many ways as possible, using one, two, three, and four body parts as a base of support.
   b. Form the rope into different letters of the alphabet by using different body parts such as the feet, elbows, or hands.
   c. Jump or hop from one side of the rope to the other in forward, backward, and sideways directions.
   d. Form the rope into different numbers by solving simple addition, subtraction, multiplication, or division problems posed by the teacher.
   e. Turn the rope forward and try different methods of jumping—rebound jump (short bounce between jumps), jump on one foot, jump on alternate feet, jump in place, and progress forward in a run.
   f. Turn the rope backward and try the latter methods of jumping.
   g. Turn the rope to one side of the body or from one side to the other in figure eight fashion while jumping in place to the rhythm of the turn.
   h. Experiment with changes in tempo while first jumping slow and then fast.

2. Long jump rope
   a. With partners holding the rope at different heights, try to jump over, as in high jumping.
   b. With partners cradling the rope from side to side, try to jump it.
   c. With partners turning the rope, try rebound jumping. Turn the rope at various speeds, starting slow and getting faster.
   d. Try to go in the ''front door'' and ''back door'' while the rope is turning.
   e. Try to jump the long rope while you try to jump a short rope you are turning alone.

3. Jump rope rhymes. Perform the activities for short and long jump ropes while singing or chanting the following rhythm rhymes*:

   a. Gypsy, gypsy, please tell me
      What my husband is going to be:
      A rich man, a poor man, a beggar-man, a thief,
      A doctor, a lawyer, an Indian chief.
   b. Down in the valley where the green grass grows,
      There sat _____ as sweet as a rose.
      She sang and she sang and she sang so sweet,
      Along came _____ and kissed her on the cheek.
      How many kisses did she receive?
      One, two, three, etc. (Turn fast and count until person misses and that's the number of kisses)
   c. Teddy bear, Teddy bear,
      Turn around.
      Teddy bear, Teddy bear,
      Touch the ground.
      Teddy bear, Teddy bear
      Show your foot (hop on one leg).
      Teddy bear, Teddy bear,
      Sling your hook (run out).
      Teddy bear, Teddy bear,
      Go upstairs (lift knees high).
      Teddy bear, Teddy bear,
      Say your prayers (clasp hand together).
      Teddy bear, Teddy bear,
      Switch out the light (hands over head).
      Teddy bear, Teddy bear,
      Wave good night.
   d. Johnny on the railway, pickin' up stones,
      Along came an engine and broke his bones.
      ''Oh,'' said Johnny, ''that's not fair.''
      ''Oh,'' said the engine driver, ''I don't care.''
   e. Have the children make up and chant or sing their own jump rope rhythm rhymes.

---

*Additional jump rope rhymes may be found in Vannier, Maryhelen, and Gallahue, David L.: Teaching physical education in elementary schools, ed. 6, Philadelphia, 1978, W. B. Saunders Co.

Fig. 1-8. Can you jump a rope blindfolded?

4. Blindfold jumping
   a. Blindfold the child and have him listen to the tempo of the rope hitting the floor. Each time the rope hits the floor, he should be in the air. As a result, he needs to anticipate and time his jump to precede the rope hitting the floor. Have the child practice jumping outside the rope while it is turning. Finally, have the child try to jump the turning rope while he is blindfolded.

CONCEPT: The concepts of auditory association and verbal encoding can be enhanced through movement experiences involving action words.

Level: Advanced.

Subconcept: Children may learn about synonyms and antonyms through movement experiences.

Materials: None.

Activities: Through the use of the accompanying movement chart (Fig. 1-9) concerning the action words, the concepts of auditory association, synonyms, antonyms, and verbal encoding may be taught to children. Synonyms are words that mean the same. Antonyms are words that mean the opposite. Auditory association is used when the teacher or child hears one word and can think of others that mean the same or opposite. Verbal encoding is used when the child can say another word that means the same or opposite, and manual encoding is used when a child can move the same or opposite to a word that is heard.

To begin the lesson, have children work in their own space and give direction cues:

Can you move at a high level? What are some other words for high? What is a word that means the opposite? Show me. Now move in a circular pathway. What are other words that mean the same? The opposite? Show me. This time move with lots of force. What are some words that describe this movement? What are some words that mean the opposite? Show me.

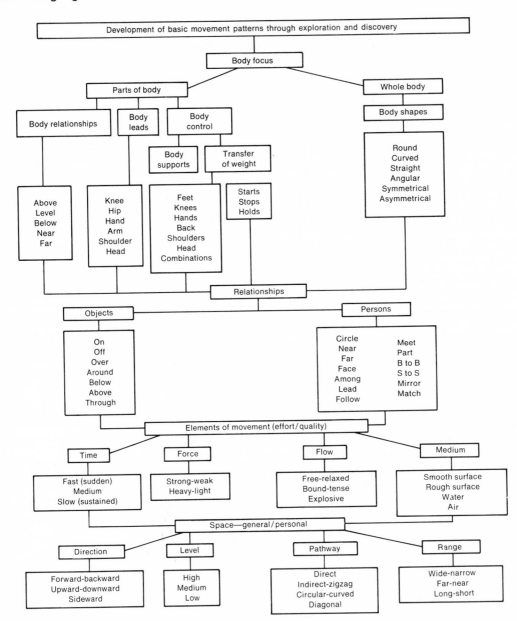

Fig. 1-9. Movement chart.

Continue with other words from the chart.

Now let's think of some action words. Let's choose the word *turning*. What are some words that mean the same? The opposite? Show me. Think of the word *vibrate*. Show through your movement some actions that fit this word and then tell me some words that mean the same (or opposite).

Continue exploring by choosing other words.

Encourage the children to verbalize as much as possible. This will expand their vocabulary and awareness of synonyms and antonyms.

If you have a mature class, give them an action word list and allow them to work with a partner. One child should say a word from the list while the second child performs an appropriate movement and then says one synonym and one antonym. Action words may be chosen more than once, but each time a new synonym and antonym must be given as an answer.

CONCEPT: Children can learn a game and use their speaking abilities to teach the game to others.

Level: Advanced.

Subconcept: A problem-solving approach to games provides children with a chance to make up their own rules and strategies within a group and explain their game to other children in the class.

Materials: Balls, hoops, bean bags, ropes, rackets, scoops, plastic bottles, balloons, etc.

Activities: Following the lesson on creative game playing in the reading and writing chapter (p. 46), have the children, placed in groups of 2 to 6, make up some games with the equipment provided. You may choose the following examples or choose your own problem solving situations:

Problem 1: With a balloon, make up a striking game at a high level, using small or moderate amounts of force.

Problem 2: With a ball and a container or target, make up a game of throwing for accuracy at a low level.

Problem 3: With a ball and some plastic bottles, make up a kicking game that stresses controlled, accurate striking at a low level.

As you supervise each group of children making up their game, encourage each group member to have some verbal input into the decision making process of the rules and strategies. Allow each group to try out their game, alter any problems they encounter (add or change existing rules and strategies), and play their game for a period of time (5 to 15 minutes). Then have one member from each group go to another group and teach them the game. Repeat this experience as often as necessary, giving each child a chance to be a leader (teacher) and to speak in front of a group.

CONCEPT: Speaking in front of groups helps develop self-confidence.

Level: Advanced.

Subconcept: Learning and performing cheers helps one develop confidence while speaking and performing in front of an audience.

Materials: None.

Activities: Upper elementary school children are often interested in cheering their favorite team (middle school, high school, college, professional, or age group team in any sport) to victory. It is a fun experience for both boys and girls to learn and perform old cheers or to make up cheers of their own. In this lesson assign the children to small groups (2 to 6 per group) and allow them to choose a cheer and make up an appropriate movement sequence to fit it. Stress group cooperation and the use of large body movements (arms and legs). Stress different directional movements for patterns also.

SAMPLE CHEERS

Football

All the way down, all the way down, all the way down the field, hey!

Push 'em back, push 'em back, push 'em *way* back!

First and ten, do it again.

We want to go *that way* (point).

Basketball

We want two!
Hey, hey, what do ya way? Take that ball the other way.

Steal it! Steal it! (Clap, clap.)

Two points (clap, clap).

(Repeat.)

Wrestling

Take down, take down (clap, clap).
Take 'em down,
Break 'em down,
Roll 'em over and pin him!

General

Lean to the left, lean to the right, stand up, sit down, fight, fight, fight!

Two bits, four bits, six bits, a dollar. All for _____ stand up and holler!

What are ya gonna do, team?
  (Reply, do not spell) WIN!
What's that?
  (Reply) WIN!
Louder.
  (Reply) WIN!
Win, team, win!

On the move, hey, hey, to win today.
Go all the way, hey hey,
We'll win today.
All right, all right, all right, hey!

Hey you, hey raiders,
You're looking all right.

Fig. 1-10. Let's all cheer together!

Hey you, hey raiders,
Let's win tonight.
Hey you, hey raiders,
Fight, fight, fight!

Singing formal cheers

Well, it looks like your team has got the boogey-woogey
    blues.
And if you can't boogey,
Your team is gonna lose.
So do the boogey,
Try the boogey,
Stand up and boogey,
LET'S DO THE BOOGEY!

One (clap)-two-three-four-five (run numbers together)
Mighty Hawks gonna skin 'em alive!
Six (clap)-seven-eight-nine-ten (together)
Back it up and let's do again.

My head is achin',
My pants too tight,
My body is shakin' from left to right.
Ooh, Ooh, I got that feelin'—yeah.
Ooh, Ooh, I got that feelin'—yeah.
(Then same as the previous cheer)

Be creative. Allow the children to make up their own cheers. After a period of working together, give each group a chance to perform their cheer with appropriate movements in front of the class. Then have each group teach the other groups their cheer, or allow each group to pick a new cheer or do a previous cheer in a new way.

CONCEPT: Reading poetry can be used as a stimulus for developmental speech, as well as creative movement for children.

Level: Advanced.

Subconcept: Voice inflection, phrasing, and mood are aspects of language one can communicate through proper speech habits.

Materials: A source book for poetry or use the children's work.

Activities: Divide the children into small groups. Allow each group to select a poem (from a book or one of the children's poems) to be read. With the help of the classroom or speech teacher help the children to develop proper speech habits—voice inflection, phrasing according to sentence structure, creating a mood by voice tone, etc. While one person reads the poem, the remaining children should develop an appropriate movement sequence. Allow time for practice before each group performs its sequence in front of the other groups. Repeat as necessary until each child gets a chance to read.

SAMPLE POEMS

Very young verses

Feet

There are things
Feet know
That hands never will.

The exciting
Pounding feeling
Of running down a hill;

The soft cool
Prickliness
When feet are bare
Walking in the summer grass
To most anywhere

Or dabbing in
Water all
Slip-sliding through toes–
(Nicer than
Through fingers, though why
No one really knows.)

"Toes, tell my
Fingers," I
Said to them one day,
"Why it's such fun
Just to
Wiggle and play."

But toes just looked at me
Solemn and still.
Oh, there are things
Feet know
That hands
Never will.
AUTHOR UNKNOWN

Action Word Poetry

Shrink and crumble
Lean way out
Then tumble, tumble.

Spin, turn, twirl
Whirl round and round
Run, leap, creep
Then gently touch the ground.

Touch gently on the floor
With fingers, knees, toes
Turn softly to the sky
With fingers, belly and nose.

Dashing, darting, to and fro
Way up high
Then very low.

Up, down
Around and through
Forward, backward
Then I meet you.
PETER WERNER

Resources

Boorman, Joyce: Dance and language experiences with children, Don Mills, Ontario, 1973, Longmans Canada Ltd.
Koch, Kenneth: Wishes, lies, and dreams, Teaching children to write poetry, New York, 1970, Vintage Books, Inc.

Other suggestions:

1. Allow children to read stories or poems from action words developed in Chapter 2.
2. Allow the children to read nursery rhymes, tall tales, myths, and fables from Chapter 2.

Chapter 2

READING AND WRITING

Reading is the ability to perceive, understand, and interpret language in its printed form. The basis for reading is spoken language. If a child has a rich background of experiences and can understand and use spoken words well, he is basically ready to deal with symbols. When a child is ready to learn to read, the only new skill he must master is word perception—the ability to respond to written symbols with the appropriate sound. As a result, the readiness stage of reading involves developing the concepts of auditory and visual discrimination, establishing the left-to-right sequence in reading, developing vocabulary, observing the relationships between letter form and sound, and seeing the relationships between the visual and auditory elements of words and phrases (sequential memory, association, and closure). If his first experiences in reading lead him to see the relationships between oral language and printed symbols, reading becomes meaningful. Success is likely to follow as the child can relate the speech patterns he already knows to the written symbols that he is trying to decode.

At a beginning reading level, children develop word recognition skills through sight vocabulary. They gradually infer meaning from context and/or pictures, use of word form clues, phonetic analysis, structural analysis (root, prefix, and suffix), and use of a dictionary. Comprehension, interpretation, and critical reading are stages that follow later as children develop independent reading skills.

Writing is the process of communicating language skills graphically. It, too, has a base in oral communication, for the child who has a rich background of experiences can begin to formulate his impressions and express them in writing. Except for the fact that the process has changed from decoding to encoding, the stages of developmental writing seem to parallel those of reading. Other than developing the gross motor and fine muscle control to make impressions on a chalkboard or piece of paper (manual encoding), the child must be able to visually discriminate among geometric shapes, letters, numbers, and words; to establish the left-to-right sequence in writing; and to establish proper use of grammar and punctuation. Generally manuscript (printing) proceeds cursive writing with the specific types of writing categorized as creative and expository writing. Creative writing includes riddles, jingles, phrases, tall tales, stories, Haiku, and other forms of poetry. Unlike creative writing, expository writing includes copying messages, letter writing, reporting information, and writing news, advertisements, and book reports of a factual, functional, or utilitarian nature. In either instance it is the role of the teacher to provide the motivation to help children write in their effort to exchange, express, and encourage their ideas.

Experiences in movement should be designed to enable a child to read and write the written language more effectively. Initial experiences in the primary grades should include visual decoding, visual sequential memory, association, closure, and manual encoding through working with letters, words, parts of speech, and sentence structure. Experiences with reading and writing various forms of composition and poetry should be developed as the child's abilities increase. Sample lessons follow.

Learning activities

Reading

CONCEPT: The world of children's literature provides a broad spectrum of resources for reading materials and possible movement experiences for children.

Levels: Beginning and intermediate.

Subconcept: Choose an appropriate story and think of ways in which the topic of the storybook could be used for activities in physical education.

Materials: Books, charts, pamphlets, etc. from the school and/or local public library.

Activities: It would be impossible to write one lesson with regard to the use of children's literature for purposes of teaching reading and creative movement. With literally thousands of books to choose from, it would be a mistake to select one as an example. Rather, it is the intention of this lesson to provide the reader with information to locate guides to children's books and a sample classification of the various categories of children's books. It is up to the parent or teacher to provide as broad a scope of reading material as possible for the children. In addition to reading, the books may be used by teachers as stimulus ideas for creative movement experiences.

Resources

Dodson, Fitzhugh: How to parent; Appendix C: A parent's guide to children's books for the preschool years (Signet), New York, 1970, The New American Library, Inc.

Larrick, Nancy: A parent's guide to children's reading, rev. and enlarged ed., New York, 1975, Bantam Books, Inc.

Categories

A. Toddlerhood
   1. Books for labeling the environment
   2. Word identification books
   3. Animals, toys, colors, machines, objects
   4. Mother Goose books
   5. Bedtime books
B. Early childhood
   1. ABC and counting books
   2. Books about sounds
   3. Nursery tales
   4. Animal stories
   5. Books about the child and his familiar everyday world

C. Preschool and primary years
   1. Nonfiction
      a. Occupations
      b. Science—physical, biological, earth
      c. Animals, birds, fish
      d. History
      e. Sports and famous athletes—especially important
      f. I can read—beginner books
      g. Biographies
   2. Intellectual and emotional development
      a. Sensory and perceptual awareness
      b. Concept formation
         (1) Relationships
         (2) Classifications by color, shape, time, number, season
      c. Basic science concepts
      d. Problem solving
      e. Scientific method
      f. Alphabet and learning to read
      g. Mathematics
      h. Self-concept
      i. Relationships with family and peers
      j. The community and its helpers
      k. The larger community—the world
      l. Children's emotions
      m. The magic of words and books
      n. Etiquette
      o. Religion
   3. Fiction and fantasy
   4. Poetry
   5. Stories, tales, and folk tales

CONCEPT: Visual decoding, visual association, and visual sequential memory are components of reading.

Level: Beginning.

Subconcept: An obstacle course may be used to help children develop better visual sequential memory.

Materials: Chairs, barrels, boxes, hoops, tires, and outdoor playground equipment such as a jungle gym or horizontal ladder.

Activities:
1. Ask one child to negotiate 2, 3, or 4 obstacles in a given order. The remaining chil-

dren must observe the order, direction, and method of execution for each obstacle. They must then perform the same movements in negotiating the obstacles.

2. Give specific directions that limit the children's performances by moving on, over, through, under, to the left of, or to the right of each obstacle.
3. Make the course sequentially more difficult by adding an obstacle each time. How many obstacles can be negotiated before someone forgets the order or method of negotiation?

■ ■ ■

Level: Beginning.

Subconcept: Balance puzzles may be used to help teach children better concepts of visual decoding, visual association, visual sequential memory, and manual encoding.

Materials: The following balance puzzles can be made by drawing with a felt-tipped marker on 8½ × 11 inch sheets of paper or by using poster board or cardboard (Fig. 2-1). The sheets or charts may be laminated for a more permanent product. A chalkboard may be needed also.

Activities: Have the children perform the following experiences according to their abilities.

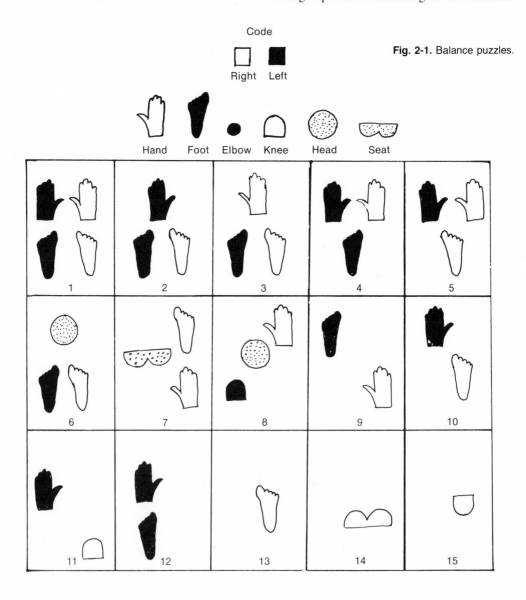

Fig. 2-1. Balance puzzles.

1. Starting with the easier puzzles, hold up one chart at a time and ask the child to balance on the body parts, as shown in the puzzle. The child must balance with the correct parts (left or right) as well as in the same position, as shown in the chart, with no other body parts touching the floor.

2. Use the puzzles as part of an obstacle course. When the children arrive at one, they must perform the designated balance task before moving on to the next obstacle.

3. Show the child a chart and then remove it from his vision. Ask the child to use his visual memory to assume the balance position.

4. Lay 10 to 20 charts out on the floor and time the children to see how quickly they can assume each of the positions as they progress from one chart to another in sequence. Use as part of an obstacle course with one chart at each obstacle.

5. Show the child 2, 3, or 4 charts and then remove them from his vision. Ask the child to perform each of the balance positions in sequence from memory.

6. Divide the children into small groups of 3 or 4. Have them develop their own coded sequences (red circle, R hand; blue circle, L hand; orange square, R foot; green square, L foot) and perform the above experiences. Using charts or a chalkboard, have one person make up the balance position (encode). The others perform the position (decode).

CONCEPT: An awareness of directionality and space is necessary as prereading skills.

Level: Beginning.

Subconcept: Directionality and spatial awareness activities may be related in such a way as to show the connection between movement and the components of letter forms.

Materials: A variety of equipment, including playground and gymnasium apparatus, balls, ropes, hoops, wands, and chalkboards.

Activities: The purpose of this lesson is to help children categorize the components of directionality with reference to similarity. If children can identify in movement and in the classroom objects and occurrences in their daily life in the environment, they may be able to trans-

fer the categorical relationship from concrete experiences to more abstract experiences of language and communication. For example, the children may learn about slanted or diagonal lines in physical education when playing on a slide, seesaw, or swing. They may make slanted or diagonal body gestures or movement patterns on the floor. They may then talk about other objects or occurrences that are diagonal in nature—stair steps, a hill, an escalator, and the roof of a house. They may then work at their desks with paper and pencil and at the chalkboard and make the letters with diagonal lines in them. Similar experiences may be repeated for each of the other directional concepts.

Directions in space
Front-back (forward-backward)
   Environmental—streets, trains, body, toe-heel, car, bus
   P.E.—pendulum of swing, linear movement
   Classroom—isles (or rows) of desks, front of line–back of line
Up-down
   Environmental—elevator, helicopter, sky-ground
   P.E.—Climbing ropes, jumping, climbing pole, bouncing ball
   Classroom—chairs, desks, letters with up and down shapes
Left-right
   Environmental—streets, arms, legs, shoes, gloves
   P.E.—move to left and right, perform with left or right side
   Classroom—metronome, letters with left or right orientation
Diagonal
   Environmental—escalator, steps, roof, hill
   P.E.–slide, seesaw, braces on a swing, body movement
   Classroom—desk top, letters with slanted lines
Curved
   Environmental—earth, globe, clock, buttons, ring
   P.E.—A jump rope, a ball, move in curved path
   Classroom—circle, letters with curves

CONCEPT: Teachers and children can use symbols to develop beginning reading and writing skills.

Level: Beginning.
Subconcept: Visually coded movement sequences can be made by the teacher or children to assist in the development of visual decoding,

visual association, visual sequential memory, and manual encoding.

Materials: A set of 3 × 5 inch cards (index) or a chalkboard.

Activities: Have the children perform the following experiences according to their abilities:

1. Teach the child a set of directional action words. For example, *run, jump, hop, skip, crawl, roll, draw,* and *cut.* Print these words on individual 3 × 5 cards and teach them to the child through a sight vocabulary method. If he has trouble recognizing the words, draw a picture of the action next to the word so that the child can associate the word with the action.

2. Practice exposing a card and have the child execute the movement indicated. Say the word out loud. Then encourage the child to move in response to only the visual cue.

3. Another way to solve the problem of word recognition is to substitute symbols or geometric designs for the words. For example, you could use the following symbols to replace words:

*	Step	/	Half turn
○	Hop	X	Whole turn
□	Jump		

Then, by using the cards or a chalkboard, make up movement sequences for the child to execute.

***○	*○	*○
Step, step, step, hop	step, hop	step, hop

4. Put on a card or chalkboard individual sentences that communicate specific movement directions for the child to execute.

   Draw 5 ○ (Draw 5 circles.)
   Jump 3 × ↑ (Jump three times forward.)
   Roll 3 × → (Roll three times to the right.)
   Draw 5 □ (Draw 5 squares.)
   Hop 5 × R (Hop five times on the right foot.)
   Hop 4 × L (Hop four times on the left foot.)

   Read the word part to the child. He is to interpret the rest of the movement directions by himself. As he learns the directional words, he should figure out the entire sentence himself.

5. As the child develops performance in this routine of visually directed movement, the sentences should be enlarged. For example: Slide 3 × ← and gallop 4 × ↓. From here he may be given three consecutive movement directions to carry out, again directed by the visualizing process.

6. Now have the child look at a direction card and perform the sequence from memory.

7. Next, reverse the routine. Give the child the task of creating a directional sentence on a card or chalkboard. The teacher or a partner should carry out the directions, with the child deciding if the correct actions were executed. The instructions should occasionally be intentionally followed incorrectly to give the child the opportunity to discover that a mismatch has been made between his written instructions (a product of his visualization) and the subsequent movement pattern.

■　■　■

Level: Beginning.

Subconcept: Visually coded movement sequences can be made by the teacher or children to assist in the development of visual decoding, visual association, visual sequential memory, and manual encoding.

Materials: Make visually coded movement sequences on task cards, as shown in Fig. 2-2. Index cards may be used. Follow a system of dots and dashes, long and short dashes, or musical notation for stimuli.* Have blank cards in case you wish to make up some sequences as you work with the child. Allow the child to make his own sequence. In case you desire a set of permanent cards, it is a good suggestion to have them dry mounted for protection.

Activities: Have the children perform the following experiences according to their abilities:

1. Look at a task card and verbally interpret what the card is telling you to perform.

---

*The goal here is for the child to learn that the question being asked of him is "What does this tell us?" and not mere word recognition. He must learn that symbols convey information to him—that each communicates a specific kind of movement.

Symbols

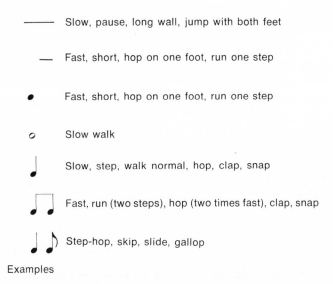

——— Slow, pause, long wall, jump with both feet

— Fast, short, hop on one foot, run one step

• Fast, short, hop on one foot, run one step

o Slow walk

♩ Slow, step, walk normal, hop, clap, snap

♫ Fast, run (two steps), hop (two times fast), clap, snap

♩♪ Step-hop, skip, slide, gallop

Examples

——— ——— ——— — Slow, slow, slow, fast
Walk, walk, walk, hop

• • • • • • • Clap, clap, pause, clap clap clap,
pause, clap, clap
Hop, hop, pause, hop, hop, hop,
pause, hop, hop

——— ——— ——— — Walk, walk, walk, hop

♩ ♩ ♩ ♫ Walk, walk, walk, run, run

♩ ♩ ♩ ♫ Clap, clap, clap, snap, snap

♩ ♩ o Hop, hop, slow walk

Fig. 2-2. Examples of visually coded movement sequences.

2. While looking at the task card, perform the movements indicated.
3. Look at a task card and memorize the sequence. Put the card down and perform the movements from memory.
4. Look at the task card and then use your hands or fingers to clap or snap through the sequence. (——--— long, short, short, short, long, short). Use other body parts to perform the same task.
5. Make up your own sequence on a card, memorize it, and then perform it.
6. Combine sequences so that you can memorize two, three, or four task card sequences at once and perform them without a break.

Letters and words

CONCEPT: Learning to recognize and reproduce the letters of the alphabet is essential to reading and writing.

Level: Beginning.

Subconcept: Movement experiences may be designed to help the child recognize letters of the alphabet.

Materials: Chalk, paint, tape, shoe polish, or a felt-tipped marker.

Activities: Put the two designs in Fig. 2-3 in one or more places on the gym floor, classroom floor, or outdoor hard surface area with an appropriate material (chalk, paint, etc.).

From these two-line configurations all the letters of the alphabet may be made. As the teacher or another child calls out or shows a spe-

Fig. 2-3. Move along the lines to form a letter or word.

cific letter on a chart, a child should be able to move to the appropriate design and map out the letter. The child may use specified forms of locomotion to complete the letter. He may also vary his time (speed), level, direction, and pathway (start at different places on the letter) as he completes each letter. While forming the letter using a locomotor pathway, the child may also trace the letter with his arms or another body part in the air. After working with the letters, the child may begin to spell words.

■　■　■

Level: Beginning.

Subconcepts: (1) Movement experiences that use an alphabet grid encourage the development of visual decoding, visual association, visual sequential memory, and manual encoding in children. (2) All letters of the alphabet are made from three different types of lines: straight, diagonal, and curved (Fig. 2-4).

- Letters made of straight lines only are E, F, H, I, L, T.
- Letters made of diagonal lines only are V, W, X.
- Letters made of curved lines only are C, O, S.
- Letters made of diagonal and straight lines are A, K, M, N, Y, Z.

- Letters made of curved and straight lines are B, D, G, J, P, R, U.
- Letters made of curved and diagonal lines are Q.

Materials: A gym or school yard with an alphabet grid similar to the one in Fig. 1-4 is needed for this activity. Alphabet charts with upper case letters and/or a chalkboard also may be used for this experience.

Activities

1. Using the alphabet charts or chalkboards, the children may categorize the letters according to shape.
2. They may make the different categories of letters with their bodies using "body alphabet" (next lesson) by themselves, with a partner, or with a small group.
3. The children may walk the shapes of the letters by changing their pathway on the floor. If a sandbox is available, the children may use their hands or feet to trace their letters in the sand.

■　■　■

Level: Beginning.

Subconcept: Movement experiences may provide children the opportunity to enhance

Fig. 2-4. The alphabet is made from straight, curved, and diagonal lines.

their knowledge and understanding of the letters of the alphabet.

Materials: None.

Activities: Using the body alphabet letters shown in Fig. 2-5, teach the children to create various body poses that resemble each of the letters of the alphabet. How many different ways can each letter be made? Can they be made in caps, then small? Can the letter be made by an individual, then by a group of children?

After learning to make the letters of the alphabet, the children may group together to spell words and sequentially spell out sentences. Groups may take turns performing and trying to figure out what words and sentences of other groups spell.

■ ■ ■

Level: Intermediate.

Subconcept: Learning the letters of the al-

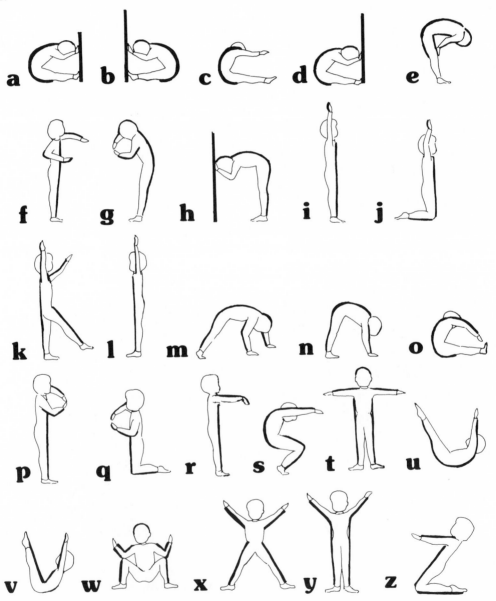

Fig. 2-5. Body alphabet.

phabet is enhanced through movement and music.

Materials: Streamers, a record player, and a choice of records to which children may move. Examples are *The Nutcracker Suite* and music from the movies *The Sting* and *Zorba, the Greek,* and ''Aquarius'' by the rock group The Fifth Dimension.

Activities: Using the charts in Fig. 2-6, have the children practice writing the letters of the alphabet in the air, paying attention to the sequential order of how the letter is made. Practice should include both capital and small letters. In their own personal space the children may vary the level, time, pace and flow of their movement. Large movements should be stressed. The children may also trace the pathway of the letters on the floor through locomotor movements as they trace the pathway of the letters in the air. To increase interest in this lesson, streamers and music may be used. The streamers create added interest in the letters because the children can actually see the letters being traced in the air. Music, sometimes smooth and free flowing, sometimes percussive in nature, encourages children to compare and contrast how the letters are made. Which letters have curved lines and can be made more easily with smooth, free-flowing music? Which letters are angular and made more easily by percussive music?

■ ■ ■

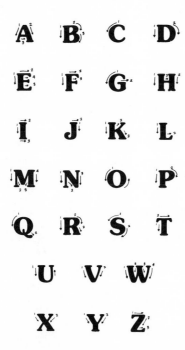

Fig. 2-6. Trace the pattern of the letters in the air.

Level: Beginning.

Subconcept: The learning of the letters of the alphabet is enhanced by movement activities.

Materials: A grid as shown either taped or drawn on the floor (Fig. 2-7).

Activities: A variety of jumping and throwing games may be played with this grid.

1. Jump, hop, etc.
2. Jump into the grid and identify each letter you jump on as you land on it.
3. Sequence the letters by jumping from each square in alphabetical order A to Y, then Y to A.
4. Jump on the consonants, hop on the vowels.
5. Jump on the grid to spell complete words.
6. Race with a friend to see who is first to "jump out" a word.
7. Toss a bean bag on the squares and identify the letter on which the bag lands.
8. Toss the bean bag on a specific letter.
9. Toss the bean bag on the letter that begins the word *ball, cat, dog,* etc.

CONCEPT: Manuscript and cursive letters are the two basic forms of the English language.

Level: Beginning.

Subconcepts: (1) The concepts of visual decoding, visual association, and manual encoding can be enhanced through movement experiences with card and grid games. (2) The children will learn that any given letter of the alphabet may take several forms but still have the same sound and meaning.

Materials: Make up a series of letter cards and letter grids for each of the following types of script:

- *Manuscript* — capital letters
- *Manuscript* — small letters
- *Cursive* — capital letters
- *Cursive* — small letters

Activities: The children may use the letter cards and letter grids interchangeably. The teacher or a child in a group may say or hold up one letter. An assigned child or group of children may try to find that letter in all its forms — capital and small, manuscript and cursive. The children may run, hop, jump, or perform any of the locomotor skills as they move from one place to another. They may use body alphabet as they try to make all forms of a given letter with their bodies. They may try to walk, hop, jump, or use any other form of locomotion as they make the pathway of each of the letters and their forms on the floor. The path-

Fig. 2-7. Spell your name.

way of the letters may also be traced in the air with various body parts. They may use the letter grids to hop or jump from one letter to another in completing their spelling words. Letters may be presented visually or the letter cards in one form and manually encoded by hopping on the proper letter in a different form on the letter grid. The teacher may verbally say a given letter, and each child may find the letter or a letter/grid, make the letter with his body, or make the pathway of the letter on the floor or in the air. Then, on command, each child should be able to make the same letter in a different form—capital, small, manuscript, or cursive.

CONCEPT: Map-reading skills may be used to develop concepts related to reading and writing.

Level: Intermediate.

Subconcept: Mapping experiences may be used to teach children better concepts of visual decoding, visual sequential memory, and manual encoding.

Materials: Use rubber matting, carpet samples, or a similar material and cut it into the shapes of simple geometric forms or human feet. A nonskid material will work best. Place the forms on the floor in a pattern, as indicated on 3 × 5 index cards already designed. Draw some map guidelines on 3 × 5 cards, as seen in Fig. 2-9. Leave other blank cards for you to make up or allow the children to make up as they progress through the activities. Home base should always be a different shape or color to serve as a reference point for the child. Some of the map guides should direct the child to step on each of the forms. Others should direct the child to go around the forms in different directions, such as making inside or outside loops. Make up stories about farming, driving a truck, flying an airplane, and similar occupations to accompany the map experiences.

Activities: Have the children perform the following experiences according to their abilities:
1. Lay 3 to 10 squares on the floor. Hand the child an index card or map while he is standing at home base. Tell him to follow the sequential guidelines from beginning to end. The task can be regulated according to the child's ability by increasing or decreasing the number of forms or guidelines.
2. Show the child a map. Then take away the map and have him attempt the pathway from visual memory.
3. Have the child fabricate a story about his

Fig. 2-8. Can you find the same letter?

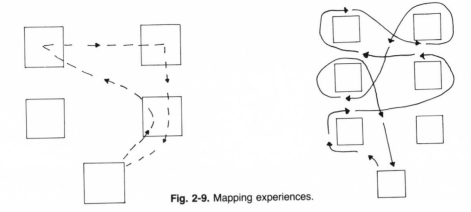

Fig. 2-9. Mapping experiences.

map experiences. If he intends to farm, he could plow various fields. If he plans to be a truck driver, he could make deliveries. Have the child think of other situations relative to the mapping experiences.

4. Have the child remove his shoes and follow the path with his eyes closed.
5. Pretend the forms are stepping-stones across a creek and have the child hop from one form to another.
6. Give the child a task care with written instructions instead of pictorial directions.
7. While working with a partner, have one child use a blank index card to design a map and sequential order of progression for the other child to perform.

CONCEPT: Orienteering and map-reading skills may be used to develop concepts related to reading and writing.

Level: Advanced.

Subconcept: Orienteering and map-reading experiences may be used to teach children better concepts of visual decoding, visual sequential memory, and manual encoding.

Materials: Paper, pencils, maps, and compasses.

Activities: Learning to read and make maps can develop into a technical adventure that may be pursued throughout life. To initiate their activities, each child may be given a compass and taught to locate the four major directions and azimuths in between. Out on the school grounds the children may use various directional points to identify the location of the school, exit points, turns, streets, and playground

equipment. They may pace off the location of each focal point and draw a map according to scale. The children can learn to make a beeline while on a hike. They can learn to play the silver dollar game or a simple compass game that will test their skills at reading a compass and using it in the field.

Learning to make and/or use road maps of the community, city, and state are other activities. Full-scale map reading by routing trips, hiking cross-country, and point or score orienteering may be pursued as familiarity with reading a map and compass increases.

Silver dollar game. The silver dollar game, as suggested by Bjorn Kjellstrom, is a simple three-legged compass walk that requires a relatively small area and little equipment. The orienter takes his "silver dollar" (a can top, a coin, or a plaque) and places it between his feet. He then sets his compass on any azimuth between 0 and 120 degrees and paces out 20 to 30 paces following the azimuth; at the end of the first leg he resets his compass by adding 120 degrees to the first azimuth and steps off the original number of paces; and at the end of the second leg, the orienter again adds 120 degrees to his azimuth and steps off the original number of paces. If he has been accurate, he will end up on his silver dollar. What he has done is completely walk the three sides of an equilateral triangle. If the orienter is incorrect or not confident, he need only start off again on a different azimuth.

You can see that it is easy to increase the complexity of the game into a four-, five-, or six-sided equilateral polygon. The pace counts

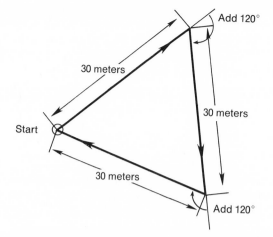

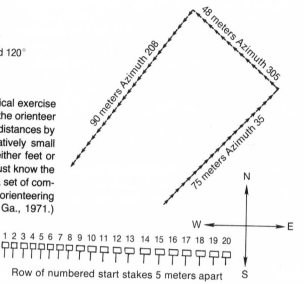

Fig. 2-10. Silver dollar game. (From The orienteering book, U.S. Army Infantry School, Fort Benning, Ga., 1971.)

Fig. 2-11. Compass game. This is another practical exercise suggested by Kjellstrom that is designed to train the orienteer in following compass azimuths and in measuring distances by walking. The game can be conducted in a relatively small area, and can be set up in a short time, using either feet or meters as the measurement base. The player must know the length of his pace to participate. Silva, Inc., has a set of compass game cards designed for feet. (From The orienteering book, U.S. Army Infantry School, Fort Benning, Ga., 1971.)

Row of numbered start stakes 5 meters apart

for each side will be identical; the angle added to each azimuth is obtained by dividing the number of sides of the polygon into 360 degrees.

Resources

Books

Fieldbook for boys and men, Boy Scouts of America, North Brunswick, N.J., 1967.

The orienteering handbook, U.S. Army Infantry School, Fort Benning, Ga., 1971 (Free).

Compass and maps, Girl Scouts of America, New York, N.Y.

Kjellstrom, Bjorn: Be expert with map and compass, American Orienteering Service, La Porte, Ind., 1967.

Films

The following are available from International Film Bureau, Inc., 333 S. Michigan Ave., Chicago, Ill. 60604

Orienteering. A 10-minute color film made at 1968 Canadian championships.

The Sport of Orienteering. Color, 34 minutes.

By Map and Compass. Color, 36 minutes.

CONCEPT: Children learn about the parts of speech, sentence structure, and punctuation to establish the proper use of grammar.

Level: Intermediate.

Subconcept: Movement experiences may enhance a child's awareness of the parts of speech—noun, adjective, verb, adverb, preposition, conjunction, and disjunction.

- A noun is the name of a person, place, or object.
- An adjective modifies a noun.
- A verb is a predicate or action part of a sentence.
- An adverb modifies a verb.
- A preposition is a word that combines with a noun or pronoun to form a phrase.
- A conjunction is a word that joins together words, groups of words, or sentences.
- A disjunction is a word that separates words, phrases, or sentences.

Materials: Newspaper.

Activities: Give each child a piece of newspaper. Instruct them to take their newspaper (home) onto the playing area (neighborhood). To reinforce personal space concepts, encourage the children to position their house (personal space) away from other people's houses (general space) so that they have a nice big yard.

Noun: on your paper find a noun. Clap the number of letters in the word. Use body alphabet to spell the word to a neighbor. Write the word in the air or spell the word on the floor while walking. Use movement to act out the noun.

Adjective*: think of an adjective that modifies one of the nouns you selected from your newspaper. Use body alphabet to spell it. Use movement to act it out. Examples are a *big* bear, a *fast* train, a *small* spider.

Verb: on your paper find a verb. Use body alphabet to spell the word to a neighbor. Write the word in the air or spell the word on the floor while walking. Use movement to act out the verb.

Adverb: think of an adverb that modifies one of the verbs you previously selected. Use body alphabet to spell it. Use movement to act it out. Examples are run *slowly,* twisting *quickly,* and punch *hard.*

Preposition: use a form of locomotion to go *over* and *around* your house. While changing level, pathway, direction, etc., move *in between* (*among, toward, away from,* etc.) your neighbor's houses.

Conjunction and disjunction: teach the children about the words *and, or either, neither, nor, but.* On or around your newspaper, do this *and* that, *either* this *or* that, *neither* this *nor* that. Examples are jump over *and* hop around your house (do both); *either* jump over *or* hop around your house (do one *or* the other, *but* not both); *neither* jump over your house, *nor* hop around your house (precludes *either* nothing is happening, *or* anything *but* jumping and hopping is happening).

■ ■ ■

Level: Advanced.

Subconcept: Concepts of proper sentence structure may be enhanced through movement experiences in physical education.

Materials: Obtain 4 cardboard boxes, decorate or paint them, and letter the outside of each with one of the 4 following words—

NOUN, ADJECTIVE, VERB, ADVERB. Develop a set of ten or more 5 × 7 inch cards for each category.

EXAMPLES:

Noun	Adjective	Verb	Adverb
dog	big	walk	quickly
cat	little	run	slowly
horse	wide	hop	smoothly
car	narrow	leap	jerky
truck	high	hurl	softly
ball	low	shrink	strongly
water	round	spin	suddenly
boat	fat	fly	weakly
kite	skinny	roll	directly
airplane	square	skip	heavily

Activities: Divide the children into small groups. Place the large cards into 4 stacks, but do not explain to the children that all the nouns, verbs, etc. are in 1 stack. On signal, a member from each team must run, hop, jump forward, jump backward, etc. to the stacks, take a card from each stack, and form a proper sentence. The children must call out their sentence when finished. Articles may be added and verb forms may be changed, if necessary—present, past, future tense. Although sentences may not be logical, they must be in proper order.

EXAMPLES

- The square boat flew heavily.
- The fat cat skipped smoothly.

After forming each sentence, the children may perform interpretive actions of their sentences and finish by placing each of the words from the sentence in the appropriate box.

A relay may also be performed in which each member of the team gets to draw 4 words from the stacks and construct a sentence. The first team to have each member construct a proper sentence will win the game.

Composition

CONCEPT: Creative and expository writing are the two types of writing.

Level: Intermediate.

Subconcept: Scripts and captions for commercials in magazines and on television and radio may serve as stimulus ideas for children's creative and expository writing and movement.

Materials. None.

---

*An excellent reference and picture book for adjectives, adverbs, and prepositions is Spier, Peter: Fast, slow, high, low, Garden City, N.Y., 1973, Doubleday Books, Inc.

Fig. 2-12. Make a sentence.

Activities: Companies making commercials to sell their products on television and in magazines often use children to advertise their wares. Examples of these commercials are Delmonte fruit and vegetables (with Bill Cosby), Sunbeam bread, Sunshine and Nabisco crackers and cookies, Oscar Mayer hot dogs, Heinz catsup, and McDonald's Restaurants. The objectives of this lesson are to encourage the children to pick a product of their choice and make up a jingle, caption, or full-scale written commercial. Following this written experience, the children may be divided into groups of 3 to 5 to add appropriate expressive movements to their commercial. A final experience may be to eliminate the verbal cues and have the children do the commercials nonverbally through creative movement.

■   ■   ■

Level: Advanced.

Subconcept: Movement experiences in dance, gymnastics, sports, and games provide a rich background for composition and creative writing.

Materials: None.

Activities: The classroom teacher, with the assistance of the physical education teacher, can encourage children to develop their skills in composition and creative writing. After participating in a particular movement experience, the children may return to the classroom and write about their involvement. The following are suggested movement and composition themes:

- What it feels like to be powerful and jerky
- How you feel when you're upside down
- The written rules to the game you created in physical education
- Your favorite sport
- Your favorite athlete
- What you like to do during your summer vacation
- When you were moving your streamers to the music you felt like . . .
- Electronic music makes you dance like . . .
- Write a tall tale about one of your creative movement experiences in physical education—a rescue at sea, the man with balloons, the bear that couldn't hibernate, and the hinge that creaked behind you.
- Your hair stood on end as you . . .
- Let's pretend: a hockey star who has a bad season, an astronaut on the moon, first prize for . . .
- You feel proud when . . .

How many more can you think of?

CONCEPT: The skills of reading and writing can be used to learn about new activities in physical education.

Level: Intermediate.

Subconcept: The qualities of movement can be used to help children learn how to classify, code, or categorize objects and events in their environment.

Materials: Balls, ropes, or any other play equipment, in the school or gymnasium.

Activities: The purpose of this lesson is to help children learn how to classify or categorize objects and events in their environment. Visual sequential memory will be used through the medium of activity. To begin the activities, the teacher may use one of every kind of ball that is available in the gym and ask the children to classify or categorize them. Possible systems of classification may be according to size, shape, and the use (some for throwing, some for striking, some for kicking).

Next, the teacher or a child may perform a sequence of movements, such as bouncing a ball five times with the left hand, then the right. Possible classification systems might be as follows: movement at a medium level, a ball bouncing or striking activity, a medium amount of force applied, a left movement followed by a right movement, movements in series of five, or a movement in personal space.

Other examples of movement sequences that may be classified follow:

- Three forward rolls, followed by three backward rolls
- A cartwheel, followed by a forward roll
- Three hops on the left foot, followed by four on the right foot
- Five skipping steps forward, then five backward
- Step, step, step, hop, step, step, step, hop (schottische)
- Any simple dance step
- Four throws for accuracy with the dominant hand

How many others can you think of?

■ ■ ■

Level: Intermediate.

Subconcept: Children can develop better reading and writing skills through an individualized or personalized approach to movement that includes the use of task cards.

Materials: Index cards (3 × 5 inches).

Activities. Currently there is a trend in education to individualize or personalize the learning environment. This approach includes the use of task cards by children individually or as a group in station teaching. In any instance the children must read the prepared task card and perform accordingly. After an introduction to the use of task cards, the teacher can encourage children to write their own task cards with appropriate movement experiences and then perform the tasks. Task cards may be written for any of the content areas of games, rhythms, and gymnastics. Some examples follow:

Balls
1. Bounce the ball in your own space with the hand you write with.
2. Bounce the ball in your own space with your other hand.
3. Alternate hands while you bounce the ball.

Fig. 2-13. Read the task card and perform.

4. Bounce the ball around your body, behind your back, through your legs.
5. Move about the room while you bounce the ball with the hand you write with. Change your direction and pathway on the floor.
6. Change hands and do no. 5.

Rhythms

1. Listen to the music. Count the beats of each measure.
2. Clap to the beats of each measure.
3. Clap to the first beat of the measure. Snap your fingers to the remaining beats of the measure.
4. Step or walk to the beats of each measure. Change your direction or pathway at the beginning of each new measure.
5. Hop or jump to the rhythm of the music.
6. Make up your own 8- to 16-count dance sequence by using walking, hopping, and/or jumping steps. Change your direction and pathway on the floor. After you get your dance sequence together, share your dance with a friend.

Balance beams and mats

1. Move along the beam, using stretched and curled shapes.
2. Move on and off the beam, showing twisted shapes in the air.
3. Make up a sequence to get on, along, and off the beam and show various balanced shapes while on the beam.
4. With a partner, move along the beam in opposite directions and try different ways to cross each other's path in attempting to cross to the other end.

■ ■ ■

Level: Advanced.

Subconcept: Movement experiences and word games ("Anagrams," "Concentration," etc.) can enhance language arts concepts.

Materials: Any equipment appropriate for a particular ball skill unit.

Activities: Word anagrams (or games such as concentration) may be used in games of all kinds as a method of keeping score and enhancing language arts concepts. When playing relays, lead-up games to any of the team or individual sports, or using a problem-solving approach to creative games, introduce the word games as a means of keeping score. Use spelling lists, actions words, words from another school subject, or a dictionary as a resource for the anagrams. Jumble the letters in the word and cover each of the letters. Work with the classroom teacher and/or children to make the concentration puzzles. Each puzzle should consist of three levels: the top number grid (25 to 30 squares), a matching code (colors, geometric shapes, dots, pictures, etc.), and the puzzle. Use book titles, movies, sayings, and the like for puzzle solutions. Then as a basket is scored, a goal kicked, a run scored, or a point made, allow the team to uncover one of the letters of the anagram or make a match in the concentration game. After each score the team is allowed to get together for a period of time (30 seconds) to discuss what they believe the word or saying to be. The first team to complete the word or saying is the winner of the round. Special note may be made here: the team that scores most does not necessarily win the round; the team that plays well and concentrates on the solution to the word game will win. Several rounds constitute a match.

■ ■ ■

Level: Advanced.

Subconcept: Action words may be used to develop an awareness of mood, feeling, and/or language vocabulary through writing and/or movement experiences.

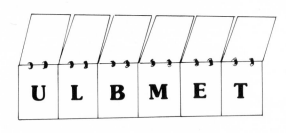

Fig. 2-14. Solve the puzzle.

Materials: None.

Activities: To begin this lesson, have the children experiment with movements appropriate to each of the single words in the movement categories. Then compare and contrast two words from either the same or different categories (run-walk, soar-slither, lift-lower, shrivel-stretch).

EXAMPLES

Traveling

run	gallop	flee	quick
walk	leap	dart	slow
hop	prance	fly	burst
skip	creep	soar	hurrying
jump	bounce	slither	rushing

Turning	*Contracting*		*Expanding*
spin	shrink	crumble	grow
whirl	bend	squeeze	stretch
twist	close		open
swivel	narrow		reach
swirl	flex		spread
twirl	shrivel		release

Rising	*Sinking*	*Starting*	*Stopping*
lift	lower	begin	freeze
up	down	go	anchor
elevate	settling	release	pause
rise	fall		hold
high	collapse		grip
	sink		perch

Percussive

stamp	punch	poking	dab
explode	pound	crashing	flick
patter	hit	smashing	

Flowing

soft	smooth	swooping	drifting
calm	gentle	waves	floating
blowing	sweeping	sailing	

Mood

happy	bubbling	upset	fear
sad	laughter	joy	desire
angry	worry	serene	want
surprise	afraid	excited	need
smiling	glee	silly	

Vibratory

| shiver | | wobble | | tremble |
| quiver | | shake | | shudder |

Or pick a theme and choose words appropriate to that theme.

Wind	*Leaves*
whipping	falling
hurrying	floating
rushing	trembling
whispering	twirling
sweeping	settling
gentle	
pounding	

Then make up appropriate rhymes or poems, first writing the sequences and then moving to the sequence.

The wind goes whipping, rushing around
As the leaves twirl and float, falling to the ground.

Shrink, bend lower, slither;
Rise up, quickly quiver.

Sweeping, soaring, floating free,
Happy turning, smiling glee.

WERNER

Resources

Boorman, Joyce: Dance and language experiences with children, Don Mills, Ontario, 1973, Longmans Canada Ltd.

Koch, Kenneth: Wishes, lies, and dreams: teaching children to write poetry, New York, 1970, Vintage Books, Inc.

■　■　■

Level: Advanced.

Subconcepts: (1) After reading task card requirements, children should be able to synthesize game rules and strategies to invent new games of their own. (2) Children should be able to analyze component parts of a game and write the rules for others to read, learn, and play.

Materials: Balls, bats, rackets, ropes, hoops, and other equipment appropriate for children's games.

Activities: Make up a series of rules, skill, and movement quality cards as seen below. Add more cards as you or the children think of additional rules and strategies.

Skill	Quality	Rule
Throwing and catching	Low level—keep ball on ground	Hit target
	Medium level	
	High level—keep ball in air	Two tries
Kicking and trapping	Lot of force—distance	Three tries

Fig. 2-15. Slither, bend, shrink.

Striking	Little force—accuracy	Four tries
Bouncing	Space	Get ball away
	Line game	
	Circle game	
	Net game	
	Field game	
Rolling	Time—fast	Continuous play
Carrying	Time—slow	Alternate play

1. Striking game
2. Medium level
3. Lots of force—with accuracy
4. Two tries on serve
5. Alternate play

To begin the lesson, place the cards in 3 piles. Divide the children into small groups of 3 to 5 each. Ask a child from each group to select one card from each pile. After bringing the cards back to the group and reading the cards, the children should invent a game that meets the requirements. For example, make up a bouncing game at a medium level in which someone tries to get the ball away from another. At a later stage more than one card can be drawn from each pile. The children may also choose 5 to 6 cards and make up a game with any three or four of the requirements.

The children may also use their abilities to analyze a game to record in writing the games being played by other groups. This may be done in the original children's games or in any of the known individual or team sports. For example, in tennis the children may write the following rules:

When approached in this manner, the children will become more analytical of game playing skills, rules, and strategies. They will be able to synthesize game qualities as they invent their own games. Also, the task card approach will help children gain independence in reading and writing as they read, make up, and write about their games.

■ ■ ■

Level: Advanced.

Subconcept: Children can use the manipulative concepts of throwing, catching, and kicking to invent games of their own, write the rules and scoring techniques for their games, and play the games of others by reading their rules.

Materials: Balls, bats, hoops, ropes and any other manipulative equipment.

Activities: The objective of this lesson or series of lessons is to encourage children placed in small groups of 3 to 5 to develop skills in problem solving and to invent games of their own. Any manipulative skill may be chosen for major emphasis, with the qualities of space, force, time, and flow receiving minor emphasis. Some suggestions follow:

1. Given a piece of equipment (ball) or more than one piece of equipment (a ball and a hoop), make up a game in which the equipment is used.
2. Given a ball and one or more hoops, make up a throwing game in which the ball passes through the hoops at different levels.
3. Make up a throwing game at a low level with a little force.
4. Make up an accuracy kicking game in which different parts of the foot are used to strike the ball.

As the children invent their own games, they will be making their own decisions regarding the rules and scoring. In turn, they will develop their writing skills as they attempt to communicate their ideas in print. This activity may be done in physical education or in the classroom with the help of the language arts teacher. In a later physical education class the groups of children may exchange game cards, read them, and attempt to play the game accordingly.

CONCEPT: Haiku poetry can be used as a stimulus idea for creative writing and for nonverbal communication.

Level: Intermediate.

Subconcept: Body posture, gestures, and imitation may be used to communicate nonverbally.

Materials: None.

Activities: Haiku poetry is a seventeen-syllable, unrhymed verse of Japanese origin that may be used as a stimulus idea for creative writing and creative movement experiences. Each poem is three lines: five syllables in the first line, seven in the second, and five in the third. Some examples follow:

Raging water run.
Canoes paddle thru the gate.
Draw, pry, and brace! Clear!
WERNER

Balls flying—near, far.
Fielders catching high and low.
Game is won. Crowd cheers.
WERNER

Clouds softly floating
White feathers in the bright sky
Silently past us.
WERNER

Fig. 2-16. "Grow delicious fruit."

Rain softly falling
Summer crops soak up the wet
Grow delicious fruit.

WERNER

Grassy river bank
Large unexpected frog
Goes splash! Scared to death!

WERNER

The purpose of this experience is twofold. First, using these examples, have the children attempt to write their own Haiku poetry. Seasons of the year, weather, animals, birds, people, trees, moods, and feelings are good topics for stimulus ideas.

Second, using the examples of Haiku written creatively by your students, develop creative movement experiences. For example, using one of Werner's poems, the children could perform the following movement sequence:

Rain softly falling
(Gentle, downward collapsing movements of body parts or the whole body.)
Summer crops soak up the wet
(Absorbent, expanding, spongelike qualities.)
Grow delicious fruit
(Get larger, rise, branch out.)

Divide the children into small groups of 3 or 4 and give them a poem with which to work. Ask them the verbal and movement images disclosed in the poem. Stress that it is not their task to represent the objects in the poem (rain or fruit); rather, they should express the feeling, mood, or movement qualities in the poem. Ask the children to find movements that express the qualities of the word images (perhaps a calm gentle evening), as they perceive it. Encourage them to use different body parts in various ways to express the idea. Try also to use different levels, locomotor, and gesture movements.

Resources

Japanese Haiku, Mt. Vernon, N.Y., 1958, The Peter Pauper Press.

Logan, Lillian M., et al.: Creative communication; teaching the language arts, Scarborough, Ontario, 1972, McGraw-Hill Ryerson Ltd.

The four seasons, Mt. Vernon, N.Y., 1958, The Peter Pauper Press.

Chapter 3

NONVERBAL COMMUNICATION

Movement, like speaking and writing, is a means of expression. It is a universal language that helps individuals communicate with others. It is vital at all levels of communication. Freedom of movement is essential if a person is to communicate ideas and feelings effectively. In communicating with others, it is the total response or interaction that determines the quality of understanding. Greetings are accompanied by gestures such as a handshake or a friendly smile. At times a person may greet someone nicely with words, but the actions may not show sincerity. A person speaks with the eyes, the voice, and the whole body and conveys ideas not only with words but also with subtle, covert actions.

Gestures are used in everyday speech to supplement words. Talking with the hands is characteristic of many people or ethnic groups. Body postures or gestures reveal a person's feelings. Various movements tell others when a person is angry, sad, lonely, or happy.

Specific words in our language often suggest movement and action. Words such as swinging, swaying, vibrating, falling, and splashing are examples of action words. Specific types of actions characterize different tasks or occupations. Mixing a cake, cutting the grass, sawing wood, and plowing a field are but a few of the tasks that can be conveyed through imitative actions.

Movement experiences offer many opportunities for children to communicate nonverbally. Dance or dramatic play can be used to help children express the movements of nature, such as a violent waterfall or a calm, sunny spring day. These movement experiences can dramatize a day on the farm, a day at the beach, a hayride during a Halloween party, and other similar situations that suggest interest to the children.

Pictures as well as other objects and ideas can often be used to help children learn to communicate through movement. Showing children pictures of animals on the prowl, butterflies fluttering in the wind, or bees collecting honey, as well as other action scenes, is a way of helping them learn to communicate through movement. Stalking an unsuspecting animal, fluttering indirectly, or buzzing in a direct line back to the hive are suggestions through which children become aware of the qualities of movement—sustained, sudden, direct, indirect, loud, soft, etc.

Moods, feelings, and emotions can also be expressed through movement. Have the children make a happy or silly body movement, facial expression, or pose. Have them say hello to another child in slow motion. Encourage them to express feelings of joy, happiness, or surprise between friends at a party. Utilize streamers or scarves to express feelings of lightness. Other objects may be used to create feelings of heaviness or other moods and emotions.

In helping children communicate through body action, the teacher might well emphasize pantomime or the art of mime. In either, posture gives the first clues to characterization. For instance, in "The Emperor's New Clothes" the body carriage of the emperor should immediately distinguish him from the weavers. In "Cinderella" the movements of the girl servant should be different from those of the princess.

When using gestures, action words, dance, dramatic play, pictures, objects, or themes for expression, it is important for the teacher to remember two factors for successful implementation. First, the stimulus is a means to an end—not an end in itself. The stimulus should be used for stimulation, not imitation. Teachers should help children learn to express themselves through their movements by using stimuli in a literal sense to express the qualities of movement that the stimuli suggest. For example, initially a child may copy a scene in a picture, wave a streamer, or pretend to try on new clothes. Gradually he may learn to use his movements to interpret his impression of emotion or mood created by the picture; he may learn to use the color, shapes, lightness, and movement patterns of the streamer; or to show the excitement and his likes or dislikes about a new set of clothes. When children can draw relationships between what they see, feel, and hear and how they move, they are using the process of abstraction. The intention, then, is to move away from the stimuli as the center or focal point of the lesson toward utilizing the various stimuli to reinforce the qualities of movement and expression.

Second, when using pictures, objects, or themes for movement experiences, avoid having the children imitate something that they really cannot be, such as an inanimate object (orange). To move like an orange is an impossible task that will create confusion in children and undesirable results. It would be better to ask the children to make their bodies into the shape of an orange and then ask them how it would move if it could move.

Nonverbal communication through body postures, gestures, imitation, dance, dramatic play, and pantomime helps persons convey feelings and ideas. Exercises should not be practiced in isolation, but as an outgrowth of meaningful situations. When this is done, they will result in animation, spontaneity, coordination, and creativity. Actions become linguistic tools of alert teachers who are quick to seize on a teachable moment. Movement helps individuals articulate their experiences, thoughts or ideas, perceptions, feelings, and emotions creatively.

Following are some sample lessons concerning how concepts regarding nonverbal communication could be taught to elementary school children.

Learning activities

CONCEPT: The human body communicates information through its actions.

Level: Beginning.

Subconcept: Gestures may be used to express greetings, moods, feelings, decisions, and ideas.

Materials: None.

Activities: A dialogue between teacher and children may develop as follows:

Hello, boys and girls. Hi. How many ways can you say "Hello" to me verbally? Hi. How are you? Good morning. Now, pretend to greet me with your body. Shake hands. Cool handshake. Give me some skin. Bow and curtsy. Say hello with just your hand. With both hands. Now do it and change your level. Make the gesture and add a step so that you move through space. Change direction as you do it.

Now say to me with your body, "I am very happy." Make me see right away how happy you really are. Show me a happy walk, a happy skip. Show me a happy gesture at a high level, a low level. Combine them. Show me all your happiness by moving about in space while changing direction and pathway.

Next, say to me with your body, "Oh, oooooh, I have an awful pain." Make sure I can see where your pain is. Show me pain with a stretch, a curl, a twist, a swing, a press, a jab, a jump, a hop. Make it faster (sudden). Make it slower (sustained). Now, I will make 10 beats on my drum and during that time, dance that pain in as many as you can.

Now, let's try to experiment with the following cues: "I smell something." "I hear something." "I like you." "I want you to be my friend." "Go away." "I hate you." "I am angry." For example, show me an angry face. Show me an angry movement with your foot, your arm. Show me that your whole body is angry. Change your level. Stretch, bend, twist. Combine all your angry movements.

Now without using your voice, say "yes" to me with your body. Say it in another way. Now, say "please." Then, say "no." Can you say "no" with your head, your arms, with your whole body? Let's make up a story for you to act out with a partner, involving "yes," "please," and "no." One of you is a parent, and the other is a child. As the child you are asking to do something or have something that you really want by saying "please" with your body. As the parent you keep saying "no." Each of you do as many gestures as you can think of by taking turns responding to each other. Move through space—advancing, approaching, negating, retreating. Let me

Fig. 3-1. We can say "Hello" in different ways.

know at the end, by your movement, who gets his way. At the end, some of you parents just might give in and say "yes." We'll practice for a minute or two and then we'll watch your sequence of gestures.

■ ■ ■

Level: Beginning.

Subconcept: Body gestures or actions can be used to express moods, feelings, and emotions.

Materials: None.

Activities: A dialogue between teacher and children may develop as follows:

I'm going to say a feeling or mood word, and I want you to show me a body shape or action that expresses this word. My first word is "surprise." What might make you surprised? (Getting a present, seeing something that is unexpected, being treated to an ice cream cone.) First, show me a surprised face. Then add your arms and whole body.

Now I'm going to give you some movement words. Show me surprise with whatever word I say. With a jump. With a run. With a stretch. With a twist. With fast moves. With slow, sustained moves. Now hold your pose. Good. Make up a sequence of movements that show your surprise. Show me a variety of shapes and moves to relate how excited or

shocked you are. Don't waste time doing the same thing over and over. Remember to concentrate and focus on your surprise. Don't worry about what others are doing.

Next, show me how you look when you are sad. Show me a body shape. Another. Show me how you move when you are sad. A sad walk. A sad hop or a sad crawl. Most of your sad body shapes and movements have been slow and at a low level. Can you change your level, your direction, your floor pathway, your speed and still be sad?

Next, show me how you laugh. With your head. With your whole body. Can you change your level while you laugh? Can you move about while you laugh? Can you laugh a little? Change, show me a big, side-splitting, belly laugh. Exaggerate your laugh with really big movements to show me how funny it is. Remember to focus on your laughter and not on anyone else.

For our next feeling let's do "desire." That word is hard to define or talk about, so let's create a movement story. Let's imagine that your dad is a farmer. His crops are planted, but it hasn't rained for a long time. The corn, oats, and wheat are dying, the ground is very dry. As a last-ditch effort to change the weather and produce rain, a rainmaker is hired.

Each of you be a rainmaker and show me through your ritual, belief, and concentration how you will produce rain. You must change the weather, and that

Fig. 3-2. What moods can you express with your body?

takes strength of mind and body. There is rain up there in those clouds, and it is dry on the ground. Make that rain come. Ready, begin. (You may wish to use music of drums in the background for accompaniment.)

As we say good-bye today, let's continue this dance of desire. Those of you who want it to be raining when you get outside, line up here. Those of you who want sun, line up over here. (You may choose two other desires—swimming versus basketball, food, drink, vacation, etc.) I'll watch to see which group is dancing with the strongest desire. Maybe when you leave we'll see a change in the weather. Ready, go, Good-bye.

CONCEPT: Props may be used to emphasize various movement qualities in nonverbal communication.

Level: Beginning.

Subconcept: Streamers may serve as stimuli to emphasize various movement qualities in nonverbal communication.

Materials: A record player and records—any music that emphasizes contrasts between free-flowing and percussive music. Suggestions are "Up, Up, and Away" and "Aquarius" by The Fifth Dimension and "Also Sprach Zarathustra" from the movie "2001, a Space Odyssey."

Activities: Streamers of different colors may be used as stimulus ideas for children to work on different qualities of movement. Children following the different action sequences listed next* will change their levels, directions, pathways (air and floor patterns), dimensions, flow time, force, locomotor movements, and body and partner relationships. Whether the children work alone, with a partner, or in a small group situation, you should remember that the children, when using streamers, must maintain focus on the movement qualities and aspects of esthetic expression, instead of using the streamers without any objective reason other than to exercise the children. Initial experiences should be done alone without music. Working with a partner or group and adding music should follow, with careful attention being paid to the phrasing, focus, sequencing, and challenge of each movement theme. As a teacher, you must encourage the children to solve each problem in a variety of ways.

1. Make your streamer fly high in the air in your own space. Now low down.

---

*Young, Jane: Using streamers to introduce creative dance, The Physical Educator **32**:207-209, Dec., 1975.

2. Move anywhere, making your streamer fly sometimes high and sometimes low.
3. Find out what happens to your streamer when you make sudden changes of direction.
4. Use leaping and spinning movements with your streamer. Do you always have to spin on your feet?
5. Make a shape with your streamer in the air. With part of it touching the ground.
6. Make your streamer stay close to you. Far away from you.
7. With a partner, develop a sequence so that you change streamers.
8. Make your streamers use the same air patterns. Different air patterns. Opposite air patterns.
9. Make up a short dance (Fig. 3-3) with the streamers, showing very strong and very light movement.
10. Select three or four movements with the streamer and make them into a movement study that can be repeated again and again.
11. Compose a duet that begins as two solos.

CONCEPT: Words create mental images we can express and communicate through movement.

Level: Intermediate.

Materials: A ball, facial tissue, and word cards. Suggestions for word cards are taken from a child's everyday vocabulary: kite, tractor, wagon, bicycle, rain, snow (Fig. 3-4), river, waterfall, machine, truck, fire, smoke, tornado, firecracker, explosion.

Activities: A dialogue between teacher and children may develop as follows:

Everyone watch. I am going to take this ball, hold it up in the air, and let it fall. Watch how fast it falls and what happens when it hits the floor. It fell at a rather fast direct rate, bounced, and tumbled or rolled when it landed. Show me how you can make your body land as the ball did.

Now, watch as I release this piece of facial tissue. Watch its falling pattern and rate of decent. How did it compare with the flight and landing of the ball? It was more slow, indirect, floating, and soft. Show me how you can make your body move through space and land as the tissue did.

So far we have used two props to notice how they fall through space when released and landed. Then,

as individuals you used your bodies to interpret that movement. Each movement had a beginning and an end, and each observed specific qualities of movement. Now, I would like you to form groups of 3 to 5 children. One child from each group will come here and draw a card out of the bag I am holding. On the card will be a word. Your group must dance that word. When you get your word, you must decide on all its characteristics. Talk with your group about it first. Decide how to start, the direction, size, level, pathway, force, speed, and how to end your action. Then do movements that fit with what you decide. Don't let other groups know your word. Each group will be given 5 minutes to make up their movements, and then we'll all take turns observing your actions. Try to make your movements like the word in every respect, and we'll judge how close you come to describing your word. Ready, go.

It is important in this lesson to allot each group enough time to prepare their movements. You as the teacher may circulate around to each group to give them clues to the movement qualities of their word.

As a matter of evaluation, it is not extremely important for each group to guess another group's word. What is important is to make them observant of the quality of action that took place. A description of "we saw light, downward falling, sometimes swirling, sometimes gusting movements that started at a high level and ended at a low level in a pile" may be a good explanation of falling snow (Fig. 3-4). As a result, this training is as beneficial to the observers as well as the dancers. Any incorrect perceptions could further evolve into correction and perfection of the movement sequence for each word.

Further suggestions for group movement experiences with word cards may stem from spelling words, words from other subjects the children are studying, vacation trips, or other events in the children's lives.

CONCEPT: Pictures stimulate images of action that may be interpreted through movement.

Level: Intermediate.

Materials: Pictures from *National Geographic Magazine, Wildlife,* or any magazine that lends itself to pictures that stimulate action or movement. Suggested pictures: a kite flying, a

Fig. 3-3. Make up a dance with your streamer.

Fig. 3-4. Being a snowfall.

seagull flying, a waterfall, a fish about to strike a lure, a deer drinking at a stream, a busy street, an auto accident, a machine or production line, a hawk circling, etc.

Activities: A dialogue between teacher and children may develop as follows:

To begin our lesson, let's all look at the picture of this kite flying in the air. Somehow this kite had a beginning to its flight. As it is flying, sometimes the winds are calm and gentle, sometimes blowing and gusting. Each kite also has an end to its flight: sometimes natural by being wound up, sometimes

Fig. 3-5. We can create the movements of a kite.

unnatural by diving quickly into a kite-eating tree or telephone wires. I would like each of you in your own space to dance the flight of a kite from beginning to end. Think of the movement qualities (Fig. 3-5) possible—smooth, flowing, rising, high level, diving, changing directions, drifting, sweeping, swooping, floating, sailing, sinking, crashing. Show these qualities in your dance. Ready, go.

Now, I would like you to get into groups of 3 to 5. One child from each group will select a picture for your group to dance. When you get your picture, you must decide what happened before the picture, what is happening in the picture, and what will happen after the picture. Your dance will have a beginning and an end. The main part of your dance will focus on all the movement qualities unique to your picture. I'll give you 5 minutes to work on your dance, and then we'll all share our dances with each other.

With the emphasis on movement qualities and on cause-effect relationships, real paintings, sculptures, and designs made out of colored construction paper may also be used as stimulus ideas for movement experiences.

CONCEPT: Mother Goose nursery rhymes* contain themes that can be expressed by movement.

Level: Beginning.

Materials: None.

Activities: This lesson is designed to encourage children to explore the qualities of space and body relationships through creative movement experiences. The medium or stimuli for nonverbal expression will be children's nursery rhymes. A dialogue between teacher and children may develop as follows:

The eency-weency spider went up the water spout,
Down came the rain and washed the spider out.
Out came the sun and dried up all the rain,
And the eency-weency spider climbed up the spout again.

Could you move like a spider, children? How do they move? At a low level? A high level? Fast? Slow? What kind of spider will you be? A scary one? One catching a fly in its web? The spider is climbing up a water spout (Fig. 3-6). What is a water spout? (A drain or gutter to catch the rain.) Could you make

*The real Mother Goose, Chicago, 1944, Rand McNally.

Fig. 3-6. "The eency-weency spider went up the water spout."

your body into the shape of a water spout? A long skinny one? An angular one? A broken one with a hole in it? *Down came the rain.* With your body could you make the sound and movement that a drop of rain makes as it falls? A soft gentle rain? A thunderous rainstorm? The rain washed the spider out of the spout. What body movements could you make to show that? *Out came the sun and dried up all the rain.* Show me how your body could interpret the warm radiancy of the sun. The hot sun relentlessly beating down. As the sun dried up all the rain, *the eency-weency spider crawled up the spout again.* Show me.

Now, let's all move to the story of Humpty Dumpty:

> *Humpty Dumpty sat on a wall.*
> *Humpty Dumpty had a great fall.*
> *And all the king's horses and all the king's men*
> *Couldn't put Humpty Dumpty together again.*

Humpty Dumpty sat. How many ways can you find to sit? All stretched out? An angular sitting position? All curled up? Partly stretched and partly curled? *Humpty Dumpty sat on a wall.* Could you get together with one or two friends and show me how Humpty sat on the wall? How many ways can you sit on the wall? *Humpty Dumpty had a great fall.*

Show me but be careful and fall safely. *And all the king's horses.* Show me how a horse might move. Fast, slow. With a lot or a little force. In different pathways. *And all the king's men.* Show me how the king's men might move. Like stiff, marching soldiers. Like a servant. Like a doctor. *Couldn't put Humpty Dumpty together again.* In your groups again, show me how the king's horses and men might have tried to fix up poor old Humpty's broken body. One person be Humpty. The others move Humpty's body parts, trying to place Humpty back into an appropriate posture.

You can use other nursery rhymes to effect creative movement with children.

EXAMPLES:

- Hickory, Dickory Dock
- Jack and Jill
- Jack, Be Nimble
- Little Boy Blue
- One, Two, Buckle My Shoe
- Rock-A-Bye, Baby
- The Mulberry Bush
- The Cat and The Fiddle
- Three Blind Mice
- Mary, Mary, Quite Contrary

CONCEPT: People can move in the same way some animals move.

Level: Beginning.

Materials: None.

Activities: A dialogue between teacher and children may develop as follows:

Who has seen a tiger? Show me how a tiger moves. Now show me how a cat moves. What is the difference between a tiger and a cat? (Size, speed, where they live.) How are they the same? (Four legs, stalk their prey, climb trees, sharp claws, tails, piercing eyes.) Cay you move like a tiger or a cat on two feet? Can you get the movement in your back (curled) to show me what their backs look like when frightened? Can you make your eyes look piercing as you stealthily creep with your paws? Show me how a tiger or cat runs or leaps. Show me how they sleep.

Now show me an alligator. Show me that wiggling alligator, but instead of moving close to the ground, keep the feeling of an alligator and move upward to a high level. We must remember that we can't really be an alligator, so we must try to get the quality of an alligator into our bodies. So our movements must be alternating from side to side, lumbering, powerful, sometimes smooth—especially when in water. Can you do that?

This time everyone use your own space to build a cage around yourself. You are now in a zoo. Which animal are you? You've already been a tiger, a cat, and an alligator, so be something else. What will you be? A lion, a bear, a monkey, a gorilla, a snake, a penguin, an elephant, a giraffe, a peacock, a bird? Do you have an idea? Good. Don't tell me what you are, but first show me how your animal rests. Show me another resting shape. Now show me how your animal moves (Fig. 3-7) in the cage. A low level, high level. Can your animal turn? How does your animal feel being caged? While concentrating on the qualities of movement or the feeling of the animal, imagine how your animal would move if its cage were opened. Would it rush out or come out slowly? If a person were at the opening of the cage, would your animal want to be petted, want to run away, or want to eat him up? Show me.

This time think of another animal, the qualities of movement, the feelings of expression. Start with a resting position, move in your cages, come out of your cages when they are opened. When you return to your cages we'll guess who you are.

It is important that the children learn to focus on the qualities of animal movements as dancers. Rather than pretending to be the animal, the attempt should be made to use the movement qualities to portray the feeling or essence of the animal.

Fig. 3-7. What are the movement qualities of your animal?

CONCEPT: Fairy tales contain themes that can be expressed by movement.

Level: Intermediate.

Materials: None.

Activities: Consider the following fairy tales for spontaneous group movement experiences:

- Hansel and Gretel—children wandering through an enchanted forest, finding a candy house, being scared by the witch
- Goldilocks and the Three Bears—Goldilocks tasting the porridge, trying out the chairs and beds of the three bears, and being found in bed when the bears came home
- The Three Pigs—the building of the different houses and the wolf trying to blow each over
- Jack and the Bean Stalk—Jack climbing the stalk and confronting the giant
- Henny Penny—getting hit on the head with an acorn and telling your friends that the world is falling
- Little Red Riding Hood—the initial meeting in the woods, the wolf in Grandma's house, the interaction between the wolf and Little Red Riding Hood, the woodsman killing the wolf

Can you think of others?

Assign groups, allow the children a fair amount of time to decide roles, determine their actions, and then take turns pantomiming the scenes.

CONCEPT: Selected sounds generate ideas that can be expressed through movement.

Level: Intermediate.

Materials: Record player or tape recorder and sound effects record or sounds from the environment taped on a cassette tape.

Activities: A dialogue between teacher and children may develop as follows:

Think of the sound a wristwatch makes. Remember that there are different types of watches: the spring wound—tick, tick, tick, tick; the electric tuning fork—humming or whirring; and the quartz crystal—tick, tick (but at a more definite, yet slower rate than the spring-wound watch). In any instance each sound is rather soft or light and smooth flowing or percussive in nature. Choose the kind of watch you want and make that sound. Now, make a selected body part on your whole body move to the rhythm of the watch.

Now think of different kinds of clocks (Fig. 3-8): an alarm clock, a grandfather clock, a sundial, a chime clock, a cuckoo clock, a clock tower (Big Ben). How are the sounds of all these clocks the same as the sound of a watch? (They are rhythmical and smooth flowing or percussive.) How do they differ? (They are louder.) The pitch of sound may be higher or lower. Some make special sounds: alarm (loud, piercing, vibrant, continuous), chime (soft, musical, alternating), clock tower (loud, bold, pen-

Fig. 3-8. We can create the movements of clocks.

dular, percussive). Choose to be one of these clocks and show me by your movement what kind of clock you are and what kind of sound you are making. Remember of focus on the movement qualities. If you like, you can make your sound verbally to accompany your movement.

What other sounds do you hear that you can interpret through your movement? (A motor running, a washing machine, a train passing, a jet flying, a squeaky door opening, a horn blowing, a frog croaking, a toilet flushing, a siren, a sneeze, brushing your teeth, the wind, rain falling.) I would like you to think of an action and the accompanying sound. Can you make the sound? Can you show me the sound through your movement? Each sound and movement should have a beginning and an end. Think of the qualities of the sound and make appropriate movements. You may focus on changing levels, making percussive, vibratory, or flowing movements, changing speeds, etc. I'll give you 5 minutes to practice, then be ready to make your sound and show us your movement together.

Sound effects records or recorded sounds may be used as stimulus ideas.

CONCEPT: Dramatic play is a form of self-expression that is spontaneous, original, and creative.

Level: Advanced.

Subconcept: Through dramatic play, people can act out their ideas, feelings, emotions, and concepts of the world.

Materials: None.

Activities: Dramatic play is a form of self-expression that is spontaneous, original, and creative. It is a forerunner of creative dramatics. Although verbalization is used, it is incidental to the characterization, role playing, and self-image development that takes place. By acting out his ideas, feelings, emotions, and concepts of the world, the child can try on life. Regardless of the role he is playing, he is working out his feelings and frustrations about his world. He expresses his ideas about his toys, tools, blocks, paints, clothes, actions, and words. He relives his family life in play. He dramatizes his own emotions, fears, doubts, loves, and hates. He organizes the world of people and current events by playing out the roles.

Categories of dramatic play or role playing situations of children may be centered around the following:

- *Activities of the home* — building, furnishing, cooking, eating, work, chores, play with toys, role playing of parent, brother, or sister.

Sample situation: You and your friend have one ball. You would like to throw and catch it. Your friend would like to bat or strike it. How could you work out your differences and play a game together with one ball?

- *Buying and selling wares* — grocery store or department store
- *Transportation* — building, piloting, racing (playing) in boats, airplanes, spaceships, cars, busses.
- *Community helpers* — policemen, fire fighters, doctors, nurses, construction crew, engineers, mail carriers
- *Playing legendary figures* — Pecos Bill, Paul Bunyan, Daniel Boone, Davy Crockett, George Washington
- *Animals* — dramatic pets and zoo animals in various situations

It is the role of the creative teacher to encourage children to use their imagination. Rather than dictate any situations, it is recommended that you work with your children and their specific interests. Create a topic, encourage original responses, give them time to think and play with their ideas, and provide them with any needed tools or props. Provide the children with enough guidance for critical thinking so that their play does not turn into chaos and confusion, yet allows enough freedom to creatively express themselves.

CONCEPT: Action situations can be used as themes to express feelings, emotions, and awareness.

Level: Advanced.

Materials: None.

Activities: Encourage the children to move to the action sets by following these guidelines:

1. Use spontaneous and not planned action — act on impulse.
2. Use the entire body to express the action — avoid timid, restrained, or stereotyped movements.
3. Use overt rather than covert action.
4. Express genuine thought and feeling.

EXAMPLES

- A child in a department store realizing he is lost
- A peddler selling his wares
- A person panicking in a stalled elevator
- A miser counting his money
- A person sewing and sticking himself with a needle
- A person smelling several kinds of perfume and deciding on which to give a loved one for a present
- A creature from Mars arriving on earth
- A person sneaking up on a deer in the woods, suddenly cracking some twigs, startling the deer, then realizing he is lost and it is getting dark
- A child selecting a favorite toy and playing with it
- A person searching for a lost object, finding it, and showing through movement what it is
- A person trying on new clothes, looking in a mirror, and deciding to buy a new set of clothes
- A person hanging out clothes on a windy day
- A neat mother trying to convince her son to clean up his messy room
- A timid salesperson trying to sell a magazine subscription to a busy homemaker.

CONCEPT: Short quotes or sayings create mental images we can express and communicate through movement.

Level: Advanced.

Materials: Source book for quotes or sayings, such as *Poor Richards' Almanac* or *Farmer's Almanac*.

Activities: Divide the children into small groups of 3 to 5 and assign or let them choose a saying to portray through movement. Emphasis of the movement sequence should be placed on the theme, focus, occurrence, or mood of each saying with respect to group direction, level, space, force, time, flow, and relationships.

Choose from the following:

- Birds of a feather flock together
- Big things come in small packages
- A rolling stone gathers no moss
- April showers bring May flowers
- The early bird catches the worm
- Never put off till tomorrow what you can do today
- A bird in the hand is worth two in the bush
- An apple a day keeps the doctor away
- A stitch in time saves nine
- Rain before seven, clear before eleven
- Sky pink at night, sailor's delight; pink in morning, sailor's warning
- March comes in like a lion, goes out like a lamb
- Rain, rain, go away, Little Johnny wants to play
- Early to bed, early to rise, makes a man healthy, wealthy, and wise
- If at first you don't succeed, try, try again
- To love and be loved, is the greatest gift
- Here comes the judge
- Better late than never
- Waste not, want not
- No man is an island
- Pretty as a picture
- Your actions speak so loud, I can't hear your words

When the wind is from the west, the fishing is best;
When the wind is from the east, the fishing is least;
When the wind is from the north, the fish come forth;
When the wind is from the south, the bait is blown in the fish's mouth.

Can you think of others? Also, have the children write their own sayings to which they may move.

SELECTED REFERENCES FOR PART ONE

Boorman, Joyce: Creative dance in the first three grades, Don Mills, Ontario, 1969, Longmans, Canada, Ltd.

Boorman, Joyce: Creative dance in grades four to six, Don Mills, Ontario, 1971, Longmans Canada, Ltd.

Boorman, Joyce: Dance and language experiences with children, Don Mills, Ontario, 1973, Longmans Canada, Ltd.

Bush, Wilma Jo: Aids to psycholinguistic teaching, Columbus, Ohio, 1969, C. E. Merrill Publishing Co.

Cratty, Bryant J.: Learning and playing—fifty vigorous activities for the atyical child, Freeport, N.Y., 1968, Educational Activities, Inc.

Cratty, Bryant J.: Active learning—games to enhance academic abilities, Englewood Cliffs, N.J., 1971, Prentice-Hall, Inc.

Cratty, Bryant J.: Intelligence in action; physical activities for enhancing intellectual abilities, Englewood Cliffs, N.J., 1973, Prentice-Hall, Inc.

Cratty, Bryant J., and Sister Mark Szczepanik: Sounds, words and actions; movement games to enhance the language arts skills of elementary school children, Freeport, N.Y., 1971, Educational Activities, Inc.

Dallman, Martha: Teaching the language arts in the elementary school, Dubuque, Iowa, 1971, William C. Brown Co.

Donoghue, Mildred R.: The child and the English language arts, Debuque, Iowa, 1971, William C. Brown Co.

Joyce, Mary: First steps in teaching creative dance, Palo Alto, Calif., 1973, National Press Books.

Karnes, Merle B . Helping young children develop language skills, Arlington, Va., 1968, The Council for Exceptional Children.

Logan, Lillian, M., et al.: Creative communication; teaching the language arts, Scarborough, Ontario, 1972, McGraw-Hill Ryerson Ltd.

McCullough, Constance Mary: Handbook for teaching the language arts, San Francisco, 1969, Chandler Publishing Co.

Moffett, James: A' student-centered language arts curriculum, grades K-13; a handbook for teachers, Boston, 1968, Houghton Mifflin Co.

Smith, E. Brooks, et al., Language and thinking in the elementary school, N.Y., 1970, Holt, Rinehart, & Winston, Inc.

Spier, Peter: Fast, slow, high, low, Garden City, N.Y., 1973, Doubleday Books, Inc.

Strickland, Ruth G.: The language arts in the elementary school, Lexington, Mass., 1969, Heath Publishers.

PART TWO

Developing mathematics concepts

Can you hop to the answer?

Mathematics textbooks often use play experiences and game situations to enhance the presentation of mathematics concepts. As an example, various types of word problems often describe physical education activities in which team scores, batting averages, kicking distances, and shooting percentages are used to teach mathematics concepts. Classroom teachers and physical education teachers should take advantage of these examples and move mathematics out of the classroom and into a movement environment. Through concrete practical examples, children may learn to understand the abstract mathematics concepts more easily. Understanding and using mathematics concepts correctly can be as much a part of the physical education period as play experiences and game situations are a part of the mathematics lesson in the classroom.

If children are to be taught mathematics concepts in physical education, teachers should be aware of the mathematics concepts that are taught at the various grade levels. Review of several mathematics textbook series and current mathematics projects such as the School Mathematics Study Group, Greater Cleveland Mathematics Program, University of Illinois Arithmetic Project, Madison Project, Stanford Project, and Minnesota Mathematics and Science Teaching Project indicate that the following mathematics concepts are taught in the elementary school level: the whole numbers, the metric system, mathematical sentences, sets, field properties of mathematics, geometry, and measuring and graphing. During the primary grades, children learn about counting, adding, subtracting, sets, the metric system, geometry, number sentences, measuring, commutative and associative properties for addition, fractions, and word problems. During the inter-

mediate grades, children learn about sets, set operations, identity properties for addition and multiplication, distributive properties for multiplication and division, geometry, measuring and graphing, mathematical sentences, fractions, decimals, and the metric system.

A number of studies have been conducted to determine the effectiveness of the integration of mathematics with physical education. Ashlock and Humphrey (1976), Gilbert (1977), and Humphrey (1974) have published books concerning research and practical implementation ideas, ranging from the integration of simple mathematics concepts such as whole numbers and counting to mathematics set theory with physical education activities. Other studies advocating integration of mathematics concepts with physical education evolved in a series of lessons combining the two subjects. Memmel (1953) illustrated lessons in which rope jumping, team games, throwing, kicking, marching, rhythms, and shooting baskets were integrated with mathematics concepts. Jensen (1971) used jump ropes in solving simple arithmetic problems and designing geometrical patterns through physical education. Lessons for the teaching of number concepts, integers, rationals, addition, subtraction, multiplication, division, averages, linear measures, time, geometric forms, and the metric system through physical education have also been presented by various other authors. In each instance the authors indicated a positive response by the children to the active learning experiences.

With the knowledge that the integration of mathematics concepts through physical education may be used effectively to teach children, the many possibilities will be examined in detail.

Chapter 4

WHOLE NUMBERS AND THE METRIC SYSTEM

WHOLE NUMBERS

The set of whole numbers contains the set of counting numbers beginning with zero (0, 1, 2, 3, 4 . . .). This set of numbers has a least member, zero, but no greater member. As a result, this set is an infinite one because no matter how many members of the set are listed, there are still additional members.

Early in a child's school experiences he learns various operations on the set of whole numbers. Initial experiences include counting, adding, and subtracting numbers. Gradually children learn about multiplication, division, fractions, and decimals.

METRIC SYSTEM

The metric system is a system of weights and measures that originated in France in the latter part of the eighteenth century. It has been adopted by law in most civilized countries of the world and is almost universally used for scientific measurements. For these reasons, within a few years the United States will adopt the system* in an attempt to adjust their system of weights and measures with the rest of the world.

The fundamental units of the metric system are the meter, the unit of length; the liter, the unit of capacity; and the gram, the unit of mass or weight.

Experiences in physical education may be utilized most applicably with reference to length and weight, and so the lessons that follow have been designed to help children learn about the meter and gram.

---

*Bill PL93-380, The Metric Education Program, was passed in 1974. Bill PL94-168, The Metric Conversion Act, was passed in December, 1975; it will take several years for implementation.

THE METRIC SYSTEM

The standard *meter* is the distance between two lines on a bar of platinum preserved at the International Bureau of Weights and Measures at Sèvres, near Paris, France. The meter is exactly 39.37 inches long. It was intended to be, and approximately is, the ten millionth part of a quadrant of a terrestrial meridian.

The *liter* is equivalent to the space occupied by one kilogram of pure water at the temperature of its greatest density (4° centigrade). It is, approximately, a cubic decimeter.

The *gram* is one thousandth of the mass of a piece of platinum deposited with the International Bureau of Weights and Measures. It was intended to have the same mass as a cubic decimeter of pure water at 4° centigrade.

The other units of the metric system are decimally related to the fundamental units; that is, each unit in each table is ten times the unit next smaller, and one tenth of the unit next larger. To express this relationship, the following prefixes are used: *milli-*, one thousandth; *centi-*, one hundredth; *deci,* one tenth; *deki-* or *deca-*, ten times; *hecto-*, one hundred times; *kilo-*, one thousand times; *myria-*, ten thousand times.*

---

*The cubic meter = 61,023.38 cubic inches; 1 kiloliter = 61,025 cubic inches.

Continued.

MEASURES OF LENGTH
Length

Metric denominations and values				Equivalents
1 myriameter	=	10,000 meters	=	6.2137 miles
1 kilometer	=	1,000 meters	=	0.62137 mile, or 3,280 feet 10 inches
1 hectometer	=	100 meters	=	328 feet 1 inch
1 dekameter	=	10 meters	=	393.7 inches
1 meter	=	1 meter	=	39.37 inches
1 decimeter	=	1/10 meter	=	3.937 inches
1 centimeter	=	1/100 meter	=	0.3937 inch
1 millimeter	=	1/1000 meter	=	0.0394 inch
1 micrometer (micron)	=	1/1,000,000 meter	=	1/1000 millimeter
1 nanometer (millimicron)	=	1/1,000,000,000 meter	=	1/1000 micrometer

MEASURES OF CAPACITY AND VOLUME

Metric denominations and values	Cu. in.	Dry measure	Equivalents Approximate Liquid measure	Cubic measure
1 kiloliter* = 1000 liters	= 61025.0	= 1.308 cubic yards	= 264.18 gallons	= 1 cubic meter* or 1 stere†
1 hectoliter = 100 liters	= 6102.50	= 2.8378 bushels	= 26.418 gallons	= 1/10 cubic meter
1 dekaliter = 10 liters	= 610.250	= 1.1351 pecks	= 2.6418 gallons	= 10 cubic decimeters
1 liter = 1 liter	= 61.0250	= 0.9081 quart	= 1.0567 quarts	= 1 cubic decimeter
1 deciliter = 1/10 liter	= 6.10250	= 0.18162 pint	= 0.8454 gill	= 1/10 cubic decimeter
1 centiliter = 1/100 liter	= 0.610250	= 0.6102 cubic inch	= 0.3381 fluidounce	= 10 cubic centimeters
1 milliliter = 1/1000 liter	= 0.0610250	= 0.0610 cubic inch	= 0.2705 fluiddram	= 1 cubic centimeter

*The cubic meter = 61,023.38 cubic inches; 1 kiloliter = 61,025 cubic inches.
†By definition, 1 stere = 1 cubic meter; that is, 1,000.027 liters, or 1.000027 kiloliters; 1 hectostere = 100 cubic meters.

MEASURES OF MASS (WEIGHTS)

Metric denominations and values			Quantity of water		Equivalents
1 tonne (metric ton)	=	1,000,000 grams	= 1 cubic meter (nearly)	=	1.102311 short tons
1 quintal	=	100,000 grams	= 1 hectoliter	=	220.46 pounds
1 myriagram	=	10,000 grams	= 10 liters	=	22.046 pounds
1 kilogram or kilo	=	1000 grams	= 1 liter	=	2.2046 pounds
1 hectogram	=	100 grams	= 1 deciliter	=	3.5274 ounces
1 dekagram	=	10 grams	= 1 milliliter	=	0.3527 ounce
1 gram	=	1 gram	= 1 cubic centimeter	=	0.0353 ounce
1 decigram	=	1/10 gram	= 1/10 cubic centimeter		
1 centigram	=	1/100 gram	= 10 cubic millimeters		
1 milligram	=	1/1000 gram	= 1 cubic millimeter		

Learning activities

Whole numbers

CONCEPT: We can form the shapes of numbers with our bodies.

Level: Beginning.

Subconcept: The whole numbers may be made from lines that are either straight, curved, or diagonal.

Materials: A chalkboard and chalk.

Activities: Each of the whole numbers may be made from lines that are either straight, curved, diagonal, or a combination of lines.

METRIC EQUIVALENTS OF DOMESTIC MEASURES

Length		
1 inch	=	2.54 centimeters
1 foot	=	0.3048 meter
1 yard	=	0.9144 meter
1 rod	=	5.029 meters
1 mile	=	1,609.35 meters

Surface		
1 square inch	=	6.452 square centimeters
1 square foot	=	0.0929 square meter
1 square yard	=	0.8361 square meter
1 square rod	=	25.293 square meters
1 acre	=	4046.87 square meters
1 acre	=	40.469 ares
1 square mile	=	259.000 hectares

Capacity		
1 cubic inch	=	16.337 cubic centimeters
1 cubic inch	=	0.0164 liter, cubic decimeter
1 cubic foot	=	28.316 liters, 28.317 cubic decimeters
1 cubic yard	=	764.539 liters, 764.559 cubic decimeters
1 cord	=	3.625 steres

1 quart, dry measure	=	1.1012 liters
1 peck (U.S.)	=	8.8096 liters
1 bushel (U.S.)	=	35.24 liters
1 fluiddram	=	3.70 cubic centimeters
1 fluidounce	=	29.57 cubic centimeters
1 fluidounce	=	0.0296 liter
1 gill	=	0.1183 liter
1 quart, liquid measure	=	0.9463 liter
1 gallon (231 cubic inches)	=	3.785 liters

English measures (used also in Canada)		
1 British quart	=	1.2009 U.S. liquid quarts
1 British quart	=	1.0320 U.S. dry quarts
1 U.S. dry quart	=	0.9690 British quart
1 U.S. liquid quart	=	0.8327 British quart

Weights		
1 grain*	=	64.80 milligrams
1 ounce, avoirdupois	=	28.3495 grams
1 pound, avoirdupois	=	0.45359 kilogram
1 short ton (2000 pounds)	=	907.2 kilograms
1 short ton (2000 pounds)	=	0.9072 metric ton
1 long ton (2240 pounds)	=	1.016 metric tons

*The troy, avoirdupois, and apothecaries' grain are the same.

METRIC SYSTEM SIMPLIFIED

Length

The denominations in practical use are the millimeter (mm.), centimeter (cm.), meter (m.), and kilometer (km.).

10 millimeters	=	1 centimeter
10 centimeters	=	1 decimeter
10 decimeters	=	1 meter
1000 meters	=	1 kilometer

Weight

The denominations in practical use are the milligram (mg.), gram (g.), kilogram (kg.), and ton (metric ton).

1000 miligrams	=	1 gram
1000 grams	=	1 kilogram
1000 kilograms	=	1 metric ton

Capacity

The denominations in practical use are the cubic centimeter (c.c.) and liter (l., L.)

1000 cubic centimeters	=	1 liter
100 liters	=	1 hectoliter

Relation of capacity and weight to length: 1 cubic decimeter is, approximately, 1 liter, and 1 liter of water weighs 1 kilogram.

Approximate equivalents

1 meter (39.37 inches) is about 1 yard.
1 kilogram (2.2 pounds) is about 2 pounds.
1 liter (0.91 dry qt. and 1.06 liquid qt.) is about 1 quart.
1 centimeter (0.39 inch) is about ½ inch.
1 metric ton (2204.6 pounds) is about 1 long ton.
1 kilometer (0.62 mile, or 3280 feet) is about ⅝ mile.
1 cubic centimeter is about 1 thimbleful.
1 nickel weighs about 5 grams.

Categorize each of the numbers by discussing the composition of each number. Draw them on the board or have the children draw them on the board according to proper category. Categories may vary somewhat according to how you teach the children to form the letters.

Straight line *1, 3, 4, 9*
Curved line *0, 2, 3, 6, 8*
Diagonal *4, 7*
Straight and curved *2, 3, 5, 9*
Straight and diagonal *4, 7*

After the children have discussed the composition and shape of each of the numbers, they may perform the following activities to the best of their abilities:

1. Make the shape of each of the numbers with your body.
2. Walk, hop, or jump the pattern of each of the numbers on the floor.
3. Make the numbers by tracing their shape in the air, using large body movements (head, elbow, whole arm, etc.).

4. Form a specific number with your body as a solution to a math problem you have been given.
5. Make up a number sequence with a group of children.

■ ■ ■

Level: Intermediate.

Subconcepts: (1) Addition is the sum of two or more numbers. (2) Subtraction is the reduction of a quantity (part) from the whole. (3) Multiplication is the process of finding the quantity obtained by repeating a specified quantity a specified number of times. (4) Division is the process of finding how many times a number is contained in another.

Materials: None.

Activities: This lesson is centered around having the children form the whole numbers with their bodies (Fig. 4-1). Have them perform the following activities according to their abilities.

1. Make each of the numbers with your body. Can you make any given number in more than one way? Can you make a number several ways at the same time?
2. Get together in groups of 2 to 5 and make up a number sequence. (In turn, have each group form their sequence and have the other groups guess the sequence.)
3. I'll call out or write a math problem on the chalkboard. Form the solution to the problem with your body.

CONCEPT: The whole numbers may be formed by tracing patterns on the floor and in the air.

Level: Beginning.

Subconcept: The human body can form numerical solutions to problems in addition, subtraction, multiplication, and division.

Materials: Use paint, chalk, shoe polish, or another marking device to design the pattern in Fig. 4-2 on a gym floor or hard surface area out-

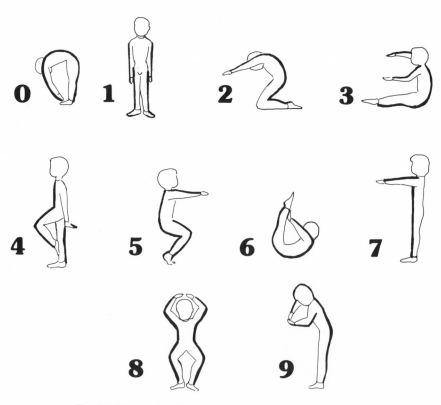

Fig. 4-1. We can form the shape of numbers with our bodies.

Fig. 4-2. Can you make the number by walking on the grid?

Fig. 4-3. Mathematics activities with small equipment.

side. Several designs may be made for the whole class.

Activities: Have the children perform the following activities according to their abilities:

1. Write a number on the chalkboard or call out a number. Then have the child trace out the number by walking the proper floor pattern. Can the child reproduce the number while walking, hopping, or jumping in forward, backward, or sideways directions?
2. Can the child perform the activity above and at the same time trace the number in the air with one or both arms while walking the floor pattern?
3. Have the child count the numbers from 0 to 9 by walking each consecutive floor pattern. Then do the same while hopping and jumping in different directions.
4. Have the child do math problems by walking out appropriate floor patterns for the numbers. For example, walk out the patterns of the 4, 3, and 1 sequentially.

CONCEPT: The shapes of numbers may be formed on the floor or in the air with props.

Level: Intermediate.

Materials: Jump ropes, paper strips or crepe paper, streamers, and a selection of records that contrast percussive versus smooth-flowing music.

Activities: The purpose of this lesson is to have the children form the whole numbers with air patterns and floor patterns. To begin the lesson, give each child a jump rope and have them place it on the floor. Then give them math problems to solve according to their ability. Have them make the answer with their rope by manipulating their rope with their feet to form the number shape. On the numbers that have curved or closed parts, have the children move from the inside to the outside using varied attempts (hop, jump, forward, backward, etc.) On the numbers that have straight or diagonal lines, have the children move along the lines, using varied attempts (walk, slide, high, low, etc). Next, give each of the children a streamer and have them trace the whole numbers in the air. With music in the background, which numbers can be traced more easily with smooth-flowing music in the background? For more ideas on the use

of streamers with music refer to the lesson on pp. 53 and 54.

CONCEPT: The whole numbers are 0, 1, 2, 3, 4, 5, 6, 7, 8, and 9.

Level: Beginning.

Subconcepts: (1) The numerical system is based on unit values of 1, 10, 100, 1000, etc. (2) The operations of addition, subtraction, multiplication, and division may be performed with. the numerical system.

Materials: Use old scraps of material or felt and dried peas, navy beans, or styrofoam pellets from old beanbag chairs. Cut the material into the shapes of geometric forms, letters, or numbers. Sew two of the same forms together with strong thread until only a small hole remains. Fill the bag with beans and complete the sewing (Fig. 4-4).

Activities: Following are some suggested activities for using the beanbags, stressing academic integration concepts.* This lesson could also be applied to letter recognition in the chapter on reading and writing (pp. 28 to 49) and the section on geometry (pp. 98 to 104).

1. Throw the number beanbag to the child and have him identify it as he catches it.
2. Give the children mathematics problems involving addition, subtraction, multiplication, and division according to their ability level and have them solve the problems by using the beanbags. Then tell them to assume the shape of the numerical answer with their bodies.

■ ■ ■

Level: Beginning.

Subconcept: The whole numbers may be used to help children develop better concepts of figure-ground perception.

Materials: Use chalk, shoe polish, water-base tempra paint, paint, or any other marking device to create number designs such as those illustrated in Fig. 4-5. Temporary designs placed on the gym floor or hard surface area outside work best because they may be changed regularly.

---

*In addition to the stress on academic integration, beanbags may also be used for balance and manipulative experiences, including throwing, catching, kicking, and striking.

NUMBER BEANBAGS

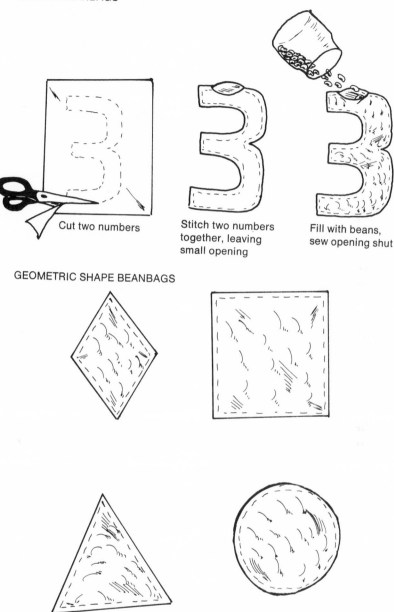

Cut two numbers

Stitch two numbers
together, leaving
small opening

Fill with beans,
sew opening shut

GEOMETRIC SHAPE BEANBAGS

Fig. 4-4. Beanbags in the shape of numbers and geometrical forms.

Activities: Have the children perform the following activities according to their abilities:

1. Walk, crawl, hop, skip, etc. along the design. Use different levels, pathways, and directions and identify each of the numbers as you move on it.

2. As a math problem is posed to you (addition, subtraction, multiplication, or division), calculate the answer in your head. Then go to the design, find the answer, and trace it with your body movement.

3. Use a piece of paper to create your own de-

Fig. 4-5. Numbers may be combined for experiences in figure-ground perception.

sign out of numbers. Then transfer your design to the floor and perform the above activities.

■ ■ ■

Levels: Beginning and intermediate.

Subconcept: The operations of addition, subtraction, multiplication, and division may be performed with the numerical system.

Materials: Use paint, chalk, shoe polish, or another marking device to design a number grid on a gym floor or hard surface area outside (see Part Two opening figure).

Activities: Have the children perform the following activities according to their abilities:

1. Jump or hop from one number to another and say the number as you land on it. Move in forward, sideways, and backward directions and change your pathway on the floor so that you can recognize the numbers from all angles.
2. See if you can count consecutively from 1 to 10 (or 1 to 50 or 1 to 100) by hopping or jumping into the appropriate boxes. When you get to the double numbers (10 and up), hop with one foot into the number for the ones column (0 to 9) and with both feet into the number for the tens column.
3. Place your body parts on a given number. For example, place your hand (R) on a 9, place an elbow (L) on a 6, place a knee (R) on a 2, etc.
4. Make up a contest with two or more friends by performing the activity in no. 3. Once a body part is placed on the floor, it must re-

main there. See how twisted or tangled up you can get before you lose your balance.
5. Do your math problems by hopping or jumping from one square to another. For example, 5 + 3 = 8: hop from the 5 to the + to the 3 to the + to the 8. Do addition, subtraction, multiplication, or division problems according to your ability. When you get to double digits, use one-foot and two-foot landings, as in no. 2.

CONCEPT: The whole numbers may be used to classify and/or seriate groups or objects.

Level: Beginning.

Subconcepts: (1) Groups or objects equal in number may be classified together. (2) Groups or objects may be seriated in order of size, weight, amount, etc.

Materials: Balls, bats, rackets, and/or any game equipment.

Activities: The purpose of this lesson is to help children group things, learn the concept of numeration, and perform simple mathematical operations. First, have the children divide into two groups—boys and girls. Count the number in each group. Now have the children divide into other groups—use hair color, eye color, height, weight, birth date, number of brothers and sisters, etc. Count the number in each group.

To become more active, have the children walk, hop, skip, jump, and gallop, using different directions, levels, pathways, and speeds, as you call out a specific size number you wish groups to form. Have the children move about the room, and when a number is called out see how quickly they can form that size group. Any children who do not find a group must freeze or squat until the next number is called, at which time they can reenter the game by finding a group. Each time, the number in each group must be exact; any extras must leave a group and form another or wait out a turn until new groups are formed.

After a period of time have the children play the same game blindfolded or with their eyes closed. Again, have them explore space as they move about, becoming more aware of their environment. Then when you call out a number, they will have to use their voices, special signals, or their sense of tough to figure out the number of children in each group.

At the end of the lesson have the children use their awareness of numbers and their abilities to classify, seriate, or group the equipment in the gym. How many balls are there? Seriate them according to size. How many sizes are there? How many in each size? How many colors do the balls have? Classify them according to colors. How many of each color are there? Seriate them according to weight or texture. Classify them according to use—inside or outside; throw, kick, or strike; etc. Do the same for all the other equipment in the gym. Classify and/or seriate the bats, racquets, gymnastics equipment, etc. according to size, color, weight, texture, or use.

CONCEPT: Counting gives order to a sequence of events.

Levels: Beginning and intermediate.

Materials: Any equipment including balls, records, and gymnastics apparatus that you may have in your teaching situation.

Activities: Rather than develop one lesson on counting, it would be more advantageous to point out several examples in which counting may be used in movement experiences. You may choose those you feel confident would work with your children. You will also no doubt think of other ways in which counting may be used.

1. While doing exercises, count the number you perform. Count from 1 up or start with a number and count down to zero. Count by using even numbers or odd numbers, by 2s, 3s, 4s, 5s, etc.
2. Count, march, or perform locomotor movements to the rhythm of the music on a record that you play by using the procedures in no. 1.
3. Count exercises in sets such as 1, 2, 2, 2, 3, 2, 4, 2 or 1, 2, 3, 4, 2, 2, 3, 4, 3, 2, 3, 4, 4, 2, 3, 4, 5, 2, 3, 4, etc.
4. Count the measures in a piece of music, using the procedure in no. 3.
5. Use your counting abilities to keep score in games such as hopscotch or shuffleboard.
6. Play a game such as basketball or volley-

ball and keep score normally or count points by 2s, 3s, 4s, etc.

7. Play a game starting with a certain number of points and count down to zero by 1s, 2s, 3s, etc.
8. Count the number of times you can jump a rope in a minute. Count by 1s, 2s, 3s, etc.
9. Count the number of times you can bounce a ball or throw a ball in 10 seconds. Count as in the preceding experience. Use different time trials and use addition or subtraction to compare the differences between trials.
10. In certain types of games such as line games where a certain number of children are caught, the number of children caught can be counted. The number of children not caught and the total number of children in the class can be used to include addition and subtraction problems.

CONCEPT: The operations of addition, subtraction, multiplication, and division may be performed on the whole numbers.

Level: Beginning.

Materials: Construct one (or more) abacus (Fig. 4-6), as seen in the picture pieces of playground equipment on your school grounds. Use various colors to paint different levels.

Another way to accomplish the same task in the gym is to suspend coat hangers with clamp clothes pins attached from a line (Fig. 4-7) hung across a gym. Pins may be painted different colors.

Activities: Have the children perform the following activities according to their abilities:

1. Have the student climb rungs or run up to the hanger and move the block laterally with his hands or feet.
2. Have the student climb rungs or move up to the hanger and move a particular color block or pin.
3. Have the student climb rungs or move up to the hanger and move a specific number of blocks or pins.
4. Have the student climb rungs or move up to the pins and move a specific number of blocks or pins either right or left.
5. Have the student identify the place value of

Fig. 4-6. Can you climb the abacus and count out the answer?

Fig. 4-7. Can you form the answer with the clothes pins?

each row of blocks or pins and then show a number using these values.

6. Have the student add or subtract numbers, using these place values.
7. Use the abacus as a vertical ladder.

■　■　■

Levels: Intermediate and advanced.

Materials: Any equipment that you have available in your teaching situation.

Activities: Because of the variety of instances in which the operations of addition, subtraction, multiplication, and division may be used in physical education, several ideas are suggested, rather than limit the material to one lesson. In addition, you will have many ideas of your own of ways to implement the operations.

1. If you have 17 boys and 15 girls in class, what is the total number of children in the class?
2. If you have five softballs, eight tennis balls, four basketballs, and three volleyballs, in the gym, what is the total number of balls?
3. If twenty-seven outs were made in a softball game and fifteen were made by fly balls caught in the air, how many were made in other ways?
4. In a game of bowling your score was 56, your two partners' scores were 92 and 87. What was your total team score? Other teams in class averaged 250. By how much did your team score differ from the average?
5. If you can jump rope twenty-seven times in 1 minute, how many times could you jump rope in 7 minutes?
6. If a football team's score was 49 points at the end of a game and only touchdowns were scored with extra points, how many touchdowns did the team make?
7. When you run it takes you five steps to cover 10 yards. How many steps would it take you to cover 220 yards?
8. If you could pace yourself and run 220 yards in 45 seconds, how many seconds would it take you to run 1,760 yards? Convert your answer to minutes and seconds.
9. If there were 28 children in your class and each averaged 3 feet 9 inches in a high jump contest, what was the total height your class

jumped? Convert figures to decimals or to inches as you compute your answer.

CONCEPT: A fraction is a quantity less than a whole, with a numerator and denominator; it can also be expressed as a decimal.

Level: Advanced.

Subconcepts: (1) A numerator is that part of a fraction written above the line. (2) A denominator is that part of a fraction written below the line.

Materials: Any equipment, including balls, bats, rhythm sticks, records, and gymnastics apparatuses or mats that you may have in your teaching situation.

Activities: Rather than one lesson fractions, it would be more advantageous to point out several situations in which fractions may be used in movement experiences. You may choose those you feel confident would work with your children. You will also no doubt think of other ways in which fractions may be used.

1. Divide the class into from two to six squads. If 28 to 30 children are in the class, several comparisons may be made. If there are four squads, each squads equals one fourth the class. If two squads are combined, you have one half the class.
2. Games are often divided into time periods. Each time period equals one fourth, one third, or one half the game.
3. Other games are divided into holes, innings, or sets. Six holes equal one third of a golf round. Six innings equal two thirds of a baseball game. Six games equal one whole set in the game of tennis.
4. One couple equals one fourth of a square dance set. If there are four square dance sets, what fraction is one couple? (1/16)
5. If there are 50 points scored in a game and player X scored 10, what fraction did he score? (1/5) If player Y scored 15, what fraction did he score? (3/10)
6. If you have 4 × 6 foot panelled mats for gymnastics and you have 5 mats, what fraction would 4 panels be? (4/20, 2/10, or 1/5) What fraction would three panels be? (3/20)
7. On a record album there are six selections on each side of the record. If you learn two

of the dances on the record, what fraction have you learned? (2/12, or 1/6) If you learn two more dances, what percentage have you learned? (4/12, 2/6, or 1/3)

8. If you have ten softballs in class, 30 children, and five bats, what is the ratio of balls to children? (10/30, 2/6, or 1/3) What is the ratio of bats to children? (5/30, or 1/6) What is the ratio of bats to balls? (5/10, or 1/2)

9. Each child in a class of 30 has two rymthm or Lummi sticks. What fraction of the sticks do 3 children have? (6/60, 3/30, or 1/10)

10. You learned a dance consisting of 8 measures, or 32 counts. What fraction is 1 measure, or 4 counts? (4/32, or 1/8)

11. Calesthenics are performed in counts or measures. For example, jumping jacks take 2 counts and squat thrusts take 4 counts. As a result, each exercise can be divided into parts or fractions.

CONCEPT: The process of division can be used in determining decimals and percentages.

Level: Advanced.

Subconcepts: (1) A decimal is a fraction with a denominator of 10 or some power of 10, shown by a point before the numerator (.5 = $^5/_{10}$). (2) A percentage is a portion, or part, of 100.

Materials: Any equipment that you may have in your teaching situation.

Activities: Rather than develop one lesson about division, decimals, and percentages, it would be more advantageous to point out several situations in which they may be used in movement experiences. You may choose those you feel confident would work with your children. You will also no doubt think of other ways in which they may be used.

1. A batter came up to bat twenty times with no sacrifice outs and no walks. He made five hits. What is his batting average? (When teaching the children about division, decimals, and percentages in this instance tell them that the total number of occurrences is the denominator or divisor. The smaller number or frequency of occurrence will be the numerator. (5 ÷ 20 = .250)

2. The field goal kicker on a football team has tried twenty-five kicks from inside the 30-yard line. He has made twenty of them. What is his average? (20 ÷ 25 = .800) He has made twelve of twenty from between the 30- and 40-yard line. What is his average? (12 ÷ 20 − .600)

3. A basketball player made five our of eight shots during the first half of the game. What is his average? (5 ÷ 8 = .625)

4. In class you made ninety attempts to throw and catch the ball with your partner. You caught the ball eighty-five times. What is your success ratio? (85 ÷ 90 = .944)

5. In a game of tag 27 out of 30 class members are caught after 2 minutes of play. What percentage of players are caught? (27 ÷ 30 = .90)

Metric system

CONCEPT: The metric unit of measurement for distance is the meter.

Levels: Intermediate and advanced.

Subconcept: One meter equals 10 decimeters.

Materials: High jump standards, a landing pit, and a measuring tape—a metric one, if possible. If you do not have high jump standards, suspend a rope or bamboo pole across some makeshift standards. A landing pit may be made from gym mats, foam rubber, or tires and inner tubes.

Activities: During a unit in track and field, you may wish to teach the high jump to the children. The scissors, straddle, and roll or flop type of jumps may be taught. No matter which style you prefer to teach, emphasize a good one-foot takeoff, vertical lift, clearance of each body part over the bar, and an efficient, safe landing. As you allow the children to develop their jumping skills, you will begin to measure and raise the height of their jumps. Table 1, listing heights and a conversion to the metric system is included for your convenience.

■ ■ ■

Levels: Intermediate and advanced.

Subconcept: One meter equals 100 centimeters.

Table 1. Metric conversions for high jump

Feet	Inches	Decimeters	Feet	Inches	Decimeters
2	0	6.096	3	7	10.922
2	1	6.350	3	8	11.176
2	2	6.604	3	9	11.430
2	3	6.858	3	10	11.684
2	4	7.112	3	11	11.938
2	5	7.366			
2	6	7.620	4	0	12.192
2	7	7.874	4	1	12.446
2	8	8.128	4	2	12.700
2	9	8.382	4	3	12.954
2	10	8.636	4	4	13.208
2	11	8.890	4	5	13.462
			4	6	13.716
3	0	9.144	4	7	13.970
3	1	9.398	4	8	14.224
3	2	9.652	4	9	14.478
3	3	9.906	4	10	14.732
3	4	10.160	4	11	14.986
3	5	10.414			
3	6	10.668	5	0	15.240

Table 2. Metric conversions for vertical jump

Feet	Inches	Centimeters	Feet	Inches	Centimeters
	1	2.54	1	7	48.26
	2	5.08	1	8	50.80
	3	7.62	1	9	53.34
	4	10.16	1	10	55.88
	5	12.70	1	11	58.42
	6	15.24			
	7	17.78	2	0	60.96
	8	20.32	2	1	63.50
	9	22.86	2	2	66.04
	10	25.40	2	3	68.58
	11	27.94	2	4	71.12
1	0	30.48	2	5	73.66
1	1	33.02	2	6	76.20
1	2	35.56	2	7	78.74
1	3	38.10	2	8	81.28
1	4	40.64	2	9	83.82
1	5	43.18	2	10	86.36
1	6	45.72	2	11	88.90
			3	0	91.44

Materials: Vertical jump standards or use a piece of chalk or another marking device to record the height of jumps on a wall; a measuring tape—preferably a metric one.

Activities: During this lesson the children will practice their vertical jump skills. Emphasis will be placed on a two-foot takeoff, good extension of the legs, and timing of the arm swing with extension at the peak of the jump. Each jump will be measured to the nearest inch or *centimeter* and recorded. Each child should stand next to the wall, reach as high as he can with an extended arm, and mark that point with the chalk. Then, taking care not to jump into the wall, he should try to jump as high as he can and mark that spot with the chalk. Finally, while standing on a chair or bench, he should record the distance between the two marks. This is the actual height of the child's jump. In case you do not have a metric measuring device, Table 2 is included for your convenience.

■　■　■

Levels: Intermediate and advanced.

Subconcept: One meter measures just a little more than 3 feet.

Materials: A measuring tape—a metric one if possible.

Activities: During this lesson the children will practice their standing long jump skills. As they develop their skills, they should concentrate on placing their toes up to the mark, getting a good arm rhythm, bending their knees and ankles in rhythm with their arm motion, and getting a good leg extension at the point of takeoff. On landing, they should concentrate on landing forward rather than falling back. In an attempt to use the metric system, the children should measure each jump to the nearest inch or *centimeter*. In case you do not have a metric measuring tape Table 3 is included for your convenience.

■　■　■

Levels: Intermediate and advanced.

Subconcept: One meter measures just a little more than 1 yard.

Materials: Softballs, footballs, soccer balls, or shot puts and a measuring tape—preferably a metric one.

Activities: During this lesson the children will throw the softball, kick the football or soccer ball, or put the shot. Good form should be stressed in whichever skill you choose to have the children practice. In each instance the children will measure and record their efforts

Fig. 4-8. Metric standing long jump.

to the nearest foot or *meter*. Table 4 is provided for your convenience in case you do not have a metric measuring tape.

■ ■ ■

Levels: Intermediate and advanced.

Materials: A stopwatch and a long measuring tape—a metric one, if possible. If you can use the track at a local middle or high school, it would be most helpful also.

Activities: This lesson could be used as part of a unit in track and field. The children could compare the distances run and times for the races for track competition in the United States at present and in Olympic competition.* Table 5 is provided for your convenience.

―――――
*In some states and in national or international competition, track and field competition has already changed to metric measurement.

After comparing each of the distances, the children could sprint the shorter distances to work on speed and run the intermediate or longer races to work on pace and endurance.

CONCEPT: The metric unit of measurement for weight is the gram.

Levels: Intermediate and advanced.

Subconcept: One pound equals 453 grams.

Materials: A scale and any equipment that may be found in the gym.

Activities: The purpose of this lesson is to introduce children to the metric system of weights. The activities might take place at any time or in any lesson, and so rather than develop one specific lesson, ideas for several ways in which the metric system may be used will be listed.

1. In a unit of ball activities, weigh various

Table 4. Metric conversions

Feet	Meters	Feet	Meters
10	3.0480	56	17.0688
11	3.3528	57	17.3736
12	3.6576	58	17.6784
13	3.9624	59	17.9832
14	4.2672	60	18.2880
15	4.5720	61	18.5928
16	4.8768	62	18.8976
17	5.1816	63	19.2024
18	5.4864	64	19.5072
19	5.7912	65	19.8120
20	6.0960	66	20.1168
21	6.4008	67	20.4216
22	6.7056	68	20.7264
23	7.0104	69	21.0312
24	7.3152	70	21.3360
25	7.6200	71	21.6408
26	7.9248	72	21.9456
27	8.2296	73	22.2504
28	8.5344	74	22.5552
29	8.8392	75	22.8600
30	9.1440	76	23.1648
31	9.4488	77	23.4696
32	9.7536	78	23.7744
33	10.0584	79	24.0792
34	10.3632	80	24.3840
35	10.6680	81	24.6888
36	10.9728	82	24.9936
37	11.2776	83	25.2984
38	11.5824	84	25.6032
39	11.8872	85	25.9080
40	12.1920	86	26.2128
41	12.4968	87	26.5176
42	12.8016	88	26.8224
43	13.1064	89	27.1272
44	13.4112	90	27.4320
45	13.7160	91	27.7368
46	14.0208	92	28.0416
47	14.3256	93	28.3464
48	14.6304	94	28.6512
49	14.9352	95	28.9560
50	15.2400	96	29.2608
51	15.5448	97	29.5656
52	15.8496	98	29.8704
53	16.1544	99	30.1752
54	16.4592	100	30.4800
55	16.7640		

Table 3. Metric conversions for standing long jump

Feet	Inches	Meters	Feet	Inches	Meters
3	0	0.9144	6	0	1.8288
	1	0.9398		1	1.8542
	2	0.9652		2	1.8796
	3	0.9906		3	1.9050
	4	1.0160		4	1.9304
	5	1.0414		5	1.9558
	6	1.0668		6	1.9812
	7	1.0922		7	2.0066
	8	1.1171		8	2.0320
	9	1.1430		9	2.0574
	10	1.1684		10	2.0828
	11	1.1938		11	2.1082
4	0	1.2192	7	0	2.1336
	1	1.2446		1	2.1590
	2	1.2700		2	2.1844
	3	1.2954		3	2.2098
	4	1.3208		4	2.2352
	5	1.3462		5	2.2606
	6	1.3716		6	2.2860
	7	1.3970		7	2.3114
	8	1.4224		8	2.3368
	9	1.4478		9	2.3622
	10	1.4732		10	2.3876
	11	1.4986		11	2.4130
5	0	1.5240	8	0	2.4384
	1	1.5494		1	2.4638
	2	1.5748		2	2.4892
	3	1.6002		3	2.5146
	4	1.6256		4	2.5400
	5	1.6510		5	2.5654
	6	1.6764		6	2.5908
	7	1.7018		7	2.6162
	8	1.7272		8	2.6416
	9	1.7526		9	2.6670
	10	1.7780		10	2.6924
	11	1.8034		11	2.7178
			9	0	2.7430

Table 6. Metric conversions for weight lifting

Pounds	Kilograms	Pounds	Kilograms
2	0.90718	52	23.58668
4	1.81436	54	24.49386
5	2.26795	55	24.94745
6	2.72154	56	25.40104
8	3.62872	58	26.30822
10	4.53590	60	27.21540
12	5.44308	62	28.12258
14	6.35026	64	29.02976
15	6.80385	65	29.48335
16	7.25744	66	29.93694
18	8.16462	68	30.84412
20	9.07180	70	31.75130
22	9.97898	72	32.65848
24	10.86616	74	33.56566
25	11.33975	75	34.01925
26	11.79334	76	34.47284
28	12.70052	78	35.38002
30	13.60770	80	36.28720
32	14.51488	82	37.19438
34	15.42206	84	38.10156
35	15.87565	85	38.55515
36	16.32924	86	39.00874
38	17.23642	88	39.91592
40	18.14360	90	40.82310
42	19.05078	92	41.73028
44	19.95796	94	42.63746
45	20.41155	95	43.09105
46	20.86514	96	43.99823
48	21.77232	98	44.90541
50	22.67950	100	45.35900

Table 5. Metric conversions for distance

Yards	Meters
50	45.72
54.66	50
100	91.44
109.36 or 110	100
218.72 or 220	200
437.44 or 440	400
546.8	500
880	804.67
1093.61	1000, or 1 kilometer
1640.4	1500, or 1.5 kilometers
1760 or 1 mile	1609.35, or 1.6 kilometers

Fig. 4-9. Lifting metric weights.

types of balls—table tennis ball, golf ball, tennis ball, softball, basketball, etc. One ounce equals 28.3495 grams.

2. Weigh each of the children in class. One pound equals 4.5359 hectograms.

3. Using a seesaw, apply the information in nos. 1 and 2 to solve balance problems. If one person weighs x grams and another weighs y grams, where will each have to sit to make the seesaw balance (R × RA = F × FA—refer to p. 126).

4. In a manipulative unit weigh different types of striking implements—tennis racket, badminton racket, golf club, etc. One ounce equals 2.83495 decagrams.

5. Weigh the different types of gymnastics equipment you use in a gymnastics unit—mats, balance board, low balance beam, horse, etc. One pound equals 0.45359 kilogram.

■　■　■

Levels: Intermediate and advanced.

Subconcept: One kilogram equals 2.2 pounds.

Materials: Use a set of barbells or a set of weights. If you do not have any, you can make a set by using pipe and pouring sand into graduated size coffee cans.

Activities: As part of a physical fitness, conditioning, circuit training, or weight training unit, the children may learn to lift weights (Fig. 4-9). The military press, jerk, bench press, arm curl, and leg lift are different lifts that could be taught to the children. Care should be taken to emphasize good form and to do the lifts properly. Lift with the large muscles of the legs and arms. Avoid straining the back by lifting improperly. Children should also learn to recognize the amount of weight they can lift for each type of lift. Lifting too much weight or showing off can lead to unwanted accidents. Since most weights are measured in pounds at the present time, Table 6 contains conversions for your convenience.

Chapter 5

MATHEMATICAL SENTENCES, SETS, AND FIELD PROPERTIES

MATHEMATICAL SENTENCES

Children learn to communicate with mathematical sentences just as they learn to communicate with words and sentences in some language arts. Symbols used in mathematical sentences follow:

- Capital letters denote a set.
- Equal signs show equality on both sides of the equation.
- Braces ({ }), brackets ([ ]), or parentheses ( ) are enclosures for members of a set.
- Symbols or names within the enclosures refer to members of the sets.
- Commas separate the symbols that represent the members of a set when the members are listed between enclosures.

An example of the symbols that have been illustrated to this point is A = (1, 2, 3, 4, 5, 6, 7, 8, 9, 10), which is read, "A is the set of numbers from 1 through 10."

- Three dots (. . .) means to continue in the indicated pattern. For example, A = (1, 3, 5 . . .), which is read, "A is the set of odd whole numbers beginning with 1 and continuing to infinity."
- Symbols to denote individual members of sets usually are lower case letters of the alphabet.
- The Greek letter epsilon (ϵ) is used to abbreviate "is a member of" or "is an element of." For example: b ϵ B, which is read, "b is an element of the set B."
- A slanted bar (/) is frequently used as a negation symbol in mathematics. For example, b $\notin$ B, which is read, "b is not an element of the set B."
- For sets A and B, the statement A $\subset$ B means that A is a subset of B and that B has at least one member that is not a member of A. For example, {1, 2} $\subset$ {1, 2, 3, 4}, which is read, "One and 2 are a subset of the numbers from 1 through 4."

- The symbols < and > denote "less than" and "greater than," respectively. For example, 4 < 6, which is read, "4 is less than 6" and 7 > 3, which is read, "7 is greater than 3."
- Set operations involving the union and intersection of sets are also capable of being represented through mathematical sentences. They will be discussed in the presentation of set theory.

SETS

Beginning in the first grade, children learn about sets. Throughout their elementary school years, concepts regarding sets are expanded to form a solid foundation on which more advanced mathematical concepts will be built in later school years. *A set is a collection of a particular kind or group of objects.* For instance, there is a set of whole numbers, a set of all animals in the dog family, or a set of implements used for striking balls in physical education. The items that make up a given set are called *members,* or *elements,* of a set. Elements of the set of whole numbers are 1, 2, 3, etc. Elements of the set of implements for striking are hockey sticks, softball bats, golf clubs, etc. Any part of a set can be viewed as a *subset.* For example, the members of the set of children in a class at any one time may be divided into two subsets, the set of boys and the set of girls. Subsets may be divided into *classifications* according to color, size, weight, sex, age, etc. A set with no elements in it is an *empty set.* The set of people who are able to fly is an empty set. A set with a specific number of members in it is called a *finite set.* The number of children in a given classroom is a finite set. A set with an infinite number of members is called an *infinite set.* The set of whole num-

82

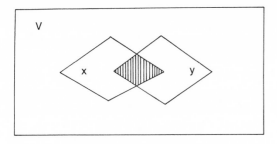

Fig. 5-1. Venn diagram.

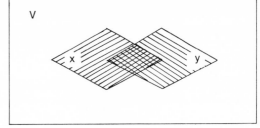

Fig. 5-2. Union of sets.

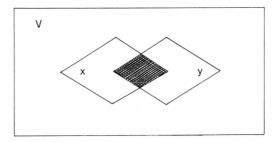

Fig. 5-3. Intersection of sets.

bers is an infinite set. A *universal set* is a master set denoting all possible sets.

Venn diagrams such as Fig. 5-1 are commonly used to represent set concepts. In general, a closed geometric figure is used to represent the universal set (U), with the understanding that the region interior to the boundary line represents the universal set. Smaller, closed, geometric figures completely contained in U represent the subsets of the universal set. Subsets often overlap or intersect. For example, if Fig. 5-1 represents a class of boys and girls in a physical education class, the girls could be designated in subset X and the boys in subset Y. The intersection of X and Y could be the number of children who have blue eyes. Blue eyes are a common element of subset X and subset Y.

Just as in addition, subtraction, multiplication, or division, operations on set concepts may also be performed. The first operation that will be illustrated in the union (∪) of sets. If X and Y are sets from Fig. 5-2, the union of X and Y (written X ∪ Y) is the set of all elements

that belong to X, or belong to Y, or belong to both X and Y.

The second operation that will be illustrated is the intersection of sets. If X and Y are sets from Fig. 5-3, the intersection of X and Y (written X ∩ Y) is the set of all elements that belong to both X and Y at the same time.

The hierarchical structure of set terminology and the set operations of union and intersection provide a vehicle by which human movement can be defined and analyzed. By viewing movement from mathematical set concepts, you may come to understand it more thoroughly and teach it more effectively.

FIELD PROPERTIES OF MATHEMATICS

In their beginning experiences with mathematics during the elementary years, children learn to compute through the use of the operations of addition, subtraction, multiplication, and division. In modern mathematics an attempt is being made to teach children concepts when common rules may be applied. These mathematics concepts are called the field properties of mathematics and are described as follows:

1. Identity element for addition and multiplication

$$1 + 0 = 1 \qquad\qquad 1 \times 1 = 1$$
$$3 + 0 = 3 \ldots \qquad\quad 3 \times 1 = 3 \ldots$$

The identity element for addition is the number zero (0). If zero is added to any number, the sum is still the number. The identity element for multiplication is the number 1. When any number is multiplied by 1, the product is still the number.

2. Commutative property for addition and multiplication

$$1 + 2 = 2 + 1 \qquad\qquad 2 \times 4 = 4 \times 2$$
$$5 + 7 = 7 + 5 \ldots \qquad\quad 3 \times 7 = 7 \times 3 \ldots$$

The commutative property of addition states that the order of two added numbers can be changed without changing the sum; that is, $1 + 2 = 2 + 1$, or, in general, if X and Y are any whole numbers, then $X + Y = Y + X$. The commutative property of multiplication states that the order of multiplying two numbers may be changed without changing the product; that is, $2 \times 4 = 4 \times 2$, or, in general, if X and Y are any whole numbers, then $X \times Y = Y \times X$.

3. Associative property for addition and multiplication

$$(3 + 5) + 2 = 3 + (5 + 2)$$
$$(4 + 6) + 7 = 4 + (6 + 7) \ldots$$

$$(5 \times 4) \times 6 = 5 \times (4 \times 6)$$
$$(8 \times 9) \times 2 = 8 \times (9 \times 2) \ldots$$

The associative property for addition states that when three or more numbers are added, the order in which they are added may be changed without altering the sum; that is, $(3 + 5) + 2 = 3 + (5 + 2)$, or, in general, if X, Y, and Z are whole numbers, then $(X + Y) + Z = X + (Y + Z)$. The associative property for multiplication states that when three or more numbers are multiplied, the order in which they are multiplied may be changed without altering the product; that is, $(5 \times 4) \times 6 = 5 \times (4 \times 6)$ or, in general, if X, Y, and Z are whole numbers, then $(X \times Y) \times Z = X \times (Y \times Z)$.

4. Distributive property

$$(2 + 4)6 = (2 \times 6) + (4 \times 6)$$
$$5(1 + 3) = (5 \times 1) + (5 \times 3) \ldots$$

The distributive property of mathematics states that when a group of two or more numbers are to be added and then multiplied by another factor, the numbers may be added first and then multiplied by the factor, or the numbers may be multiplied by the factor first and then added together. In either order the product remains the same: $X(Y + Z) = (X \times Y) + (X \times Z)$.

Other field properties of mathematics, such as the property of closure, have little or no practical application in movement experiences. As a result, they will not be discussed in this text. The reader is encouraged to become familiar with the math sentences, sets, and field properties that have been discussed and to be innovative in applying them to situations in movement experiences.

Learning activities

Mathematical sentences

CONCEPT: Movement sentences can be written by using mathematical sentence terminology.

Levels: Beginning and intermediate.

Subconcept: Various symbols are combined to make up a sentence.

Materials: None.

Activities: Children may learn to use mathematical sentence terminology while exploring the elements, or qualities, of movement. As you guide them through exploration and problem-solving challenges with reference to space, force, time, and flow concepts, consider the following possibilities:

1. $E = S, F_o, T, F_1$. The elements or qualities of movement are space, force, time, and flow.
2. $S, F_o \subset E$. Space and force are subsets of the elements of movement.
3. {Fast, medium, slow} ϵ time: Fast, medium, and slow are elements of time, or the rate at which one moves.
4. {Strong, medium, weak} ϵ force: Strong, medium and weak are elements of force, or the amount of effort one uses to execute a movement.
5. $F_o \notin T$: Force is not an element of time.

6. {Direction, level, . . .} ∈ space: Direction, level, pathway, and range are elements of space.
7. {Forward, backward} ⊂ direction: Forward and backward movement are subsets of directional movement.
8. Direction ∉ pathway: Direction is not an element of pathway.
9. Shapes = {twisted, curved, and angular}: Twisted, curved, and angular are menbers of the set of body shapes.
10. Levels = {high, medium, and low}: High, medium, and low are members of the set of body levels.

■ ■ ■

Level: Beginning.

Subconcepts: (1) The symbol < means less than. (2) The symbol > means more than.

Materials: None.

Activities: Children may learn about the concepts of "less than" or "more than" through the use of task cards placed at various teaching stations. Several examples are provided as illustrations. You are encouraged to make up your own task cards to fit the ability levels of your children and your teaching situation.

Exercises

1. Perform less than (<) five push-ups.
2. Perform more than (>) ten sit-ups.
3. Perform < fifteen toe touches.
4. Perform > five leg lifts.
5. Perform "greater than or equal to" (≥) 10 seconds in a flexed arm hang position.
6. Run in place > 30 seconds, but < 2 minutes.

Gymnastics

1. Do > three forward rolls.
2. Do < five backward rolls.
3. Do > four cartwheels.
4. Do < five different vaults over the horse.
5. Try > four, but < ten different ways to cross the balance beam.

Ball skills

1. Bounce the ball < thirty times with your right hand.

2. Bounce the ball > forty times with your left hand.
3. Throw and catch the ball < twenty-five times against the wall.
4. Throw and catch the ball with a partner > fifteen times without dropping the ball.
5. Shoot the ball at the basket until you make > ten, but < twenty baskets.

Rope jumping

1. Place the rope on the floor and walk along it > four different ways.
2. Place the rope on the floor and jump over it < five different ways.
3. Jump a long rope turned by 2 others > twenty times.
4. Jump a short rope by yourself < fifty times.
5. Jump a short rope > fifteen times, but < twenty-five times before you change to the other foot.

■ ■ ■

Levels: Intermediate and advanced.

Subconcept: Various symbols are combined to make up a sentence.

Materials: None.

Activities: Locomotor activities may be used to emphasize the application of mathematical sentences to walking, running, hopping, jumping, and other locomotor skills. As you work with the children, consider the following factors:

1. L ⊂ U: Locomotion is a subset of the universal set of all movement patterns.
2. {Walking, running} ⊂ L: Walking and running are subsets of the concept of locomotion.
3. {Transferring one's weight from one foot to the same foot, one foot to the other, two feet to two, two feet to one foot, and one foot to two} = five methods of weight transfer on feet.
4. {Walk, run, leap} = transfer of weight from one foot to the other.
5. {Jump} = transfer of weight from two feet to two feet.
6. {Hop} = transfer of weight from one foot to the same foot.
7. {Skip} = walk, hop
8. {Walking, hopping, skipping, jumping} ∈ L: Walking, hopping, skipping, and

jumping and other movements are elements of the set of locomotor patterns.

9. {Throwing} ∈ L: Throwing is not a locomotor pattern.

10. Basketball = running, leaping, sliding, jumping: Basketball is a game in which the locomotor skills of running, leaping, sliding, and jumping are used.

■ ■ ■

Levels: Intermediate and advanced.

Materials: Different types of balls.

Activities: Ball activities may be used to emphasize the application of mathematical sentences. As you work with the children on throwing, catching, bouncing, kicking, or striking, consider the following factors:

1. M ⊂ U: Manipulation is a subset of the universal set of all movement patterns.

2. Propulsion ⊂ M: Propulsion, or giving force to objects, is a subset of manipulation.

3. {Batting, volleying, heading, . . .} Striking: Batting, volleying, and heading are members of the subset of striking skills.

4. {Throwing, catching, kicking, . . .} ∈ M: Throwing, catching, kicking, and other propulsive and absorptive patterns are elements of the set of manipulation.

5. {Batting, kicking, dribbling, . . .} ∈ striking: Batting, kicking, dribbling, and other propulsive actions where there is only momentary contact with the ball are elements of the skill of striking.

6. Running ∈ M: Running is not an element of manipulation.

7. Throwing ∈ striking: Throwing is not a member of the set of striking skills.

8. {Catching, trapping} = absorptive patterns: Catching and trapping are methods that the body uses to absorb or receive force from objects.

9. Basketball = {bouncing, passing, catching, shooting}: Basketball is a game in which the manipulative skills of bouncing, passing, and shooting are used.

10. Softball = {throwing, catching, batting}: Softball is a game in which the manipulative skills of throwing, catching, and batting are used.

Sets

CONCEPT: A set is a collection of a particular kind or group of objects or ideas.

Level: Beginning.

Subconcept: A subset is a part, or portion, of a set.

Materials: Different types of equipment that you may have in your teaching situation.

Activities: The purpose of this lesson is to introduce children to set theory in a movement environment. The children themselves compose a set. Subsets of children may be derived from sex, hair color, eye color, age, month of birthday, height, weight, etc. Each of these subsets may be used to categorize children into teams for purposes of play. These subsets may also be used for dismissal techniques at the end of class.

All movement may be classified as being part of the universal set of basic movement patterns (p. 87). Movement patterns may be classified into subsets of body-handling patterns and object-handling patterns. Stability and locomotion are subsets of body handling patterns. The elements of the set of locomotion are walking, running, hopping, etc. The elements of stability are balance, rolling, bending, stretching, etc. Absorptive and propulsive patterns are subsets of manipulation. The elements of the absorptive patterns are trapping, catching, and carrying, and the elements of propulsion are throwing, kicking, striking, and so forth. An example of an infinite set would be any of these movements; one could choose walking, for instance, and vary the speed, force, direction, pathway, etc. an infinite number of ways. An example of a null, or empty, set would be the number of children who can high jump 7 feet, long jump 25 feet, etc.

Equipment in the gym may also be categorized into sets—a set of balls, striking implements, gymnastics equipment, etc. Each set again can be further divided into subsets. For example, there are subsets of balls categorized by those that are used primarily for kicking, throwing, or striking. The number of balls or any other pieces of equipment in the gym at any time is a finite set because they can be counted—there is a specific or end number.

DEVELOPMENT OF BASIC MOVEMENT PATTERNS

Body handling patterns		Object handling patterns
Stability	*Locomotion*	*Manipulation*

Stability	*Locomotion*	*Absorptive*	*Propulsive*
Balance	Walking	Absorptive	Propulsive
Rolling	Running	Trapping	Lifting
Springing	Hopping	Catching	Throwing
Bending	Skipping	Carrying	Kicking
Stretching	Galloping		Striking
Twisting	Sliding		Pushing
Sitting	Jumping		Pulling
Rotation	Dodging		Blocking
Swinging	Vaulting		Bouncing
Standing	Combinations		Rolling
Supports			
Curling			

CLASSIFICATION OF QUALITIES OF MOVEMENT

Space	*Force*	*Time*	*Flow*
Levels	Strong-weak	Slow	Free
High	Heavy-light	Medium	Bound
Medium	Tight-loose	Fast	Sequential
Low	Hard-soft		
Ranges	*Directions*	*Emphasis of movement*	
Wide-narrow	Forward-backward	Sudden	
Far-near	Upward-downward	Explosive	
Long-short	Sideways	Sustained	
	Pathways	Staccato	
	Direct path	Relaxed	
	Circle pattern		
	Diagonal patterns		

For purposes of activity you may choose to practice any of the movement skills while emphasizing the application of movement patterns to set theory.

CONCEPT: The operations of union and intersection may be performed on sets.

Level: Intermediate.

Subconcepts: (1) The union of sets is the combination of all members of two or more sets. (2) The intersection of sets is the number of elements that belong to two or more sets at the same time.

Materials: Record player, several records that provide for change in tempo, flow, mood, and even and uneven rhythmical patterns.

Activities. It is common for children to combine the qualities of movement in their exploratory experiences. It is often done in the early grades, but by grade 5 children are capable of understanding combinations of movements in terms of the intersection of sets. If the qualities of movement are considered the universal set, then space, force, time, and flow may be considered subsets (see chart above). Within the set of space movements the subsets are moving at different levels, ranges, and directions. Within the set of force movements the subsets are comparisons of hard and soft, strong and weak, heavy and light, and tight and loose. Within the set of time movements, the subsets are moving at different speeds. The set of flow movements also has a subset of movements. During this lesson the children will explore the union of two or more qualities of movement. Music will be provided to vary the tempo, flow, mood, and even and uneven rhythmical patterns that the children will explore. Stability and loco-motor movements will also be explored. The teacher will stimulate the children's movement by posing stimulating problems. What types of movements occur when the set of space move-ments unite with the set of force movements? What types of movements occur when range movements are united with time movements? (After uniting movements from two elements, the children may be asked to explore the union of three movements.) What types of movement occur when children are asked to unite the sets of flow movements, force movements, and space movements at the same time? How many different variations can the children think of in which the qualities of movement are inter-sected?

■ ■ ■

Level: Intermediate.

Materials: None.

Activities: During this lesson the children will explore the locomotor movements of walk-ing and hopping. They will find that the union of the set of walking patterns with the set of hopping patterns (Fig. 5-4) will permit them to move in an infinite variety of ways. They may walk forward, backward, fast, slow, smoothly, jerkily, with long steps, and with short steps. They may move any way they wish with respect to the qualities of movement. They may per-form the same exploratory movements with re-gard to the set of hopping movements. In ad-dition, they may explore the movements that occur when they combine walking and hopping movements at the same time. Movement pat-terns such as step-hop (skip), step-step-hop,

step-step-step-hop (schottische), hop-hop-step, hop-hop-step-step, and a variety of others may occur.

With respect to the intersection of sets, the only movements that will be permitted are those in which walking and hopping occur at the same time. The intersection of the two sets (Fig. 5-5) thus limits the children with respect to what they may perform. No longer can they perform only walking or only hopping; they must combine the two sets at the same time. They may only perform the step-hop (skip), step-step-hop, step-step-step-hop (schottische), step-hop-hop, and a variety of other combina-tion movements. Thus the skip, schottische, etc. may be best thought of as the intersection of two sets. It should also be pointed out that the children may still vary the space, time, force, and flow of their movement as they at-tempt these intersection movements.

In follow-up lessons the children may wish to unite and intersect other locomotor sets. For example, what movement patterns evolve when running and leaping intersect? (Hurdling, long jump, stag leap.) What movements occur when jumping and hopping are united? (Hopscotch, dancing.) What movements occur when leaping and walking intersect? (Slide, gallop.)

■ ■ ■

Level: Advanced.

Materials: Basketballs.

Activities: During a unit on basketball the children will learn the skills of dribbling, shoot-ing, passing, and guarding. Each of these skills provides an opportunity to teach children about the set operations of union and intersection (Fig. 5-6). Basketball can be thought of as a combination of locomotor and manipulative sets. At times a player is moving without the

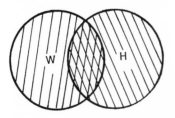

Fig. 5-4. Union of walking and hopping.

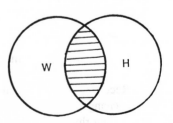

Fig. 5-5. Intersection of walking and hopping.

ball—jumping for a rebound, guarding, and running down the court or to get open to receive the ball. These are all locomotor skills. At times a player is manipulating the ball without moving—various types of passes. At other times a player is performing locomotor and manipulative skills at the same time. A jump shot may be thought of as the intersection of a vertical *jump* and *shooting* (a form of *throwing* the ball). A lay-up may be thought of as the intersection of a *leap* and *shooting* the ball. Dribbling is the intersection of *running* and *striking* the ball. Can you think of other examples of set operations in basketball? Can you use set operations in other sports?

■ ■ ■

Level: Advanced.

Materials: Gymnastics mats and any available apparatus pieces.

Activities: During a unit on gymnastics the children will learn various types of rolls, balance, and support positions with different bases of support. Each of these skills provides an opportunity to teach children about sets and set operations by focusing on stability concepts and the qualities of movement. Several examples follow:

Sets

Symmetrical movements—forward roll, cartwheel, skin-the-cat, handspring, head and hand stand, handstand, tip-up, tripod, squat vault, straddle vault, etc.

Assymetrical movements—one-arm cartwheel, scale, head and hand stand with one leg bent, flank vault, sheep vault, etc.

Movements at a low level—forward roll, backward roll, tip-up, tripod, etc. (Fig. 5-7).

Movements at a high level—cartwheel, handspring, handstand, head and hand stand, etc.

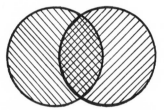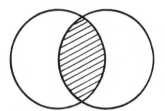

Fig. 5-6. Union and intersection of basketball activities.

Fig. 5-7. Set of low level body positions.

Movements using the hands as a base of support—
tip-up, handstand, lever, vaults, etc.
*Movements that may be performed on more than
one piece of equipment*—forward roll on mats,
balance beam and parallel bars; hip on mats,
parallel bars and horizontal bars; handspring,
mats and vaulting horse; and skin-the-cat on
parallel bars, hanging rings, ropes, and horizontal bar

Union of sets

*Movements at a low level and rolling move-
ments*—any body position at a low level
(stretched or curled), any rolling movement,
and any movement that combines a low level
with rolling at the same time, i.e., forward roll,
backward roll, etc.
*Body movements with one base of support and
body positions in a stretched shape*—any body
position with one base of support, any body
position that is stretched, and any movement
that combines a stretch with one base at the
same time, i.e., one-arm cartwheel, scale, etc.

Intersection of sets

*Movements in which the body is supported by
the hands and movements performed at a low
level*—the movements that are performed on the
hands and at a low level at the same time, i.e.,
tip-up, lever
*Movements at a high level and symmetrical move-
ments*—cartwheel, handspring, handstand,
etc.

Field properties of mathematics

CONCEPT: The property of identity helps define or state the uniqueness of a given object,
number, or skill.

Level: Beginning.
Subconcept: Movement concepts have identity by their definition.
Materials: None.
Activities: As children learn about the identity elements of addition and multiplication,
they are essentially learning about the uniqueness of a given number. For example, when
zero is added to another number, the sum remains the same. When a given number is multiplied by 1, the product remains the same. As
a result, the uniqueness of the number remains
separate from all others. It stands apart or by
itself.

In physical education, each movement skill
has identity elements. What is it that makes
walking a unique skill? A person can walk forward, backward, straight, with much or little
force, etc., and yet there are certain characteristics that can be identified as walking. Walking is placing one foot after another on the
ground with *continuous contact with the surface*. What are the identity elements of running,
hopping, jumping, skipping, and galloping?
What makes each of these a unique skill? Discuss these with the children as you practice each
of the above skills.

What are the identity elements of carrying
objects, throwing objects, and striking objects
(pp. 162 to 171). What makes each of these a
unique skill? What helps to differentiate one
skill from another? A person can carry an object
with the right or left hand, while moving fast or
slow, etc. just as long as the object remains in
continuous contact with the body. A person can
throw the ball overhand, sidearm, underhand,
with much or little force, etc. just as long as
there is a *buildup of momentum prior to release*.
A person can strike an object with the arm or
leg, with or without an implement, etc. just as
long as the *momentum of the body is developed
prior to making momentary contact with the object*. Discuss these concepts with the children
as you practice each of the skills.

CONCEPT: The properties of commutation,
association, and distribution show that groups of
objects or numbers can be combined in different
ways without affecting the sum or product.

Levels: Intermediate and advanced.
Subconcept: Movement activities often ex-
hibit the qualities of the commutative, associative, and distributive properties of mathematics.
Materials: Balls and a set of softball bases.
Activities: While participating in a number
of softball or baseball activities, the children
can learn about the properties of commutation,
association, and distribution. With respect to
the commutative property ($a + b = b + a$ or
$a \times b = b \times a$) the children can play catch
with a partner. While playing catch the two
partners may be labeled a and b. When player
a starts throwing and player b receives and returns the throw, one complete rotation is made.

Fig. 5-8. Movement activities help children learn the properties of mathematics.

If player a then returns the ball to player b, the ball has been thrown a total of three times (2 + 1). During the next turn, if player b initiates the first throw to player a, then player a returns the ball to player b and b throws to a again, the ball has been thrown a total of three times again (1 + 2). If the players made five throws three different times in comparison to three throws five different times, the total in each instance would be fifteen throws (5 × 3 = 3 × 5). This is an example of the commutative property for multiplication. If this rotation of three throws were repeated five times, a total of fifteen throws would be made. The total would remain the same no matter whether player a or player b initiated the throws. (1 + 2)5 = (2 + 1)5 = (1 × 5) + (2 × 5) = 15 shows the distributive property for mathematics.

In addition to the application of the field properties to throwing experiences, the children may run the bases (Fig. 5-8). If 2 players start at home plate and run around the horn back to home plate, they have executed the associative property of addition for mathematics (1 + 2 + 3 + 4 = 4 + 3 + 2 + 1).

■ ■ ■

Levels: Intermediate and advanced.

Materials: None.

Activities: During this lesson the children will perform a number of relay activities to demonstrate the application of the associative property for mathematics. As an example, suppose there are 30 children in class and they are divided into six groups of 5 each. Each child will then be given a number by counting off.

For purposes of placement and illustration line up each relay team in different numerical order:

5	1	2	3	4	5
4	5	1	2	3	2
3	4	5	1	2	4
2	3	4	5	1	3
1	2	3	4	5	1

Then, have the children perform a variety of running, hopping, jumping, sliding, and galloping relays. Point out to the children that the order of their turn or the sum of the addition sequence remains the same in each relay regardless of the way they are lined up. For example, $[(1 + 2) + (3 + 4) + 5 = 1 + (2 + 3) + (4 + 5)]$. After each relay have the first person in line go to the last position for the next relay emphasizing again that the order of the turn or addition sequence bears no consequence in the sum, or end, experiences.

Chapter 6

QUANTITATIVE IDEAS, GEOMETRY, AND MEASURING AND GRAPHING

QUANTITATIVE IDEAS

From their earliest experiences, children learn about quantitative ideas. A full baby bottle for an empty stomach, a big warm blanket, and a cold drink are examples. As children grow through their preschool years and enter the elementary school, experiences in the classroom and physical education can be designed that deepen and expand their understanding and awareness. Following are some of the concepts that children should learn to master:

- *Size*—little-big, small-large, half-whole, tiny-huge, fat-skinny
- *Length or distance*—long-short, near-far, tall-short, wide-narrow, high-low
- *Quantity*—few, many, some, all, less than–greater than, shorter than–taller than, faster than–slower than, smaller than–bigger than
- *Weight*—heavy-light
- *Amount*—full-empty, some, much, enough, many, few
- *Position*—up-down, right-left, first-last, above-below, between, around, in-out, through, beside, on, over-under, front-back
- *Form*—circle, line, curved, straight, beginning-middle-end, square, triangle, diamond, rectangle
- *Time*—year, month, week, day, hour, minute, second, season, today, tomorrow, yesterday, noon, early-late, day-night
- *Speed*—fast-medium-slow, sudden, sustained
- *Climate*—cold-hot, warm-cool, snow, ice, rain, drizzle, sleet, sunny, fog

GEOMETRY

As children enter school, it is expected that they are able to recognize and reproduce the simple geometrical forms. These include the straight, curved, vertical, and horizontal lines,

cross, square, circle, rectangle, and triangle. Later, mastery of the diagonal line, diamond, and complex geometrical forms such as the parallelogram, rhomboid, and trapezoid are involved. To be consistent with learning the recognition and reproduction of these forms, the study of geometry in the primary grades should include forms, space, points, lines, angles, shapes, sizes, patterns, and designs. In the intermediate grades, work in geometry should include symmetry, open and closed curved figures, convex figures, inside, outside, and geometrical forms. Children also perform more advanced work on topics from the primary grades. Geometry can be related to movement experiences through rhythms, movement exploration, and games and sports.

MEASURING AND GRAPHING

Measuring and graphing are used in elementary school mathematics and science to present facts about aspects and properties of objects in an effort to describe them precisely and to understand them. Measurement makes it possible to define, predict, and control. To measure a quantity means to find out how many times a standard unit is contained in a given object. To measure means to pictorially represent or describe a collection of data.

Children pass through several stages while learning to measure. At the lowest stage of premeasurement, the child describes objects in indefinite quantitative terms such as large, small, big, and little. Next, he measures objects through comparison such as longer than, shorter than, bigger than and smaller than. At a still higher level the child learns to use one object

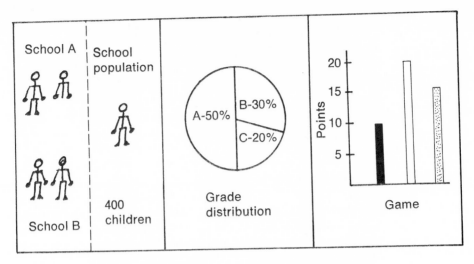

Fig. 6-1. Graphs help children interpret learning experiences.

to help describe another object. For example, he may say, "This ball is about two times as heavy as an orange" or "This book is almost two times bigger than that book." Later the child will directly use units of measurement to compare height, weight, distance, etc. Units of measurement may be the length of an arm or a foot, a baseball bat, a sidewalk square, and similar familiar amounts.

At the highest level the child actually uses a measuring device to measure or describe an aspect of something with a number. Thus he may use a yardstick or metric stick to measure how far or high he can jump, a tape to measure how far he can throw a ball, or a stopwatch to time how long it takes someone to run 100 yards or 100 meters.

As children enter the intermediate grades, they become capable of using graphs to represent collections of data. Graphs that children use depend on the kind of data to be presented and the competence level of the children. Types of graphs most commonly used are the pictograph, circle graph, and bar graph or histogram (Fig. 6-1).

Learning activities

Quantitative ideas

CONCEPT: Comparison of size, length, quantity, weight, position, form, time, speed, and cli-

mate expands our awareness of the environment through quantitative ideas.

Level: Beginning.

Subconcept: Exploring space, level, direction, pathway, force, time, and flow concepts helps us learn about quantitative ideas.

Materials: None.

Activities: Any activity in which children explore the qualities of movement will automatically include the quantitative ideas from mathematics. For purposes of this lesson, quantitative ideas will be explored with reference to two movement concepts—stability and locomotion. First, the children will assume various body postures and gestures as well as balance positions in response to questions and challenges posed by the teacher. Then they will explore locomotion.

How small can you make your body (Fig. 6-2)? What do you do with your body when you assume a small shape? Can you make your body assume a shape larger than your small shape? How large can you make your body? What do you do with your body when you assume a large shape? Can you be larger than, smaller than, before? Can you think of other words that convey concepts of size? (Little, big, tiny, huge.)

Next, let's think of length and distance. How long can you make your body? How short can you make your body? Can you make your body long and large at the same time? Now make your body wide,

Fig. 6-2. How small can you make your body? How large?

then narrow. What are some other words for length and distance? (Tall, near, far, high, low.) Can you assume these body positions with one, two, three, or four supports as bases on the floor? Can you assume a small body pose in which your head is lower than (position—above, below) your hips? Can you assume a medium-level body position with one arm between and one arm beside your legs? How many other body poses can you create with reference to these quantitative ideas?

Now that you have warmed up, let's begin to move about the room. You may choose to walk, hop, jump, skip, or perform any other type of locomotor movement. How fast can you move? How slow? Can you move faster than, slower than, before? As you take your steps, make them larger than before. Now, shorter. Can you take long fast steps, short fast steps, long slow steps, short slow steps? As

you move, can you assume a low body position? Can you be tall as you move? Wide? Narrow? Can you be heavy as you move? Light? Can you move with more force, less force, than before? As you change the force with which you move, can you move to the right, left, forward, backward? Can you move in a straight line, a circular, diagonal, or zigzag pathway? How many other ways can you combine these quantitative ideas as you move about exploring locomotor movement?

■ ■ ■

Level: Beginning.

Subconcept: Designs on the floor help us learn about quantitative ideas regarding form, size, climate, and time.

Materials: Use chalk, paint, or another proper marking device to place the diagram or one similar to it on the gym floor or hard-surface area outside. The gym floor may serve as a medium to help children in primary grades relate to quantitative ideas. Children may line up for circle games and rhythmical activities by positioning themselves on a day of the week, month, season, or direction. They may stand inside, on or outside the circle or any other geometrical form in the gym. Different geometrical shapes should be painted on the floor for form recognition. Some figures should be large and others small for comparison of size. Some figures should be outlined only to emphasize the idea of empty. Other figures should be painted in tall and full to emphasize the concept of full. Walls can be used as target areas and to measure height (tall, short). Other gym designs are left to the imagination of each individual teacher for communication of quantitative ideas.

Activities: Before beginning to play a game or rhythmical activity, have the children line up around the circle or on one of the geometrical forms to practice their quantitative awareness. On command, have the children move to another position or geometrical form. You may have them move high, low, heavy, light, fast, slow, etc. as they change. If they are on a day,

have them change to another day. If they are on a month, have them find another month. If they are on a season or direction, have them change season or direction. Those children selecting the forms should move inside, outside, far away from, near, and in the full, empty, large, or small forms.

After a short period of practice involving these quantitative ideas, you may choose an appropriate circle game or rhythmical activity according to the children's interest level and ability. If you wish to play a different type of game, the children may be divided into teams according to geometrical forms, days, months, seasons, or directions to create further quantitative awareness.

■　■　■

Level: Beginning.

Subconcept: Moving up, down, left, right, over, under, around, through, between, in, out, high, low, fast, and slow among objects helps us learn about position and speed.

Materials: An obstacle course made out of gymnastics equipment, hoops, a ladder, traffic cones, and similar objects.

Activities: At the beginning of this class period use the portable equipment and permanent equipment to design an obstacle course for the day (Fig. 6-4). The children may also be given the opportunity to place the equipment in new sequences or designs. The idea is to encourage them to be aware of the concepts of up, down, right, left, over, under, between, around, through, and other quantitative ideas as they design the obstacle course or move through it. To encourage as much continuous participation as possible, have the children start at different points of the course, rather than wait in line and take a turn. The objective is quantitative awareness and not a race to see who can negotiate the course the fastest. Talk about moving fast, slow, little or big steps, and heavy or light steps between pieces of equipment.

To further enhance the learning of quantitative ideas, you may tell the children or use signs to indicate how they must move between the obstacles. Moving at high or low levels, fast or slow speeds, many or few steps, and straight or curved pathways are among the

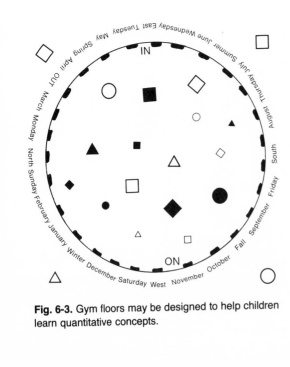

Fig. 6-3. Gym floors may be designed to help children learn quantitative concepts.

many choices available, each of which conveys a quantitative idea.

■ ■ ■

Levels: Intermediate and advanced.

Subconcept: Creative storytelling can create an awareness of quantitative ideas about climate, season, time, weight, and speed.

Materials: None.

Activities: The purpose of this lesson is to emphasize quantitative ideas through creative movement in dance. Begin by fabricating a story about the seasons of the year and pull in situations that are peculiar to the envoronment in which you live. As you tell the story, emphasize certain points and allow the children to move between sentences. An example follows:

Today, boys and girls, we are going on a trip through the seasons. Let's begin with a winter morning as you awake and get out of bed. Oh, it's so nice and warm and comfortable under those covers. The floor is so very cold to the touch of your feet. After you get up, get dressed, and eat your breakfast, you peek outside and see that it snowed last night, and you want to go out and play. You put on your heavy coat, snow pants, and big galoshes or boots and go outside. Oh, it's cold. Show me how you move with all those heavy clothes on when it's cold. The snow has drifted so high you have to use snowshoes. Show me how you walk with those heavy clothes and big snowshoes. Next, you decide to go skiing. Will you move faster or slower on skis? Sometimes you will race downhill in a slalom course, and at other times you will go cross-country, sometimes up and sometimes down hills. Show me how you could go up a hill on skis. After skiing you decide to go ice-skating. It is your first time on skates. Show me how you wobble over the slippery ice. With more experience you can perform spins and fancy figures (pathways) on the ice and make up a duet with a partner (relationships—near, far). Toward the middle of the day the sun gets so warm that the ice and snow begin to melt. You decide to make a snow figure, fort, or have a snowball fight. The snow packs real well, but it is also very heavy compared to the light powdery snow when you were skiing in the morning. How will you move in the heavy snow as you play?

Continue the story by changing seasons. Compare and contrast movement and play activities in different climates. Playing in the rain in spring, stamping through puddles, building dams, surfing or waterskiing during the summer, walking in water (low, medium, or high levels) at the beach, walking through crinkling

Fig. 6-4. Learning quantitative concepts by moving through an obstacle course.

leaves, over, under, around, and between trees in the woods in the fall, hiking a mountain trail in the hot sun, and trying to move in the fog, sleet, hail, or coming hurricane or tornado are other examples. Create the story as you go along. Use the children's ideas as cues for other movement suggestions.

Geometry

CONCEPT: Geometry is the study of lines and shapes.

Level: Beginning.

Subconcepts: (1) Circles, lines, triangles, rectangles, and squares are different kinds of geometrical shapes. (2) We can form geometrical shapes with our bodies.

Materials: A jump rope for each child.

Activities: During this lesson the children will explore five different geometrical shapes with their body and with a jump rope. A *line* is a thin, threadlike mark on a surface that may be straight or curved. A *circle* is a curved line that has no beginning and no end. All points on a circle are equal distance from the center. A *triangle* is a geometrical shape, constructed from three intersecting lines, that has three angles. A *rectangle* is a four-sided geometrical shape with four right angles—two sides are

long and two are shorter. A *square* is a four-sided geometrical shape with four equal sides and four right angles.

To begin the lesson, the children may explore various body shapes in which their body forms different lines.

How many different curved and straight lines can you make with your body? Next, how many ways can you make a circle with your body? Can you make a circle with just your fingers? Can you make a circle with your arms or legs? Can you use your whole body to make a circle? Now change and make your body into a triangle. How many different ways can you balance on the floor with three different points of contact? Can you make a triangle with your two arms and one leg touching the floor? How many other ways can you make a triangle? Can you make your body look like a box? How many different ways can you make your body look like a rectangle? Can you make a rectangle with four body parts touching the floor? Can you work with a partner and make the shape of a rectangle in different ways? Can you make one with your arms only, with your legs only, and with your arms, trunk and legs at the same time? Can you and your partner make the shape of a square with your bodies?

After exploring different body shapes without equipment, the children should begin using the rope. First, have the children stretch the rope out

Fig. 6-5. We can make the same shape with the rope and with our bodies.

on the floor. The path of the rope may be straight or curved.

How many different ways can you move along the line? Walking, hopping, skipping, crawling, etc. may be explored at different levels and speeds. Now make the rope into a circle. How many different ways can you move from the outside of the circle to the inside and then back to the outside? Can you move from the outside of the circle to the other side without touching the inside? Can you walk around the circle while keeping your balance? Now make a triangle with your rope. How many different ways can you move along the triangle? Can you jump from the top to the bottom of the triangle? Next, make a rectangle with your rope. Explore different ways to move around the rectangle. Last, do the same exploratory activities with a square.

■ ■ ■

Level: Beginning.

Subconcept: The use of geometrical forms in movement and balancing activities creates an awareness of color, shape, size, and direction.

Materials: Use pieces of cardboard from large appliances boxes or thin sheets of styrofoam to construct the obstacle course forms. Circles, triangles, squares, diamonds, rectangles, and other forms can be cut out. Vary the dimensions from 2 to 4 feet, allowing for a 2-inch border, and cut out the center of the form so that the child can crawl through it. Paint the forms various colors. A base should be made for each form from a piece of 2 by 4, as

seen in Fig. 6-6. Each base should be about 4 inches long. A groove should be cut in each base, ½ inch deep and ¼ inch wide. Insert the forms into the bases and make an obstacle course.

Activities: Have the children perform the following activities according to their abilities:

1. Tell the child to crawl through a specific form with a corresponding color. For example, crawl through a red circle or blue square.
2. Tell the child to crawl through a specific form with a corresponding size. For example, crawl through a large rectangle or a small triangle.
3. Tell the child to crawl feet first or head first through each of the forms. Challenge him to change body positions and have his front or back facing the floor as he passes through the forms. Tell the child to try not to touch the forms as he passes through them.
4. Combine the previous items into auditory sequential commands of two or more factors in complexity. For example, crawl feet first through a small, red triangle or head first through a large, red square.
5. Set up an obstacle course with the forms and other objects, such as balance beams, springboards, and chairs. As the child's skill improves, time him to see how long it takes him to progress through the course.
6. Lay the forms on the ground and use them for self-testing activities. For example:

Fig. 6-6. Geometrical obstacle course forms.

a. Have the child stand in the center of the form. Can he balance on one base of support? Can he bounce a ball while standing or kneeling within his form?

b. Can the child jump in and out of the form without touching it? How many ways can he move around the form? How many ways can he move in and out of the form on two bases of support?

7. Lay the forms on the ground and use them to play hopscotch.

8. Use the forms as targets and try to throw beanbags through them at varying distances.

■   ■   ■

Level: Beginning.

Subconcept: Specially designed targets and beanbags may be used to create an awareness of geometrical shape.

Materials: Targets with simple geometrical forms cut out can be made from pieces of plywood or cardboard boxes. If possible, back supports should be made to allow the target to be placed at various angles toward which the child can aim. The targets can be painted to create a more complete and attractive project (Fig. 6-7). Instructions for making beanbags in the shape of letters, numbers, and geometrical forms can be found on p. 71 in Fig. 4-4.

Activities: Have the children perform the following activities according to their level of ability.

1. Have the child trace his fingers around the openings in the target to identify various forms. Perform first with the eyes open and then with the eyes closed.

2. Tell the child to toss objects through specific holes in the target by aiming at specific geo-

Fig. 6-7. Children can throw objects through geometrical shapes.

metrical forms on command. Throw a triangle beanbag through the triangle hole, a red B through the circle hole, etc. Balls may be used if you do not have beanbags.

3. Have the child stand at various distances from the target and try to throw objects such as beanbags through the holes.

4. Vary the angle of the target from perpendicular to the floor to parallel with the floor and have the child try to toss objects through the holes.

5. Throw the letter, shape, or number beanbag to the child and have him identify what it is, as the class watches.

6. Have the children spell words with the letter beanbags. Then have them assume the shapes of the word's letters with their bodies.

7. Give the students mathematics problems involving addition, substraction, multiplication, and division according to their ability level and have them solve the problems by using the beanbags. Then tell them to assume the shape of the numerical answer with their bodies.

■ ■ ■

Levels: Beginning and intermediate.

Subconcept: Circles, lines, squares, triangles, rectangles, trapezoids, diamonds, parallelograms, and rhomboids are different kinds of geometrical shapes.

Materials: Use paint, tape, chalk, or any other type of marking material to place the grid in Fig. 6-8 on an indoor or outdoor playing area. For a whole class of children, more than one design is needed.

Activities: Have the children identify the various shapes by moving on them in challenging ways.

Find a curved, straight, or diagonal line and move across it going forward. Can you move on the same line going backward, sideways, at a high level or low level, fast, slow, and with a lot or a little force? Can you combine the factors as you move across your line?

Now identify a circle, square, rectangle, triangle, diamond, parallelogram, or rhomboid and move along your shape. Change your method of locomotion. Can you walk, hop, jump, skip, gallop, or slide along your shape? Can you use parts of your body in addition to your feet to move along your shape? Can you change directions, speeds, levels, etc.? Can you trace the same shape in the air with

Fig. 6-8. Geometrical grid.

your arms, elbow, hands, or head as you move along the shape on the ground?

CONCEPT: Geometry is the field of mathematics that deals with the properties, measurement, and relationship of points, lines, planes, and solids.

Level: Intermediate.

Subconcepts: (1) The human body can assume various geometrical lines and shapes. (2) The human body can trace lines and shapes by moving in various pathways on the floor and in the air.

Materials: Record player, elastic ropes, streamers, and a selection of records with contrasting smooth-flowing and percussive music.

Activities: The purpose of this lesson is to help children learn to define space through dance. Space is length, width, and height. The body has certain dimensions of length, width, and height when motionless and can be carried through space to describe other shapes of length, width, and height. During this lesson the children will extend their knowledge of two-dimensional shapes into three-dimensional shapes through movement in dance.

To begin the lesson, have the children extend their awareness of a circle into a cylinder with various properties (Fig. 6-9). By moving through space, their bodies may be used to describe the dimensions of the cylinder. How long, wide, and high is it? Their movement should also indicate how the cylinder is related to the floor. Is it tall and straight? Is it wide or only large enough to fit your body inside? Is it lying on the floor, possibly able to roll, or is it leaning at an angle? The students should be allowed to work for a short time with music as background only. At this point they are defining the shape and not the rhythm of the music. After a period of experimentation the teacher should emphasize the round qualities of a cylinder in contrast to straight or angular lines of other geometrical figures.

In the next step of the lesson the teacher should ask the children to develop a short sequence with a beginning pose, a movement of short duration, and an ending pose. Each stage should be characteristic of the cylinder, defining its properties of length, width, and height. The children may now choose to continue defining their shape or relate their sequence more to the rhythm of the music—smooth and flowing.

This lesson can be practiced with variations.

Fig. 6-9. Geometrical awareness through movement.

After a period of time the children will be able to concentrate on a body focus or lead to describe the cylinder. Changing levels, direction, time, force, and range of motion could be added as points of concentration. Equipment such as an elastic rope or streamers may be used to help define the shape of the cylinder.

Through similar directions the teacher can guide the children to experiment with other geometrical shapes such as the cube being an extension of a square or a pyramid being an extension of a triangle. Although the qualities of length, width, and height remain, the obvious differences compared to a cylinder are now those of straight and diagonal lines jointed with angles of various sizes.

■ ■ ■

Levels: Intermediate and advanced.

Subconcept: Geometry includes the study of both concave and convex forms; acute, right, and obtuse angles; and symmetry.

Materials: None.

Activities: As the children begin this lesson by performing warm-up exercises, point out the ones that are symmetrical versus assymetrical. The jumping jack, sit-up, push-up, and pull-up

are symmetrical. The windmill or alternate toe touch is an assymetrical exercise. Ask the children to think of other exercises or body poses that are symmetrical or asymmetrical. To continue with the concept of symmetry, you may explore various gymnastics and locomotor activities with the children. Which activities in gymnastics are symmetrical? (Forward, roll, tip-up, tripod, headstand, hip, squat vault, sheep vault.) Can you think of others? Which locomotor skills are symmetrical? (Jump.) Which are asymmetrical? (Walk, hop, slide, skip, gallop.)

In addition to becoming more aware of symmetrical relations, children may also become more aware of curvilinear and angular relationships. Curved lines may be explored through various body poses or designs painted on a floor. Because concavity and convexity (Fig. 6-10) are a matter of orientation, use the front of the body as a point of reference. A person bending or flexing at the elbow or hips creates a concave body line. A convex body line can be created by hyperextending the hips or looking at the back side a bent (flexed) arm. Because the knee joint oriented opposite to the elbow, a bent knee creates the opposite refer-

Fig. 6-10. Can you make your body assume a concave or convex shape?

Fig. 6-11. Creating angles with the body.

ence—the front of the knee is convex, the back of the knee is concave. When moving on a curved line or circle, the inside of the line is concave. The outside of the line is convex.

Angular relationships may be explored by using the joints of the body (Fig. 6-11).

An acute angle is one of less than 90 degrees. Can you bend one body part at an acute angle? Two? Three? Four? A right angle is 90 degrees. How many body parts can you bend at 90 degrees? An obtuse angle is one of more than 90 degrees. Can you create different body poses with one or more joints bent at obtuse angles? Can you create body poses with one joint bent at an acute angle, one at a right angle, and one at an obtuse angle? Can you move across the floor on your hands and feet with your legs at acute angles and your arms at obtuse angles (crab walk)? Can you move across the floor on your feet with one leg bent at an acute angle and one at an obtuse angle? While bending the joints at acute, right, and obtuse angles, can you create symmetrical and asymmetrical body poses? Which geometrical forms have acute, right, or obtuse angles? Which forms have concave or convex lines? How many other ways can you think of to use symmetrical, curvilinear, and angular lines?

Measuring and graphing

CONCEPT: Measurement tells us how many times a standard unit is contained in a given object.

Level: Beginning.

Subconcept: The hand, or foot, a stick, a bat, a ruler, and yardstick may be used as measuring devices.

Materials: Rulers and yardsticks.

Activities: Initial experiences with measuring should help children become familiar with different units of measurement. Because it is difficult for children to identify with the standards of an inch, foot, and yard, they might enjoy measuring with more familiar devices. They may choose to use the width of their hand, the length of their foot, forearm, or body, a stick or bat, or the length of their stride.

During the movement activities for your lessons you may choose to have the children hop, jump, throw, and kick for distance. They can then measure and record their attempts in particular unit values. For example, one child might be able to hop 10 hands, jump 5 fore-

Fig. 6-12. The distance to the base is 8 bats.

arms, have a walking stride of 1 stick or bat length (Fig. 6-12), throw 25 walking strides, etc.

As the students become more familiar with counting and their own units of measurement, they will become more ready to convert to the standard units of measurement. They will be able to understand better the necessity for standard units because each child's hand, foot, body length, stride, etc. are different. Although 2 children may perform at the same level, their measurements are different because their standards are different. If a person wants to compare his performance with others, he must have a common unit. Thus the reason for an inch, foot, yard, centimeter, or meter becomes important, and children may readily convert to the standard units. Further practice should follow that allows the children to convert their performances to standard units of measurements.

CONCEPT: Measuring and graphing help us describe and record information exactly.

Level: Intermediate.

Subconcept: Measuring and graphing play fields to scale makes it possible to define and pictorially represent the surfaces on which games are played.

Materials: A long measuring tape, paper, and pencils.

Activities: This lesson may take place as a part of a unit in mathematics or as a part of one of any number of units in physical education. The purpose is to teach the children basic concepts in measurement and to make drawings to scale (blueprint drawing). As a result, rather than develop one lesson, several suggestions follow that provide opportunities for the specified activities while concentrating on movement experiences.

1. As a part of a unit on volleyball, measure the length and width of the court. Measure the height of the net. Compute the area of the court. Make a drawing of the court to scale (½ inch = 1 foot), including all boundary and service lines.

2. As a part of a unit on basketball, measure the length and width of the court. Measure the height of the basket, distance of the free throw line from the basket, width of the free throw lane, distance from the boundary line to the hall court line, and diameter of the basketball hoop. Compute the area of the court. Make a drawing of the court to scale (½ inch = 1 foot), including the boundary lines, center circle, half court line, and free throw lines and lanes.

3. As a part of a unit on softball, measure the distance from home plate to first and third base, from home plate to the pitcher's mound and second base, and, when the playing field has a fence, from home plate to the left, center, and right field fence. Compute the area inside the base paths. Make a drawing of the field to scale (1 inch = 1 yard), including all the boundary lines, fences, bases, and pitcher's mound (Fig. 6-13).

4. Make a diagram of the outdoor playground or an obstacle course that you have developed with hoops, tires, ropes, etc. Make the diagram to scale, including the placement and distance between objects.

■ ■ ■

Level: Advanced.

Subconcept: Measuring, recording, and graphing data from exercise and human physiology helps us understand our level of fitness.

Materials: Jump ropes, a bench, and a stopwatch.

Activities: To begin this lesson, teach the children to find their carotid artery and to take

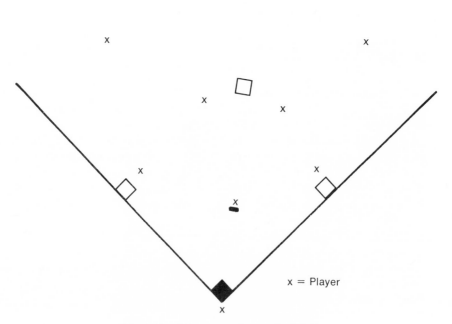

Fig. 6-13. Make a map of the softball field.

their pulse for 1 minute. (Count 1001, 1002, 1003, etc.) If you desire, you can have them take their pulse for 10 seconds and multiply by 6. Start with their resting pulse rate. Is there a difference between pulses when lying down and sitting at rest? Why? (The body is performing a minimal amount of work while maintaining a sitting posture.)

Next, have the children perform different types of exercise for 1 minute. They may walk, perform calesthenics, throw and catch balls, jump rope, step up and down on the bench (one rotation every 2 seconds), run, or perform any other type of movement activity. After each exercise period have the children take their pulse immediately. Then, after 1 minute of rest, have them take their pulse again.

The children should record and/or graph the following types of information: their resting heart rate in comparison to others in the class, a rank order of activities from easiest to most strenuous, the difference between resting and postactivity heart rates for each activity, and the rate of recovery 1 minute after each activity.

After recording this information, the students may participate in a unit that stresses physical fitness. Then they may again record the same types of information. A comparison with pre-vious experiments and graphs should help them discover several facts about their bodies and basic fitness:

1. The resting heart rate of a person with good cardiorespiratory fitness is usually lower than that of one who is not in good condition.
2. The heart rate of a person in good condition immediately following exercise may be higher than that of a person not in good condition because the heart has responded well by carrying oxygen to the muscles and lactic acid products to the lungs to exchange for more air.
3. The heart rate of a person in good condition will recover back to its normal resting heart rate more quickly than that of one who is not in good condition.
4. To establish a good level of fitness, a person should perform some type of exercise to get the heart rate over 100—preferably 120, but not over 180—for 3 to 30 minutes every day.*

■   ■   ■

*Morehouse, Laurence E.: Total fitness, New York, 1976, Pocket Books.

Fig. 6-14. You can make a graph of your heart rate changes.

Levels: Intermediate and advanced.

Subconcept: Measuring and graphing the ability to jump for distance and height over a period of time shows improvement in performance.

Materials: High jump standards, a high jump landing pit, a long jump pit, and a measuring tape.

Activities: The learning experience is intended to be extended over a series of lessons. During the first lesson the details of measurement can be shown. In the high jump the measurement is made from the top of the high jump bar to the ground. The measurement is made in feet and inches. In the long jump the measurement is from the board to the nearest point of impact when landing. The measurement is

made in feet and inches. In each of the events the children should also be instructed as to the number of trials and how a foul is committed. After they understand the details of measurement, the students can be taught the essentials of graphing. The bar graph (Fig. 6-15) is most appropriate for measuring improvement in jumping skills.

During this first lesson a sample bar graph for each of the events should be provided for the students. In the bar graph for the high jump the horizontal scale will represent the number of the trial and the vertical scale, the height in feet and inches. In the bar graph for the long jump the horizontal scale will represent the number of the trial and the vertical scale, the distance in feet and inches. In both the graphs the children will

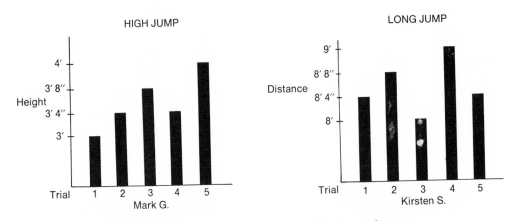

Fig. 6-15. You can use a graph to record your jumping performance.

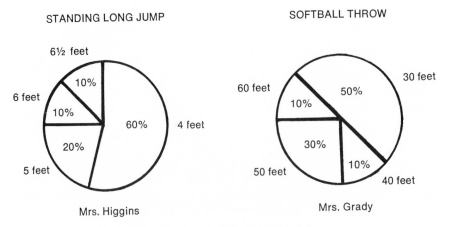

Fig. 6-16. How well did your class do?

be taught how to show the height or distance of the jump in succeeding jumps.

As the children begin jumping, divide them into two groups. One group can work on high jumping skills and the other group on long jumping skills. The groups will be subdivided to include some children who are measuring, some who are recording the bar graphs, some who are taking care of the pits, and some who are jumping. Children will rotate positions within the group and will change jumping events at an appropriate time to allow all a chance to perform at each station.

During succeeding lessons the students can learn how to construct their own bar graphs as measuring devices. As children improve in each of the skills, the bar graphs will indicate the amount of improvement for each child.

CONCEPT: Graphs represent collections of data.

Levels: Intermediate and advanced.

Subconcept: Some types of graphs are pictographs, bar graphs, and circle graphs.

Materials: The equipment used can vary according to the activity in which the children engage.

Activities: The last two lessons used the bar graph,* or histogram, to record performances. It is the purpose of this lesson to suggest ways in which the pictograph and circle graph may be used to record performances.

1. After a unit on jumping or throwing activities in which the performances of the children were recorded, use a circle graph to indicate levels of performance in various events. Display the graphs on a bulletin board* for the children to read and interpret (Fig. 6-16). For example, in the standing long jump, 60% of Mrs. Higgins' class jumped 4 feet or less, 20% jumped between 4 and 5 feet, 10% jumped between 6 and 6½ feet, and 10% jumped 6½ feet or better. In the softball throw 45% of Mrs. Grady's children threw the ball 30 feet or less, 20% threw it between 40 and 50 feet, 25% threw

---

*You may use the circle graph or pictograph or bulletin boards as motivational devices for children to read and interpret. Any activity may be chosen for purposes of recording performances. You may choose to record percentages, distances, heights, times, boys' versus girls' performances, and one class versus another. As the children become skilled at using the graphs, they may make their own on the bulletin boards.

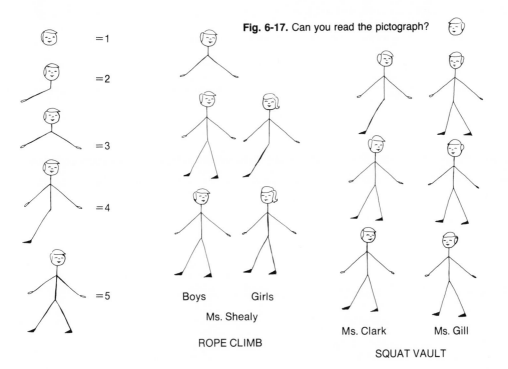

Fig. 6-17. Can you read the pictograph?

= 1

= 2

= 3

= 4

= 5

Boys   Girls

Ms. Shealy

ROPE CLIMB

Ms. Clark   Ms. Gill

SQUAT VAULT

it between 50 and 60 feet, and only 10% threw it 60 feet or more.

2. During a unit on gymnastics or stability skills, use pictographs displayed on a bulletin board to record levels of performance (Fig. 6-17). The children may read and interpret the performances of the boys versus the girls or their class compared to other classes of the same grade. For example, in the rope climb the boys from Ms. Shealy's class had 13 climb to the top of the rope, and the girls had 9 climb to the top of the rope. In vaulting, 14 children from Ms. Clark's room could perform the squat vault compared to 16 from Ms. Gill's room.

SELECTED REFERENCES FOR PART TWO

Ashlock, Robert B., and Humphrey, James H.: Teaching elementary school mathematics through motor learning, Springfield, Ill., 1976, Charles C Thomas, Publisher.

Brandes, Louis Grant: Mathematics can be fun, Portland, Me., 1956, J. Weston Walch, Publisher.

Copeland, Richard W.: How children learn mathematics, New York, 1974, Macmillan Publishing Co.

Devine, Donald F., and Kaufmann, Jerome E.: Mathematics for elementary education, New York, 1974, John Wiley & Sons, Inc.

Dienes, Zoltan Paul: Mathematics through the senses: games, dance and art, New York, 1973, Humanities Press.

Duker, Sam: Individualized instruction in mathematics, Metuchen, N.J., 1972, Scarecrow Press, Inc.

Garstens, Helen L., and Jackson, Stanley B.: Mathematics for elementary school teachers, New York, 1967, The Macmillan Co., Publishers.

Gilbert, Anne Green: Teaching the three R's, Minneapolis, 1977, Burgess Publishing Co.

Grossnickle, Foster E., and Brueckner, L. J.: Discovering means in elementary school mathematics, New York, 1973, Holt, Rinehart, & Winston.

Hollands, Ray: Mathematical games and activities for first schools, London, 1971, Chatto & Windus Ltd.

Howard, Charles F., and Dumas, Enoch: Teaching contemporary mathematics in the elementary school, New York, 1966, Harper & Row, Publishers.

Humphrey, James H.: Child learning through elementary school physical education, Dubuque, Iowa, 1974, William C. Brown Co., Publishers.

Jensen, Terry M.: Creative ropes, Journal of Health, Physical Education, and Recreation 32:56-57, May, 1971.

Keller, J. J.: Metric system guide. Vols. I and II, Metrication in the United States, Neenah, Wis., 1976, J. J. Keller & Associates, Inc.

Kennedy, Leonard M.: Games for individualizing mathematics learning, Columbus, Ohio, 1973, Charles E. Merrill Publishing Co.

Kovach, Ladis D.: Modern elementary mathematics, San Francisco, 1968, Holden-Day, Inc.

Kramer, Klaas: The teaching of elementary school mathematics, Boston, 1967, Allyn & Bacon, Inc.

Lovell, Kenneth: The growth of understanding in mathematics; kindergarten through grade three, New York, 1971, Holt, Rinehart & Winston, Inc.

Marks, John L.: Teaching elementary school mathematics for understanding, ed. 3, New York, 1970, McGraw Hill Book Co.

May, Lola June: Teaching mathematics in the elementary school, ed. 2, New York, 1974, The Free Press.

Memmel, Rudolph L.: Arithmetic through play, Journal of Health, Physical Education, and Recreation 24:31, June, 1953.

Miller, Arthur G., Cheffers, J. T., and Whitcomb, V.: Physical education; teaching human movement in the elementary schools, ed. 3 rev., Englewood Cliffs, N.J., 1974, Prentice-Hall, Inc.

National Council of Teachers of Mathematics: An analysis of new mathematics programs, Washington, D.C., 1965, The Council.

National Council of Teachers of Mathematics: Sets, Washington, D.C., 1965, The Council.

National Council of Teacher of Mathematics: The whole numbers, Washington, D.C., 1965, The Council.

School Mathematics Study Group: Mathematics for the elementary school, grades 1-6, 3 vols., rev. ed., New Haven, Conn., 1963, Yale University Press.

Sherman, Helene: Common elements in new mathematics programs, New York, 1972, Teachers College Press.

Smith, Eugene P., et al.: Discoveries in modern mathematics, Columbus, Ohio, 1968, Charles E. Merrill Publishing Co.

Smith, James A.: Setting conditions for mathematics in elementary school, Boston, 1970, Allyn & Bacon, Inc.

Swenson, Esther J.: Teaching mathematics to children, Sydney, 1973, Collier Macmillan Australia.

PART THREE

Developing science concepts

Roller skating involves a combination of several scientific principles.

Because of the technological age and culture in which we live, children in the elementary schools must be exposed to a variety of meaningful science experiences that leads them to an understanding of the world about them. If children are to be provided with meaningful learning experiences in science, classroom teachers and physical education teachers should make an attempt to coordinate their efforts when possible. Because of this philosophical attitude toward correlating subjects, we reviewed several science series as well as science supplement textbooks for teachers and children to discover which science concepts could best be related to physical education. We reviewed books concerned with subject matter to be presented in grades 1 through 6. We found that science concepts were based on and taught through units in the biological, physical, and earth sciences. Concepts in the physical sciences were most naturally applicable to physical activity. Concepts in the physical sciences that were related to physical activity and mentioned most often in the science textbook series and science supplement books are machines, levers, Newton's laws of motion, types of motion, factors affecting motion, resistance, friction, gravity, centrifugal force, sound, buoyancy, energy, force, inertia, and momentum.

Chapter 7

STABILITY

Stability or balance is an extremely important factor to consider in all physical activity. A stable position is important for maintaining balance, regaining balance, and producing, giving, and receiving force. To effectively maintain a balanced position in any of these situations, one must understand the concepts of gravity and base of support. *Gravity* is a force pulling downward toward the center of the earth. A center of gravity exists within all masses or bodies that pulls each toward the earth. Gravity is the reason why all objects sent into the air return to the earth. The center of gravity for a geometrical or symmetrical shape is in its center. The center of gravity in asymmetrical objects or bodies may be determined by a system of weighing and balancing. A line of gravity is established by extending an imaginary line through the center of gravity to the earth in a vertical direction. The *base of support* is that part of the body which is in contact with the supporting surface or ground. Usually the feet are a base of support, but there are times when other points of contact act as the base of support—when lying down, sitting, performing a headstand of a handstand. Sometimes a person has a wide base of support and sometimes a narrow base. The interrelationship of a center of gravity and the line of gravity to a base of support determines the amount of stability. If a line of gravity falls outside a base of support, the object falls. If a body has a wide base of support with a low center of gravity, it is in a stable position (Fig. 7-1).

The cerebral cortex, lower brain centers, and various sensory organs of the body are important centers for the monitoring of a person's stability. The motor, premotor, and prefrontal areas of the cortex act through the pyramidal and extrapyramidal tracts to control and refine voluntary and involuntary motor behavior. The cerebellum is an essential integrative center for postural adjustment, locomotion, and many other reflex and motor activities that are monitored by a complex feedback loop. The vestibular apparatus in the inner ear facilitates a person's awareness of his position in space. The semicircular canals are most sensitive to rotary motion, whereas the otoliths and saccule are most sensitive to linear motion and the force of gravity or its sudden loss. As a sensory organ the eyes play an important role in the maintenance of body balance. One can readily learn how much a person relies on vision for balance and all motor acts when those same acts are executed with the eyes closed. In an effort to use the eyes to enable good balance and motor coordination, they should be focused in the direction of the intended movement. The eyes help determine the relative position of the body. An individual can usually control his position better if he focuses them on a fixed target than if the eyes are closed or allowed to wander randomly. The awareness of the position of one's body in space is also greatly enhanced by the proprioceptive end organs in the skin, muscles, tendons, and ligaments. These sense organs enable a person to be aware of texture, touch pressure, pain, temperature, and amount of flexion or extension in the joints.

Following are some sample lessons concerning how concepts regarding stability could be taught to elementary schoolchildren.

Learning activities

CONCEPT: To move well, a person must control his balance while in static and dynamic postures.

Level: Beginning.

Subconcepts: (1) Gravity is a force pulling downward toward the center of the earth. (2) A

Fig. 7-1. The body remains balanced when the center of gravity and line of gravity fall within the base of support.

body is most stable when the center of gravity is directly over the base of support. (3) Static balance activities are those in which the center of gravity remains in the same position. (4) Dynamic balance activities are those in which the center of gravity is constantly shifting.

Materials: A record player and the record ''Going Out of My Head'' and ''Can't Take My Eyes Off of You'' from ''And the Beat Goes On'' by Ambrose Brazelton.

Activities: In an attempt to accomplish the specified objectives, a dialogue between teacher and children may develop as follows:

Today we are going to work on balance. Sometimes we will move on balance and other times we will move off balance. What happens to you when you move on balance? (Your muscles hold you upright and you don't fall down.) What happens to you if you move off balance? (You fall.) What is it that makes you fall when you are off balance? (Gravity.) Why can't you move in any position like an astronaut does in space? (Gravity.) Everyone stand up and hold your hands and arms over your head. Now relax your arm muscles as much as you can just let go. What made your arms fall down to your sides? (Gravity.)

Now think about holding a ball out in front of you and then letting go of it. What happens? Why wouldn't the ball stay right there in space where you put it? (Gravity.) We all know that our muscles are strong enough to hold us up to walk even though gravity is pulling down on us all the time, but are your muscles able to hold you in any position? Let's see!

Spread out over the floor so that you can work in your own space and then make a balanced shape. Hold it. On what are you balanced? That is called your base of support. Your base of support is the part of your body that touches the floor and supports your weight. Now make a different shape and hold it very still. Are you on or off balance? How big is your base of support? Can you make it even bigger? Are you still on balance? You are if your weight is over your base of support. Now see if you can make your base of support much smaller and make a balanced shape. Can you still be on balance over that little base of support? Is it easier or harder to be on balance with a little base of support? (Harder.) (See Fig. 7-2.)

Now let's have everyone travel throughout the room, using as many different body parts as you can to support yourself as you move.

Keep changing the body part that is touching the

Fig. 7-2. Who is the most stable?

floor. Keep trying to make different shapes as you move, but when you hear or see my signal, freeze in the position that you are in. Now as you travel, move at different levels while changing the body parts on which you are balanced. Remember to hold your position very still when you hear the signal. Let's see if you can take a balanced curled position. Can you change the body part on which you are taking your weight and still show a curled position? Keep trying to find different body parts on which you can balance and show several different curled positions. Can you curl your body without holding your legs in with your arms? Is your head tucked in? Now can you move throughout the gym in a curled position? Change your curled position and see if you can move. Remember to keep away from each other as you move.

Let's see if you can take a balanced stretch position. Keep changing the body part on which you are balancing. Emphasize different stretch positions. Reach away from the base of support with all free body parts. (See Fig. 7-3.)

Now get a partner close to you and see how many different shapes you and your partner can make together. Be sure to work with your partner in making these shapes. Let's see if you and your partner can make a big, rounded shape together. Try to make an-

other big, rounded shape. Can you make a small rounded shape? Now let's see if you can make a very long, straight, and narrow shape. Can you make a twisted shape? Next, make the widest shape that the two of you can.

So far we have been trying to be on balance. Let's work on moving off balance safely and rolling out to a new position. Everyone make some kind of balance shape and listen to my signals. Very carefully lean out of your shape until you move off balance. Then curl your body, making it very round, and roll out to your feet. Balance with a big base of support, lean, roll over, recover. Next, balance with a narrower base of support, lean, roll, and recover.

Continue with these variations while the children experiment with levels, body leads, directions, and body shapes.

CONCEPT: The sensory organs of the body enable a person to maintain his stability by sending clues to the brain concerning his position in space.

Level: Intermediate.

Subconcepts: (1) A person's sensory organs in the skin, muscles, joints, and ligaments send

Fig. 7-3. Balanced stretch positions.

clues to the brain concerning his position in space. (2) The vestibular mechanism in the inner ear helps a person be aware of linear and rotary motion. (3) The eyes help a person locate his position in space. (4) When moving in a linear or rotary manner, keep the eyes open and focused on a continual point of reference.

Materials: Balance beams, vaulting boxes, mats, wagons, scooters, and moving dollies.

Activities: To begin the lesson, have the children close their eyes and assume various body positions with different bases of support. Have them concentrate on the awareness of their body parts by kinesthetically "feeling" where each body part is located. What relationships can they create between the arms, head, trunk, and legs? How does it feel to be supported by the hands and head, with your head at a lower level than your legs? How does it feel to be in a tuck, or curled, position? How does it feel to be in a stretch position? Which body parts are near each other and which are far from each other in the examples given? Even though the children have closed their eyes, they can still feel where body parts are located in space because of the sense receptors in the skin, muscles, and joints.

While still keeping their eyes closed, have the children move about the room. Have them move slow at first, then faster. Have them change their directions and pathways. Even though the children cannot see where they are going, they can feel their way about the room through the sense receptors in the skin, muscles, and joints Also, their ears help them locate the position of other children through sound.

In addition to the sound clues regarding the proximity of other children, the ears give children clues as to the type of motion in which they are engaged. To emphasize this point, use a wagon, scooter, or moving dolly and allow the children to give each other rides. The person receiving the ride should close his eyes. The pusher should vary the pathway of the scooter from straight to zigzag and circular movements. Changes in direction should also occur. The rider is aware of the tension placed on the body to initiate turns and changes of direction by the pusher. In addition, the ears help the rider be aware of linear and rotary motion. In the same way a person is aware of the linear or rotary motion of a car accelerating, decelerating, and turning; an elevator going up or down; or a carnival ride spinning around. Encourage the chil-

Fig. 7-4. Walking on a balance beam helps children learn about stability.

dren to think of other examples in which the ears help make a person aware of linear or rotary motion.

To this point the children have been working with their eyes closed. The next part of the lesson will emphasize the importance of using the eyes to help maintain one's balance. First, have the students balance on one leg with their eyes closed, then with their eyes open. It will be obvious that the eyes help them keep their balance. Next, have the children walk across a balance beam with their eyes open and then closed. Again, it will be obvious that the eyes help maintain balance. To emphasize the use of the eyes in conditions other than static or linear motion, have the children jump in the air from the floor or off of the vaulting boxes and execute quarter turns, half turns, and full turns with their eyes open and closed. It should be pointed out to them that when turning their body, they should keep their eyes open and focused on one continual point of reference. This is how dancers, divers, ice skaters, and roller skaters are able to turn and spin without losing their balance. This concept is difficult to master for any performer and could become a series of lessons in itself.

CONCEPT: The stability of the body is affected by the size and shape of the base of support and the relationship of the center of gravity to the base of support.

Level: Intermediate.

Subconcepts: (1) When carrying or lifting a heavy object, keep the object close to the body. (2) To regain balance, raise the arms or legs on the side of the body opposite the direction in which the balance is lost.

Materials: Balance beams or pieces of 2 × 4 inch lumber cut into 10-inch lengths, as well as some weighted objects.

Activities: When it becomes her turn, have each child stand on the end of the balance beam opposite the end where a weight has been placed. The child should walk to the other end of the beam, pick up the weight, make a 180-degree turn, and return to the starting end of the beam. Allow each child to experiment balancing her own body weight and the weight of the object while on the beam. Have each student carry the weight near to and far away from her body while holding the weight in front and to the sides of the body. (See Fig. 7-4.)

After each child has tried this routine several times, discuss how the children balanced themselves from start to finish. How did they regain their balance if it was ever lost? Did they carry the weight best near to or far away from their body? Why? The students should realize that balance can be regained by adjusting the arms or legs on the side of the body opposite the direction in which balance is lost. To lift and carry the weighted object efficiently, the student should carry it close to his body.

■　■　■

Levels: Intermediate and advanced.

Subconcepts: (1) To maintain balance, the center of gravity must be within and above the base of support. (2) The body is more stable when it is supported by a large base of support than when it is suppored by a small base. (3) The stability of the body is increased by lowering the center of gravity.

Materials: Books, records, pencils, golf balls, table tennis balls, and empty tubes from rolls of toilet tissue or paper towels.

Activities: Have the children use some of the objects and balance them in various positions on the floor. Once each object is balanced in a given position, ask the students to apply force to tip the objects over. For example, have the

children balance a book, pencil, or paper roller on end and then flat on its side. In each instance ask the child to try to tip the object over. In addition to learning that an object with a low center of gravity is stable, the children will learn that an object with a large base of support is more stable than one with a small base. Use leading questions to get the children to discover these concepts for themselves. (See Fig. 7-5.)

Now have the children balance the same objects on their finger in an effort to find out where the center of gravity of each object is located. The center of gravity is located in the geometrical center of the object. Have them balance the objects in vertical and horizontal positions. They should be led to discover that an object with a low center of gravity is easier to balance (horizontal position of the object) than one with a high center of gravity (vertical position of the object). (See Fig. 7-6.)

To further emphasize this point, have the children place a table tennis ball and golf ball in opposite ends of a paper roller. Have them try to balance the paper roller on their finger in a horizontal position. They will find that the center of gravity of the paper roller has changed toward the end with the golf ball. Next, have

Fig. 7-5. Objects can be balanced in different positions.

Fig. 7-6. It is easier to balance an object when the center of gravity is low rather than high.

Fig. 7-7. Which athlete is the most stable? Why?

Fig. 7-8. What foot position enables you to stop quickly and maintain your balance?

them stand the paper roller first on one end and then the other. Ask them to push the roller over when the golf ball is closest to the base of support and when the table tennis ball is closest to the base of support. The children will again discover that an object is more stable when it has a low center of gravity.

Explain to the children that their bodies are subject to the same rules. As long as their center of gravity is within the base of support, they will be in a balanced position. When their center of gravity falls outside the base of support, they will fall over. Their bodies are most stable when they have a large base of support and a low center of gravity. Challenge the children to assume body positions that place their center of gravity at high, medium, and low levels with various bases of support. Have them show you different body positions that are unstable (small base of support and high center of gravity). Then have them show you different body positions that are stable (large base of support and low center of gravity).

Finally, explain to the children that the location and relationship of their body parts affects the location of their center of gravity. Have them experience moving their arms and legs in-

to different positions and discuss this effect on a person's stability. Have them stand on tiptoe with their arms at their sides and then with their arms fully extended overhead. Discuss how elevating the weight of the arms raises the body's center of gravity. Have them stand with their feet close together and with their feet apart. In which position is the body more stable? Have them support their body weight with one, two, three, and four or more bases of support. Under what conditions is the body most stable?

■ ■ ■

Levels: Intermediate and advanced.

Subconcepts: (1) To stop linear motion quickly, bend the knees, ankles, and hips and spread the feet in the direction of the motion so as to lower the center of gravity and keep it over the base of support. (2) When stopping a rotary movement, land with a wide base and a low center of gravity that is over the base of support.

Materials: Vaulting boxes, minitrampolines, and mats.

Activities: Previous lessons have concentrated on stability concepts with reference to static balance. The same concepts apply to bodies in motion and those stopping their motion. The wide base of a baseball pitcher during delivery or infielder picking up a ground ball and the low profile of a football runner or wrestler are all examples of the application of the concepts of stability when the body is in motion. Encourage the children to think of other examples of balance control while the body is in motion. Have them bring in newspaper and magazine pictures showing these concepts. (See Fig. 7-7.)

For the purpose of activity, these concepts can be best illustrated by concentrating on body relationships when stopping motion. Have the children run as fast as they can and come to a quick stop. Have them take sliding steps to the side and stop quickly. What conditions enable efficient stopping action—a high center of gravity or a low center of gravity, a large base of support or a small base of support? In what direction should the feet be placed when stopping forward or sideways movement? (See Fig. 7-8.)

Next, have the children run straight, jump or vault off a box or minitrampoline, and come to a quick stop. How can they best stop their linear motion? Finally, have them perform jumping turns in place, from a run, and from a height. How can they best stop their rotary motion?

Chapter 8

LEVERS

Throughout their elementary school years, children learn about the six different types of simple machines. They learn about the lever, inclined plane, screw, pulley, wedge, and wheel through studying about machines that are used at home and work. Inclined planes are used on loading ramps and conveyer belts. Levers are used to throw a ball, pry off a hubcap, open a bottle, and crack a nut. Screws are used in all types of carpentry work. Pulleys help an automobile mechanic lift an engine out of a car or lift a heavy load in steel construction. Wedges are used in splitting wood with an ax. Wheels are used in cars, bicycles, and all forms of transportation. Many machines are complex, or combinations of more than one simple machine. For example, a crane is a combination of a pully and lever system. Each type of machine helps perform work.

A *lever* is defined as a rigid bar that turns around an axis, or fulcrum. In the human body the bones represent the rigid bars and the joints, the fulcrums. The muscles of the body provide the effort, force, or resistance necessary for movement. There are three different types of levers, which may be analyzed according to the relationship between the fulcrum and the point of application of force and resistance.

FIRST-CLASS LEVERS

A first-class lever is one in which the fulcrum is located between the resistance and the force arms. When the force arm is longer than the resistance arm, such as in balancing on a seesaw (Fig. 8-1, *A*), force is favored. When the resistance arm is longer than the force arm, as in rowing a boat (Fig. 8-1, *B*), speed and range of motion are favored. Other examples in which first-class levers are employed include use of a crowbar and cutting with a scissors. Can you think of others?

SECOND-CLASS LEVERS

The second-class lever is one in which the resistance is located between the fulcrum and the point of application of force (Fig. 8-2). This type of lever favors force because it can lift a heavy load rather easily. Force is gained as an advantage at the expense of speed and range of motion. Examples of this type of lever are the wheelbarrow, nutcracker, and door when it is opened with a knob. There are few examples of a second-class lever in the human body. One example is the foot when it supports the body's weight.

THIRD-CLASS LEVERS

The third-class lever is one in which the force application is located between the fulcrum and resistance. This type of lever favors speed and range of motion at the expense of using a large amount of force. The human body often uses a third-class leverage system. Examples of third-class levers are throwing a ball and kicking a ball. In fact, most athletic skills involve the use of a third-class lever (Fig. 8-3).

Sometimes a particular movement can be a combination of leverage systems, as evidenced in shoveling with a spade or paddling a canoe. When the top arm acts as the fulcrum, a third-class lever is used. When the bottom arm acts as the fulcrum, a first-class lever is used. Can you think of other examples?

OTHER FACTS ABOUT LEVERS

Mechanical advantage is a ratio that indicates the number of times a force is multiplied by a machine. It is the ratio, or conversion factor, between the resistance or length of the lever arm and the force, much like the gear ratio in a set of wheels or the transmission of a car. When a lever converts a small force exerted over a large distance into a larger force operating over a

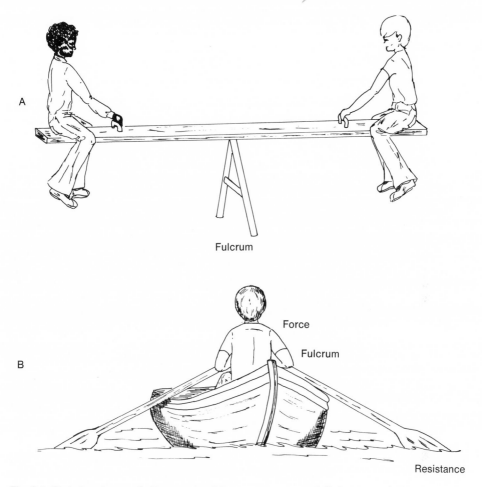

Fulcrum

Force

Fulcrum

Resistance

Fig. 8-1. First-class levers. **A,** Force and resistance arms are equal. **B,** Longer resistance arm favors speed and range of motion.

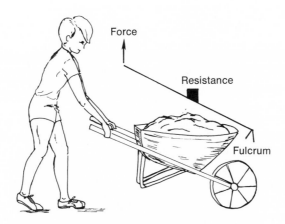

Force

Resistance

Fulcrum

Fig. 8-2. Second-class lever.

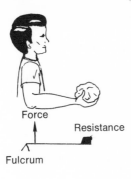

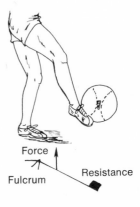

Fig. 8-3. Third-class levers.

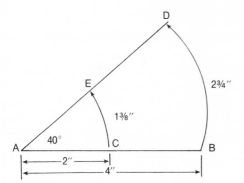

Fig. 8-4. Mechanical advantage is gained through the use of levers.

lesser distance or utilizes speed, it can gain mechanical advantage. Thus range of motion and speed are critical to the application of force. If two softball bats (Fig. 8-4) move through an angle of 40 degrees at the same speed, the tip of the longer bat *(AB)* travels much farther than the tip of the shorter bat *(AC)*, and because it covers this longer distance *(BD)* in the same time that the shorter lever covers the shorter distance *(CE)*, it must travel faster. Because of the added range of motion and faster speed of the longer bat, the mechanical advantage gained will allow a person to strike a ball farther than can be done with the shorter bat.

The term *moment of force* is used to describe the amount of force necessary to produce motion. The moment of force is calculated by multiplying the amount of the force by the length of

the force arm and equating it with the amount of resistance times the length of the resistance arm. When a lever is in a state of equilibrium, the moment of force is equal for the force arm and the resistance arm. Any additional effort from the force arm or the resistance arm causes motion. For this reason the formula $F \times FA = R \times RA$ is used to calculate the moment of force. When any three of the quantities are known, the fourth can be calculated. If a person is trying to move a 400-pound rock (Fig. 8-5) with a crowbar that is 9 feet long, how much force would he have to use to move the rock if the fulcrum was placed 1 foot from the rock?

$$F \times FA = R \times RA$$
$$F \times 8 = 400 \times 1$$
$$8F = 400$$
$$F = 50$$

As calculated in this problem, a force of 50 pounds or more would be needed to move the rock. Other examples such as a seesaw, crane, or throwing a ball could be used to help children understand how to calculate the moment of force.

The reaction of a lever indirectly is proportional to its length. A relatively easy, yet sustained, movement at the end of a long lever arm causes a short but powerful reaction at the other end. The longer the force arm, the greater the amount of force about the fulcrum. As a result, one can readily see that a long force arm requires less energy to move or balance the resis-

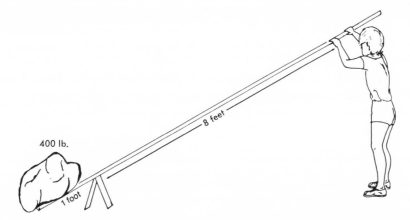

Fig. 8-5. Moment of force may be calculated to find the amount of force needed to produce motion.

tance. On the other hand, a long resistance arm or heavy weight requires more force to move or balance the resistance. Thus for strength tasks a lever with a long force arm in relation to the resistance arm should be used, such as a wheelbarrow, or second-class leverage system. When movements requiring speed, range of motion, or light weights are desired, the resistance arm should be lengthened, as in throwing, or a third-class leverage system.

Children should learn that the human body uses predominantly a third-class leverage system. It should be pointed out that the body is built for speed and range of motion at the expense of having to use large amounts of force. From a practical point of view, this means that children's muscles should be developed to be strong and that nutrition should be good to supply the necessary force and energy for body movements, especially in strenuous activities.

A lever system may operate to absorb force from external objects, as well as to apply force to objects. For example, when an individual catches a ball that is moving fact, a leverage system is used to diminish the shock of the catch by sequentially reducing the speed of the ball until it comes to rest. This is sometimes called "giving" with the ball as a person bends at the shoulders, elbows, wrists, and fingers to receive the ball.

In addition to absorbing force from objects, the body uses a leverage system to absorb its own force during a fall or a jump. By bending at the hips, knees, and ankles, one gradually reduces the body's force and comes to a gradual stop. The lever system incorporates an increase in distance, time, and surface area to absorb force during fall.

Following are some sample lessons of ways in which the concepts involving the use of machines, with a specific emphasis on the use of levers, can be integrated with physical education at the elementary school level.

Learning activities

CONCEPT: The lever, inclined plane, screw, pulley, wedge, and wheel are types of simple machines.

Level: Beginning.

Subconcept: Machines help a person do work.

Materials: A record player and any of several records available that contain sound effects or electronic music and are suggestive of twisting, curling, bending, stretching, and percussive movements ("To Move Is To Be" by Jo Ann Seker or "Electronic Sound Patterns" by Daphne Oram)

Activities: The purpose of this lesson is to teach children to understand that machines help persons do work. At the beginning of the lesson you may discuss the different types of machines: the lever, inclined plane, screw, pulley, wedge, and wheel. Have the children cite examples of machines found in everyday life with which they are familiar. Examples may be the hammer, screwdriver, ax, bicycle, wagon, automobile, wheelbarrow, crane, and steamroller.

As machines help people do work, they perform tasks such as pulling, pushing, bending, stretching, twisting, and carrying. During this lesson have the children explore the various movements that machines perform. Use sound effects music or electronic music to allow the students to explore the movements of machines with which they are familiar and of machines they create in their imagination. At times have the children move to the percussive sounds of a hammer, the twisting and rotating of a screwdriver or mixer, the creaking of an old door slamming shut, and the rolling movements of a bicycle, wagon, automobile, or steamroller. Use electronic music to allow the students to move as imaginary machines. Ask them to explore various levels of space, force, time, and flow. Sometimes have the children work individually, at other times, grouped together to combine movements and produce the effects of a large machine with many complex working parts.

As a result of the lesson, the children will better understand several concepts. Machines in factories and in the home make work easier for everyone. A human is a machine whenever he does work. All machines operate on the basis of rhythm as they do work. Any machine that does not sound as if it is working rhythmically is probably broken and needs fixing.

■   ■   ■

Level: Intermediate.

Subconcepts: (1) Machines help a person do work. (2) A lever is a rigid bar that turns around a fixed point, or a fulcrum. (3) A lever is composed of a fulcrum, a force arm, and a resistance arm.

Materials: A 30- to 40-foot rope at least an inch or more in diameter and fifteen individual ropes.

Activities: The purpose of this lesson is to teach the children about simple machines and about levers in particular. A machine is something that helps a person do work. Types of simple machines are the lever, inclined plane, screw, pulley, wedge, and wheel. Ask the children to name several examples of each type of machine.

A lever is a rigid bar that turns around a fixed point or a fulcrum. A lever is composed of a fulcrum, a force arm, and a resistance arm. Examples of levers are the wheelbarrow, scissors, and nutcracker. Ask the children to name other examples of levers.

In this lesson ask the children to consider how the body works as a machine when pulling objects. Have them play the game tug-of-war. Hold individual and team contests. During individual contests, tell each contestant to grasp one end of the rope. The middle of the rope is over a center line. Each game is won when either person pulls the other player over the center line. For maximum pulling force, each child must get his body close to the ground by lowering his center of gravity. He can do this by bending his legs at the knee and placing the feet in stride position in the direction the team wishes to pull (Fig. 8-6). When working together as a group, instruct the children to pull together by establishing a cadence, or rhythm, in which they pull, step back, and recoil or get ready for the next pull. By pulling together at the same time, a team can overcome inertia (Chapter 9) and pull the other team off balance.

As the children play tug-of-war, they are a machine. In actuality they are a lever with the force coming from their bodies. The resistance is from the other team. The fulcrum is their feet. The children may not understand what class lever they are, but they can learn what a lever is and what its parts are.

CONCEPT: There are three classes of levers.

Level: Intermediate.

Subconcept: A first-class lever has the fulcrum located between the resistance arm and the force arm.

Materials: Seesaws out on the playground.

Activities: The purpose of this lesson is to

Fig. 8-6. Use good leverage in a tug-of-war contest.

teach the children about the first-class lever. In a first-class lever the fulcrum is between the force and resistance arms. An example is a water pump or a scissors. In the pump the water is the resistance. The force comes from the person pushing the handle of the pump. The fulcrum is the pivot point on the pump. Ask the children to name other examples of a first-class lever.

The seesaw, a piece of playground apparatus, provides a good example of a first-class lever. The resistance is the down end of the seesaw; the force arm is the up end. The fulcrum is the point at which the board balances on the pivot. The children have played on the seesaw many times before. During this lesson have them experiment with the varying weights and lengths of the force and resistance arms by manipulating the placements of the board on the fulcrum. The students will find that 1 child can lift the weight of 2 children if he is allowed to have a long force arm. If the weight of 3 children are equal, 1 child can lift 2, provided the length of the 1 child's force arm is twice that of the 2 children's resistance arm. The students can also experiment with 3 children being lifted by 1 child. This is a practical example of a first-class

lever. This is another way in which a body serves as a machine.

■ ■ ■

Level: Intermediate.

Subconcept: A second-class lever has the resistance located between the fulcrum and the point of application of force.

Materials: None.

Activities: The purpose of this lesson is to teach the children about the second-class lever. In a second-class lever the resistance is between the force arm and the fulcrum. An example is a wheelbarrow. Ask the children to name a few more second-class levers.

During this lesson have the children pick a partner of equal size and strength. Instruct them how to perform the wheelbarrow stunt. The child who is the wheelbarrow has both hands on the floor. By moving his arms forward, placing one hand in front of another, he will move forward like a wheel. The child who is the wheelbarrow should keep his arms, back, and legs as straight as possible. The one who is the carrier of the wheelbarrow should pick up the legs of the wheelbarrow at the knees. If the child cannot carry the wheelbarrow at the knees because of a weight problem, he can lift the wheelbarrow at the thighs. Instruct the carrier of the wheelbarrow to let the wheelbarrow set the pace. Place emphasis on form and not on racing. Often the carrier wants to go too fast, causing the wheelbarrow to fall head first to the floor.

The hands of the child being the wheelbarrow are the fulcrum. The weight of the child being the wheelbarrow is the resistance. The carrier of the wheelbarrow provides the force. This is an example of a second-class lever. Have the children move forward, backward, sideways, go up and down inclined planes, or move through an obstacle course that has been set up as they play during this lesson.

■ ■ ■

Level: Intermediate.

Subconcept: A third-class lever has the force application between the fulcrum and resistance.

Materials: A record player and any record that contains a 4/4 tempo.

Activities: The purpose of this lesson is to teach the children about the third-class lever. In a third-class lever the force is between the fulcrum and the resistance arm. An example is a person bouncing a ball or throwing a ball. Ask the children to name some other examples of third-class levers: shoveling snow or dirt, lifting a weight, or writing with a piece of chalk on a blackboard.

During this lesson have the children experiment bouncing a playground ball to the rhythm of the music. You may ask then to try to make up a routine to the music, such as bounce the ball with one hand, two hands, alternating hands, and trying to bounce the ball through their legs. While the children are bouncing the ball, the ball is the resistance, the muscles of the forearm are the force, and the elbow, wrist, or shoulder is the fulcrum.

CONCEPT: Levers help a person do work.

Level: Intermediate.

Subconcepts: (1) Machines can be used to change the direction of a force. (2) The longer the force arm, the greater the force produced.

Materials: A crowbar, fulcrum, and heavy

Fig. 8-7. Pulleys help do work.

box; a set of pulley-rope hoists for rings or climbing ropes.

Activities: The purpose of this lesson is to demonstrate to the children that machines sometimes do work by changing the direction of a force. First, show the children that by pulling down on the hoist rope in a pulley system, the rings or climbing ropes in a gym are pulled up to the ceiling. In doing work, the direction of the force is changed. (See Fig. 8-7.)

Next, show the children how the direction of a force is changed through the use of a crowbar. Use a box that is too heavy to be lifted by one person. By placing the crowbar under the box, using a fulcrum, and pushing down on the crowbar, the box can be lifted. In doing work, the direction of the force is changed. The longer the force arm of the crowbar, the greater the force produced and the easier the work. To emphasize this last point, you may have the children lift the box with the crowbar by applying the lifting force at various points along the crowbar. The farther away from the fulcrum

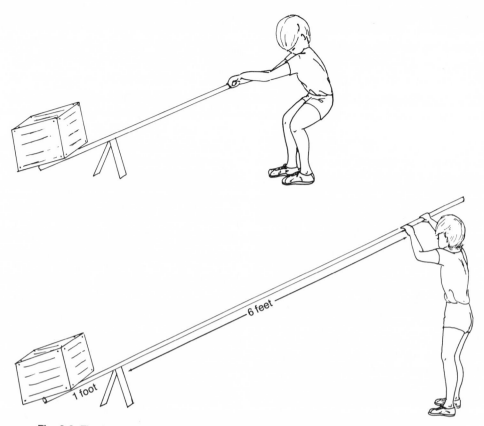

Fig. 8-8. The farther away from the fulcrum the force is applied, the easier to lift the box.

that the force is applied, the easier it is to lift the box. (See Fig. 8-8.)

In these two examples, one machine is a pulley and one is a lever. Both machines change the direction of a force to produce work. Ask the children to name other examples in which a machine changes the direction of a force. Examples in physical education are batting a pitched ball or kicking a ball that is moving. The bat or a person's leg provides the force to change the direction of the moving ball. In a lever the resistance is working in one direction and the force is working to overcome the resistance in the opposite direction.

Following this introduction, you may proceed to teach the children an appropriate lesson about striking or kicking or one in gymnastics that uses the climbing ropes and rings.

CONCEPT: The human body is designed to predominantly use a third-class lever when it moves.

Levels: Intermediate and advanced.

Subconcept: A third-class lever gains speed and range of motion at the expense of using a great force.

Materials: Four each of the following: softballs, playground balls, basketballs, volleyballs, soccer balls, yarn balls, and footballs.

Activities: During this lesson have the children throw different kinds of balls in a movement exploration setting. As a person throws a ball, the body utilizes a third-class lever system. The ball is the resistance. The muscles of the arm are the force, and the fulcrum is the shoulder joint. The force arm is between the fulcrum and the resistance arm, making the action a third-class lever.

Explain to the children that all throwing, striking, and kicking sports involve the use of third-class levers. Tennis, golf, badminton, hockey, softball, football, and soccer involve the use of third-class levers. Challenge the students to figure out some examples of third-class levers used in everyday life: peddling a bicycle, pushing a grocery cart, cutting food with a knife, and digging with a shovel. Even such locomotor movements as walking, running, jumping, and hopping involve the use of third-class levers.

After the children understand this concept, you may have the class begin doing different kinds of throwing activities. Ask them to change the level of their throws by changing from kneeling, sitting and standing positions. The level may also be changed by throwing high in the air or close to the ground. Explore aspects of force and time by having the children throw for speed, accuracy, or distance, as well as underhand, overhand, and from other body positions. Tell them to use one or both hands for throwing. In a more structured situation have them practice chest passes, bounce passes, or other specific means of throwing balls. In all cases the application of force to a ball involves the use of a third-class lever.

The lesson could be adapted for use in a unit on kicking, throwing, or striking activities. After the children explore various types of kicking, throwing, or striking movements, you may select appropriate lead-up games to team sports that they may play. For example, if a unit on throwing and striking activities is being taught, appropriate lead-up games to softball that could be taught are workup, one old cat, team pepper, and five hundred. Team softball could be played at the end of the unit with children in the upper elementary grades.

■ ■ ■

Levels: Intermediate and advanced.

Subconcepts: (1) A third-class lever gains speed and range of motion at the expense of using a great force. (2) Mechanical advantage is the number of times a force is multiplied by a machine. (3) The longer the resistance arm at the time of release, the faster the action. (4) Throwing with a straight arm or using a striking implement as an extension of the arm enables a person to throw or propel an object faster and farther than when the arm is bent or no implement is used.

Materials: Tennis balls, whiffle balls, softballs, yarn balls, and/or paper balls (large wadded paper balls); tennis rackets, badminton rackets, table tennis paddles, nylon hose rackets, and/or softball bats.

Activities: To begin the lesson, have the children play catch with a partner. In an effort to help the students discover mechanically efficient patterns of throwing, have them start by facing their partner and throwing with their forearm so that the elbow is held in a stationary position at the side. The wrist and forearm provide the force for the throw. Next, have the children throw with their whole arm by getting a good arm extension at the time of release. Sequentially, have the children add trunk and leg movements to the throwing action, allowing them to discover good throwing concepts. A good throw involves the use of a good base of support, leg opposite the throwing arm extended, trunk and shoulder rotation, and extension of the throwing arm. In a given time period an extended throwing arm moves a greater distance at a faster rate of speed than an arm held close to the body. As a result, the children will discover that they use a third-class lever and can throw better and farther with an extended arm than when the arm is held close to the body. To gain this speed, range of motion, and efficient throwing action, however, great force must be used. (See Fig. 8-9.)

Next, have the children use a ball and racket to discover efficient striking patterns. While going through the same progression in the throwing sequence, they will find the striking action to be the same as the throwing action. They will discover that they can strike a ball better when the racket is held away from the body than when it is held close. Again, a third-class lever is used. However, with the use of a striking implement, more leverage or mechanical advantage is gained. The striking implement moves through a greater distance at a faster rate of speed than does a throwing arm.

Fig. 8-9. To throw well, use good leverage.

To gain speed, range of motion, and efficient striking action, even more force must be used than in the throwing action.

After practicing their throwing and striking skills, you may have the children progress into playing appropriate games in which they can use the above concepts.

CONCEPT: Levers help a person gain mechanical advantage.

Level: Intermediate.

Subconcept: Mechanical advantage is the number of times a force is multiplied by a machine.

Materials: Softball balls and bats, tennis balls and rackets, or golf balls and clubs.

Activities: Present this lesson during a unit on striking activities. The children already know that when a person uses a bat, racket, or club, it works as a lever. The purpose of this lesson is to show the students that mechanical advantage is involved when using a striking implement. The bat, racket, or club is an extension of the striking implement and allows up to 3 to 4 feet of additional leverage. Because the extension of the bat, racket, or club allows the arm to be three or four times as long, the child has the potential to propel the ball three to four times as far as with the arm alone. This means that the mechanical advantage of the striking implement is 3 or 4.

As the child swings the striking implement, it moves through an arc. In a fraction of a second the striking movement is made. The end of the bat, racket, or club moves much faster and travels a larger distance than do the hands (Fig. 8-10). To gain this speed, distance, and mechanical advantage, a large amount of energy must be used by the children to swing the striking implements. However, if the bats, rackets,

Fig. 8-10. Rackets, bats, or clubs help gain a mechanical advantage when striking objects.

or clubs are too long or heavy for them to manipulate efficiently, any mechanical advantage that may be gained is lost because the child cannot exert the force necessary to strike the balls. Thus it is important for educators to select equipment properly for children so that they can use it well in an effort to gain any mechanical advantage for which it was intended.

Have the children play striking games according to the skill level of the children and the particular sport chosen.

■   ■   ■

Level: Advanced.

Subconcept: Mechanical advantage is the ratio of the load to the applied force that allows a machine to multiply force and do work.

Materials: A seesaw and other playground equipment.

Activities: The purpose of this lesson is to have the children learn ratios and how to do mathematical problems related to mechanical advantage. To accomplish this, have the students do problems on balancing the weight on each side of a seesaw. (See Fig. 8-11.)

The seesaw is 20 feet long. The fulcrum is

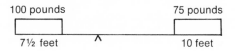

100 pounds   75 pounds

7½ feet   ∧   10 feet

Fig. 8-11. Balancing on a seesaw.

the middle of the seesaw. Ten feet are on each side of the fulcrum. Two boys are going to balance on the seesaw. One boy weight 100 pounds and the other, 75 pounds. If the 75-pound boy sits at the end of the seesaw, where does the 100-pound boy have to sit to balance the seesaw?

$$F \times FA = R \times RA$$
$$75 \text{ lb.} \times 10 \text{ ft} = 100 \text{ lb.} \times RA$$
$$750 \text{ ft.-lb.} = 100 \text{ lb.} \times RA$$
$$\frac{750 \text{ ft.-lb.}}{100 \text{ lb.}} = RA$$
$$7.5 \text{ ft.} = RA$$

The 100-pound boy has to sit 7.5 feet from the fulcrum to balance the seesaw. Do the first problem on a blackboard in the classroom or gym. After this have the children take their pencils and papers out to the playground and experiment with different weights and lengths on a seesaw.

Fig. 8-12. Landing properly requires good stability and leverage.

CONCEPT: Levers are used when producing and receiving force.

Level: Intermediate.

Subconcept: When receiving force from an extermal object as in catching, landing from a jump, or recovering from a fall, the center of mass moves in the direction of the force and gradually diminishes the forces.

Materials: Vaulting boxes, chairs, or any other type of equipment from which children may jump.

Activities: As children jump from a height, they need to learn how to land properly. Those who absorb the force of impact when landing with the body and legs straight are subject to injury. By increasing the distance, surface area, and time over which the force is absorbed and using as many joints as possible to absorb the force, children will learn proper methods of landing. The more gradual the absorption of force from landing, the less likely the danger of injury from the force. (See Fig. 8-12.)

Have the children begin by jumping off the floor (vertical momentum) and landing softly. They should experiment with several techniques and notice what their body does to absorb the force of the jump. They may land in a stride position in the direction in which they are moving (increase of distance or base of support over which the force is absorbed). They may land and bend at the ankles, knees, and hips (use of as many joints as possible) to absorbe the force. They may land and perform a forward roll or shoulder roll (increase of time and surface area) to absorb the force.

Then have the children move to jumping off the boxes and again explore several techniques to absorb the force of landing. Soon they will learn how to land quietly and smoothly, "giving" to the floor to absorb the force of landing.

As the children learn how to land properly, have them explore various qualities of space, force, time, and flow as they jump: how high they can jump, how many shapes they can make, how much force they can create, how many levels they can use, what type of body relationships (touch elbow to knee) are possible, etc.

As the students analyze their movements, have them practice again to take advantage of what they have learned. Further exploration of absorption of force may involve the absorption of (1) horizontal momentum (quick stops after running), (2) a combination of vertical and horizontal momentum (landing from a running long jump), and (3) the force of balls thrown by self and others.

Chapter 9

NEWTON'S LAWS OF MOTION

Motion is one of the most interesting phenomenon in the world. It takes place all the time and everywhere, particularly in physical education when movement of bodies and objects in space is a constant factor. Yet as common as it is, people generally know little about motion.

Teachers of children should help them become more aware of motion, what causes it, and what factors influence it. When an object is changing its position, it is said to be in motion. A force is required to start an object's motion, to slow it down or stop it, to change the direction of its motion, or to make it move faster. All these types of motion are influenced by three laws that were discovered by Sir Issac Newton. Examples of Newton's laws of motion are in evidence in daily living. Anything movable always follows these laws, which describe how things move and make it possible to predict the motion of any object.

NEWTON'S FIRST LAW

A ball that is placed on the floor remains in a stationary position unless someone or something causes it to move. Once movement of the ball is initiated, it remains in motion at the same speed and keeps moving in the same direction unless it is acted on by an outside force, such as friction, gravity, or a muscular action. This example illustrates Newton's First Law of Motion: an object at rest tends to remain at rest (Fig. 9-1), and an object in motion tends to remain in motion at the same speed and in the same direction. Another example illustrating Newton's first law occurs when a car, airplane, train, or bus starts or stops quickly. When the vehicle starts suddenly, the passengers are pressed back against their seats. When the vehicle that is traveling fast stops suddenly, the passengers are thrown forward. This is the result of inertia. *Inertia* is the tendency of a body to remain at rest or to remain in motion until it is acted upon by an outside force. In this case the outside force occurred when the vehicle started or stopped suddenly. In most instances seat belts are used to keep persons in their seats against the tendency of inertia to keep them moving forward when the vehicle stops.

Momentum is another factor related to Newton's first law. *Momentum* is the quantity of stored-up energy of a moving body. Momentum is less for a large mass with little speed than for a large mass with great speed. Momentum tends to cause an object or mass to remain in motion. For example, a person who is roller skating discovers that the tendency to continue rolling is much greater if he is moving at a fast speed than if he is moving at a low speed. (See Fig. 9-2.)

If a person is moving fast and is told to stop, is it harder for him to halt his movement than if he is moving slowly. Why? Why does a person who jumps run or swing his arms to build up as much force as he can before he jumps? Why does a ski jumper go down a long, steep hill before leaving the jumping platform? Inertia and momentum and the answers.

NEWTON'S SECOND LAW

The speed of an object is proportional to the force applied and inversely proportional to the object's mass. This is a statement of Newton's Second Law of Motion and is somewhat difficult to understand. It means simply that for a given object, application of large force will result in a great speed. If the same amount of force is applied to two objects of different mass, the one with the smaller mass will move faster. The resulting rate of acceleration or deceleration of objects is continually a factor in physical education when people and objects of varying masses and shapes manipulate or are manip-

Fig. 9-1. Inertia causes the ball to drop down into the jar when the cardboard is "shot out" from underneath the ball.

Fig. 9-2. Momentum causes the person on the skates to remain in motion after he stopped exerting force.

ulated by other people or objects of varying mass and shape. For example, a child pushing another in a wagon soon realizes that he must push harder to make the wagon travel faster. He is also aware that when 2 or 3 children are in the wagon, he has to push much harder to at-

tain a fast speed than when only 1 child occupies the wagon.

NEWTON'S THIRD LAW

After inflating a balloon, did you ever release it without having tied the end? As the air rushes out of the opening in our direction, the balloon flies away in the opposite direction. This is a simple example of the concept of action and re-action, referred to as Newton's Third Law of Motion. For every action there is an equal and opposite reaction. The statement may seem puzzling at first until some common activities are observed. For example, when a person swims in the water, the arms and hands push the water in a backward direction. The resulting reaction is that the body moves forward in the water. If a person jumps, he pushes down against the ground and his body travels up and away. When an airplane flies, the propellers force the air in a backward direction as the plane moves forward.

The principle of action-reaction means that whenever one body exerts a force, a second body exerts an equal force in an opposite di-rection to the first force. If there were not an equal and opposite reaction, people would be unable to swim, jump, fly, etc. (See Fig. 9-3).

Even bodies at rest have equal but opposite forces acting upon them. A book lying on a table remains in a stationary position because the table provides an upward force equal to the downward force of gravity. Children can see this more readily if a heavy object is placed in their hands. They can feel that the object exerts a force downward in their hands and that they must use their muscles to provide an opposite force to counteract it.

Learning activities

CONCEPT: Newton's First Law of Motion states that a force is required to start an object in motion, stop it, or change its direction.

Level: Intermediate.

Subconcepts: (1) An object at rest will re-main at rest unless acted upon by an outside force. (2) A push or a pull must be exerted for an object to be set in motion. (3) A push or a pull must be exerted to change the direction of a moving object.

Materials: A ball and bowling pin or plastic bottle for each child.

Activities: A ball placed on the floor re-mains motionless unless acted upon by an out-side force. The ball, when picked up, thrown, or kicked, moves in the direction of the applied force. Have the students experiment manipulat-ing their ball in various directions with different

Fig. 9-3. The principle of action-reaction enables people or objects to move through space.

body parts. What body parts can they use to make the ball travel? What types of forces can be supplied by the children? How can the ball be made to move to the left, right, forward, or backward? From their experience help them discover that a push or a pull from their muscles is needed to get the ball moving. Once the ball is in motion, it moves in the direction of the push or pull.

Next, have the students set their ball in motion by rolling or kicking it along the floor. Instruct them to follow the path of the moving ball and apply a second force to change its direction. Unless a new force is applied, the ball continues in the same direction. How many different ways can the children effectively change the direction of a moving ball? Encourage them to think of examples in sports and everyday life in which this concept is applied. A baseball batter uses a bat to change the direction of a pitched ball. Soccer players kick the ball back and forth to each other when moving it downfield to score a goal. Machines of all types are used to change the direction of moving objects, as when products are assembled on a conveyer belt.

Finally, have the children move their ball toward their bowling pin or plastic bottle perhaps trying various kinds of throws, rolls, and kicks as they try to knock over the object. Allow them to predict the direction in which the object will move when hit by an outside force. What happens when the object is hit from the left or right side? The students will discover that the object remains at rest until it is hit by the ball. On being hit, the object moves in the direction of the applied force. Bowling is a sport in which this concept is applied. Encourage the children to think of other examples.

CONCEPT: Newton's First Law of Motion is about inertia and momentum.

Level: Intermediate.

Subconcepts: (1) Momentum is the tendency of an object to stay in motion. (2) Momentum is dependent on the mass of an object and the speed with which the object is moving.

Materials: Benches, vaulting boxes, and mats.

Activities: To begin this lesson, ask the children to move about the room while changing their level, direction, pathway, force, and flow and, on hearing a drumbeat, clap, or the command "Freeze," to hold their pose. With your guidance, have them experiment with the quality of time—sometimes moving fast, sometimes slow. When moving fast, the children will discover that it is more difficult to come to a halt and hold a pose on signal than it is when moving slow. You may use some of the larger children in class as examples to show that it is difficult to stop the momentum of a large mass moving at a fast rate. You could combine this aspect of the lesson with one of the stability lessons, which emphasize that when coming to a stop, it is best to have a low center of gravity with a wide base of support in the direction of movement.

After the children have practiced stopping their body momentum on the floor, have them use the benches and vaulting boxes. Tell them to move onto the apparatus and come to a freeze position. Then have them move off or vault the apparatus and come to a freeze position on landing. In each instance have the children vary their speed when moving on and off the objects. Again, the students will discover that it is more difficult to stop their body motion when moving fast than when moving slow.

■   ■   ■

Level: Intermediate.

Subconcept: There are many forces that stop the inertia of moving objects.

Materials: Soccer balls, pinnies, and goals.

Activities: During this lesson have the children play modified soccer. In this game all the fundamental skills of soccer are used, plus corner kicks, goal kicks, and penalty kicks. There are 8 to 11 children on each team. The playing area is 30 by 60 yards. The object is to advance the ball across the other team's goal line. The game is like regular soccer without position play. Players may advance the ball by kicking it. They may not touch the ball with their hands. Each team has a goalkeeper who may touch the ball with his hands. The rest of the players are either guard or forward as the ball is moved down the field. One point is scored when the ball passes over the opponent's goal line. (See Fig. 9-4.)

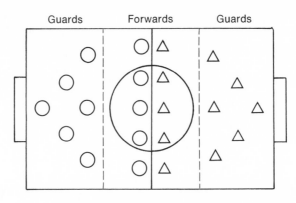

Fig. 9-4. Formation for modified soccer.

The balls and the children themselves operate under Newton's first law. There are several reasons why the inertia of an object is stopped. The forces that stop the inertia of a moving object are friction, air resistance, gravity, and a person's muscles. A stationary object such as a wall will change the direction of a moving object but will not stop the inertia of the object. A person's muscles—through kicking, heading, blocking, or trapping actions—may initiate the movement of a stationary ball, change the direction of a moving ball, or stop the inertia of a moving ball. Encourage the children to think of examples in which different forces stop the inertia of a moving object. Apply examples from the game of modified soccer first. The friction between the ground and the ball will stop the inertia of the ball. Also, the wind may stop the inertia of the ball. Gravity will carry a ball that is in the air to the ground and stop its inertia. Then encourage the children to think of examples from other sports.

CONCEPT: Newton's Second Law of Motion is about acceleration and deceleration.

Level: Intermediate.

Subconcepts: (1) Momentum is directly proportional to the mass of the object and to the speed at which the object is moving. (2) If objects have equal mass, a greater speed will yield greater momentum. (3) If bodies are moving at equal speed, a greater mass will yield greater momentum.

Materials: A scooter, pair of roller skates, or skateboard for each group of 3 children; a

straight line should also be marked off across the play area.

Activities: Have the children work together in groups of 3, those in each group having different size and mass. Ask them to experiment pushing each other on the scooter, roller skates, or skateboard up to a designated line near the middle of the play area. For the sake of safety, have all children travel in the same direction. Once the line of the floor is reached, tell the pusher to stop pushing and to observe and record the distance that the child on the scooter, skates, or skateboard travels beyond the line. This distance traveled beyond the line is the result of momentum that was built up by the pusher before the line was reached. Which child travels farther beyond the line? Does the mass of the child influence the distance traveled? Does the speed of pushing have any influence on the distance traveled? The children will discover that a child on the scooter who has a great mass and is being pushed at a slow speed does not travel as far beyond the line as a child who has a small mass and is being pushed at a high rate of speed. When 2 children of equal mass are pushed at unequal speeds, the students will discover that the child traveling with greater speed has more momentum and travels farther beyond the line. When 2 children of unequal mass are traveling at equal speeds, the child with more mass has more momentum and travels farther beyond the line. As the children discover these concepts, encourage them to think of examples in sports and everyday life in which they have practical application. (See Fig. 9-5.) Momentum is a factor that must be

Fig. 9-5. The child with more mass has more momentum and travels farther.

considered when high jumping, long jumping, and pole vaulting in track and field. It is also a factor in the traveling speeds and stopping times of cars, trucks, and motorcycles. Discuss with the students the importance of this concept in accident prevention. Can you and the children think of other examples in which momentum is an important concept to be considered?

■   ■   ■

Level: Intermediate.

Subconcepts: (1) The greater amount of force applied to an object, the greater the speed that the object will travel. (2) If the same amount of force is applied to bodies of two different masses, the less massive object will move faster. However, once inertia is overcome, the heavier mass will exert a greater force on something it contacts.

Materials: Bowling balls, playground balls, Indian clubs or plastic bowling pins, and gym mats.

Activities: Allow the children to work together in small groups for this activity. Set up a group of three clubs or pins in a small triangle on one side of the room for each group of children to aim at. Block the wall with mats for

protection. Have the students stand from 10 to 20 feet away from their pins. To begin the activity, have the children shove the bowling ball and playground ball toward the pins with the side of their foot and then perform the same activity by rolling each ball with their arms. Tell them to take turns setting up the pins or clubs that are knocked down. Encourage the students to experiment with kicking or rolling the balls at different speeds. Have them observe how different speeds of the ball affect the resulting flight of the pins that are knocked down. Which type of ball is harder to accelerate? (The bowling ball.) Why? (It has the greater mass.) Which ball accelerates more rapidly when similar forces are applied to each? (The playground ball contains less mass.) How can the bowling ball be given the same acceleration as the playground ball? (By the application of more force.) If the balls are traveling at the same speed, which one has more momentum to aid in knocking over the pins? (The bowling ball.) Why? (Because it has more mass.)

■   ■   ■

Level: Advanced.

Subconcepts: (1) The heavier the object and the faster it is moving, the more force required to overcome its moving inertia or to absorb its momentum. (2) The heavier the object, the more force needed to accelerate or decelerate it. (3) Of two unequal forces on objects of equal mass, the greater force will cause greater acceleration. (4) Of two unequal masses under the influence of equal forces, the larger mass will have the smaller acceleration.

Materials: Cage balls, beach balls, and regulation size volleyballs.

Activities: Have the children work together in small groups. Allow them to experiment with passing, kicking, and catching the regulation size volleyball within the group. Encourage the students to manipulate the ball in as many different ways as they can—passing fast, kicking soft, kicking hard, throwing high, rolling the ball slowly, etc. Next, switch to the beach ball and repeat the process. Finally, allow each group to try to manipulate the cage ball.

Now discuss with the children the differences they noticed in handling the three balls of different size and mass. Did they notice that when the heavier cage ball came to them at high speed, to catch or stop it took more effort than with a beach ball traveling at the same speed. It also took more force to throw the heavier cage ball. Sometimes you may have a child strike the regulation size volleyball softly and sometimes very hard. The child will draw the conclusion that of the two different force applications (heavy and light) on the same ball, the great force application will cause the ball to travel faster. If a child strikes the beach ball with the same force that he strikes the cage ball, he will note that the cage ball travels through a lesser distance and more slowly than the beach ball. Air resistance must be a factor to consider with the beach ball, however.

Once these concepts are understood, allow the children to continue kicking, passing, catching, and striking the balls within their groups to observe and explore Newton's second law.

■   ■   ■

Level: Advanced.

Subconcepts: (1) The heavier the object, the more force needed to accelerate or decelerate it. (2) If the same amount of force is exerted upon two bodies of different mass, greater acceleration will be produced on the lighter or less massive object. (3) The heavier object will, however, have greater momentum once inertia is overcome and will exert a greater force than the lighter object on something that it contacts.

Materials: Balls of different size and mass, such as basketballs, tennis balls, shot put, medicine balls, softballs, and cage balls.

Activities: During this lesson have the children explore throwing and catching movements in relation to objects that differ in terms of mass and weight. Take the children out to the playground and divide them into groups of 3. Have 1 child in each group throw the ball, 1 mark the spot where the ball lands, and 1 retrieve and mark the spot where the ball stops its roll. Make sure the children rotate and take turns. First, have them *toss* the ball easily onto the field. Next, have the children *throw* the ball at the same angle as hard as he can. Again, mark the spot where the ball lands and stops. Why did the second throw go farther in the air and on the roll? (More force was applied, it was traveling faster, it had more velocity, it had more momentum.) What caused the ball to come to a stop? (Gravity, friction, and air resistance.) Was the decelerating force the same in both the toss and throw? (Yes, momentum was the only reason the thrown ball rolled farther and longer.)

Now have the children throw balls that differ in weight or mass. They will discover that it takes more force to throw a heavy object a given distance than it does to throw a light object the same distance. For example, a child could throw a softball 10 feet with much less force than he would have to use to throw a medicine ball or shot put 10 feet.

Next, have the children emphasize the catching of objects that differ in weight or mass. The children will discover that it takes more energy to catch or absorb the force of a heavy object than it does to catch a light object. For example, it is harder to absorb the force from catching a cage ball than it is to absorb the force from catching a tennis ball. By absorbing the force of a heavy object over a large surface area and/or over a longer time period, it is possible to catch a heavy object, but the fact still remains that it takes more energy to catch a heavy ball.

Finally, have the children try to use the same amount of force to throw balls of different masses. They will discover that the lighter balls travel a greater distance.

CONCEPT: Newton's Third Law of Motion is about action and reaction.

Levels: Intermediate and advanced.

Subconcept: For every action there is an equal and opposite reaction.

Materials: Scooters, roller skates, bowling pins, and bleach bottles.

Activities: The children have seen airplanes and jets flying in the sky. At the beginning of this lesson, point out the use of Newton's third law in an airplane's flight. As the propellers push the air back, the air pushes the plane ahead. Encourage the children to identify other examples in which action-reaction is used: jumping, swimming, and similar sport activities.

Have the children put this principle into action when they play on their scooters. The type of scooter available on the market with the four wheels and plywood base built close to the floor is best suited for this activity. If the school does not have these you may substitute roller skates. Encourage the students to explore several ways to move about while assuming various body positions on the scooter. No matter which body part is used to create the propulsive force, the law of action-reaction applies. Set up an obstacle course with the bowling pins or plastic bottles to challenge the children into making direction changes. As the child pushes in one direction, the floor pushes the body in a reverse direction. Thus the child receives a ride by using the concept of action-reaction.

■   ■   ■

Levels: Intermediate and advanced.

Subconcept: For every action there is an equal and opposite reaction.

Materials: A swimming pool.

Activities: The medium of aquatics provides an excellent opportunity to teach children about motion. When a boat is rowed or a canoe is paddled, Newton's third law is being used. The oar or paddle pushes back against the water. The water, in turn, exerts a force against the paddle and boat, pushing the boat forward. For every action there is an equal and opposite reaction.

When a person learns how to swim, he uses his body as a boat. The arms are used as the paddles. To begin this lesson, have the children experiment with using their arms and legs to paddle the water in various directions. When in a vertical position, either treading water or supported in an innertube, have the children push the water to the left or right. A push to the left will result in a turn to the right. A push to the right will result in a turn to the left. A downward push on the water will result in elevation of the body in the water. An upward push on the water will result in submersion of the body in the water. Instruct the children that in a horizontal position in the water, each stroke should be performed so as to push the water backward. The water, in turn, pushes the child forward. For every action there is an equal and opposite reaction.

Have the children swim freestyle, backstroke, or breaststroke. To provide for competition, they can have swimming races.

Chapter 10

FACTORS AFFECTING THE HUMAN BODY AND ITS MOVEMENT

MASS

Mass is any quantity of a solid, liquid, or gaseous substance that has weight or takes up space. Sometimes mass is thought to be the same as weight. In actuality, however, weight is the gravitational pull on the mass of an object. Objects, whether on earth or in outer space have the same mass, but they are weightless in space because there is no pull exerted by gravity. Baseballs and tennis balls are about the same size, but one is heavier and has more mass than the other. A beach ball may be much larger yet have less mass than a soccer ball. The mass of two objects may be the same, but their shape may differ. A football has about the same mass as a basketball. As a result, one can learn that mass is determined by the measure of quantity of matter in an object and not by the object's size or shape. Because of this fact, it must be considered that the mass of an object also affects its motion. It is more difficult to move an object with greater mass than it is to move a smaller one.

FORCE AND WORK

A force is a push or a pull exerted against an object in an effort to start, stop, accelerate, decelerate, maintain, or change its motion. One or more forces that are always in operation affect the motion or stability of an object. The forces that cause the human body to move are produced internally by muscles and externally by another person, a machine, an animal, the wind, etc. and by gravity.

Work is a force acting upon mass through a distance. In simpler terms, work means the ability to push or pull an object over a distance. Work may also mean the ability to complete a task. Many times children think of work as a chore to perform around the house. In teaching, work may be a chore or any task that requires movement. Even games, play, dance, or tumbling activities of children can be considered work.

As children learn about the concept of work, several points must be considered. How can work be measured? At a beginning level, children should learn that work equals force times distance moved, or $W = F \times D$. Later the concept of work per unit of time can be introduced: $\frac{W = F \times D}{T}$ (work equals force times distance moved divided by the time needed to complete the task). Other points to be considered are the amount of force required to perform the work, the place where the force should be applied, and the effects of friction and resistance on work.

ENERGY

Energy is required to produce force and move objects from one place to another. The human body applies force in the form of muscular energy. This muscular energy may be applied directly to an object through a continual force such as pushing, pulling, carrying, or lifting; over a period of time while motion is developed and followed by a release, as in throwing; and by instantaneous contact such as in striking. This energy of motion is called *kinetic energy*. The body may also apply forces to objects indirectly through the use of *potential energy*. The drawn bow, stretched slingshot, and taut spring are examples of potential energy that becomes kinetic energy on release (Fig. 10-1).

To move an object, the forces acting upon it must be unbalanced. A heavy object requires a lot of force or energy to move it. A light ob-

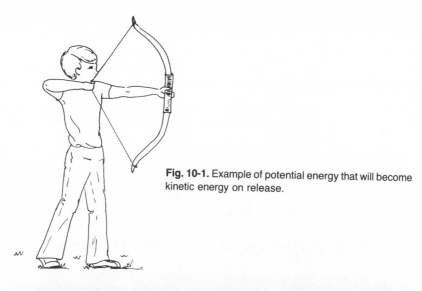

Fig. 10-1. Example of potential energy that will become kinetic energy on release.

Fig. 10-2. Force should be applied in the direction of the intended movement.

ject requires less energy to move it. If an object is to be moved over a great distance, more energy is needed to do the work. More energy is necessary to propel an object at a fast rate of speed than to propel it slowly.

APPLICATION OF FORCE

When performing work, a person needs to consider where he should apply the force in an effort to move the object efficiently. Forces should be applied in the direction of the intended movement (Fig. 10-2). When moving an object in a vertical direction, a person should stand as close to the object as possible so that force can be applied either up or down. When moving an object in a horizontal direction, several factors should be considered. Most of the force should be applied by the legs because they contain the strongest muscles. As explained in the chapter on stability, one should have a wide base of support, with the legs spread in the direction of the intended motion. An object can be controlled most effectively if one's hands are spread apart and placed in line with the center of gravity. If the hands are placed close together and/or not in line with the center of gravity, rotary motion of the object may result. If the hands are placed too high or too low when applying the force, loss of control may occur and the object may tip over because of the tendency toward rotary motion. A person should also contact the object to be moved and prepare the muscles for the task before exerting the pushing force.

FRICTION AND RESISTANCE

Resistance is an opposing force that makes it difficult to move an object. Friction is a type of resistance between the surfaces of two objects. The amount of friction between two objects depends on the types of surfaces and the weights of objects. Rough surfaces cause more friction than smooth ones. Heavy objects cause more friction than light ones.

Friction is necessary to start and stop motion. To gain efficient movement, it is desirable to create enough friction for movement to take place but not too little or too much that inefficiency of execution results. For example, there must be some friction between the surface of an athletic shoe and the surface of the ground or playing floor. To gain efficient movement, various athletic shoes are specially designed, such as football, baseball, and basketball shoes, to give athletes traction on the surfaces on which they move. In some instances it is desirable to reduce the amount of friction between surfaces to enable more efficient movement. Ice skates, roller skates, and skateboards are examples.

There are three circumstances in which friction affects motion: (1) starting friction, (2) sliding friction, and (3) rolling friction. *Starting friction* exists when a person begins to move an object. This type of friction causes greatest resistance to movement and is the hardest to overcome. *Sliding friction* exists when an individual attempts to drag or slide one object over another. *Rolling friction* exists when a person rolls one object over another. Rolling friction

is the easiest to overcome. Children will find that a heavy object placed on wheels or a dolly system is easier to move than if dragged across the floor. Still another aspect of friction to consider is the amount of surface area from the two objects that come into contact. The less surface area in contact with another object, the easier it is to move.

AIR RESISTANCE

Air resistance is a force that is always present and slows the speed of a moving object because of the flow of air around it. The effects of air resistance on an object are dependent on its size, shape, and form. Air resistance also affects the velocity, or rate of speed, of an object. A light object with a large surface area falls more slowly than a small object with great mass. This is why a badminton shuttle, beach ball, balloon, and golf ball, when dropped from a height, do not fall to the earth at the same rate of speed. They also have a different flight pattern when they are hit.

LINEAR MOTION

Linear motion is motion in a straight line, or a direct pathway. This type of motion may be directed horizontally forward, backward, and sideways; vertically up and down; and diagonally. Linear motion can occur under several circumstances in physical education. The body itself can move in a linear pathway by utilizing various locomotor patterns. It can be carried by an object such as a scooter board or roller skates. The body can also propel other objects such as balls in a linear pathway. In the latter two instances the body and/or object travel together at the same rate of speed in the same direction until either or both are acted upon by an outside force.

ROTARY MOTION

Rotary motion is movement of a body around an axis. This type of motion may occur in any or all of three body planes—around the vertical, horizontal, and transverse axes. In rotary motion a short radius causes a fast rate of rotation. A long radius causes a slow rotation rate. Performing a dive in a tuck position causes a faster rotation than if the dive is executed in a pike or layout position. The same is true for forward and backward rolls and handsprings. Ice skaters, roller skaters, and dancers are able to turn or spin faster by pulling the arms in toward the body. When they wish to stop the spinning action, they extend their arms out to the side (Fig. 10-3).

At times rotary motion does not make a complete turn around an axis. This is called *pendular action*. In a pendular type of rotary motion when an object turns about a fixed point, there is a critical time during which tricks may be performed. It occurs when the effects of the inertia are cancelled out by the effect of gravity (Fig. 10-4). The time to execute a stunt on the swinging rings, ropes, or horizontal bar is at the top of the swing—at the time when all motion is cancelled. The most dangerous time is at the bottom of the swing when the greatest

Fig. 10-3. Use your arms to help stop rotary motion.

Fig. 10-4. Execute a stunt at the top of the swing.

Fig. 10-5. Children learn to pump a swing.

stress factors occur—the forces of inertia and gravity are at their maximum.

To accomplish the pumping action while swinging, one must lengthen the radius of rotation while working with gravity. When moving against gravity in an upward direction, one must shorten the radius of rotation (Fig. 10-5). The *radius of rotation* is the distance between the center of gravity and the fulcrum, or axis of rotation. One may achieve a long radius by establishing a low center of gravity on the down phase of the swing. One may achieve a short radius by establishing a high center of gravity on the up phase. For example, when children learn to pump a swing in a standing position, they learn to bend the knees on the down phase and to stand up straight on the up phase.

CENTRIPETAL AND CENTRIFUGAL FORCE

Two additional factors affect the motion of a person or an object when moving in a circular pathway: centripetal and centrifugal force.

Centripetal force is the name given to any force directed inward toward the center of a circular path of motion. Centrifugal force is the inertia tendency of a body in motion to move out or away from the center of the circular path. Centrifugal force causes an object to travel in a straight line if it is in some way released from the axis of rotation. An example may best illustrate and define the factors. When a person throws a ball, the windup establishes a rotary motion while the ball is held. The muscles of the arm and hand serve as the centripetal force by pulling the ball inward and keeping the ball in contact with the hand as it travels in a circular pathway before release. On release, centrifugal force causes the ball to move away from the body in a straight line, tangent to the point of release (Fig. 10-6). Other situations in which centripetal and centrifugal force must be considered are playing on a merry-go-round, throwing a discus, and driving a car around a curve. Can you think of others?

Following are sample lessons concerning

Fig. 10-6. Example of centrifugal force.

how concepts or factors affecting humans and their movement could be taught to elementary school children.

Learning activities

Mass

CONCEPT: Mass is anything that has weight and takes up space.

Level: Intermediate.

Subconcepts: (1) A large object may have less mass than a small object. (2) Two objects may have different shapes but have the same mass. (3) Two objects may be the same size but have different masses. (4) More force is necessary to move objects with great mass than to move those with less mass.

Materials: Large balloons, small playground balls, footballs, soccer balls, baseballs, and tennis balls.

Activities: Allow each child to work with a partner. Give each pair a playground ball, balloon, football, soccer ball, baseball, and tennis ball. First have the children manipulate the balloon and playground ball by striking, throwing, and bouncing each. Noting the large size of the balloon compared to the smaller playground ball, ask which object seems to have the greater mass. Which object requires a greater force to move it? Even though the balloon is larger, the playground ball has more mass and requires more force to move it.

Next, introduce objects with different shapes and the same mass. This time have the children manipulate the football and soccer ball by striking, kicking, and throwing each. Again, ask which ball has more mass. Which takes more force to propel? Even though each ball has a different shape, the masses are equal and require equal forces to propel them.

Finally, introduce objects that are the same size but have different masses. This time have the children manipulate the tennis ball and baseball by striking and throwing each. Ask which object has greater size. Which has move mass? Which object takes more force to propel? Even though both balls are the same size and shape, the baseball has more mass and requires more force to move it.

At the conclusion of the lesson discuss each of the concepts that were presented. Mass is anything that has weight and takes up space. It should be emphasized that mass is not equal to weight but rather depends on gravitational pull on the object. Size is not necessarily an indication of mass. A large object may have less mass than a small one. Two objects may have different shapes but the same mass. Two objects may be the same size but have different masses. The object having the greater mass requires more force to propel it.

Force and work

CONCEPT: Work is the ability to push or pull an object.

Level: Beginning.

Subconcept: One or more forces are always in operation that affect the stability or motion of an object.

Materials: Climbing ropes, tires, parallel bars, side horse, and mats.

Activities: During this lesson divide the children into several small groups to work at the educational gymnastics activities suggested in the following list. As the students climb onto a piece of apparatus (mount), perform a stunt while on the apparatus, or climb off a piece of apparatus (dismount), they are using their muscles to push or pull their bodies on, over, around, and off the equipment. The children are performing work as their muscles provide the pulling and pushing forces.

With balance beams and mats:
1. Move along the beam by using stretched and curled shapes.
2. Move on and off the beam, showing twisted shapes in the air.
3. Make up a sequence to get on, along, and off the beam, showing various balanced shapes while on it.
4. With a partner, move along the beam in opposite directions and try different ways to cross each other's path in attempting to cross to the other end.

With 4 tires, 2 jump ropes, and mats:
1. Make a stretched shape as you pass over the rope. Then roll into a curled shape and end in a balanced stretched shape.
2. Find a way to move over the rope in a curled shape.
3. Make twisted shapes as you move over and under the ropes.
4. Find a way that all of you can keep moving over and under the rope by using different shapes.

With pommel or vaulting horse and mats:
1. Find a way to get on the horse by using a curled or twisted shape.
2. Move over the horse, showing a twisted shape.
3. Lead your body over the horse with your elbows, knees, or head.
4. Find a way to get off the horse by using a curled or twisted shape. When you land on the mat, roll and balance.
5. Find a way for 2 or 3 of you to move on the equipment at the same time.

With uneven or even parallel bars and mats:
1. Get on the bars by using a curled shape.
2. Travel along the bars, making twisted shapes.
3. Travel from the lower bar to the higher bar in any way you can.
4. Make up a sequence with a partner that shows two different shapes.
5. Get off the bars by moving your body in several different ways.

With climbing ropes and mats:
1. Keep the rope still and climb to where you are safe. Make two shapes before you come down.
2. Make a shape, holding on with one hand.
3. Hang upside down on the rope and make a curled or stretched shape.
4. Make a shape while you swing, then drop on to the mat and roll and balance.

CONCEPT: Work is a force acting on mass through a distance.

Level: Intermediate.

Subconcept: It takes more energy to do work fast than it does to do work slowly.

Materials: A record player, one of the several records available containing rope-jumping

Fig. 10-7. Jumping rope is work.

rhythms, and sixteen 8-foot jumping ropes and eight 16-foot jumping ropes.

Activities: During this lesson have the children jump rope to the rhythm of the music (Fig. 10-7). Some of the music has a slow tempo, and the boys and girls should jump with a slow pace. Other music is faster and requires a faster jumping rate. As the students jump fast, it requires a lot of force and energy. The slower jumping rate requires less force and energy. A good way for the children to measure the amount of force and energy that they use while jumping rope is to teach them how to count their pulse rate. They can take their pulse rate by feeling the carotid artery on the side of the neck just under the jaw. Have the children count their pulse rate for 30 seconds and multiply by 2 to get their heart rate for 1 minutes. Have the students take their resting heart rate, as well as their heart rate after jumping to a slow tempo and after fast jumping. The faster a child jumps, the more force and energy required to do the work.

Work is a force acting on mass through a distance. While jumping rope, the child is the mass, the force is provided by the leg muscles, and the distance is the jumping into the air. The faster or the higher a child jumps, the greater the heart rate and amount of work done.

CONCEPT: A force is a push or pull exerted on an object.

Level: Beginning.

Subconcept: It takes more force to propel an object fast that it does to propel an object slowly.

Materials: Scooter boards.

Activities: During this lesson have the children explore different ways to propel their bodies across the floor on a scooter board. The children will discover that they can sit, kneel, stand, and lie down on the scooter board. The main propelling forces come from the arms and legs. When exploring the concept of force, guide the children through some simple activities. The students should give a gentle shove with their arms or legs. What happens? What is the rate of speed and distance traveled? (Slow rate of speed, short distance.) Next, have the children apply a vigorous force to the floor. What happens? What is the rate of speed and distance traveled? (Fast rate of speed, far distance.) As a result, the children have discovered that it requires more force to propel an object fast than it does to propel an object slowly.

For the remainder of the lesson the children may further explore other movement concepts on their scooters. Can they change their pathway on the floor? (Straight, zigzag, circular.) Can they vary their direction of movement? (Forward, backward, sideways.) Can they lead with various body parts as they move about the room? (Head, feet.) The students could also experiment with their scooters in general and personal space.

■   ■   ■

Level: Intermediate.
Subconcepts: (1) The forces that cause the human body to move are internally produced by muscles and externally produced by another person, a machine, an animal, the wind, etc., and gravity. (2) Work equals force acting on mass through a distance over a period of time.
Materials: A stopwatch and fifteen 8-foot jump ropes.
Activities: During this lesson have the children learn how to calculate the amount of work they do. Work equals force acting on mass through a distance over a period of time. When children jump rope, the force is provided by the children's muscles. The mass is the weight of each child. The distance is the height of each jump. The period of time is the length of time each child jumps. A jump of 1 foot in the air for a duration of 30 seconds will be used as an illustration. A person who weighs 100 pounts should demonstrate. The child should jump thirty times in 30 seconds.

$$\text{Work} = \frac{\text{Mass} \times \text{Distance}}{\text{Time}}$$

$$= \frac{30\,\text{Jumps} \times 1\,\text{ft.} \times 100\,\text{lb.}}{2\,\text{min.}}$$

$$= \frac{30\,\text{ft.} \times 100\,\text{lb.}}{\frac{1}{2}\,\text{min.}}$$

$$= \frac{3000\,\text{ft.-lb.}}{\frac{1}{2}\,\text{min.}}$$

$$= 3000\,\text{FP} \times \frac{2}{1}\,\text{min.}$$

$$= 6000\,\text{ft.-lb. per minute}$$

Using a blackboard, have the students compute the amount of work done by children who weigh different amounts, jump different dis-

tances, for different periods of time. A lightweight child can do the same amount of work as a heavy child if the former jumps higher or faster for a given period of time.

After the children learn this subconcept, have each child work with a partner. They can jump rope for different periods of time, take turns counting the number of jumps for their partner, and compute the amount of work they do.

CONCEPT: A human body can exert force to perform work.

Level: Beginning.
Subconcepts: (1) A heavy object will need a great force to move it. (2) A light object will need less force to move it.
Materials: Several heavy balls such as medicine balls or shot put and several light balls such as 6- or 8½-inch playground balls.
Activities: During this lesson have the children explore the amount of force needed to roll or throw heavy and light objects. They may choose various distances to roll a medicine ball or rubber-covered shot put to a partner. They may also try to throw the medicine balls through the air to a partner. Playground balls should be rolled or thrown various distances to a partner in the exploration of the manipulation of light objects. As the balls are rolled or thrown, the children should experiment with a lot of force and a little force to propel them. They should also try to propel the objects fast and slowly. The children should discover that it takes more force to overcome the inertia of a heavy object. They should also learn that it takes more energy, or force, to stop the momentum of a heavy object than it does a light object that is moving at the same speed.

After the exploratory experiences the children may be divided into several small teams for passing relays. Heavy and light balls should be used by alternate teams. Because of the added weight, clumsiness, and extra energy required to pass the medicine ball, the teams that pass the playground ball should win each relay.

CONCEPT: Application of forces affects the way in which an object will travel.

Level: Intermediate.
Subconcept: Application of force should

be in the direction of the intended motion—the feet should be placed in a stride position with the legs in the direction of the intended motion, the hands placed apart for better control of an object, and the center of gravity low.

Materials: Parallel bars, vaulting horse, balance beam, and apparatus transporter.

Activities: The purpose of this lesson is to have the children learn about moving heavy objects. The heavy objects that they should move are gymnastics apparatus. The children should experiment by moving the apparatus with different methods. It takes more force to move a heavy object that it does to move a light object. This fact should be apparent to the students.

Divide the children into three groups and assign one group to each piece of equipment. The students should experiment with moving the apparatus around the gym. They should discover several conclusions. If they push the apparatus at one of the sides, rotatory motion takes place. If they push the apparatus at the top or bottom, it is hard to move because there is a tendency for rotatory motion. The best place to push is near the object's center of gravity. The children can control the apparatus better if they have their hands apart rather than close together. As they push or pull the apparatus, they should have a stride position, with their legs in the direction of the intended motion. This allows for a wide base of support and low center of gravity. Application of force should be in the direction of the intended motion.

After the children learn about the best way to push or pull an object, they may learn any activity appropriate for their grade level on each piece of apparatus. When the class period is over, reemphasize the purpose of the lesson by having the children put the apparatus away.

CONCEPT: A force is a push or a pull exerted on an object in an effort to start, stop, accelerate, decelerate, maintain, or change its motion.

Level: Advanced.

Subconcept: For an object to move, the forces acting upon it must be unbalanced.

Materials: Horizontal bar, balance beam, parallel bars, and tumbling mats.

Activities: The children already know that movement is necessary to do work. During the lesson they should learn that for an object to move, the forces acting upon it must be unbalanced. On the tumbling mats have the boys and girls perform rolling movements such as the forward roll, backward roll, log roll, or egg roll since the first grade. The purpose of repetition in this particular situation is to emphasize unbalanced forces. In a forward roll the child is in a crouched or curled position with the legs close together. He places his hands on the floor near the outer side of his feet. Then he leans forward, raises his seat into the air, and tries to place the back of his head on the mat. As he does this, he loses his balance and rolls over. As the child stays in a tuck position, he should take hold of his ankles and roll over to the beginning position. The point is that the actual roll is not initiated until a loss of balance occurs. The center of gravity must fall outside of the base of support for this movement to occur. The extent to which the roll is successful is determined by the efficiency with which the loss of balance is controlled and regained. Other rolls may also be explained in a similar fashion, with the emphasis on beginning the roll with a loss of balance.

The children can also attempt to perform rolling or rotating movements on the horizontal bars, balance beam, and parallel bars. Forward and backward rolls may be attempted on the balance beam and parallel bars. Hip circles or Flip the Pancake are stunts that may be tried on the horizontal bar. To initiate movement in each of these stunts, the children must put their bodies in a position of imbalance. As the body becomes unbalanced, the child should rotate around an axis and perform the stunt desired.

Energy

CONCEPT: Energy is required to do work.

Level: Beginning.

Subconcepts: (1) If an object is moved a great distance, much energy is needed to do the work. (2) If an object is moved a short distance, less energy is required to do the work.

Materials: Softballs, yarn balls, playground balls, or any other type of ball that the children may throw.

Activities: During the first two grades, children learn that work is the ability to push or pull an object. This implies that a force is involved and that an object moves over a distance. By the third grade, children should be ready for a more sophisticated definition. Work is force acting upon mass through a distance. During this lesson the children will learn about throwing a ball for distance. The force comes from the muscles of the person who is throwing the ball. The mass being acted upon is the ball. The distance is the length of windup over which force is applied to the ball. If a child throws efficiently, the amount of force provided will determine the length of the throw. A lot of energy will propel the ball a great distance. A small amount of energy will propel the ball a short distance.

The following guided discovery approach may be used to teach throwing. It emphasizes the correct throwing style and the summation of the parts of the body to achieve the best throw.

First, have each child stand facing a partner and throw the ball to the partner by using only the muscles of the forearm. The ball will travel only a short distance. Next, have each child throw by using the whole arm. The ball will travel farther. Next, have each child experiment with the throwing motion by stepping forward with the leg on the same side as the throwing arm, then with the leg on the opposite side. The addition of body parts will allow the child to gain momentum and throw farther. As the students get the idea that the whole body should be used to develop an efficient throw, point out to them that they could get an even better throw if they would use the trunk and shoulder muscles. This means that gradually a summation of forces must be applied to obtain the most efficient throwing action. After the stepping action of the legs, the trunk and shoulder muscles should be added to the building momentum. To do this, the children must discover which leg has to be used to step forward to gain an efficient throw. If the leg on the same side of the throwing arm is used, the trunk and shoulders become locked in position, and no rotation is permitted. Thus the children should learn that they must step forward with the opposite leg to permit the muscles of the trunk and

shoulders to contribute to the throw. After the legs, trunk, and shoulders establish the forward throwing motion sequentially, the muscles of the upper arm, forearm, hand, and fingers complete the throw. With emphasis on following through, stepping toward the target, keeping their eyes on the target, and flexing the muscles of the fingers as the ball leaves the hand, the children should develop an efficient throwing style. The more energy used, the farther the ball will travel.

CONCEPT: There are two types of energy: kinetic and potential.

Levels: Intermediate and advanced.

Subconcept: The human body applies force in the form of muscular energy in three ways: directly to an object through a continual force such as pushing, pulling, carrying, or lifting; over a period of time while motion is developed, followed by a release as in throwing; and by instantaneous contact as in striking.

Materials: Balls, slingshots, bows, and arrows.

Activities: During this lesson have the children practice various manipulative skills as they learn about the three situations in which energy is applied to objects and also the two types of energy. The first energy application or situation occurs when a person applies force continuously to an object, as when he pushes, pulls, carries, or lifts different objects. The second situation occurs when a person applies force to an object over a period of time while motion is developed and follows with a release, as in throwing. The third situation occurs when a person applies force to an object through instantaneous contact, as in striking, volleying, kicking, and heading. Each concept may be taught through discovery by asking the children how many different ways they can apply forces to objects. Can they apply continuous forces to objects? Can they apply force to an object over a period of time while motion is developed, and follow with a release? Can they apply instantaneous force to objects? Which manipulative concepts are related to each of the situations? Allow the children time to practice to ensure discovery before moving to the different types of energy.

The two types of energy are potential and

kinetic energy. As examples, you may choose to use a slingshot or bow and arrow. When the slingshot and bow are drawn, each has stored-up, or potential energy. A stretched rubber band has potential energy. On release, kinetic energy propels each object into motion. Even a book resting on a table has potential energy. If the table were quickly pulled out from underneath, the book would drop to the floor. Can you think of other examples in which potential and kinetic energy are evident? To emphasize these subconcepts, you could develop a unit on archery.

Friction and resistance

CONCEPT: Friction is a force at the surface of an object that makes it difficult to move another object.

Level: Beginning.

Subconcept: Friction is necessary to start and stop an object's motion.

Materials: None.

Activities: Friction is a helping as well as hindering force (Fig. 10-8). Too much friction causes machines to act inefficiently and break down easily. However, it is necessary for a machine to have a minimal amount of friction to begin its motion. Race cars must have spe-cial tires to allow proper road traction during a race. A person must wear tennis shoes to provide proper friction as he runs while playing basketball or other sports. During this lesson have the children try an experiment of their own. Divide the boys and girls into four teams. Two teams should wear tennis shoes and the other two teams, stockings and no shoes. Have them run an obstacle course designed so that the children can change directions quickly and start and stop often. The boys and girls will discover that those with slippery feet run the course in a slower time. The conclusion will be that friction between surfaces is helpful when a person tries to start, stop, or change directions.

CONCEPT: Air resistance is a force that is always present and slows the speeds of moving objects because of the flow of air around them.

Level: Intermediate.

Subconcept: The effects of air resistance on objects is dependent on the size, shape, and form of the object.

Materials: A box of tissue paper, newspaper, balls, and shoes.

Activities: During this lesson the children

Fig. 10-8. Friction may help or hinder one's motion.

will explore the rate and flow of falling objects. To begin the lesson, have the children hold a ball high in the air, release it, and watch it fall, bounce, roll, and come to a halt. Then have them attempt to do the same type of movement with their bodies. After a jump into the air and a direct fall to the floor, they may bounce and roll several times before coming to a halt. Next, have them drop one of their shoes from the same height, again observing its fall, and then attempt to do the same type of movement with their bodies. Except for a possible tumble and halting in a sideways or awkward position, the flight of the ball and shoe were much the same. Both fell directly and at a fast rate.

Next, have the children hold a piece of newspaper at a high level and then drop it. How does it fall when held in a vertical or horizontal position? Compare the flight of the newspaper with the ball and shoe, noting the size, indirect flight pattern, and rate of fall (Fig. 10-9). Have the children attempt to do the same type of movement with their bodies beginning at a high level, performing changes of pathway, direction, and various bends and stretches, and grad-

ually coming to rest on the floor. Finally, have each child use a piece of tissue paper with the ball, shoe, and newspaper, noting the size, indirect flight pattern, and rate of fall. Have the children attempt to do the same type of movement with their bodies.

At the conclusion of the lesson call the children together to discuss the subconcept they have discovered. Air resistance is a force that is always present and slows the speed of moving objects because of the flow of air around them. The effect of air resistance on objects is dependent on their size, shape, and form. Did the ball and shoe fall at the same rate? (Yes.) What were their flight patterns? (Fast and direct.) How did the newspaper fall to the floor? (More indirect.) In which position did the newspaper fall the fastest? (When held in a vertical position.) Why? (Less air resistance.) What would have happened if they had crumpled the newspaper into the shape of a ball? (Its shape would be smaller, have less air resistance, and fall at a fast direct rate, like the ball and shoe.) How did the tissue paper fall to the floor? (It was the slowest in rate of descent, with an indirect

Fig. 10-9. Air resistance affects motion.

flowing motion.) Why? (It was the smallest and lightest, and thus air resistance affected its flight the most.)

CONCEPT: Resistance is a condition that makes it difficult to move an object, whereas friction is a force at the surface of an object that makes it difficult to move another object.

Level: Intermediate.

Subconcepts: (1) Resistance is necessary to start and stop an object's motion. (2) Starting, sliding, and rolling friction are three types of friction.

Materials: Roller skates and a starting block.

Activities: At the beginning of this lesson you should discuss with the children the different types of friction and the role that resistance plays in movement. Starting, sliding, and rolling friction are the three different circumstances when friction is present (Fig. 10-10). To begin any type of movement, one must overcome the inertia of a body at rest. As a result, starting friction is the most difficult to overcome. To initiate movement, there must be a proper amount of resistance for efficient movement to take place. At this point you may introduce sliding and rolling friction to emphasize the importance of resistance in the initiation of movement. If the conditions exist, the children may attempt to run on sand, ice, grass, and/or pavement. If the children try to run on sand or ice in their shoes or with their bare feet, they will slip a lot because the surface does

not provide enough resistance. These are examples of sliding friction. The use of ice skates is also an example of sliding friction. Next, the children may try to roller skate on a floor or pavement. This is an example of rolling friction. In each instance, once motion is initiated, a proper balance between friction and resistance is necessary. If there is not enough, a person slips and falls. If there is too much, his movement is hindered.

In the opposite respect, resistance is also necessary to stop a person's motion in each of the examples used. Once a person is moving on the ice, sand, grass, floor, or pavement, there must be a proper amount of resistance for efficient stopping movements to take place. Ice skating, roller skating, or running in the sand are conditions in which it is difficult to stop because of the tendency to continue sliding or rolling. There is not enough resistance to stop motion efficiently.

In many sports, athletes wear special shoes to obtain the friction and resistance necessary for fast starts, stops, and changes of direction. Baseball players wear spikes. Football players wear cleats. Soccer players wear cleats. Basketball and tennis players wear special kinds of tennis shoes designed to provide good traction on the playing surface. Track participants wear a special kind of spike. To get added help in making a fast start, track athletes use starting blocks to provide added resistance. The starting block provides an opposition to the back-

Fig. 10-10. There are three different circumstances when friction is present.

ward force of the leg and allows the person to move ahead quickly without slipping. Each step a person takes pushes the ground back so that he can move ahead (Newton's third law). Without friction the person would slip or not move ahead at all. During the remainder of this lesson the children may test themselves while running the 50-yard dash. They may run several times with the starting block and several times from a standing start. Their times with the starting block should prove to be better.

CONCEPT: There are three types of friction: starting, sliding, and rolling.

Level: Advanced.

Subconcepts: (1) More force is required in starting friction because inertia must be overcome. (2) The amount of force required to slide an object over the surface of another is determined by the size at the surface contacting the floor, the weight of the object, and the physical characteristics of the object and the floor. (3) Less force is required to overcome rolling friction than to overcome sliding friction.

Materials: Parallel bars, a vaulting horse, a balance beam, and an apparatus transporter.

Activities: When the children come to class, the equipment is often already in place for them. During this experiment the children learn gymnastics stunts on the heavy apparatus. Before they perform on the apparatus, however, have the students set the equipment up and make it ready for use. Instruct them to try to carry or slide the apparatus into place. The equipment is heavy and presents problems for the children to move even when a group work together. Putting a heavy object into motion is difficult because of the weight of the apparatus. The size of the surface contacting the floor and the physical characteristics of the object and floor are other factors that determine the amount of sliding friction. A light, small, smooth-surfaced object slides more easily than a heavy, large, round-surfaced object.

Next, have the children use the apparatus transporter to move the equipment into place. The transporter lifts the apparatus off the floor and permits transportation by the use of wheels, or rolling friction. Perhaps 1 or 2 children can easily control the apparatus and move it into

place under these circumstances because less force is required to overcome rolling friction. Thus a heavy object that is put on wheels is easier to move than when it is resting flat on the floor.

After the children learn about the different types of friction and the use of wheels in overcoming friction, they may learn any activity appropriate for their grade level on each piece of equipment. When the class period is over, you may reemphasize the purpose of the lesson by having the children put the equipment away.

Linear and rotary motion

CONCEPT: Linear motion is motion in a straight line, whereas rotary motion is movement of a body around an axis.

Level: Beginning.

Subconcept: In rotary motion the length of the radius of the circle will influence the speed of rotation.

Materials: None.

Activities: This class should begin with a discussion of pathway and direction of movement. *Direct movement* is movement in a straight line and is called linear motion. The *direction of movement* refers to whether the movement is forward, backward, or sideways. Ask the children to show you how many ways they can vary a direct movement (pathway) while changing their direction; allow them to perform their solutions. They could change their form of locomotion (walk, run, hop, skip, etc.). They could also change their speed and the amount of force as they move from one point in the room directly to another. Zigzag movements may also be performed as a change in pathway because they, too, are a form of linear motion in which a person chooses to move directly to one point, change course (tack), and move directly to another point. In their own personal space the children can perform various bends and stretches as they change body level and dimension when moving directly from one pose to another.

In addition to direct and zigzag movement, a person may choose to move in a curved or circular pathway. Such movement around an axis is called rotary motion. The children may choose to perform different locomotor movements in a circular pathway while varying their direction, speed, and force. In their personal space they can isolate body parts and move each in a circular pathway as they change body level and dimension. The speed, force, and flow of their movements may also be changed. How many of their body parts can the children use to create rotary motion?

To conclude the lesson, the students can experiment with a special form of rotary motion called spinning or rolling. This type of motion may be done in a vertical (upright) plane, as when a dancer, roller skater, or ice skater turns or pivots around an axis, or in a horizontal plane, as when a gymnast performs a forward roll, backward roll, or hip circle. In each of the examples, if the performer desires to rotate around the axis at a high speed, the radius of the circle of rotation is small. If the performer desires to rotate more slowly or to halt the rotary motion, the radius of the circle of rotation is increased. Have the children practice various turning, rolling, and spinning movements. What can they do with their arms, legs, and body to influence the speed of their rotary motion? (To spin fast in a vertical plane, create a small base of support and hold the arms in close to the body after the motion is initiated. To stop rotation in a vertical plane, create a wide base of support and extend the arms out to the side. To turn fact in a horizontal plane, bend or tuck the body into a small, curved [ball-like] shape. To turn more slowly in a horizontal plane, extend or stretch the body away from the center of rotation.)

CONCEPT: Children are able to learn to pump a swing by learning about rotary motion.

Level: Intermediate.

Subconcept: In a pendular type of rotary motion, a pumping action can be achieved: when working with gravity, increase the radius of rotation; when working against gravity, shorten the radius of rotation.

Materials: If outdoors, use playground swings; if indoors, use indoor swings, climbing ropes, hanging rings, or suspended automobile tires.

Activities: The purpose of this lesson is to have the children discover how to accomplish efficient pumping actions when swinging in a pendular fashion. Allow each child to work with a partner. Have the students take turns swinging in a standing or sitting position. Some children may take a short run to start the swinging motion. Others may have their partner give them a push to get them started. Still others may use body lean and leg action to initiate their motion. After the initial swinging motion is begun, the students should attempt to increase the height of their swing by developing an efficient pumping action. Ask them to be aware of what they are trying to do with their body in relationship to gravity as they move through their pendular arc. Partners should watch, observing from the side so that they have a good view of what the body of the swinger is doing to "pump" the swing.

After the children have experimented on the swings, a discussion should take place. What were the legs doing to keep the swing moving? Where was the center of gravity on the downswing? When each child reaches the top of a swinging arc, he should lower his center of gravity to gain momentum on the down phase of the swing. A high center of gravity on the up phase of the swing helps reduce resistance. Thus, to accomplish more efficient pumping action while standing, the children should bend their knees on the down phase of the swing. When trying to pump the swing while sitting down, they should straighten the knees on the down phase and bend the knees on the up phase.

After discussing this concept with the children, allow them to return to the swings and explore this method of efficient pumping. Encourage them to be aware of the motion of their bodies while swinging and pumping.

Centrifugal force

CONCEPT: Centrifugal force affects the motion of persons and objects traveling in a circular pathway.

Level: Intermediate.

Subconcepts: (1) Centripetal force is the name given to any force directed toward the center of a circular path of motion. (2) Cen-

Fig. 10-11. Centrifugal force affects when one should release an object thrown at a target.

trifugal force is the inertia tendency of a body in motion to travel in a straight line and is the reaction to centripetal force. (3) An object under the influence of centrifugal force will travel in a straight line tangent from the point where it was released.

Materials: Hula-Hoop; traffic cones or weighted plastic bottles for targets.

Activities: To begin this lesson, have the children find a space on the floor where they can move without touching anyone else. Explain that you would like them to turn or spin around in one place. You may caution the children to focus their eyes on one spot so that they do not get dizzy, but for purposes of this lesson you should emphasize what is happening to their arms. Have the children relax the muscles of their arms, letting them hang at their sides. As the students start and continue to spin, what happens to their arms? (They move out to the side like the propellors of a helicopter.) Why? (Centrifugal force.) Why don't the arms detach and fly away from the body? (The muscles of the upper arm and shoulder hold them in—centripetal force.)

Next, give each child a hoop. Have the children stand in one spot and hold the hoop loosely in one hand by using finger-thumb opposition. Instruct them to hold their arm out to the side parallel to the floor. What is the position of the hoop? (Vertical.)

While the children continue to hold the hoop loosely, ask them to begin spinning. What happens to the hoop? (It moves out to a position parallel to the floor.) Why? (Centrifugal force.) What is holding the hoop in or keeping it from flying away from the hand? (The muscles of the hand—centripetal force). What would happen if the hoop were released? (The hoop would take off in a direction tangent to the point of release.) To emphasize this point, use the traffic cones as targets and ask the children to perform the spinning movements, exploring the problem of when they need to release the hoop to get it to ring the target (Fig. 10-11).

■   ■   ■

Level: Advanced.

Subconcepts: (1) Centripetal force is the name given to any force directed toward the center of a circular path of motion. (2) Centrifugal force is the inertia tendency of a body in motion to travel in a straight line and is the reaction to centripetal force. (3) An object

Fig. 10-12. The object moves in a line tangent to the point of release.

under the influence of centrifugal force will travel in a straight line tangent from the point where it was released.

Materials: Playground balls or yarn balls.

Activities: During this lesson have each child work with a partner to explore different ways of imparting force to an object while using a circular motion. To begin, encourage the children to think of as many different ways as possible to throw a ball by using a circular windup. For example, they may use a clockwise or counterclockwise windmill motion. They may also whirl around like a discus thrower. In each instance the ball travels in a circular pathway during the windup. The muscles of the arm and hand provide the centripetal force to hold the ball. Ask the children to be aware of when they release the ball as they use the various windups. They should discover that on release, centrifugal force causes the ball to travel in a straight line tangent to the point of release (Fig. 10-12). They should then be able to use this information

to discover where they should release the ball when using different windups to throw it directly to a partner or at a target.

Next, discuss with the children the application of this concept when using an implement to strike a ball. When swinging a golf club, tennis racket, badminton racket, or baseball bat, what is the path of the implement? (Circular.) If one were to let go of the implement during the swing, what would happen? (It would fly off in a straight line tangent to the point of release.) What causes the racket to be controlled? (The muscles of the arm and hand provide the centripetal force to hold the implement.) When contacting the ball or bird, in what direction does it move? (The ball or bird moves in a straight line tangent to the point of contact.) The children may then practice striking various types of balls with an overhand, underhand, forehand, or backhand swing and try to strike the objects at selected targets in various locations in space (up, down, right, left, etc.)

Chapter 11

PRODUCTION, APPLICATION, AND ABSORPTION OF FORCE

Since motion is initiated by a force, it should be obvious that force and motion are closely associated. It is important for children to understand how force is produced and how it can be used most effectively. The source of force in the human body is strength derived from the muscles through good nutrition and efficient oxygen consumption. Force is needed to move the body, to stop the body's motion, and to stop objects with one's own body. The topics to be discussed in this chapter are production of force, application of force, including projectiles, and absorption of force.

PRODUCTION OF FORCE

The amount of force needed for a particular task depends on the purpose of the movement. Since the muscles supply force for each movement, a person should be aware of certain facts about them and how they work so that he may use them efficiently. The large, strong muscles of the body will be able to exert more force than the smaller, weaker muscles. The muscles of the legs, hips, and thighs are larger and stronger than those in the arms, shoulders, and back and therefore should provide most of the force when lifting heavy objects. Even in the small muscle coordination tasks such as cutting, pasting, and writing, the small muscles should be as strong as possible to work efficiently. Thus physical fitness is needed in both the large and small muscles.

Whenever possible, several muscles or muscle groups should work together to provide the force for moving a heavy object. For example, the muscles of the legs, hips, thighs, shoulders, arms, and back should work together to prevent strain on any one muscle group.

Muscles are able to exert more force when they are placed in a stretch position before they contract. This is the reason for the backswing before striking a golf ball, the windup before throwing a ball, and the backswing before stroking a tennis ball.

The most efficient and effective total force is developed when the force from each contributing part of the body is applied in a single direction in a sequential order over as long a period of time as possible. The summation of forces from each contributing body part enables a greater number of muscles to apply the force over a longer distance and greater period of time until momentum reaches its maximum at the point of application of the force or release of the object. The sequential contribution of various body parts to the force of the throw also allows for greater leverage, which will increase the force and efficiency of the throw. For example, as a person throws a ball, momentum is initiated by the movement of the legs. The rotation of the hips and shoulders increases momentum until the arm uncoils sequentially— shoulder, elbow, and wrist. Finally, the ball is released by the fingers after maximum force has been applied. At the time of release the full weight of the body is behind the throw, and the whole body is acting as a third-class lever. All this force is then transferred to the ball, and it acquires the same rate of speed at which the hand is moving at the time of release. The same rules apply when kicking and striking the various balls in the different sport activities.

The follow-through motion is important in that the center of the arc of the throwing movement is at the point of release and the maximum amount of speed and force is transferred to the object. If the momentum is stopped immediately after release of an object or at impact,

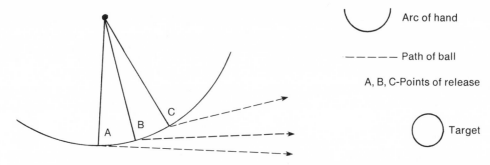

Fig. 11-1. The object should be released at a point where the arc is tangent to the desired target.

a jerking motion results. The arc of the movement is shortened, and the speed of the hand is slowed before the object leaves the hand. A shorter, more inaccurate throw results. Following through with throwing, striking, and kicking patterns also serves as a safety factor in terms of reducing possible strain of the muscle groups involved if momentum is stopped immediately.

APPLICATION OF FORCE

As discussed in the concept concerning work, a force should be applied to an object as directly as possible in the direction it is to go. To move an object upward, the force should be applied through the center of gravity of the object in the desired direction. When the force is applied away from the center of gravity, rotary motion will occur. Any force applied in a direction other than the one desired is a hindrance and waste of effort. For example, when the arms are swung from side to side while running, forward motion is hindered.

The direction that an object which is thrown, struck, or kicked takes is a line tangent to that in which the arm, implement, or foot is moving at the point of release or impact (Fig. 11-1). If accuracy is desired, the object should be released at a point where the arc is tangent to the desired target. If distance is desired, the object should be released at a point that allows it to be projected at an angle of 45 degrees.

Projectiles

A projectile is an object that is propelled into space. Many activities involve projection of the body or objects into space. The body is a pro-

jectile as it moves through space after jumping, diving, or rebounding off a trampoline or diving board. A ball, hoop, or other object becomes a projectile as it is thrown or hit into the air. The flight of a projectile in space is affected by gravity, air resistance, angle of release, spin, and amount of initial force that launched it.

ABSORPTION OF FORCE

When absorbing the force from a fall or receiving the force of an object, as in catching a ball, there should be a gradual reduction of force. Absorption of a force should be spread over as large an area as possible, as long a distance as possible, and as long a time period as possible. A baseball glove helps disperse the impact of a ball over a large area of the hand, as well as lengthening the time it takes for a ball to slow down. When falling or performing a forward roll, a person tries to land and roll by using a large portion of the body, as well as absorbing the force over as long a distance as possible. When diving into the water, a person tried to enter the water gradually with the body as vertically aligned as possible to distribute the impact over as long a time period as possible. Bending at the hips, knees, and ankles when landing from a jump allows the body more time to absorb its momentum. As a person prepares to absorb a force, he should also be aware of assuming a stable position in line with the oncoming force, with the body weight low and over the base of support. Reception of the force anywhere other than through the center of gravity initiates rotary motion whereby a person loses his balance and loses control of the object.

■ ■ ■

Following are sample lessons of ways in which the concepts involving production, application, and absorption of force can be integrated with movement experiences and taught to elementary school children.

Learning activities

Production and application of force

CONCEPT: The muscles of the human body may be used to produce and apply force to objects.

Levels: Beginning and intermediate.

Subconcepts: (1) As more muscles are used, more force is produced. (2) As the muscles act faster, more force is produced. (3) If a heavy object is to be moved, the force should be exerted by the large muscles of the legs, hips, thighs, shoulders, arms, and back in the direction the object is to go. (4) To lift a heavy object, keep the back straight and use the muscles of the legs. (5) To move an object upward, the force must be directed vertically. (6) To move an object forward, the force should be applied through the center of gravity of the object in the desired direction. (7) If the force is applied away from the center of gravity, a rotary motion will result. (8) The amount of force imparted to an object is dependent on the mass of an object and the distance and speed necessary for the purpose of the movement.

Materials: Large cardboard appliance boxes filled with balls, a gym mat, or any other equipment that makes the boxes too heavy and cumbersom for one child to lift; cases of groceries from the school cafeteria would also serve.

Activities: This lesson is a review of the concepts that were learned in the chapters concerning stability, Newton's laws of motion, and factors affecting human motion. Depending on the size of the boxes, you may ask the children to work individually, in pairs, or in small groups. A box as large as a refrigerator carton filled with gym mats would accommodate as many as 3 or 4 students. Ask the children to push the box across the floor as they experiment with qualities of movement and concepts relating to production and application of force.

Can the children push the box across the floor in a direct, linear pathway? Can they start, stop, and change directions? Where do they apply the force to achieve linear and rotary motion? Can they push the box fast? Can they use a slow, sustained, forceful motion? What muscles of the body should be used to produce the force? Why? Can the children lift the box in the air and carry it? Where is the force applied to achieve vertical movement? Which muscles of the body should be used for lifting movements? (See Fig. 11-2.)

Discuss each of the above subconcepts after a period of exploration and then tell the children to return to the boxes to further explore the movement concepts involved. You may have the activity culminate in the making of an obstacle course in which the children move under, over, around, and through the boxes in different ways.

CONCEPT: A windup for preparatory movement helps the body to exert a maximum amount of force.

Level: Intermediate.

Subconcepts: Muscles exert more force when they are placed in a stretch position before they contract.

Materials: Soccer or playground balls and bowling pins.

Activities: At this age level many of the students have seen or participated in an actual game of bowling at a bowling alley. They have already seen the importance of the backswing windup of the throwing arm in bowling. Ask the students if they can think of other examples in which a windup is used to place muscles in a stretch position before they contract to achieve effective force action. A baseball windup, the backswing before hitting a golf ball, and the backward extension used before hitting a badminton birdie are all examples. Have the class divide into small groups. The groups can explore production of force concepts by playing two variations of bowling. Set up ten bowling pins in triangular fashion on the floor as they are at a bowling alley. Place a line 10 to 15 feet back from the headpin. In both the following variations have the students deliver the ball directly from the line.

Fig. 11-2. What is the most effective way to lift a heavy object?

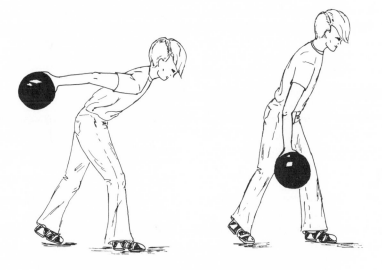

Fig. 11-3. Windup is important to an effective throw.

Variation I: Play according to regulation bowling rules except that no arm backswing or leg approach is allowed. Have the students stand at the line and throw the ball from the normal resting position of the arm and hand. Keep score as in a regulation bowling game or by simply adding together the number of pins that are knocked down.

Variation II: Use the same rules as in the first game. Have the students stand at the line when delivering the ball. This time, however, allow them to use the backswing arm motion when delivering the ball down the floor or alley. Keep score as in the first game.

The students will notice more effective total force in the second game because the arm is allowed to stretch before it contracts. Scores from the variation I and the variation II games may be compared. The score from the latter may be higher. (See Fig. 11-3.)

CONCEPT: The most effective total force is developed when the force from each contributing part of the body is applied in a single direction in a sequential order.

Level: Intermediate and advanced.

Subconcepts: (1) The greater the length and number of levers that are brought into action in successive fashion, the longer the time provided for force to develop. (2) There is a summation of forces as each body part contributes its share until momentum reaches its maximum at the point of application of force or the release of the ball. (3) The direction an object takes is a line tangent to that in which the arm or implement is moving at the point of release or impact (centrifugal force). (4) A sport implement (bat, racket, club) becomes a part of the body and is used as a third-class lever when applying force to an object. (5) A sport implement enables a person to contact a ball with more momentum and range of motion at the expense of using more force to generate the motion. (6) More velocity can be achieved with a long lever, but a long lever is often difficult to control. (7) The linear motion of a projectile can often be increased if the person develops rotary motion prior to throwing or striking the object. This is the reason for the windup and rotation of the shoulders and hops in a throwing motion and

for a shotputter's rotation of the whole body prior to putting the shot. (8) A follow-through in all hitting, throwing, and kicking activities ensures maximum application of force and allows time for gradual reduction of momentum.

Materials: Volley balls, playground balls, tennis balls, and tennis rackets.

Activities: At first glance this lesson may seem overwhelming because of the long list of subconcepts. Many of them, however, have been stressed in other lessons in previous chapters on levers and factors affecting human motion. The purpose of this lesson is to use striking activities for review, with an emphasis on production and application of force.

Give each child a ball and instructions to strike it with the hand against a wall, allowing it to bounce one or more times before striking it a second time against the wall. After a short time question the children about their performance. Can they hit the ball better when the arm is held close to the body or when the arm is extended away from the body? With which leg do they step forward? Can they hit the ball better if they keep their shoulders, trunk, and hips rigid or use body rotation? What type of leverage is used to propel the ball forward? In which direction does the ball travel on being struck with the hand? Why is follow-through important? What happens if no follow-through occurs? (The center of the arc of the striking motion is at the point of impact. At this time the maximum amount of speed and force is transferred to the ball. If momentum is stopped immediately after impact with the ball, a jerky motion results, the arc is shortened, and the speed of the hand is slowed. A throw or strike without a follow-through is therefore short and inaccurate.)

After the children strike the ball against the wall with the hand, change hands, and vary the force application, have them perform the same activities with a ball and a racket. Repeat the same questions after a period of activity and, in addition, ask the children about leverage with reference to force application. What is the role of the racket in striking an object? What advantages are gained? What if the racket is too heavy?

Follow each period of questioning by an

activity period during which the students are allowed to apply the concepts they have learned. This may be in the form of further individual play, partner play, or small group play in which children are allowed to make up games showing good striking concepts with reference to proper production and application of force.

CONCEPT: The way in which forces are applied affects efficiency of movement.

Level: Beginning.

Subconcept: Application of force should be as even as possible so that all the force is used to overcome resistance, not to overcome inertia.

Materials: Scooters (if not available, topless boxes that are large enough for a child to sit in may be used) and floor-marking tapes.

Activities: Divide the gym in half lengthwise. On one half place three evenly spaced lines horizontally across. Let the other half remain unmarked. Have the children work together in small groups, each group using one scooter or box to experiment with. Place the groups so that half the class is working on the marked portion of the gym and half on the unmarked portion. Refer to the diagram in Fig. 11-4.

Now instruct the class that each child is to push another child on the scooter to the opposite end of the gym. The children on the tape-marked half of the floor lose contact with the child they are pushing every time they reach a piece of tape on the floor. In other words, the pushers on the marked side of the gym must

pause momentarily each time they reach the tape before they may continue pushing to the other end of the gym. Later have the children switch sides so that everyone takes a turn on both the marked and unmarked runway.

Ask the children what difference they noticed between the two halves of the gym. Why was the unmarked half easier and faster? Why did the marked half take more energy? With the even application of force on the unmarked half, all force could be used to overcome resistance and build up momentum. On the marked half the children had to repeatedly pause. After each pause they had to overcome inertia, which led to inefficient force application and more energy expended.

CONCEPT: To accomplish a complete turn or rotation in the air, a person must establish the turning force before leaving the ground.

Level: Intermediate.

Subconcepts: (1) A twisting movement is movement around an axis in which limited motion occurs because of a base, or anchor point. (2) A turning or rotating movement is movement around an axis in which full motion is permitted.

Materials: A record appropriate for twisting and turning movements, such as "To Move is to Be" by Jo Ann Seker* and a record player.

Activities: Begin this lesson by discussing

---

*Educational Activities, Inc., Freeport, N.Y.

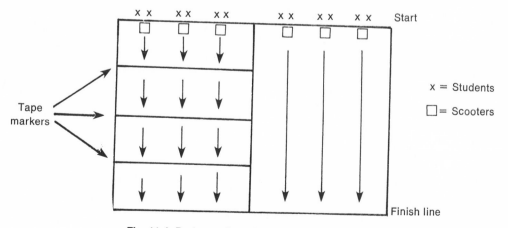

x = Students

□ = Scooters

Tape markers

Start

Finish line

Fig. 11-4. Push or pull continuously for best results.

with the children the differences between a twist and a turn or rotation. What is a twist? What is a turn or rotation? How do they differ? A person may twist the wrist or forearm or twist around the trunk of the body when the feet are anchored to the floor, or he may rotate the whole arm around the shoulder joint or jump into the air and turn around.

After learning about twisting and turning movements, the children may begin experimenting with the performance of each type of movement. Which body parts can they use to twist? Can they perform twisting movements with more than one body part at a time? Can they create twist poses at different levels in space? Can they perform twisting movements on opposite sides of the body that are symmetrical or asymmetrical? What body parts can they use to turn or rotate? How many can they rotate at one time? Can they turn their whole body around (rotation) by jumping into the air?

Encourage the students to start with quarter turns in the air, then to try half turns in which they face the opposite direction from which they started. Once these turns are accomplished, ask them to try turning a complete circle while in the air. Encourage them to concentrate on using their arms and legs in the take-off. They may wish to try turning around from a standing or running take-off, then leaps with the turns. When is a turning movement started? When is the force that causes the turning motion being applied? The children will discover that to accomplish a continuous turn in the air, they must first establish the turning force before leaving the ground.

CONCEPT: The angle at which an object is struck or released will affect the distance it travels.

Level: Advanced.

Subconcepts: (1) A ball that is projected at a large angle (vertical) at the time of impact will travel high in the air for a short distance and be in the air longer than a ball projected at a small angle. (2) To project a ball or object into the air and over as great a distance as possible, the angle of release should be 45 degrees. (3) The linear motion of a projectile can be increased if the person develops rotary motion prior to throwing or striking the object. (4) The direction an object takes is a line tangent to that in which the arm or implement is moving at the point of release or impact (centrifugal force).

Activities: During the lesson have the children work on the striking concepts of bumping, setting, and serving in volleyball, beginning by working individually with a ball. Ask the children if they can find a way to strike the ball so that it goes straight up. Have them pick a spot on the floor to see if they can strike the ball and make it land or bounce on that spot. Where do they need to contact the ball? (Under.) What should their body position be? (Low, with the knees and hips bent and back straight to permit the arms to get under the ball.) How should they contact the ball? (Since carrying the ball is not permitted in volleyball, cup both hands together for an even or flat surface. This permits more control than a one-arm hit.) Ask the children if they can continually strike the ball into the air by using an underhand pattern (bump) and allow the ball to bounce once on the floor between each hit. How much force should they apply to the ball? (Moderate force will allow a high trajectory, permitting the child to get under the ball each time.) Next, ask the children if they can perform the same underhand striking pattern continually without allowing the ball to touch the floor.

A follow-up to the individual work would be to have the students perform the underhand striking pattern with a partner, first allowing a bounce and gradually moving to continuous striking in the air. When bumping the ball to a partner, how does the movement change? (It is exactly the same except that the ball is contacted more to the side, allowing it to be projected a distance rather than in a straight or vertical pattern.) If they wanted to make the ball travel a large distance, at what angle would the ball be projected? (At 45 degrees.)

In a different group or lesson, have the children practice the same sequence by using an overhand striking pattern. (Set.) Stress the same concepts in both individually and with a partner. (Get under the ball, have a wide base of support, strike the ball with two hands, use a moderate force to project the ball high yet under control.)

In a third group or lesson have the children learn how to serve the ball. Instruct them to use an underhand or overhand striking pattern while applying good body mechanics. (Opposite foot forward, good trunk and shoulder rotation, wide base of support in the direction of movement, eye-hand coordination, follow-through). You may also point out that in preparing to serve, the striking arm is moving in an arc, or circular pathway, and that on contact the ball will travel in a line tangent to the point of impact (Fig. 11-5). As a result, you may ask the children where a serve should be placed. (Deep into the opponents' court.) How can that be accomplished? (By hitting under and to the back of the ball—get a good angle).

CONCEPT: The angle of refraction equals the angle of reflection.

Level: Intermediate.

Subconcept: A ball will bounce back from the floor, wall, racket, bat, paddle, or club at the same angle at which it hit (angle of refraction).

Materials: Basketballs, traffic cones or chairs, playground balls, a tennis racket and tennis ball, a softball, and a softball bat.

Activities: For this lesson have the students experiment with application of force by moving from station to station. Explain that a ball bounces back from the object it hits at the same angle at which the ball originally hit. As the children move from station to station, encourage them to experiment by throwing or batting the ball at different angles and observing the resulting angles at which the ball bounces back. Some stations that may be used follow:

1. Partners bounce-pass a basketball to each other. Lengthen or shorten the distance between the partners so that they may observe different angles of refraction.

2. Have each student dribble a ball while standing in one spot and observe how the ball

Fig. 11-5. The ball travels in a line tangent to the point of impact.

Fig. 11-6. A ball rebounds at the same angle at which it is hit.

bounces back from the floor vertically.

3. Set up two or three traffic cones or chairs in a line about 6 feet apart. Have students dribble in and out of the objects in a zigzag fashion (Fig. 11-6).

4. Have each student stand about 5 feet from the wall and experiment passing a playground ball against the wall and catching his ball after it bounces off of the wall. Tell them to throw the ball at as many different levels as possible (high on the wall, middle of the wall, and low on the wall) so as to observe different angles of refraction.

5. At this station you may have a student use a tennis racket to hit a tennis ball against the wall, observing the angle of the tennis ball as it bounces off the wall so as to be in a ready position to hit the ball again.

6. You may have a student practice hitting a softball with a softball bat. If the bat is swung downward, the ball will travel in that direction. If the bat is swung upward, the ball will bounce off of the bat in an upward direction.

CONCEPT: The point of force application on an object affects the manner in which it will spin.

Level: Advanced.

Subconcept: As a ball is passed, various spins may be imparted to it that will cause it to bounce in different ways.

Materials: Basketballs.

Activities: Have each student work with a partner in this lesson to experiment with spins on a ball. Tell the class that each member of the pair should bounce-pass the ball back and forth to each other. Encourage the students to try placing different spins on the ball each time they pass it and to observe the influence that each spin has on the ball as it bounces from the floor. By placing different spins on the ball, the students can try to prevent their partners from catching it. When the children are finished experimenting, discuss with the class the effects of spin on a ball. What results did they observe in their passing? What effects did different spins have on the bounce of the ball? A ball that spins to the left curves to the left and bounces to the left as it comes in contact with the floor. One that spins to the right curves to the right and bounces to the right as it comes in contact with the floor. A ball with top spin drops fast and has a long, low bounce. One with back spin rises in the air, travels farther, and has a high, short, bounce. After this discussion, allow the students to exchange partners and continue bounce-passing the ball, continuing to place spin on the ball and observe the ef-

Fig. 11-7. After moving through the air, landing by absorbing the body's force.

fects of the spins that were previously discussed.

Absorption of force

CONCEPT: Children can learn to efficiently absorb the force of their body's movement.

Level: Beginning.

Subconcepts: (1) When absorbing the force of one's body, there should be a gradual reduction of force over as large a surface area as possible and over as long a period of time as possible. (2) When receiving a force, a person should get in line with the oncoming force, assume a stride position in the direction of the force, and have the body weight low and over the base of support.

Materials: Vaulting boxes, wooden boxes, and/or stable cardboard or plastic boxes (beer cases or milk cases).

Activities: The purpose of this lesson is to have children experience the concept of moving through the air with an emphasis on a proper landing. It may be taught as a separate lesson or in conjunction with lessons on stability and production of force. Ask the children to move off the boxes in different ways. Can they use a one- or two-foot takeoff? How far can they

jump? How high can they jump? Can they jump off in different directions? Can they create bent, stretched, symmetrical, asymmetrical, and other body poses while in the air? Can they land and stay in one spot? Can they land and perform a rolling movement?

Place emphasis on the takeoff and landing. To get a good takeoff, one should use the whole body. The summation of forces from the action of the arms, hips, and legs is important. To jump high, the force should be applied in a vertical direction. To jump far, the force should be applied through the center of gravity at a 45-degree angle. To land efficiently, there should be a gradual reduction of force over as large a surface area as possible and over as long a period of time as possible. This means that a person should land with a wide base of support in the direction of movement and bend at the hips, knees, and ankles to absorb the body's force* gradually (Fig. 11-7).

---

*If a trampoline, minitrampoline, or innertube from a car tire is available, the concept of absorption of force may be further emphasized. A person wishing to stop the bouncing motion should land with a wide base and bend at the hips, knees, and ankles to absorb the force of motion.

Chapter 12

SOUND

A sound is a stimulus that can be heard. Sounds are produced by vibrations in the air. These vibrations, or air waves, are received by the ear and decoded. The process of decoding sounds is called hearing. The source of the vibrations a person hears may be a human voice, an instrument playing, a hammer striking a nail, a bat hitting a ball, or any of thousands of other stimuli.

Objects vibrate at different rates and different volumes. This causes sounds to be heard in different ways. The word *pitch* is used to describe the highness or lowness of a sound, determined by the frequency of vibration of the sound waves. Objects that vibrate at a fast rate of speed produce high-pitched sounds. Those which vibrate at slow speeds produce low-pitched sounds. The density, length, and thickness of an object affect the rate of vibration and thus the pitch of a sound. In general, low-density, long, and thick objects produce low-pitched sounds. High-density, short, and thin objects produce high-pitched sounds. (See Fig. 12-1.)

Just as sounds vary in pitch, so do they in tempo. *Tempo* is the rate at which successive sounds are heard. In music, for example, a person may hear instruments being played at a fast or slow tempo. The *volume* of sound that a person hears refers to dynamics. Some sounds are loud; some are soft.

By listening to sounds a person can learn much about his environment. A study of sounds can help children become aware of listening as a conscious process. Good listening habits are necessary to succeed in school. Children need to learn to listen to sequential auditory directions. The areas of dance and music are rich with experiences such as beat, measure (meter), accent, tempo, phrasing, and intensity. Such experiences encourage children to be aware of

sounds they hear. Children should gradually recognize that it is possible to make distinctions among the various types of sounds (figure-ground) and learn to identify events (water running) and objects (car horn blowing) in the environment by listening to the sounds associated with them. Children should be able to recognize these sounds at night as well as in the daytime, just as a blind person uses sound to learn an awareness of the environment.

Following are lessons that involve the teaching of concepts on sound to elementary school-children.

Learning activities

CONCEPT: Sounds are produced by vibrations in the air.

Level: Beginning.

Subconcepts: (1) A person can recognize the direction from which a sound is coming. (2) A person can recognize different sounds at night. (3) There are reasons why a person cannot hear some sounds.

Materials: Blindfolds.

Activities: Conduct this whole lesson in the dark by blindfolding the children. Have them start in mass or scatter formation and tell them that when you call out a number, they should form that size group. Call out "Two" first and instruct the children that after they have found a partner, they should sit down and be quiet until everyone has found a partner. Next, ask the partners to establish a sound (finger snap, series of two claps, etc.) or a word (color, blue; vegetable, carrot; etc.) that they can use to relocate their partner later. Then call out "Three" and ask the children to form groups of 3, using the same procedure. The groups of 3 should establish their own sound or word cue. Do the same for groups of 4 and 5. By now the chil-

Fig. 12-1. Balls sound different when they are bounced.

dren should be scattered. You can all out any number you desire and watch how the children use their special codes to locate each other. At the beginning it is difficult because the scattered individuals are not able to hear their coded sounds, but as groups find each other, they will sit down and be quiet so that the remaining groups can hear where their members are located. (See Fig. 12-2.)

■ ■ ■

Level: Beginning.

Subconcept: There are reasons why a person cannot hear some sounds.

Materials: A record player and records: "Exercise is Kid Stuff," "To Move is to Be," and "Jumpnastics"* or any other exercise record for young children. A radio or tape recorder is necessary.

Activities: The purpose of this lesson is to show the children that sometimes a person cannot hear sounds for two reasons. The first situation occurs when a sound is so loud or its source is so close that it drowns out any other sound (figure-ground problem). One example is the

*Educational Activities, Inc., Freeport, New York, N.Y.

television or radio being played so loud a person cannot hear what is being said on the telephone. Another example is a car radio drowning out the noise of an approaching railroad train. The second situation in which a sound cannot be heard occurs when it is too faint or the source is too far away. The only time an individual can hear a watch tick is when he holds it up to his ear. The sound is always there, but it is sometimes too faint to be heard an arms' length away. What are some other examples of situations in which sounds are not heard? Why?

After the children understand, tell them to find a space on the floor that no one else occupies and have them follow the directional cues on one of the records you have selected. After an initial period of hearing normally, begin to vary the sound source. Make it play loud and then so soft that only those nearest the record player can hear it. Add a second record, tape, or radio as a distracter. Make one play loud and the other soft. Use your voice or a whistle as a distraction. In addition to learning better listening skills with respect to auditory discrimination and figure-ground perception, the children will learn the reasons why some sounds cannot be heard.

Fig. 12-2. Can you find your way back to your group?

CONCEPT: A sound represents something that can be heard.

Level: Beginning.

Subconcept: A person can recognize events by listening to sounds.

Materials: Blindfolds, a record player, and the record "Muffin in the City"* or any similar record—a sound effects record or personally made audiotape with sounds that children can imitate through voice and action.

Activities: The purpose of this lesson is to have the children listen to, identify, and move to sounds that they might hear in the dark. Create a situation in which the children may experience this lesson in the dark: shut off the lights and cover the windows of the room or gym or have the children wear blindfolds. The latter is preferable because the teacher may observe the children.

Begin the lesson by discussing with the students the different types of sounds that they may hear every day: loud, quiet, harsh, pleasant, shrill, percussive, flowing, etc. Some sounds are pleasing to the ear (music); others are annoying or distracting (noise). The children may wish to give examples of the different types of sounds. Emphasize the idea that sounds are sometimes frightening in the dark. Teach children that if they remain calm and attempt to figure out the source and reason for sounds in the dark, these sounds become less frightening.

After the discussion use the record "Muffin in the City", any sound effects record, or personally made audiotape to encourage the children to identify different sounds and move creatively as a response to the sound. How would a person move when hearing a loud sound? Soft sound? Percussive or vibratory sound? Flowing sound? How would children move to interpret a scream in the night? A fire siren? A toilet flushing? A car passing? A train moving through town? A door squeaking? How many different examples of sound effects can you create to help children interpret different sounds at night?

■ ■ ■

Level: Intermediate.
Subconcept: By listening carefully to

---

*Young People's Records, New York, N.Y.

Fig. 12-3. Find your balloon.

sound, a person can follow the movement of an object.

Materials: Balloons.

Activities: The purpose of this lesson is to let the children experiment with a balloon to learn some basic concepts about sound.

Have each child find a space on the floor for himself and his balloon. Let the children blow up their balloons slowly, encouraging them to listen to the sound of the air entering it. The vibrations of air inside the balloon are causing the sound. Have the children release the air from the balloon slowly, noticing the sound coming from the mouthpiece (you can also have them stretch the mouthpiece to get a squeaky sound).

Next, have the children blow up the balloon again in the following manner—two slow blows, two fast blows, two slow blows, etc., noticing the difference between the resulting sounds. When the balloon is full, have the children let go of the mouthpiece completely, listen to the sound of the air rushing out of the balloon, and watch the balloon's flight.

Now have the students close their eyes. Tell them to be very quiet, to stay in their area of the gym, and to listen carefully for the sound of their own balloon. When they all have their eyes closed, tell them to blow up their balloons, release it when full, and listen very carefully to its flight so that after the balloon has landed, they can walk over and pick it up without even seeing it. Each child will know exactly where the balloon went by listening to its sound in flight. (See Fig. 12-3.)

Finally, have the children blow air into their balloons, tie them, and see if they can tap their balloons continuously in the air while their eyes are closed. They should be able to know where the balloon is by using their sense of touch (where and how hard did they tap the balloon) and their sense of hearing.

CONCEPT: Different sounds are produced by different kinds of vibrations.

Level: Intermediate.

Subconcept: (1) Objects that are dense and vibrate at a high speed produce a high-pitched sound. (2) Objects that are not dense and vibrate at a slow speed produce a low-pitched sound.

Materials: A drum, tambourine, triangle, cymbal, glass of water, and guitar.

Activities: At the beginning of this lesson have the children experiment with making sounds by using the various instruments. Have a child place a penny or another small object on the drum and strike the drum. What happens? (The penny vibrates on the drum because of the sound being made.) Have a child place a glass of water next to a cymbal and strike the cymbal. What happens? (The cymbal causes the water in the glass to vibrate.) The children will also discover after a period of experimentation the pitch that the different instruments make. What type of sounds does the drum make? (Low pitch, large surface area but hollow or not dense, percussive in nature.) What type of sound does the triangle make? (High pitch, long surface area and high density, free-flowing.) What type of sounds are produced on the other instruments? On the guitar, which strings produce a high pitch? A low pitch? On a specific string, how can the pitch be made higher or lower?

After experimenting with the instruments themselves, the children may begin to move creatively. Ask one or more children to produce sounds (or you may wish to do it yourself). Have the children make bent or stretched shapes when they hear high- or low-pitched sounds; change their body pose, level, pathway, or direction when they hear free-flowing or percussive sounds; and perhaps make up sequences of alternating movements to high- and low-pitched sounds. The complexity of the movement sequence depends on you and the ability level of the children. An example of a simple sequence might be to make up an 8-count movement of bends and stretches to four alternating high- and low-pitched sounds. A more complex sequence might be adding the quality

Fig. 12-4. Listen to the sounds of the instruments.

of flow to the same simple sequence. Emphasize alternating percussive (drum) and free-flowing (triangle) sounds so that the children move suddenly or percussively into a stretch position and then smoothly into a curled position. A change of levels in the sequence makes it even more complex.

CONCEPT: A person can learn to recognize movement by listening to sounds that are made.

Level: Intermediate.

Subconcept: Locomotor movements such as walking, running, skipping, and galloping may be identified by their rhymical sounds.

Materials: A drum and blindfolds.

Activities: Emphasize this lesson on sound in a unit on locomotor activities or dance. The purpose is to teach the children about weight transfer and rhythm. As the students refine their skills and awareness, use blindfolds to encourage auditory awareness.

Begin by having the children work on weight transfer skills: how to move from one foot to the opposite foot, one foot to the same foot, two feet to two feet, one foot to two feet, and two feet to one foot. Each of these movements constitutes a walk, run, leap, hop, and jump. Each is considered an even rhythm. Use a drum or clap to beat out these rhythms and ask the children to perform. How would the movements differ with fast and slow beats? Loud and soft beats? Can the children do these movements while changing their pathway, direction, amount of force, etc.?

Next, talk to the children about combination, or uneven, rhythm locomotor movements. They are the gallop, slide, and skip, which are a combination of a leap and walk (gallop), slide, and walk and hop (skip). The rhythm is uneven in that there is unequal emphasis on the beat (slow-fast, long-short, or loud-soft). Again, use a drum or clap to beat out these rhythms and ask the children to perform. Can the students execute the combination movement patterns to the imposed uneven rhythm pattern? Can the children vary their movements to include a change in direction, pathway, level, force, and time?

As the children become refined in their movement patterns and auditory skills, have them begin to experiment with their eyes closed or while blindfolded. Can they listen to a rhythm (even or uneven), identify it, and perform appropriate actions? Can the children listen to one child performing a locomotor skill without any imposed accompaniment and tell whether that child is running, walking, hopping, jumping, skipping, galloping, or sliding? Have them take turns guessing each other's movements.

CONCEPT: There is a difference between music and noise.

Level: Intermediate.

Subconcepts: (1) Music is made from combinations of vibrant sounds based on octave scales. (2) Noise is a combination of sounds that are not pleasing to the ear.

Materials: A record player and one or more of many available folk dance records that children can learn; also a whistle, bat, starting gun, and any other available object with which to make noise.

Activities: The purpose of this lesson is to teach the children that music and noise are both sounds produced by objects, but the regular sound vibrations of music are pleasing to the ear, whereas the irregular sound vibrations of noise are unpleasant.

One or more records could be used to show the children that music contains several elements which make the sounds pleasing to the ear. Music is made of combinations of vibrant sounds based on octave scales. Notes that sound well together are called *harmonious*. Music is made in a definite pattern, like a sentence. Each beat is a word. Several beats makes a measure. Several measures make a phrase. Several phrases make up a song, which compares to a sentence or story. Have the children listen to the records and help them distinguish between a measure and a phrase. Then tell them to make movement sentences to the records. Have them choose curled and stretched body poses by changing levels, body dimension, and body relationships on each new beat or at the beginning of each new measure. Have the students combine body poses in a way that flows from one position to another and make up a sequence that can be repeated—a movement sentence or dance.

Fig. 12-5. Dance to the music of your homemade instruments.

Next, talk with the children about noise. A noise is a combination of sounds that is not pleasing to the ear. The sound may be called *inharmonious*. An extremely loud sound may be a noise. A whistle may be used to show this. A sound that is flat or not in tune to the intended sound may be a noise. Boys and girls singing off key is an example. A sound that breaks continuity may be called a noise. A whistle, clap, or drumbeat used to stop or freeze the motion of the children's continuous locomotor patterns may be employed as an example. A starting gun that cracks the silence may also be called a noise and used as an example.

Music is pleasing to the ear. Noise is not pleasing to the ear. But a noise sometimes has a purpose: a whistle stops the rhythm of a game; a car horn warns a child not to cross the street.

CONCEPT: Children can make instruments, learn how to play them, and make up simple dances to their music.

Level: Intermediate.

Subconcept: The pitch of sound is affected by the surface area, density, and velocity of an object.

Materials: Homemade instruments from available materials such as flower pots, jars, and pieces of wood.

Activities: One lesson does not suffice to teach children how to make instruments, learn how to play them, and dance to the music played. It would require a series of lessons. The science and art teachers can help the children make and decorate the instruments. Those most appropriate for children to make and play are percussion and string instruments. The music teacher has already taught the students how to read music and can teach them how to play a few songs. The physical education teacher can teach the children to dance to the music. Perhaps you can have the children learn to play music and dance to a simple schottische, folk dance, or a simple chord to which square dancing could be executed. If these rhythms are too difficult for the children to learn, have them learn to beat out locomotor rhythms such as walk, run, hop, jump, gallop, or skip or rhythms for creative dance on their percussive instruments. The children could then perform appropriate steps or creative dance movements to the beat of the music. (See Fig. 12-5.)

Chapter 13

OTHER SCIENCE CONCEPTS THAT RELATE TO PHYSICAL ACTIVITIES

Although no attempt will be made to illustrate sample lessons, many additional concepts in biological, earth, and physical sciences can be integrated with physical education. Trends from projects such as the Science Curriculum Improvement Study, Science Concept Development in the Elementary School Through Inquiry Training (Science Research Associates) Project, Conceptually Oriented Program in Elementary Science Project, University of Illinois Elementary School Science Project, Elementary School Science Improvement Project, American Association for the Advancement of Science Project, and Individually Guided Education Project are highly related to physical education. Realizing that not all facts and pieces of information can be taught to children, teachers in science, physical education, and other academic disciplines are turning to conceptual learning—thus the emphasis of this book.

Children are learning through discovery and problem-solving; these methods of inquiry are now used in science and physical education, as well as in other areas of the curriculum. Rather than being told a specific answer, children are being led through a set of experiences designed to enable them to discover the answer for themselves. School experiences in science include activities dealing with classifying objects, quantifying and qualifying objects, observing, comparing objects, grouping, ranking information in order of importance, measuring, recognizing space-time relationships, convergent and divergent thinking, investigating, inventing, and planning and carrying out experiments. In physical education classes, students can classify, quantify, and qualify various balls, sporting implements, and large apparatus according to size, shape, sound, and function.

They can observe a group of different-type balls, compare those which are larger or smaller than an object of a given size, and rank the balls according to the sport for which each is appropriate. Other experiences in physical education, such as moving over, under, around, and through different objects, help teach quantification and qualification (tall, short, larger than, smaller than, etc.) to children, as well as increase their awareness of laterality, direction, and space. Many situations in physical education offer opportunities to measure. Children measure how far they can throw or kick a ball, how high they can jump, how far they can run, and the size of different fields for different sports. Space-time relationships occur often in physical education and are especially evident in rhythmical or dance experiences. Children can use convergent and divergent thinking when discussing the similarities and differences in movement skills (underhand throwing pattern—softball pitch, bowling, badminton serve) or when making up strategies for effective game playing. They can investigate new movement skills and invent new games to implement these skills. They can also plan and carry out experiments in physical education. For example, children can learn how to count their pulse rates at the carotid artery for a minute. They can then jump rope at different speeds or for varying amounts of time, after which they measure their pulse rates. Thus they will learn that the faster or longer they jump rope or do work, the faster their pulse rates, and as a result, the harder their heart has to work.

Many other experiments can be carried out regarding all the concepts in this book. Following are additional ideas concerning the integration of physical education with the biological, earth, and physical sciences.

BIOLOGICAL SCIENCES

The elementary school years provide children with many introductory experiences to the biological sciences. Concepts from biology, botany, zoology, physiology, and other biological fields may be related to physical education. During the early elementary years young students learn about plants and animals. In physical education they may create a movement sequence involving the cycle of planting, growing, and harvesting various crops or flowers with which they are familiar. As they learn about domestic pets, farm animals, and animals in the zoo, they may move like the various animals. Other movement sequences may involve the transition of a catepillar to a butterfly or a bird hatching out of an egg and gradually learning how to fly.* Even movement patterns of the earthworm or fish may be observed and then adapted in physical education. During the upper elementary years, children learn the basics of physiology through units emphasizing the various systems of the body. Line, circle, scatter, tag, and relay games can be played in physical education by adapting new words or titles to old rules of activities. For example, ''blood cell tag'' or ''systems relay'' might be innovative titles to games that children play. In this manner students are encouraged to relate classroom learning to activity-oriented lessons. They learn about the muscular, skeletal, nervous, excretory, circulatory, endocrine, respiratory, and reproductive systems in a meaningful learning situation.

In addition to learning the names of the muscles or bones of the body, children can also learn their functions. They can learn about flexion, extension, and which muscles help them perform various activities. As examples, the biceps help a person perform chin-ups; the abdominal muscles, sit-ups; the quadriceps and hamstring muscles, running and kicking movements; the triceps muscles, push-ups and throwing movements. By learning the major muscle groups and the joints over which the movements take place, the children learn how their bodies move, as well as where and why their bodies move. As they become more aware of

*The reader is directed to a series of records, *Dance-a-Story*, by Anne Barlin, RCA Victor.

laterality, direction, and other concepts of spatial relationships, children function better in their movements in physical education and are move knowledgeable in their science experiences.

EARTH SCIENCES

During their elementary school years, children are introduced to many concepts concerning the earth sciences. Several concepts from anthropology, astronomy, geology, and other earth sciences may be related to physical education. In a theme related to environmental education and ecology, children may learn about various surface textures involved in soil conservation. In physical education, surface textures may be related to the amount of traction needed to move efficiently. Various types of shoes are used in different sports for efficient movement: spikes in track, cleats in football, skates on ice, etc. Children may also learn the feel of different textures on their body (smooth, rough, coarse, etc.). For example, they love to run barefooted in the grass or walk through soft sand.

As students learn about geology, they may pretend they are on a rock hunt and jump from one rock to another or hurdle a wide crevice. They may move as if they are as heavy as a rock or use group formations to build mountains or pyramids. As children learn about water, lakes, rivers, and streams, they may wish to learn about water safety, swimming, canoeing, and other water sports. They may play the game ''Over the Creek'' or build bridges in partner activities, finding several ways to move their bodies over and under the bridge that their partner creates.

When studying related astronomy topics, the children may learn about the solar system in physical education. They may compare movements here on earth under the influence of gravity and then attempt to move as if they were weightless or walking on the moon. They can also learn the names of all the planets and their relative distances from the earth and adapt various tag games and relay races to this information. Different group settings or pyramids may also be used in an attempt to model various star formations.

Other movement experiences integrating concepts from the earth sciences with physical education may be initiated if teachers make an effort to relate the disciplines whenever meaningful.

PHYSICAL SCIENCES

Each of the preceding chapters in Part Three emphasized the integration of the physical sciences with physical education. Additional concepts concerning the physical sciences appear in elementary school science textbooks but are not emphasized to the extent that a separate chapter or section is devoted to each concept in this text. A brief description of two such concepts follows.

Buoyancy

Stated briefly, Archimedes' principle of buoyancy is that a fluid such as water exerts a buoyant force upon a body placed in it. When a body is placed in a fluid, the fluid exerts a buoyant force equal to the weight of the fluid the body displaces. Stated in terms that a child in the elementary school can more easily understand, objects that are heavy for their size will sink when placed in a liquid; objects that are light for their size will float when placed in a liquid. Many locomotor, stability, and manipulative activities can readily be utilized in physical education to teach children about buoyancy through the action of their bodies in the water. Unfortunately, however, few elementary schools have access to a swimming pool, which is the reason for brevity in this context.

Arc of pendulum

Pendulum action is used in several instances in physical education. When children swing on outdoor swings or on ropes or poles in the gym, certain laws regulate the action that occurs. Each pendulum has an arc through which it moves over a specific period of time. The time if takes for an object to swing from one end of its arc to the other depends only on the length of the pendulum. No matter how much an object weighs, if the pendulums are the same length, the objects will swing from one end of their arc to the other in the same period of time. An object will swing as far to one side of the center of its arc as to the other. These concepts can be learned through practical experiments with activities in physical education. The children may time the period of the arc. The length of the pendulum may be varied by changing the height of the swing or grasp on a swinging rope. Different weights can be compared by allowing different-sized children to swing. Thus they learn about pendular action through guided discovery, or exploration.

SELECTED REFERENCES FOR PART THREE

Barnard, J. Darrell, Stendler, Celia, and Spick, Benjamin: Science for tomorrow's world, grades 4-6, New York, 1966, The Macmillan Co., Publishers.

Barr, George: Here's why: science in sports, New York, 1965, Scholastic Book Services, Division of Scholastic Magazines, Inc.

Bloom, B. S., et al.: Taxonomy of education objectives; handbook 1, cognitive domain, New York, 1956, David McKay Co., Inc.

Blough, Glenn O., and Schwartz, Julius: Elementary science and how to teach it, New York, 1969, Holt, Rinehart & Winston, Inc.

Boyer, Madeline Haas: The teaching of elementary school physical education, New York, 1965, J. Lowell Pratt & Co.

Brandwein, Paul F., et al.: Concepts in science, grades 4-6, New York, 1966, Harcourt, Brace & World, Inc.

Broer, Marion: Efficiency of human movement, Philadelphia, 1973, W. B. Saunders, Co.

Bucher, Charles Augustus, and Reade, Evelyn M.: Physical education and health in the elementary school, New York. 1971, The Macmillan Co., Publishers.

Bunn, John: Scientific principles of coaching, Englewood Cliffs, N.J., 1964, Prentice-Hall, Inc.

Carin, Arthur A., and Sund, Robert: Teaching science through discovery, Columbus, 1970, Charles E. Merrill Publishing Co.

Corbin, Charles B.: Becoming physically educated in the elementary school, ed. 2, Philadelphia, 1976, Lea & Febiger.

Dauer, Victor Paul, and Pangrazi, Robert P.: Dynamic physical education for elementary school children, ed. 5, Minneapolis, 1975, Burgess Publishing Co.

Deason, Hilary J.: The AAAS science book list for children, Washington, D.C., 1972, American Association for the Advancement of Science.

Dunn, Lois E.: Motion; investigating science with children, vol. 4, Darien, Conn., 1968, National Science Teachers Association, Teachers Publishing Corporation.

Elliot, Margaret E., Anderson, Marion H., and LaBerge, Jeanne: Play with a purpose, ed. 3, New York, 1978, Harper & Row, Publishers.

Fabricius, Helen: Physical education for the classroom teacher, Dubuque, Iowa, William C. Brown Co.

Gallahue, David L., Werner, Peter H., and Luedke, George C.: A conceptual approach to moving and learning, New York, 1975, John Wiley & Sons, Inc.

Gilliom, Bonnie Cherp: Basic movement education for children: rationale and teaching units, Reading, Mass., 1970, Addison-Wesley Publishing Co., Inc.

Halsey, Elizabeth, and Porter, Lorena: Physical education for children, New York, 1963, Holt, Rinehart & Winston, Inc.

Hare, Elizabeth B., Joseph, Alexander, and Victor, Edward: A sourcebook for elementary science, New York, 1971, Harcourt, Brace & Jovanovich, Inc.

Humphrey, James Henry: Child learning through elementary school physical education, Dubuque, Iowa, 1974, William C. Brown Co., Publishers.

Humphrey, Louise, and Roos, Jerrold: Interpreting music through movement, Englewood Cliffs, N.J., 1964, Prentice-Hall, Inc.

Kirchner, Glen: Physical education for elementary school children, ed. 4, Dubuque, Iowa, 1978, William C. Brown Co., Publishers.

Kuslan, Louis I., and Stone, A. Harris, Teaching children science: an inquiry approach, Belmont, Calif., 1968, Wadsworth Publishing Co., Inc.

LaSalle, Dorothy: Guidance of children through physical education, New York, 1946, A. S. Barnes & Co., Inc.

Lewis, June E., and Potter, Irene: The teaching of science in the elementary school, Englewood Cliffs, N.J., 1970, Prentice-Hall, Inc.

Lockard, J. David: Sixth report of the International Clearinghouse on Science and Mathematics Curricular Developments 1968, Commission on Science Education, American Association for the Advancement of Science, Science Teaching Center, University of Maryland, 1968.

Mallinson, George G., Mallinson, Jacqueline B., and Brown, Douglas G.: Science, grades 4-6, Morristown, N.J., 1965, Silver Burdett Publishers.

Miller, Arthur George, Whitcomb, Virginia, and Cheffers, John: Physical education in the elementary school curriculum, Englewood Cliffs, N.J., 1974 Prentice-Hall, Inc.

Navarra, John Gabriel, and Zafforoni, Joseph: Today's basic science, grades 4-6, Evanston, Ill., 1965, Harper & Row, Publishers.

Neal, Charles D., and Perkins, Otho E.: Science skill test, grades 4-6, Columbus, 1966, Charles E. Merrill Books, Inc.

Nelson, Pearl Astrid: Elementary School Science Act, Englewood Cliffs, N.J., 1970, Prentice-Hall, Inc.

Plitz, Albert, and Sund, Robert: Creative teaching of science in the elementary school, Boston, 1968, Allyn and Bacon, Inc.

Rowe, Mary Budd: Teaching science as continuous inquiry, New York, 1973, McGraw-Hill Book Co.

Saffran, Rosanna B.: First book of creative rhythms, New York, 1963, Holt, Rinehart & Winston, Inc.

Schneider, Herman, and Schneider, Nina: Science in our world, grades 4-6, Boston, 1965, D. C. Heath & Co.

Schurr, Evelyn L.: Movement experiences for children, Englewood Cliffs, N.J., 1975, Prentice-Hall, Inc.

Science for children, The University of the State of New York, State Education Department, Bureau of Elementary Curriculum Development, Albany, N.Y., 1965.

Smalley, Jeanette: Physical education activities for the elementary school, Palo Alto, 1956, The National Press.

Ubell, Earl: The world of push and pull, New York, 1964, Atheneum Publishers.

Vannier, Maryhelen, and Gallahue, David L.: Teaching physical education in the elementary schools, Philadelphia, 1979, W. B. Saunders Co.

Victor, Edward, and Lerner, Marjorie S.: Readings in science education for the elementary school, New York, 1975, Macmillan, Inc.

PART FOUR

Social studies

Jump the stick.

The producers of educational materials have developed numerous attractive and effective teaching aids for social studies. Insofar as possible, we reviewed these in preparation for selecting the type and extent of learning materials to be included here. An attempt has been made to select for inclusion here only those activities in which the child's physical activity serves to extend and enhance the learning experience. Emphasis has been placed on gross motor activities, and for this reason, pantomiming and play-acting have not been included. We believe these teaching techniques could be more effectively used in relation to dramatics.

Down through the ages, in all parts of the world, people have played and danced. Using these activities as a learning medium enables children to envision how play and dance have been an integral aspect of all cultures. It provides an opportunity for them to compare and contrast the development of such cultural factors as occupations, customs, rituals, and celebrations. For example, the children will discover that their ancestors' religious ceremonies involved a great deal of physical activity. They will see how these people worshiped with their entire bodies. They will also discover how cultural festivals and celebrations centered around traditional and spontaneous games and dances. Today's children will also be able to recognize the role of physical activity in education. They will see how human survival has been dependent on the ability to obtain food, clothing, and shelter and on self-defense, Prior to automation, these were all physical activities. By actively playing and dancing, the children who lived in former cultures learned the skills and developed the strength, endurance, and agility necessary to survive. Play and dance also provided a channel for the transmission of the culture because each generation learned by participating in traditional activities. These facts are particularly evident in the section on American Indians in Chapter 16.

Not all the activities presented here are traditional movement forms. In some instances physical activities were especially created to review and reinforce specific concepts; the types of activities selected reflect as nearly as possible the nature of the people or the situations represented.

The learning activities presented in this section were selected according to the following criteria:

1. Require a minimum amount of materials and/or equipment that the children can make.
2. Provide practice and application of familiar movement skills. (This saves valuable teaching time, as well as providing the basis for .comparison of similar activities.)
3. Reflect the true characteristics and attributes of people and cultures.
4. Will have maximum carry-over value because the children enjoy them and can participate in them outside the school.
5. Bring together related content from several curricular areas (Examples are social studies, physical education, music, art, language arts, and mathematics. Selecting one culture and devoting a period of time to studying its people by integrating information from all the different subject areas is extremely effective; for example, having a Greek Day or an Indian Week.)

Additional activities may be found in the references listed at the end of Part Four. The information contained in these references will also assist you in presenting a more complete description of the origin and significance of the activities included here.

Chapter 14

LIVING AND WORKING TOGETHER

The first portion of this chapter contains activities that emphasize understanding and helping others. These are followed by concepts concerning the community and the government.

Many of the concepts included in this chapter are closely related to those of Chapter 15. In Chapter 14 the focus is on social concepts, whereas in Chapter 15 emphasis is placed on the physical environment. However, because human beings are socially interacting in this physical environment, there is no clear division between these areas. For this reason you may desire to combine some of the content as you plan learning sequences for particular groups of children.

Learning activities

Social interaction

CONCEPT: I should have an awareness of the kinds of things other people like and how they feel about things.

Levels: Beginning and intermediate.

Materials: A recording of the song "My Favorite Things" from *The Sound of Music*.

Activity: Play the song "My Favorite Things." Ask the children to name some of the favorite things mentioned in the song. Discuss why they think children like these things. Ask the children what kinds of things they like and to describe how these things make them feel. Challenge them to move through general space like their favorite things make them feel.

Variations

1. Have all the children who selected the same kinds of favorite things form a group (e.g., food, toys, pets). Ask them to discuss how these things make them feel and then to move by expressing these feelings. Have each group perform for all the other groups.

2. Divide the class into small groups. Have them discuss their favorite things and take turns moving like these things make them feel. Tell each group to select three of these favorite things and make up a story about them. Then have the group develop a movement sequence that tells this story nonverbally.

CONCEPT: I must know how to help in different kinds of emergencies.

Level: Beginning.

Subconcepts: (1) There are different kinds of emergencies, such as home accidents, fires, traffic accidents, tornadoes, and near drownings. I must know how to help myself and other people in an emergency. (2) In an emergency I must first stop and think about what I should do. (3) There are people who will help me, such as neighbors, police, firefighters, doctors, and ambulance drivers.

Materials: Cards with printed descriptions of emergency situations such as the following:

Your little brother falls off his bicycle while riding in the street. He tells you his elbow hurts and it feels like he can't straighten his arm.

You are playing in your yard one morning when you see smoke coming out of your neighbor's house. You know that no one is home there.

You are watching television while your mother is visiting the lady next door. Suddenly the announcer tells you a tornado has been sighted and a tornado watch is in effect for your town.

You are on a picnic with your family. There are children wading and swimming near a pier. Suddenly you hear one of them call for help.

Activities

1. Divide the children into groups of 2 to 5. Give each group a card with an emergency situation written on it. Instruct them to read

through the description and decide on the best course of action, then develop a movement sequence that pantomimes the action they would take. Have each group perform their sequence. Following each presentation, discuss how the situation was handled, whether this was the best course of action, and possible alternate actions.

2. Ask the children to think of emergency situations they have seen in real life or on television or have read about. Let them prepare a presentation that demonstrates how they could have helped.

CONCEPT: I can be helpful to others if I use the telephone correctly.

Level: Beginning.

Subconcepts: (1) When I dial the telephone, I must dial all seven numbers in the correct order. (2) I should be sure I have the correct number and be careful when I dial so that I do not bother people by calling the wrong number. (3) When I answer the phone, I should tell the caller who I am. (4) I should be well mannered and helpful when I use the telephone.

Materials: A simulated telephone line with two telephones, a local telephone directory, and ten cards numbered 0 through 9. The line and telephones can be constructed by making a hole in the bottom of two paper cups or two small tin cans. One end of the string is put through each can and a button tied to the end of the string to keep it securely fastened.

Activities: Fasten the cards to the floor in a circle approximately 2 meters in diameter. The cards should be in the same position as the numbers on the telephone dial. Have 1 child stand beside each card, facing counterclockwise. Have 2 children stand in the center of the circle. Give these 2 children the telephones. Assist one of them in looking up the other child's telephone number in the directory. Write this number on the blackboard.

Have the child who looked up the number dial it. To do this he stands beside the card containing the first digit in the telephone number. For example, if the number is 325-6841, the child who is dialing, or the "caller," would stand beside the number 3. Then all the children forming the dial hop three steps clockwise, and hop three steps back to place. Next, the caller stands beside the number 2 and the children hop two steps clockwise and two steps back to place. This continues until all seven digits have been dialed. When the children have returned to their places after dialing the last digit in the telephone number, they shout "Ring, ring, ring."

The child who has been called answers the phone by saying "Jones residence, Susan speaking." The 2 children then proceed to have a conversation. After they hang up, have these two exchanges places with 2 other children in the circle and repeat the activity.

Variations

1. Have the caller ask to speak to the "answerers"—mother, father, brother, sister, or grandparent. Instruct the child who answers to say "Just a minute please," then run to get the person being called. Repeat this activity and have the answerer just yell for the person or drop the phone without saying anything to the caller. Discuss the contrast between these situations and the previous one.

2. Have the answerer take a message for someone who is to return the call.

3. Have the children make emergency calls to various people.

4. Have the children jump, walk, slide, or skip the number of steps being dialed.

5. Have the caller use a push-button phone. Arrange the children as shown in Fig. 14-1. Have the child who is dialing move among the numbers and touch the top of each child's head. When a digit is touched, that child pretends he is the button on the tele-

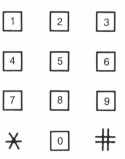

Fig. 14-1. Formation for pushbutton phone game.

phone: he crouches down and jumps back up to a standing position.

CONCEPT: It is necessary for each person to obey the rules for everyone to have fun and play safely.

Level: Beginning.

Materials: A playground ball.

Activities: Explain to the children that there are rules which must be followed in order for people to have fun playing together and to prevent accidents. Then take them out to the playground.

1. Have 2 children play together, cooperatively rolling and bouncing the ball to each other. Then have them fight over the ball; when one of the children gains possession, have him run off with the ball. Discuss how the 2 children were able to play together in the first instance, but how the game was ruined in the second instance because the children did not follow the rule of taking turns.

2. Take the children on a tour of the playground. Have them take turns playing on the various pieces of equipment, then have them all try to get on one piece. Discuss how crowding occurs and the ways in which it may lead to someone being hurt.

3. Have 3 or 4 children line up, ready to take turns climbing on a piece of equipment. Then have them swiftly take their turn on the equipment and go to the end of the line. Point out how smoothly the traffic flows because each person is obeying the rule of taking turns. Have the children line up again and this time have them demonstrate what happens when they crowd and push. Discuss how this ruins everyone's fun and may also cause accidents.

4. Walk around the playground, pointing out to the children how various areas have been designated for certain purposes (i.e., softball diamond, free play area, marked blacktop area, challenge course). Explain how these areas have been laid out so that the children can all play safely. Discuss how failing to obey the rules relative to playing in the appropriate area interrupts the play of others and may cause someone to be hurt.

CONCEPT: A community gradually grows and changes.

Level: Intermediate.

Materials: Pictures of the downtown area of the city at different periods in its history, string laid out on the floor or playground to form the original streets of the city, and signs.

Activities: Select children to represent the principal buildings in the downtown area of the city, as shown in Fig. 14-2. Signs for each of the children help to add the dimension of realism. Have the children take their places one by one along the streets. Discuss the functions served by each of the buildings. Point out how these changed over the years. As old buildings were torn down and replaced, have new buildings take the place of old ones. If the buildings are very large, such as those constructed in shopping centers, several children may group together to form them.

Discuss the factors that determined where certain buildings were located (i.e., proximity to a railroad depot, on the top of a hill, close to another key building).

Variation: Add the automobile. Have several children imitate the movements of automobiles converging to the downtown area, with the drivers making several stops at different buildings. Show the effect of the construction of shopping centers by having about half the "cars" going to one or more of these centers.

Community safety

CONCEPT: Traffic signals tell us when to move and when to stand still.

Level: Beginning.

Subconcepts: (1) Red tells us to stop. (2) Green tells us to go.

Materials: A piece of red cardboard approximately 8½ × 11 inches, a piece of green cardboard the same size, or a cardboard traffic signal (Fig. 14-3). This may be constructed by using a rectangular cardboard box approximately 15 × 30 centimeters. Cover the box with yellow construction paper. Paste red circles near the top of the front and back of the box and green circles near the bottom of both sides. Cut a small hole in the bottom of the box and insert a broom handle or a dowel rod, cut to a length of approximately 1 meter. Secure this

Fig. 14-2. Major buildings of a downtown area.

Fig. 14-3. Simulated traffic signal.

handle at the top by driving a tack through the box into the end of the stick.

Activities: Have the children line up behind the starting line. Show them the red and green cards. Tell them to run toward the goal line when you hold up the green card and to stop as quickly as possible when you hold up the red one. After all the children have crossed the goal line, have them line up behind it and run back toward the starting line when the signal is given. Encourage the children to stop as quickly as possible when the red signal appears.

Variations

1. Repeat the previous activity but use the cardboard traffic signal. Instruct the children to run when the green signal is turned to face them and to quickly stop when the red signal is facing them.

2. *Red light, green light.* Choose one child to be the police officer. This child stands near the goal line with his back to the class. Have the rest of the children line up behind the starting line. When the police officer calls out "Green light," the children cross over the starting line and cautiously move toward the goal line. When the police officer calls

Fig. 14-4. Children forming a traffic signal and moving through an intersection.

out "Red light," he quickly turns to face the children. If he sees any child moving, this child must go back to the starting line. The first one to cross the goal line becomes the traffic police officer for the next game.

CONCEPT: To cross the street safely, I must obey the traffic signals and walk in the pedestrian lanes.

Level: Beginning.

Subconcepts: (1) I can cross the street when the red light tells the cars to stop. (2) I must not try to cross the street when the green light is telling the cars to go.

Materials: A traffic intersection may be formed in the classroom by arranging the desks or by drawing lines on the floor. On the playground the lines may be marked in the dirt, painted on the pavement, or formed by ropes or string (Fig. 14-4). Four sashes, shirts, or pinnies (the type used to designate team membership in physical education activities), two red and two green, and a whistle are also needed.

Activities: Designate 4 children to be the traffic signal, 4 to be cars, 1 to be the police officer, and the rest to be pedestrians. Have 2 of the children who are to be the signal wear green sashes and the other 2 wear red. These 4 children stand back to back, forming a square in the center of the intersection. The 4 children who are the cars get down on their hands and knees in the places designated in Fig. 14-4. The police officer stands near one corner of the intersection, with the pedestrians on the corner.

When everyone is in position, the police officer blows a whistle. The cars facing the green light proceed cautiously through the intersection, and the pedestrians walk across between the crosswalk lines. When everyone is safely across, the traffic signal makes a quarter turn to the right, allowing the other cars to move and the pedestrians to cross in the other directions. If anyone attempts to cross against the signal or walk outside the pedestrian lane, the police officer blows the whistle and takes him out of the game.

Have the children change roles often.

Variations

1. Place groups of pedestrians on all the corners and add more cars.
2. Use a cardboard traffic signal instead of having the children form the signal.

3. Add some children who pretend to be riding bicycles.
4. Add another intersection or modify the existing one so that there are YIELD signs on two of the corners.

CONCEPT: Signs tell us what to do to move safely along streets and highways.

Level: Beginning.

Subconcepts: (1) STOP signs are red; they tell us to stop and look both ways before crossing the street. (2) YIELD signs tell us we must slow down, and if someone is coming along the other road, we must wait for them to pass. (3) RAILROAD CROSSING signs form an X. They tell us to slow down, listen, and look up and down the railroad track before crossing. (4) Other traffic signs also give us important messages that help us drive safely.

Materials: Cardboard signs made in the shape and color of traffic signs; a roadway laid out in the classroom, hallway, gym, or on the playground (Fig. 14-5).

Activities: Have the children line up single file or with partners behind the traffic signal. Tell them that when the traffic signal turns green, they are to begin walking along the roadway. Lead the children, pausing at each sign to read it aloud and discuss its message. Then have the children practice ''driving'' along the roadway. Have a follow-up discussion in which the safety rules of the school are reviewed and related to comparable traffic regulations.

Variations

1. Have the children execute different locomotor movements between each of the signs. (For example, *run* from the DO NOT PASS sign to the ONE WAY sign, *skip* along the curve, *jump* from the YIELD sign to the

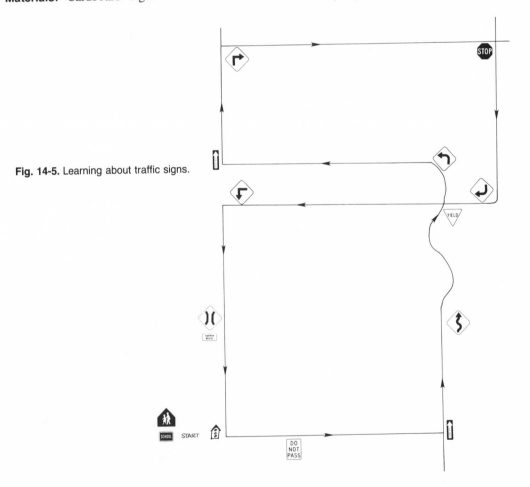

Fig. 14-5. Learning about traffic signs.

NO LEFT TURN sign, then *hop* to the DO NOT ENTER sign, *slide* to the STOP sign, *gallop* back to the traffic signal.)

2. Have the children execute a stunt or an exercise at each of the signs. Example of stunts that could be used follow:

Sign	Stunt
DO NOT PASS	Bear Walk
ONE WAY	Rabbit Jump
CURVE	Lame Puppy Walk
RAILROAD CROSSING	Duck Walk
YIELD	Inch Worm
NO LEFT TURN	Frog Hop
DO NOT ENTER	Crab Walk
STOP	Seal Walk

Our government

CONCEPT: Each branch of the federal government has a specific responsibility, or function.

Level: Intermediate.

Subconcepts: (1) The legislative branch (Congress) makes the laws. This branch consists of the Senate and the House of Representatives. (2) The judicial branch interprets the laws. This branch is the Supreme Court. (3) The executive branch enforces the laws. This is the President.

Materials: Jump ropes and sets of six cards with the following words printed on them:

Executive	Enforces
Legislative	Makes laws
Judicial	Interprets

Activities: Make circles on the floor with the jump ropes. Place a set of six cards inside each circle. Divide the class into groups containing no more than 5 children. Tell each group to stand behind a line approximately 3 meters from their circle. Have one of the children in each group hop to the circle and attempt to select two cards that go together. When the child is successful, have him hold up the pair of cards to be checked, then put them back in the

Fig. 14-6. Grid game for studying about the three branches of government.

circle and hop back to his group. Continue until all the children have had a turn.

Variations

1. Place in the circle the three cards that state the functions of the branches of the federal government. Hold up one of the cards that states the name of a branch. Have the first child in each group hop to the circle and pick up the card which indicates the function of that branch.
2. Add cards with the names of the persons currently holding office in each branch (i.e., the name of the president, names of members of the Senate and House of Representatives, names of Supreme Court Justices). Require the children to match all three related cards.
3. Use cards with the names and functions of offices on the local and/or state level (i.e., Mayor, City Council, Governor, State Legislators).
4. Vary the locomotor movements used to progress to the circle and back (i.e., jump, skip, run).

CONCEPT: Facts relative to the three branches of the federal government are reviewed.

Level: Intermediate.

Materials: A grid drawn on heavy plastic or sets of cards fastened to the floor to form a grid (Fig. 14-6); beanbags.

Activities: Have the children stand behind a line and take turns tossing a beanbag into the grid. When the child's beanbag lands in the square, he states as many facts as possible about that aspect of the government. For example, if the beanbag lands on the square labeled *House,* the child might answer:

Elected
Elected every two years
Number based on population
Names of different congressmen

If the child's beanbag lands on *Supreme Court,* the child could answer:

Appointed by the President
Serves as long as physically able
Nine members
Names of Supreme Court justices

Children are awarded 1 point for each correct answer. The child with the most points after a predetermined number of turns is declared the winner.

Chapter 15

OUR HOME, THE EARTH

There is a critical need for children to feel a personal relationship with their physical environment. Just as their physical bodies provide a home for their inner beings, the earth provides a home for their bodies.

The activities in this chapter are designed to help children see the world in relation to themselves. They are introduced to this way of thinking by envisioning their bodies as physical objects that have a relationship to all other objects and spaces. After this they identify the major environmental directions—north, south, east, and west—by focusing on where these directions are located in relation to their bodies. The concept of direction is then extended to mapping, and the child's relationship to the physical features is depicted on maps.

The activities in the section on nature are designed to assist the children in feeling closer to their natural environment and to stimulate their desire to preserve and protect it. The last section is devoted to concepts concerning transportation. By relating these concepts to those given earlier in the chapter, the children will be able to see how technology has evolved and also how its effects must be controlled to preserve the natural environment.

Learning activities

Environmental directions

CONCEPT: My body is a physical object that occupies space.

Level: Beginning.

Subconcepts: (1) I have a personal space that moves with me wherever I go. (2) As I move about from place to place, I move through general space.

Materials: None.

Activities

Personal space: Have the children scatter out around the room and sit down on the floor. Use a variety of verbal cues to guide their exploration of their personal space. (See Fig. 15-1.) Examples follow:

Move one hand all around your body.
Move it about your head.
Move it in front of you, behind you.
Move it around your legs and your feet. Now move both hands all around your body, in front of you, to the side, in back of you.
Reach as high as you can.
What must you do to reach higher? That's right, let's all stand up and reach way up.
Reach as high as you can s-t-r-e-t-c-h.
Now reach low. Reach clear down to the floor. Now reach high again.
This time I want you to reach into all the spaces clear around your body. Let's start up high and reach all around you. Let your hands touch all the space around your shoulders, your chest, your tummy, your seat, your legs, and clear down around your feet.

Explain to the children that the space they have just explored has a name. It is called personal space.

The concept of the size of their personal space may be reinforced by having them pretend they are holding a big paint brush and are painting the inside of their personal space.

General space: Tell the children there is another kind of space. It is called "general space." Explain that general space is all the empty space in the room. It is all the space that is not being used by another person or an object. Have the children point to some of the empty space.

Challenge them to explore general space by moving into all parts of the room. Caution them

Fig. 15-1. Exploring my personal space.

to remember that they must stay out of everyone else's personal space. Have the children move about slowly at first, then gradually increase the tempo of their movements as they evidence the ability to perceive empty spaces and to control their movements.

CONCEPT: I can move up and down, forward, backward, and sideward.

Level: Beginning.

Subconcepts: (1) Upward is above me. (2) Downward is below me. (3) Forward is in front of me. (4) Backward is behind me. (5) Sideward is to my right or left side.

Materials: None, except that no. 6 requires making a set of cards.

Activities

1. Have the children scatter out around the room and find a personal space. Guide their exploration of the spatial dimensions by giving them verbal instructions as follows:

    Point to something that is above you.
    Point to something below you.
    Point up. Point down.
    Sit down. Stand up.

Point to the right with your right hand.
Point to the left with your left hand.

2. Instruct the children to move in the direction you point. Use your whole arm to point as you call out the directions up, down, forward, backward, to the side, to the other side. Slowly change from one direction to the other at first, then gradually increase the speed of the changes.

3. Instruct the children to move in the different directions as you call them out.

4. Have the children execute different locomotor movements in each of the directions (i.e., hop forward, jump backward, slide sideward).

5. Have the children move through general space, changing directions each time you clap or beat the drum.

6. *Direction game.* Use four sets of six to eight cards, each set a different color. On the cards are written directions concerning how the children are to move (e.g., Forward 4 steps, Backward 2 steps, Forward 1 step, Backward 3 steps). The directions on each set of cards are the same. *Instructions:* Di-

vide the children into four teams. Name each team the color of one set of cards. Have the teams line up at the end of the playing area in relay formation. Shuffle all the cards together. Take a card from the top of the pile. Call out the color of the team that is to move and read the directions from the card. Each child begins beside the child who moved just before him. The team that reaches the goal line first wins. Vary the game by adding different locomotor movements to the directions (e.g., Hop forward 4 steps, Jump backward 2 steps, Skip forward 3 steps, etc.).

CONCEPT: The location of the directions north, south, east, and west can be learned in relation to one's own body.

Level: Beginning.

Materials: Four signs with the directions North, South, East, and West written on them.

Activities

1. Place one of the direction cards on each wall. Have the children identify objects and surfaces located in each of the different directions.
2. Have the children stand facing north. Ask them to point to the north. Tell them to raise both arms straight out to the side. Ask them what direction their right arm is pointing (east) and what direction their left arm is pointing (west). Have them put their right arm straight out in front of their body and their left arm straight back. Ask them in what directions their right and left arms are pointing.
3. Ask the children to face the direction where the sun rises, then the direction where the sun sets.
4. Have the children execute various locomotor movements while moving in different directions (e.g., walk north, leap south, jump west, skip east).
5. Have the children continue to face in one direction such as north while they move in another direction (e.g., if they move south, they will be moving backward; if they move east or west, they will be moving sideward). Vary this activity (and no. 4) by specifying both the direction and the locomotor movement (e.g., hop south, slide west, jump east).

Map and globe skills

CONCEPT: A map is a representation of a real place.

Level: Beginning.

Subconcepts: (1) A map has the same shape as the place it represents. (2) Lines are used to form the shape of a map.

Materials: Several long jump ropes, a map of the school district and the city, and signs.

Activities

1. Lay the jump ropes on the floor in the shape of the room. Point out how the shape is the same as that of the room, but the size is different. Have the children walk around the boundary formed by the ropes.
2. Have the children use wooden blocks to construct representations of the objects located within the room. Tell them to place their blocks inside the rope boundaries in the same relative positions as the objects within the room.
3. Take the children on a tour of the playground, then have them map the playground in the same way they mapped the schoolroom. Rather than use the blocks to represent the structure on the playground, you can have the children stand in the relative positions and use their bodies to illustrate the shape of the structures.
4. Take the children on a walk around a block near the school. Lay out jump ropes on the floor to simulate the street around the block. Designate certain children to represent various structures or features within the block. Have these children stand inside the jump ropes in the relative positions to the actual structures within the block. Discuss what each child represents.
5. Mark the location of each child's residence on a map of the school district. Use ropes or string to make an outline of the map on the floor. Have each child stand on the map in the relative location of his residence. Form a group of from 3 to 5 children who live within the same area. Point out that all live in the same neighborhood. Have the children in each group decide on a stunt or exercise they like to do. Make a plan of how the groups can rotate from one neighborhood to the next, visiting each one in turn.

Ask the children to select one child to serve as the neighborhood leader. This child remains in his own neighborhood and leads each group in the stunt or exercise as they visit his location.

6. Assist the children in locating on a city map the position of important sites such as the Courthouse, City Hall, Fire Stations, Police Stations, Libraries, Post Offices, and Parks and Recreation Centers. Assign each child to be one of the sites and give each a sign to wear, identifying the name and address of the site. Pick out three or four of the main facilities such as the Courthouse, City Hall, main Library, and main Post Office. Have the children who represent these sites assume a position within the room that simulates the location of that site on the map. Next, have the children who are branch libraries or post offices take their places. Add the remaining sites.

Interest may be added by briefly discussing what type of facilities are contained within each location. Each child could be assisted in locating where he lives in relation to certain sites. Certain kinds of facilities, such as police stations, fire stations, or parks, could be used as stations for an exercise circuit such as the one described in no. 5.

CONCEPT: North is always at the top of a map or globe, and south is always at the bottom.

Level: Intermediate.

Materials: A map mounted on the north wall of the room.

Activities

1. Have the children stand in a scattered formation facing the map. Point out that the top of the map is north and the bottom corresponds to south. Tell the children to raise both arms overhead. Discuss the fact that the top of their body is pointing in the same direction as the top of the map and this is designated as north. Point out that their feet are at the bottom and this is comparable to south on the map. Take the map off the wall and lay it on the floor. Point out that the map is now in the same position as when it is laid on the

children's desks. Ask the children to lie down. Point out the similarity between the position of their body and that of the map. Review the concept that the top of their body is still comparable to the top of the map and this is north.

Have the children sit up. Discuss the fact that they can lay the map in any position, but the top of the drawing on the map always corresponds to north.

3. Remove an old world globe from the stand (or mark the outlines of continents on a rubber ball). Point out that the directions on the glove are the same as those on the map. Roll the globe across the floor. Show the children that no matter how the globe turns, the directions of the drawings on the globe remain the same. Have the children execute forward and backward rolls to simulate the movements of the globe. Point out that no matter how they roll, the structure of their bodies always remains the same.

CONCEPT: The lines, colors, and symbols on a map represent the location of real rivers, mountains, roads, cities, and recreation areas.

Level: Intermediate.

Materials: Several copies of a map of a county, state, region, or country and several long jump ropes laid out on the floor in the shape of the map.

Activities: Divide the class into groups. Assign each group a certain kind of feature represented on the map (e.g., a mountain range, a river, a lake, roads, railroads, recreation areas). In a large class additional children may be assigned to represent certain cities, campgrounds, airports, etc.

Give each group a copy of the map. Tell them they are to study the location and characteristics of their assigned area and then decide how they can use their bodies to represent these features (Fig. 15-2). When the groups are ready, have them assume their positions in an area in the room. Have the natural features such as mountains, rivers, or lakes take their places first. Next, have the roads and railroads take their places. Discuss how the roads and railroads had to be laid out in relation to the natural features. Then have the recreation areas

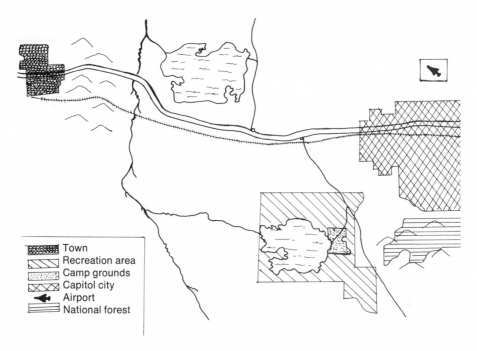

Town
Recreation area
Camp grounds
Capitol city
Airport
National forest

Fig. 15-2. Features on a map that can be formed by the children's bodies.

assume their places. Discuss the reasons these areas have been designated as recreation areas for public use. Finally, have the cities, towns, airports, etc. take their places. Discuss the relationship of these to each other and the preceding features.

Variations: Use maps that depict population, climate, or locations of natural resources. Have the groups develop movement sequences that portray these features.

CONCEPT: Children can learn to identify specific points on a map.

Level: Intermediate.

Materials: Several copies of a map of a county, state, region, or country, several sets of 3 × 5 cards with the name of a city or landmark written on each, and several dry marks.

Activities: Mount the maps on the wall at the end of the playing area. Divide the class into groups containing not more than 5 children. Have the groups line up in relay formation behind the starting line. Place a set of cards on the floor in front of each map. Give the first child in each group a dry mark. Tell the children that when you give a starting signal, the first child

in each line is to run to the pile of cards, pick up one, locate the city or landmark on the map, and draw a circle around it. This player then runs back to his group, bringing his card with him. He hands the dry mark to the next child in line, who repeats the activity. When all the students have had a turn, take the maps off the wall and give them to the group. Have them check for accuracy.

Give each group another set of cards and let them work together to locate the features named on the cards.

CONCEPT: A map tells me in what direction to move and where to locate certain places.

Level: Intermediate.

Materials: A treasure map for each group of children, a treasure for each group, and an area in the gym or on the playground with station markers at the locations indicated on the map (Figs. 17-1 and 17-11).

Activities: Divide the class into five groups. Give each group a treasure map mounted on the color of paper that specifies the team color. Have the groups locate the stations marked with their color and explain that this is where they are to begin. Tell them to follow the instructions on their treasure map, progressing until they locate their treasure. For a full description of treasure map activities, see the Mexico treasure hunt, pp. 232 and 233.

CONCEPT: The globe is divided by two sets of imaginary lines around the earth's surface; one set runs east and west, the other north and south.

Level: Intermediate.

Subconcepts: (1) Latitude is distances north or south of the equator, measured in degrees, and forming lines running around the earth parallel to the equator. (2) Longitude is distances east or west on the earth's surface, measured in degrees, and forming lines running from the north to the south pole.

Materials: None.

Activities: Have 5 children join hands and make a line facing north. Tell them they are the equator. Divide the rest of the class into groups containing 5 children. Have the groups make lines in front of and behind the equator (Fig. 15-3). The number of children in the lines can be increased or decreased, but all the lines should have an equal number of children. Explain to the students that they are forming lines which resemble latitude. Tell them all to drop hands, turn facing west, and join hands with the children who are now next to them. Explain that the lines they now form resemble longitude.

Select two students who are not in the lines to be an "It" and a "runner." Tell them they may run around and between the lines, but they cannot break through or duck under the joined hands. Explain that when you call out "Latitude," they are to drop hands and turn back to their original positions, forming new pathways through which It may pursue the runner. Call our "Latitude" and "Longitude" frequently. When It tags the runner, have them exchange places with 2 of the children in the lines.

CONCEPTS: The land area of the United States is divided into fifty states, and each state has a headquarters, which is called a capital.

Level: Intermediate.

Materials: A large outline map of the United States drawn on the floor or on the playground (p. 4).

Activities: Challenge the children to indicate where certain states and capitals are located by placing different body parts on the location specified or by using different locomotor movements to travel from one location to another. Examples follow:

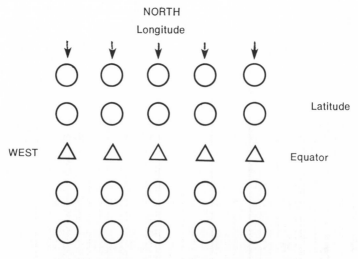

Fig. 15-3. Formation for longitude and latitude game.

Can you put one foot in Alabama and the other foot in Texas?

Can you put your left knee on Baton Rouge and your right elbow in Tallahassee?

Can you hop from Kansas to Connecticut, naming each you cross?''

Can you jump on each state capital between California and Iowa, naming the capital when you land on it?''

Can you slide from the Atlantic Ocean to the Pacific Ocean, naming each state you cross?

Can you jump into each state between Mexico and Canada, naming the state as you land on it?

Variations

1. Make a set of task cards with the previous activities and several others stated on separate cards. Have one child read the cards to one or more other children while they practice completing the task.
2. Have the children make up problems and develop task cards.

CONCEPT: The United States is divided into regions.

Level: Intermediate.

Materials: An old sheet or large piece of plastic with an outline map of one of the regions of the United States drawn on it, cards with the names of the states within this region printed on them, and cards with the names of body parts written on them (e.g., hand, foot, elbow, knee, forehead).

Activities: Have a child pick the name of a state from one bag and the name of a body part from another. Designate 1 to 5 other children to take turns placing their body parts in the state listed on the card. Continue until each child has four or five body parts on the map.

Variations

1. Make an outline map of the countries with-

in a certain area of the children's home state. Substitute cards with the names of the counties and the county seats.

2. Make an outline map of the continent and cards with the names of countries and major cities.

CONCEPT: Each of the states has a capital city.

Level: Intermediate.

Materials: A playground ball.

Activities

1. Have the group form a large circle with 1 child in the center, who calls out the name of a state and bounce-passes the ball to one of the children forming the circle. That child must call out the capital of the state as the ball is caught. If unable to answer correctly by the time the ball reaches him, he must change places with the child in the center.
2. Give each child forming the circle the name of a state capital. The child in the center of the circle calls out the name of a state and tosses the ball up in the air. The child who is the capital of that state must catch the ball before it has bounced more than once.
3. Give each child in the class the name of a state. Tell the children to scatter out on the playground and find a large personal space. Instruct them to draw a circle approximately 0.75 meter in diameter around their feet. One child is ''It.'' He stands with his back to the rest of the class and calls out the names of two states. The 2 children who are those states must change places, and it tries to get into one of the circles. Whoever is left out becomes it. Also try the following variations:

   a. Have It call out several states.

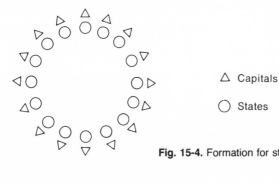

△ Capitals

○ States

Fig. 15-4. Formation for states and capitals game.

b. Use the names of countries, counties, or cities.

4. Give half the class names of states and the other half names of capitals. Have the class make a large double circle with the states on the inside and the capitals on the outside (Fig. 15-4). Instruct the children forming the inside circle to walk clockwise and those forming the outside circle to walk counterclockwise. On signal the children on the outside (the capitals) scatter and the children on the inside try to locate and tag their capital.

CONCEPT: There are several large waterways in the United States.

Level: Intermediate.

Materials: Two or more large maps of the United States and two or more set of cards containing the names of waterways (i.e., Mississippi, Missouri, Columbia, St. Lawrence, Ohio).

Activities: Fasten the maps to the wall at one end of the playing area. Divide the class into groups containing no more than 5 children. Have each group line up at the end of the playing area opposite the map. Give each child a card. Have the children take turns running to the map and attaching their card to the correct location of the waterway.

Variations

1. Let the children have a relay race, and the team finishing first with all the cards in the correct place is declared the winner.
2. Use cards containing the names of states, capitals, lakes, mountains, parks, etc.

Nature

CONCEPT: The world of nature is filled with sounds.

Level: Beginning.

Subconcepts: (1) There are sounds of living things. (2) There are sounds of weather. (3) There are sounds of the earth and the sea.

Materials: A recording of natural sounds and pictures of scenes from nature.

Activities: Play a recording of certain kinds of sounds from nature, such as those that are low, soft, and melodious. Ask the children to identify the source of these sounds, then ask them how these sounds make them feel. Encourage the students to convey their feelings by moving their hands and upper body. Have them

extend the range of their movements by using their whole body and moving through general space.

Play a recording of contrasting sounds such as loud, harsh, and jarring. Challenge the children to describe the source of these sounds and the feeling states they evoke. Have them respond in movement.

Ask the children to name and describe different sounds of nature and have the group respond in movement. Some of the sounds that may be named follow:

Rain—quiet or hard	A waterfall
Wind—a breeze or a gale	A rock rolling down a ledge
Thunder	Animal or bird sounds
Waves	

Encourage the students to describe the characteristics and qualities of the sound to suggest ways of moving that express these.

CONCEPT: We associate different tastes and smells with different seasons.

Level: Beginning.

Materials: Properties associated with the four seasons of the year.

Activities: Encourage the children to think about how nature enriches their sensory world by providing stimulus sources associated with each of the seasons. Extend the learning experiences by having the students describe the feelings involved in terms of different tastes and smells, then responding in movement to these feeling states. Instruct the older children to relate similar and contrasting sensations by developing and performing a sequence of movements that portray these factors. Examples of some stimulus sources follow:

- *Autumn*—fruits, vegetables, and nuts produced locally; burning leaves (if legal)
- *Winter*—fruit and vegetables that are easy to preserve or readily available commercially, such as apples, oranges, potatoes, carrots, celery, coconuts, and peanuts; spices commonly used in cooking, such as cinnamon, nutmeg, sage, oregano, and chili powder; the smell of pine boughs and of logs burning in a fireplace
- *Spring*—edible seeds such as sunflowers seeds and peanuts; Easter eggs and candy; the smell of spring flowers and the earth after a spring shower
- *Summer*—fresh vegetables and fruits; the smell of

summer flowers and the smoke from a charcoal broiler

The sensory sources can be related to holidays and special events that have special significance for the children, such as Thanksgiving, Christmas, and Easter.

CONCEPT: A house is a safe, warm place that provides protection.

Level: Beginning.

Materials: Pictures of animal and human houses.

Activities: Discuss with the children how they feel when they are safe, warm, secure, and cozy. Ask them to describe how they feel when they are unsafe, lost, or afraid. Have the students portray these feelings in movement.

Instruct 12 children to form the walls and roof of a house. Ask 3 others to go inside the house; give them a game or some toys and tell them to play with each other. Have 3 other students stand outside the house. Tell the class you are going to call out different weather conditions and the children inside and outside the house are to move the way they would feel. Some of the weather conditions you may use follow:

A gentle rain	Snowing
Raining very hard	The hot sun beating down
A gentle wind	Nightfall and darkness
Wind blowing hard	

Ask the students on the outside how they felt and moved under each of these conditions. Stop after each one and have those who were on the inside describe and demonstrate their feelings. Discuss the contrast and how the house seemed to protect the children on the inside and insulate them from the elements of nature.

Show the class pictures of different kinds of animal houses. Talk about the safety factors in each and their protective qualities. Have some of the children simulate the structure of these animal houses and others imitate the feelings and behavior of the animals inside and outside of the houses.

CONCEPT: Animals have physical characteristics that help them survive in their natural environment.

Level: Beginning and intermediate.

Materials: Pictures of animals illustrating some of the characteristics that help animals survive.

Activities: Ask the children to describe some of the characteristics of animals that help them to survive in their environment. List them on the board:

Ability to run fast	Sharp claws and teeth
Ability to climb trees	Ability to live long
Ability to swim	periods without water
Ability to dig	Physical size

Beside each characteristic, write the names of the animals that have these traits.

Set up an obstacle course in the gym or on the playground, in which the children move like some of the animals just listed. Place pictures of the animals along the route the children are to follow. Fig. 15-5 illustrates how the route could be arranged.

The stunts listed in Fig. 15-5 are appropriate for the primary grades. On the intermediate level you may substitute the Frog Jump, Crab Walk, Measuring Worm, and Kangaroo Jump for the first four stunts in the diagram. The Seal Walk and the Antelope Run* can be used with both levels.

When the children have finished moving through the obstacle course, discuss the char-

---

*Antelope Run is simply running as fast as you can. Descriptions of all the other stunts may be found in the Appendix.

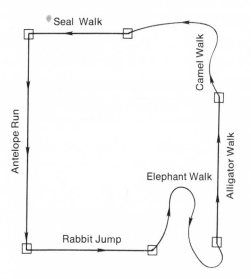

Fig. 15-5. Obstacle course involving stunts.

acteristics of the animals they imitated and how these characteristics help the animals to survive.

CONCEPT: It is essential to harvest some game animals, but this must be carefully controlled.

Level: Intermediate.

Subconcepts: (1) Animals can be hunted only during certain times of the year. (2) Game preserves are essential for the protection of wildlife.

Materials: Jump ropes or string.

Activities

The hunter and the hunted. Lay the ropes or string on the ground to mark off the areas for the river and the two game preserves (Fig. 15-6). Select 1 child to be the hunter (the ''It''). Divide the class into two equal groups and assign one group to each game preserve. Have the hunter stand midway between the game preserves. Explain that the children in the game preserve are animals that will be hunted. The rules of the game follow: The hunter calls out the names of different months. While he is calling out any of the months other than October or November, the game animals may freely roam anywhere in the playing area. But when the hunter calls out either ''October'' or ''November,'' the animals must move across the open area *and* the river and run into the game preserve on the other side. The hunter attempts to tag the children as they cross the area. Anyone who is tagged becomes It and must assist the hunter in catching the rest of the animals. Play continues until all the children are caught. The last one caught begomes the hunter at the beginning of the next game.

It may be necessary to establish outside

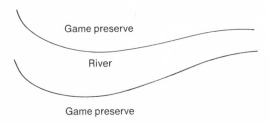

Fig. 15-6. Playing area for the game the hunter and the hunted.

boundaries so that children must stay within a certain area.

CONCEPT: Natural forces are continually working to change the environment.

Level: Intermediate.

Materials: Pictures of a volcano, glacier, and forest or range fire.

Activities: Have the children read about the cause, characteristics, and effects of the forces listed, as well as others such as earthquakes and erosion.

Divide the class into groups of no more than 5 children. Tell each group to select one of the natural forces and discuss what they have learned about it. Have each group develop a movement sequence based on actions suggested by some aspect of the natural force they selected. Ask each group to perform their sequence. Use the performances as the basis for discussing how each of these forces changes the environment.

CONCEPT: The natural environment is clean and healthy, and a polluted environment is unhealthy.

Level: Intermediate.

Materials: A recording of lively, happy music and sad, depressing music; pictures of healthy animals in a clean environment and sick or dead creatures in a polluted environment.

Activities: Show the children the pictures portraying the effects of pollution. Discuss what happens to the plants and animals when the area becomes polluted.

Play the lively, cheerful music. Relate the sound of the music to the feelings and behavior of healthy, happy animals, birds, fish, etc. Other sources of imagery you can suggest are a clear, free-flowing stream; a gentle, refreshing breeze; and a clean, floating snowflake.

Play the sad, depressing music. Ask the children to describe how that music makes them feel and to relate these feelings to the condition of creatures that must try to survive in a polluted environment.

Challenge the children to move like creatures who live in each type of environment.

Variations

1. Challenge the children to think of words that describe aspects of a clean environment

and a polluted one. Have them move like these words make them feel.

2. Ask the children to write a poem or a short story about some aspect of the effects of pollution. Then have them develop a movement sequence that portrays the feeling states suggested in what they have written.
3. Have the children draw pictures illustrating the effects of pollution. Ask them to express in movement what they have drawn.

Machines and transportation

CONCEPT: We use many different kinds of transportation.

Level: Beginning.
Subconcepts: (1) Some machines are used to move us from plact to place (car, bus, train, plane). (2) Some machines move the things we use (truck, train, plane, boat).
Materials: Pictures of different kinds of machines used in transportation and recordings of sounds made by planes, trains, and boats.

Activities

1. Ask the children how they got to school (walked, rode in car or bus). Select one of the children who walks to school to lead the class in follow the leader, simulating the way he walks to school. Give verbal cues to assist the children in recalling how he moves (i.e., turning corners, stopping before crossing the street, moving fast and slow, skipping). Have the children move through general space by using the same kinds of movements.

   Select one of the children who rode to school in a car. Ask the child to describe the movement of the car (directions in which it moved, stopping and starting, speed). Challenge the children to move through general space by imitating the different movements and sounds made by the car.

   Ask one of the children who rides on the bus to describe how the bus moves. Have groups of 4 or 5 students form a bus by standing single file with their hands on the hips of the child in front of them. Challenge the groups to move through general space by imitating the movements and sounds of a bus.

2. Inquire if they have ever taken a trip a long way from home. Ask them how they got

there. If any have traveled by train, plane, or boat, have them describe the movements and challenge the class to imitate these. If none of the children has had these experiences, ask if they would like to travel in these ways. Then tell them to imagine how they would move and to describe these movements. Challenge them to move their bodies in these ways. Playing recordings of the sounds made by trains, planes, and boats will assist in evoking a variety of movements.

3. Discuss how people will become space travelers in the future. Ask the children how they think it feels to travel in different kinds of spacecrafts. Have them move through general space by exploring these movements.
4. Ask the children how they think various objects were transported from the factory to the school (e.g., books, desks, playground equipment). Challenge the children to move like the trucks or trains move when going fast and slow, up and down hills, and hauling light and heavy loads.

CONCEPT: The vehicles and machines we use for transportation move in different environments.

Level: Beginning.
Subconcepts: (1) Some vehicles move on land. (2) Some vehicles move on and in the water. (3) Some vehicles move in the air.
Materials: Pictures of vehicles moving in different environments.

Activities

1. Challenge the children to think of many different kinds of vehicles and machines that move on land. List these on the board. Discuss how they are similar to, and different from, each other. Have the children imitate the movements of the different types of vehicles and machines (e.g., tricycle, bicycle, wagon, tractor, jeep, car, truck, bus, motorcycle).
2. Repeat no. 1, substituting vehicles that move on or in the water (e.g., rowboats, canoes, sailboats, motorboats, ships, submarines).
3. Repeat no. 1, substituting vehicles that move in the air (e.g., airplanes with propel-

lors, jet airplanes, gliders, balloons, helicopters, spaceships).

CONCEPT: The vehicles we use for transportation are powered by energy obtained from different sources.

Level: Beginning.

Subconcepts: (1) The sources of energy used as power to move vehicles are people, animals, the wind, and mechanical devices. (2) The type of power used determines how fast the vehicle can move and the size of the load it can carry.

Materials: A child's wagon, pictures of people and animals carrying and pulling loads, a picture of the wind moving a sailboat, and pictures of motor-driven vehicles.

Activities

1. Show the children pictures of people carrying loads in different ways. Have them move as though they were carrying a load on their head, on their back, and in their arms. Tell them to imagine that the load is very heavy.

2. Show the children pictures of animals carrying people and other loads. Have the children imitate the movements of these animals (horses, elephants, camels, reindeer).

3. Show the children a picture of a sailboat. Challenge them to move like a sailboat when there is just a breeze, in a strong wind, in a storm, and when there is no wind at all.

4. Have 1 child bring a wagon to school. Let the children take turns pulling the wagon when it is empty and when other children are sitting in it. Discuss how the wagon pulls harder when it is loaded. Show the children a picture of a team of horses pulling a wagon. Discuss the fact that the horses can pull bigger, heavier loads because they are bigger and stronger than people and smaller animals. Have the children pretend they are a team of horses pulling a very light load and a heavy load. Show the children a picture of a big truck. Discuss why the truck has more power than the horses. Relate the size of the motor in the truck to the size and weight of the load it can carry. Have the children move through general space imitating a truck carrying a heavy load and moving fast and slow, up and down hills.

Review these four activities, pointing out that in the first three the force to move people and objects was created by muscles. In the last activity the force was created by a machine. Explain how people are not as strong as some animals, and so they invented machines to do their heavy work. In a follow-up lesson the children can explore the movement of different kinds of small and large machines.

CONCEPT: Different kinds of transportation gradually and progressively developed.

Level: Beginning.

Subconcepts: (1) The first types of transportation were people and animals carrying or dragging their loads. (2) The invention of the wheel made it possible to pull heavier loads in carts and wagons. (3) The invention of the engine enables humans to build vehicles that can carry much larger loads.

Materials: Several well-wrapped and tied packages containing old catalogues or other heavy materials; a rope for each group of children, a child's wagon, and pictures illustrating different types of transportation.

Activities

1. Mark off an area with a starting line at one end and a finish line at the other. Divide the class into groups containing no more than 5 children. Space the groups evenly along the starting line. Place one of the packages behind the finish line opposite each group of children. Have the first child in each group run down to the finish line, pick up the package, carry it back, and hand it to the next child in the group. The second child then carries the package back to the finish line, puts it down, runs back to the group, and touches the hand of the third child. The third child repeats the action of the first, and this process continues until they have all had a turn.

2. Tie a piece of rope to each package. Repeat no. 1, having the children drag the package.

3. Have all of the children get into one group and sit down in the middle of the floor. Select one child to pick up and carry as many of the packages as possible at one time. Select another child to drag as many as pos-

sible. Discuss how many each child was able to transport by carrying and by dragging. Have a third child load all the packages in a wagon and pull it around the area. Discuss how using the wagon made the task so much easier.

4. Show the children pictures of trucks and trains. Discuss how the invention of the engine made it possible to substitute mechanical power for muscular power. Relate this to the fact that it makes work easier but it also prevents many persons from getting enough exercise to keep their bodies physically fit.

5. Older children can review these basic concepts and then develop movement sequences that demonstrate the evolution of transportation and its effects on the lives of people.

CONCEPT: The mail is transported in different kinds of vehicles as it travels from the sender to the receiver.

Level: Beginning.

Subconcepts: (1) Mail travels at different speeds in various types of transportation. (2) The mail moves through different stations.

Materials: Eight or more pieces of cardboard with house numbers written on them (Fig. 15-7), two signs with the name of a city written on each, and a slip of paper for each child with one of the house numbers written on it.

Activities: Set up a series of stations similar to those shown in Fig. 15-7. Pin one of the address slips on each of the children. Tell the children they are a letter and they must move from the address where they are sent to the address written on the slip of paper. Walk the children around the stations so that they will understand where they are to go. Next, instruct them to move in a certain way between the different signs, delivering mail. Have them hop or jump as they move from one mailbox to the next, stopping at each one. Last, tell them to pretend they are riding in a truck as they move between the post offices and the airports. Challenge them to pretend they are in a plane as they fly between the airports.

Variations

1. Discuss what is happening at each point along the letter's journey and then have the children move like these events would make them feel. For example, the person mailing the letter might feel happy and would skip around the mailbox and back to the house. When the letter is being sorted in the post office, the children can pretend to be moving along a conveyor belt and jump off when they get to the right mail sack. As they move between the airports, they might pretend they are birds flying. When they get to the address to which they are being sent, they can move like the person who is very happy to get a letter. To express this feeling, they might jump up and down and clap their hands.

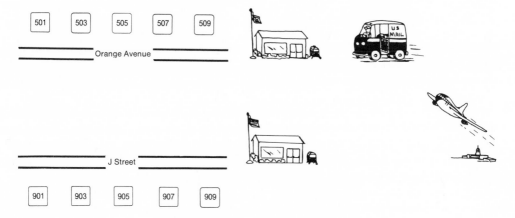

Fig. 15-7. Tracing the route a letter follows.

2. Substitute having the letter travel by train, semitrailer, or boat instead of by plane.
3. Add a variety of stunts the children can perform at different points along the way. Examples follow:

Sender's address	Rooster Hop
Sender's post office	Rabbit Jump
Sender's airport	Wicket Walk
Receiver's airport	Measuring Worm
Receiver's post office	Kangaroo Jump
Receiver's address	Jack-in-the-Box

4. Substitute methods of transporting the mail in different historical periods: (1) In ancient times, marathon runners carried messages; (2) in pioneer days, letters were carried by pony express riders and by stage coaches; (3) where the railroad was built, the mail was transferred from one train to another until it reached its destination. The children can form relay teams that simulate the mail being carried by these different types of transportation.

CONCEPT: When more people began moving faster in less space, it became necessary to develop traffic laws.

Level: Beginning.

Materials: Rope or string to mark an intersection on the floor or playground.

Activities

1. Have 3 children move about through general space. After a few minutes tell each of these children to select another child who will also move in general space. Repeat until all the children are moving.

   Instruct the children to walk fast, changing direction often. Then tell them to run. Stop the activity and discuss what happened to their available space when they added people and what problems were created when they all moved faster.

2. Construct an intersection by using ropes or string. Instruct the children to move slowly through the intersection in any direction. After a few minutes challenge them to move faster. Stop the activity and discuss the effect of their being required to move in lim-

ited space and their moving faster in such a small space. Ask the students for suggestions relative to improving the flow of their movements through space. Some suggestions follow:

Mark off traffic lanes
Install a traffic light
Install traffic signs such as STOP, YIELD, and ONE WAY
Limit the speed

Implement the children's suggestions one by one and discuss the effect of each. You may conclude the activity by discussing the similarities between traffic regulations, school regulations, and rules in games.

CONCEPT: People have invented machines that make work easier.

Level: Intermediate.

Subconcepts: (1) A machine that makes human work easier is called a "laborsaving device." (2) Machines have parts that work together to perform a certain task.

Materials: Pictures of common laborsaving devices such as washing machines, dishwashers, lawnmowers, vacuum cleaners, and mixers.

Activities

1. Ask the children to name several machines they have at home. Discuss some of the facts about the essential parts of a machine (e.g., it has gears that have been developed from wheels, it is powered by a motor, the parts are designed to work together create a mechanical advantage). Talk about what certain machines do and how these same tasks were performed by hand.

2. Divide the class into small groups of from 3 to 5. Challenge each group to select or invent a machine and to illustrate how the machine works by using their body parts as the moving parts of the machine. Have each group perform and challenge the class to guess what type of work is done by each machine.

Chapter 16

OUR COUNTRY'S HERITAGE

The purpose of this chapter is to enable children to relive the historical heritage of the United States and experience the origin of their country's traditions. The content is designed to accurately portray the people and their way of life. For this reason, the activities in this chapter focus on the American Indians and the early settlers at work and play. Also included is a section designed to acquaint the children with the origin of the traditional celebrations in the United States.

Television does not always present a true picture of the American Indian. Therefore the activities relative to the Indians are being presented as a complete unit. It is intended that this format exemplify how the other subjects in this chapter, as well as those in Chapter 17, could also be presented as a unit of work rather than as an isolated topic.

Indian games and dances can be effective ways of conveying accurate concepts concerning these people. The children will be able to identify with the original Americans because they will see how the Indians liked the same kinds of things they do, such as music, dance, nature, being out of doors, and being free. Because so much of the Indian's way of life involved physical activities, it is natural for the children to learn about them by actually participating in these activities.

Indian games and dances were purposeful. Individuals usually participated in them for amusement, as training for hunting and war, or as a part of their religious ceremonies. The skills and strategies essential in tracking and killing the birds and animals that fed the tribes were practiced in games. Games also taught Indian boys how to use weapons and participate in battles. The Indians believed certain dances could bring the rain, heal the sick, cause their crops to grow, and ensure success in hunting and victory in war.

The study of Indian life is more meaningful if it is approached as a complete unit, involving related learning experiences from other curricular areas such as art, music, mathematics, and language arts. Some of the teaching aids and related learning activities that could be used follow:

Teaching aids
- Pictures that portray the Indian's way of life.
- Pictures of Indians dancing and/or playing games.
- Indian costumes and artifacts.

Related learning activities
- Take a trip to a museum to view displays portraying art, crafts, costumes, and other objects related to Indian life.
- Assist the children in constructing a model of an Indian village.
- Assist the children in building a teepee on the playground and making Indian costumes and implements.
- Study Indian symbols and art, relating these to how the same kinds of thoughts and feelings are portrayed in the movements that comprise the Indians games and dances.
- Assist the children in constructing musical instruments resembling those used by the Indians (instructions are given in Mason [1946] and Saloman [1928], as well as in the instructor's manual for the record "Authentic Indian Dances and Folklore," Kimbo LP 9070).
- Have the children create rhythmic phrases to accompany their Indian dances. Devise different measures of distance and quantity that might have been used by the Indians; for example, (1) stepping off the distance of a playing field or the circumference of a circle, (2) measuring distance with a stick or a leather thong, or (3) using bowls of different size to measure quantity.
- Encourage the children to read and write poems and stories about Indians.

- Have the children write a story that uses Indian symbols.
- Challenge the children to use their bodies to form the shape of Indian symbols.

In the section of this chapter devoted to the physical activities associated with United States history, the children will see how some of the early American pioneers did not believe in playing. However, they will also discover that most of the early settlers found play to be a necessary release from the demands of their hard life. These immigrants brought their traditions with them, and games and dances were an essential aspect of these customs. In time, the rules and conduct of these activities were adapted to their way of life in the new land, and characteristic American games, dances, and contests developed. Studying about American history through the evolution of these activities provides a realistic link with the past.

Offering children an opportunity to experience their American heritage by dancing can be an effective learning medium. They can explore the four kinds of folk dances indigenous to the United States: (1) play-party games, (2) round dances, (3) line dances, and (4) square dances. Each of these evidences the influence of the traditions brought by immigrants (particularly the English), as well as the events and the characteristics of the people that molded this nation. As children participate in these dances, they should be encouraged to readily express the feeling states evoked by the dance movements. For example, clapping, stomping, and shouting are characteristic American behavioral patterns. The children should feel free to interject these and other rhythmical responses as long as their actions are appropriate and do not interfere with the conduct of the dance.

Americans love to celebrate. Their celebrations include traditions brought from other countries and those associated with the development of the United States, as well as local customs. The activities in this chapter are examples of how active games, contests, and dances can be used to help children develop an understanding of traditional American holidays.

Learning activities

AMERICAN INDIANS

Games

CONCEPT: The game lacrosse was used to train Indian braves for war.

Level: Intermediate.

Subconcepts: (1) Lacrosse is the oldest American sport. It was played by the Indians to develop the strength, endurance, speed, and skill necessary in war. (2) The game was named after the stick used to carry the ball (Fig. 16-1). The early French settlers thought the stick resembled the staff with a cross at the top that was carried in front of the bishops in their churches; thus they named the game by the French words meaning ''the cross.'' (3) The original game has been modified and is now a

Fig. 16-1. Modern lacrosse stick.

popular sport played in many colleges in the United States and Canada.

Materials: A playing field or gym with appropriate markings, a scoop for each player (these can be made from plastic jugs and may be decorated with Indian symbols), and a tennis ball.

Activity: Scoop lacrosse.

Playing area: Any square or rectangular area with a minimum length of 25 meters and a maximum length of 70 meters can be used. The area should be marked with the lines and circles shown in Fig. 16-2. Goals 2 meters apart should be marked at each end and a goal circle made. Road cones can mark the goals, but interest can be added by using poles the children have decorated with Indian symbols.

Players: There are 12 players on an official lacrosse team, and each has a designated position (Fig. 16-2). The number of players and their positions can, however, be modified so that all children in a given class may actively

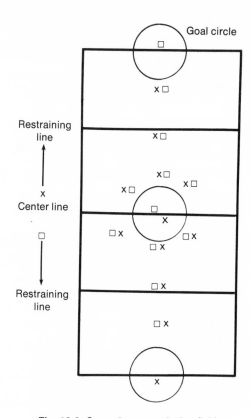

Fig. 16-2. Scoop lacrosse playing field.

participate. The prime considerations are that (1) the number of players should be limited so that each has sufficient space in which to freely move about and (2) the playing positions should be designated so that all of the children will not be converging into any one area at one time.

The teams may be designated as the red team and the yellow team to introduce the concept that to the Indian, red is the color of east and yellow the color of west (Fletcher, 1915). The teams can be identified by the color of their scoops, or players may wear red or yellow headbands. Another way of naming the teams would be to let them select the names of Indian tribes that inhabited adjacent areas (i.e., the Mohawks versus the Iroquois or the Chippewa versus the Sioux).

Each team should be divided so that half the players are the offensive and the other half are the defensive

Rules: Play begins by the umpire tossing the ball into the air between the two players in the center circle. The player who succeeds in catching the ball may run with it in his scoop or may pass it to a team member. (The ball must be passed when the player carrying it reaches the center line or one of the restraining lines.)

A goal is scored when a team succeeds in tossing the ball over the goal line (the distance between the two goal markers). One point is scored for each goal. The winning team is the one with the most points at the end of the designated time period. The game may be as short as 15 minutes or divided into 10-minute halves; if a longer time period is available, it may be divided into quarters.

A violation occurs as follows:

• When the ball goes out of bounds
• When the ball is touched by the hand or kicked
• When any player except the centers steps into the center circle before the ball is caught, or any player other than the goalkeeper enters the goal circle
• When a player who is running with the ball steps on or over one of the restraining lines or the center line

The penalty for a violation is that the opposing team is awarded the ball at the spot on the field where the violation occurred.

Unnecessary roughness is a *foul*. The penalty

is that the ball is advanced toward the goal of the team committing the foul. The distance the ball is advanced depends on the size of the playing area and the extent of the foul. Deliberate and unreasonable roughness results in a severe penalty and removal of the offender from the game.

Encourage players to use the playing space well (avoid crowding into certain areas), to throw and catch accurately, and to keep the game moving by running fast and passing often.

CONCEPT: The spear-the-fish game was used to teach children the skill of spearing fish.

Level: Intermediate.

Subconcepts: (1) Adults as well as children played the game. (2) It was played in different forms by the Indian tribes that lived from the tip of South America to Alaska and also by the Eskimos.

Materials: An implement made from a small board, a leather thong, and beef leg bones cut crosswise (Fig. 16-3).

Activities

Spear-the-fish.* This game may be played individually, with a partner, or with a small group. The purpose is to spear the objects in the way that will yield the highest number of points.

The spear is held in the dominant hand, and the bones in the other. The player tosses the bones into the air and attempts to catch them with the spear. The players take turns; a turn means a player has had an opportunity to spear all the bones.

A player's score is the total number of points accumulated by catching the various bones. More points should be awarded for catching the bones with the smaller holes. For example, 1 point might be given for catching bones with the large hole, whereas 2 points would be given for catching those with the small hole. The winner is determined by who reaches a specified number of points first (e.g., 15 or 20), provided that all players have had an equal number of turns. An alternate method is to declare

---

*Descriptions of how the Indians played this game, as well as directions for making an implement closely resembling those used by the Indians, may be found in Joseph (1972) and Salomon (1928).

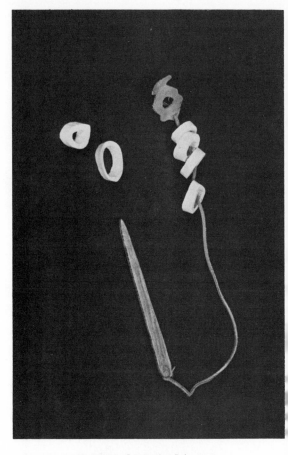

Fig. 16-3. Spear-the-fish game.

that the person with the most points at the end of each round of turns is the winner.

Contests

CONCEPT: Footraces were an important activity among the Indians because they liked to run and also because running developed endurance.

Level: Beginning.

Materials: Low obstacles over which children can jump.

Activities: Group the students according to size and ability so that smaller or less able children are not competing against those more highly skilled.

Challenge the children to run varying distances—from short sprints of 45 meters to endurance runs of up to 550 meters. Match the distance to the size and endurance level of the children.

Fig. 16-4. A, Hand wrestling; **B,** thunderclap; **C,** pullover; **D,** pull away; **E,** one-hand wrestle; **F,** rooster fight; **G,** knee wrestle; **H,** elbow wrestle; **I,** foot wrestle.

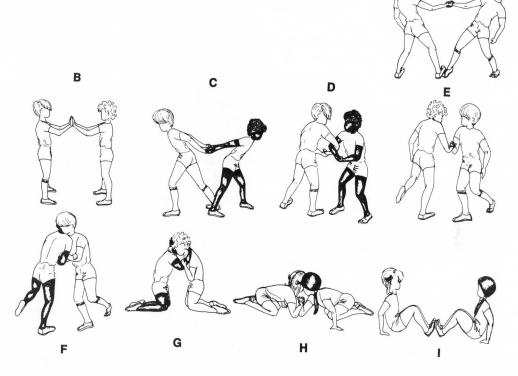

Stimulate additional interest (1) by placing low obstacles along the way so that the children have to leap over them and (2) by including relay races.

Encourage the students to set achievement goals so that they will be challenged to increase their speed and the distance they can run.

CONCEPTS: An Indian brave's survival often depended on his ability to defend himself in hand-to-hand combat. For this reason, combatives were a natural part of Indian play, as well as an essential aspect of their training.

Level: Intermediate.

Materials: None.

Activities: Point out to the children that no written records were kept by the Indians, and so we do not really know exactly how they did their combatives. Because they used their whole body when they participated in physical activities, we can assume they had contests like those which follow. In fact, hand wrestling and arm wrestling are often referred to as "Indian wrestling."

Hand wrestling. Opponents stand in a stride position, with their right hands clasped and their right feet touching. On the signal "Go," both participants attempt to force their opponent to move either foot (Fig. 16-4, *A*).

Thunderclap. Opponents stand in a sideward stride position, with the palms of their hands touching. The objective is to push against the opponent's hands so hard that he moves either foot (Fig. 16-4, *B*).

Pullover. Opponents stand back to back in a forward stride position, with both hands clasped and right feet touching (Fig. 16-4, *C*). The objective is to pull on the opponent's hands, forcing him to move either foot.

Pull away. Opponents stand facing each other, with right elbows hooked and their own hands clasped. The objective is to pull or twist forcefully enough to cause the opponent to release his grasp (Fig. 16-4, *D*).

One-hand wrestle. Opponents stand on the right foot facing each other with right hands clasped. The objective is to push the opponent off balance, causing him to touch the lifted foot to the floor (Fig. 16-4, *E*).

Rooster fight. Opponents stand on the right foot facing each other, with their arms clasped over their own chest. The object is to push against the opponent, forcing him to touch the lifted foot to the floor (Fig. 16-4, *F*).

Shoulder wrestle. Opponents kneel facing each other, with their shoulders touching and their hands locked behind their own back. Participants may move about on their knees, but they must keep their shoulders touching while attempting to push each other off balance.

Knee wrestle. This is the same as shoulder wrestling except that the hands and arms may be used in any way to push or pull the opponent off balance (Fig. 16-4, *G*).

Elbow wrestle. Opponents assume a prone position facing each other, with right elbows on the mat and right hands grasped (Fig. 16-4, *H*). The objective is to push the opponent's right hand and forearm to the floor. The elbow wrestle may also be done with the participants on their hands and knees.

Leg wrestle. Opponents lie on their backs side by side, facing opposite directions. On signal, they raise their inside legs and lock knees. The objective is to push against the opponent's leg, forcing him over backward far enough that some part of his leg or foot touches the floor.

Foot wrestle. Opponents sit facing each other, with their hands on the floor. Their legs are lifted so that the soles of their feet are flat together (Fig. 16-4, *I*). The objective is to push the opponent off balance or to push her feet far enough that the winner's legs are straight.

Dances

CONCEPT: The Indians lived close to nature and felt a kinship with the natural world.

Level: Intermediate.

Materials: The record "The Brave Hunter" from the *Dance-a-Story* series by Paul and Anne Barlin, which is available from RCA Records.

Activities: Play the side of the record that has narration and music while showing the children the pictures in the booklet. Discuss the following facts relative to the story:

• Significance of the Deer Dance

Fig. 16-5. Movements suggested by lightning, rain, and the moon.

- Feelings of the Indian boy (i.e., love for the deer, sorrow, fear, happiness, pride)
- Ways in which animals and objects moved (i.e., the deer, bear, canoe)
- Movements suggested by the elements of nature (i.e., clouds, thunder, lightning, rain, wind, moon, stars, sun, air [Fig. 16-5])
- Actions of the Indian boy (i.e., paddling the canoe, shooting with the bow and arrows, carrying the deer, walking slowly and swiftly, and soaring, swooping, and diving like the eagle

Play the record again, challenging the children to respond in movement to the body actions and feeling states portrayed by the music and the narrative.

Variations: Read poems or stories written about the Indians. Challenge the children to develop rhythmical movement sequences that express the themes and thoughts of these narratives.

CONCEPT: Some Indian dances were traditional, and others were creative.

Level: Intermediate.

Materials: The record "Authentic Indian Dances and Folklore," Kimbo Records LP 9070.

Activities

Rain Dance. Play the part of the record that contains the historical background of this dance, as described by Chief Little Elk. Then play a section of the drumbeat and the Indian drums and chants.

Demonstrate the basic step of the Rain Dance—the toe-heel step (Fig. 16-6). Instruct the children to practice the step while standing

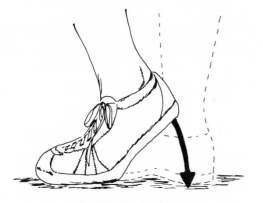

Fig. 16-6. Toe-heel step.

in place, then have them execute this step while moving clockwise in a circle.

Introduce the formation and sequence of movements in the dance. After the children practice these, have them move to the rhythm of a drumbeat as they dance.

Discuss the meaning and significance of the movements in the dance. Point out that this is a traditional dance of the Chippewa Indians and was passed down from one generation to another.

Encourage the children to add their own variations to the dance, as suggested in the written instructions.

Variations

1. Teach some of the other traditional Indian dances. The references by Buttree (1930), Mason (1944), and Shafter (1927) contain resource material and instruction for traditional Indian dances. Additional recordings with instruction are (a) "Indian Dance-Prayer for Rain," Folkraft 1192, and (b) "Indian War Dance," available from Educational Activities, Inc.

2. Have the children write a story that uses Indian symbols such as those shown on p. 15 of the Kimbo record instruction manual. Then challenge them to create a dance that tells their story in movement.

CONCEPT: The dances of the Indians expressed their feelings about the things in the world of nature.

Level: Intermediate.

Materials: None.

Activities: Divide the class into nine groups. Give each group a slip of paper with one of the following words written on it.

night	lightning	wind
moon	thunder	clouds
stars	rain	sun

Challenge the groups to develop a short sequence of movements that express the qualities and actions of their word. Have each group demonstrate their sequence. Combine the three groups in each of the columns above. Challenge them to make up a story containing their three words and to tell this story by moving. Have each group tell their movement story to the rest of the class.

Variations

1. Give the children names of animals that were important to the Indians, for example:

bear	antelope	eagle
deer	beaver	dog
buffalo	coyote	horse

Instead of combining the groups, have each group make up a story about their animal and tell the story by developing movement sequence.

2. Give the children Indian names (or let them make up their own names). Some examples that contain movement themes follow:

Brave Warrior	Yellow Moon
Mighty Hunter	White Cloud
Straight Arrow	Rushing Bear
Swift River	Running Deer
Bright Sun	Soaring Eagle

Have each child select another child whose name has a related theme (e.g., Mighty Hunter and Straight Arrow; White Cloud and Soaring Eagle). Challenge each pair of children to develop a movement sequence that expresses the characteristics of, and tells a story about, their names.

CONCEPT: The sounds produced by instruments were an essential part of Indian dances.

Level: Intermediate.

Materials: Indian instruments made by the children* (e.g., bells, rattles, drums, wooden sticks).

Activities: Divide the class into small groups and give each group an instrument Challenge them to experiment with the different sounds they can create by varying the pitch, tempo, and dynamics. As each group demonstrates the range of sounds they can create, challenge the rest of the class to move like these sounds make them feel. Some of the sounds and accompanying movement possibilities follow:

- *High pitch*—movements that extend the body upward into space, such as standing on tiptoe and arms stretched overhead

---

*Instructions for making these instruments are given on pp. 16 to 19 of the instructor's manual for the record "Authentic Indian Dances and Folklore," Kimbo LP 7090. Additional authentic instruments are described by Mason (1946).

- *Low pitch*—crouching and kneeling
- *Moderate tempo*—walking, jumping, hopping, sliding, swaying, bending, turning
- *Fast tempo*—running, rapid shuffling steps, jumping or hopping rapidly
- *Slow tempo*—walking stealthily, bending, twisting, turning, swaying
- *Loud*—sudden, strong explosive movements such as stamping
- *Jumping*—forcefully flexing and extending different body parts
- *Soft-light*—quiet, gentle movements

Have the children select various sounds and the movements these stimulate. Challenge them to fit these movements together to form an Indian dance.

Tribes

CONCEPT: Each Indian tribe had a name.

Level: Intermediate.

Materials: None.

Activities

Indian tag games. Have the students number off from 1 to 4. Give each group the name of an Indian tribe, for example; Apache, Iroquois, Navajo, and Seminole. Tell the children to line up along one side of the gym. Select one child to be the "chief" and have him stand in the center of the gym. (See Fig. 16-7.)

Explain that the chief will call out the name of one of the tribes. The children who are this tribe must run across the gym to the other side.

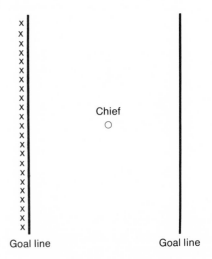

Fig. 16-7. Indian tag game.

While they are running, the chief attempts to tag them. Each Indian that is tagged must join the chief in the center and assist him in attempting to tag the other children as they run across the center.

Variations

1. Have the chief call out the names of more than one tribe or say "All Indians run."
2. Have two tribes line up on each side of the gym. The chief calls out the name of one tribe on each side or says "All Indians run." This adds the challenge of requiring the students to dodge those running in the opposite direction.
3. Use only the names of the Indian tribes that lived in a certain region of the country. For example, if the region is the Northeast, the groups would be named Mohawk, Cayuga, Seneca, and Iroquois.

CONCEPT: Several different Indian tribes lived in each region of the country.

Level: Intermediate.

Materials: None.

Activities: Have the children sit in a circle. Give each player the name of an Indian tribe that lived within a certain region. For example, if the region is the Northwest, the names that might be used are Yuma, Hopi, Navajo, and Apache.

Select one child to be "It." Have this child stand in the center. Explain that he is to call out the name of one of the tribes and everyone in that tribe must exchange places with another player from the same tribe. While they are exchanging places, It attempts to get into one of the places. The player who is left without a place to sit becomes It, and the game is repeated.

UNITED STATES

Games

CONCEPT: The English settlers brought with them the game of townball (also called boundary ball).

Level: Intermediate.

Subconcepts: (1) This game evolved into the present-day game of soccer (called football in Great Britain). (2) It is recorded that in 1602

A.D. the playing field was 3 or 4 miles long, and two or three parishes (similar to our counties) united to paly against a similar number from another area (thus the teams may have consisted of a large number of persons). (3) By 1801 the size of the playing field had shrunk to 80 to 100 yards long, with goal posts 2 or 3 feet apart. (4) The original ball was the inflated bladder of an animal (later, shoemakers made leather covers for these). (*Encyclopaedia Britannica*, 1960.)

Materials: Soccer balls.

Activities

Mass soccer. Mark end lines at opposite ends of the playground and a center line in the middle. Establish sidelines only if necessary for safety. Divide the class in half. Each group represents all the players from one township. Appoint a student to be the Mayor (Captain) of each group. Identify the members of each group (e.g., have them wear a certain color sash, scarf, or shirt). Instruct each mayor to line up players behind the endline. Place a partially deflated soccer ball in the middle of the center line. On the starting signal all the players rush toward the ball and attempt to kick it over their opponents' end line. There are no assigned positions, but the mayor may assign certain players to guard the end line. If sidelines have been prescribed and the ball goes over one of these, the referee simply throws it back in. Touching the ball with the hands is a violation, and the other team is awarded the ball. One point is scored when a team kicks the ball over their opponents' end line below shoulder level.

After the children have played for a while, stop the game and discuss how it could be made safer and more fun by adding more rules. Point out that when the game was played as the students have been playing it, many people were injured, and the game was at times outlawed because it became so violent because of the wild kicking, hitting, and pushing. Introduce rotation soccer to show the children how the concept evolved of playing positions in a limited area according to rules.

CONCEPT: The American games baseball and softball and the British games cricket and rounders all evolved from primitive contests in which a player with a ball tried to defeat another player who had an implement.

Level: Intermediate.

Subconcepts: (1) According to the first history of Plymouth Colony, this type of game was played in America in 1621. (2) The game was called "stoolball" because it was originally played by milkmaids who used their stools (called crickets) as the target. (Vinton, 1970.)

Materials: One or more stools or targets, a softball or tennis ball, and a 1 by 4 inch board approximately 2 feet long. One end of the board may be cut to form a handle (Fig. 16-8).

Activities

*Stoolball.** Two players assume the positions shown in Fig. 16-9. The contest consists of the pitcher attempting to throw the ball so that it hits the stool (or target). The defender attempts

---

*Adapted from the description given by Vinton, 1970, pp. 47 and 48.

Fig. 16-8. Modified cricket bat.

to hit the ball. If the pitcher hits the stool or catches a fly ball hit by the defender, the 2 players exchange places.

Variations

1. If a board is not available, the game can be played by having the defender simply stop a thrown tennis ball with the palm of the hand. When played in this manner, there would be no fly balls.

2. A winner may be determined by awarding the defender 1 point for each time a thrown ball is hit. The winner is the person ahead at the end of a certain number of innings or a certain length of time.

3. Stoolball may become a team game by simply adding more players in the positions shown in Fig. 16-10. Additional rules become necessary when the number of players is increased. Therefore a second stool is placed as indicated in Fig. 16-10. After hitting the ball, the defender runs to the second stool (or base). He must wait there until the ball is hit by another player before running back to the first stool (home base). The runner may be put out (a) by being tagged, (b) by a member of the defending team touching the no. 2 stool with the ball

Fig. 16-9. Stoolball.

as the runner approaches it, or (c) by an opponent touching the first stool with the ball if the runner is forced to run because a teammate has hit the ball. Each time a defender reaches the second stool, ½ point is scored, and another ½ point is awarded if the defender gets back to the first stool. When the defending team has three outs, the teams change places.

Discuss with the children the similarities and differences between this game and the American lead-up game to softball called ''long base.''

CONCEPT: The first baseball bats were sticks, the balls were homemade, and the diamond was any available playing space.

Level: Intermediate.

Materials: A stick, a homemade ball, and an improvised baseball diamond.

Activities: Show the children a baseball or softball bat. Discuss how it is made from a certain kind of hardwood and has been carefully

manufactured to be a certain size and weight. Ask them where they think the bats of the early settlers came from. Do they think they could find something around home that could be used as a bat? Ask them to bring it to school.

Show the children a baseball or a softball. If possible, have an old one sawed in half so that they can see the inside. Discuss the fact that the ball is also carefully manufactured to be a standard size and weight. Ask the children what they think the early settlers used for a ball. Suggest that the settlers may have made balls out of yarn or out of a small pouch stuffed with sawdust or rags. Show the children how to make a ball out of a sock (Fig. 16-11). Discuss how the pioneer women had to spin the yarn and knit the socks for the family, and so maybe they made balls for the children similar to the one you made.

When the students bring their improvised bats, assist them in developing a game of stickball by using their bats and the stocking ball. Help them lay out a diamond that uses natural

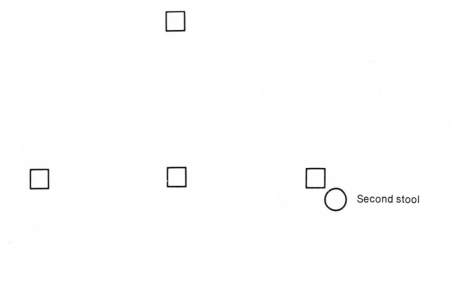

Fig. 16-10. Team stoolball.

Fig. 16-11. Making a ball out of a sock.

objects as bases (trees, a clump of grass, a spot near a fence or near the school building). Determine the size of the infield by having a child hit the ball as far as possible. (There is no point in having outfielders placed farther away than the ball will travel.) You may decide to modify or eliminate rules that do not appear necessary.

After the children have played, discuss the following points:

- Which of the improvised bats worked the best and why
- Why the stocking ball does not travel as far as a regular softball or baseball
- How they think the games of softball and baseball evolved from stoolball and games using improvised equipment
- The relative value of playing by official rules (i.e., how they might modify rules to create games involving greater participation and fun for everyone when they are playing just for fun and practice)

CONCEPT: The only major sport originating in the United States is basketball.

Level: Intermediate.

Subconcepts: (1) Basketball was invented in Massachusetts in 1891 by James Naismith, who developed it to fill the need for an indoor activity that could be played in the winter. (2) The first basketball games were played with soccer balls, and each team had 9 players. (3) The goals were peach baskets nailed to the walls at each end of the gym. (4) Since the

peach baskets has bottoms in them, each time a player made a basket, someone had to climb a ladder and get the ball. (*Encyclopaedia Britannica,* 1960.)

Materials: Two peach baskets (or round plastic laundry baskets), two step ladders, a soccer ball, and a playing area approximately the size of a basketball court.

Activities: Have the children assist you in attaching the baskets to poles or the walls. Discuss how they are placed just a little bit higher than the best jumper can reach when jumping. Select two teams with 9 players on each. Go over the following original rules of the game:

1. Play begins by a jump in the center circle and is resumed by a center jump after each basket.
2. Players must dribble or pass; they cannot run with the ball.
3. Fouls are called for rough play and body contact.
4. Any player on the team may shoot the free throw after a foul (i.e., the shooter does not have to be the player who was fouled).

Select 2 children as referees and 2 others to climb the ladders and retrieve the ball after a basket is made.

After the students have played the game, discuss some of the following points with them:

- How does the modern game differ from the original game?
- Why do they think these changes were made?
- Have one child dribble a soccer ball and another dribble a basketball. How does the bounce compare?
- Why should children use a smaller ball and lower baskets than those used by adults? (Because they are shorter and smaller.)

CONCEPTS: Ninepins was an early form of bowling brought to America by people from the Netherlands (Holland). It was a popular game played by the Dutch settlers in New Amsterdam (later named New York by the English settlers).

Level: Intermediate.

Materials: Nine Indian clubs or plastic bowling pins and two wooden balls or playground balls.

Activities

Ninepins. Set the pins in two concentric cir-

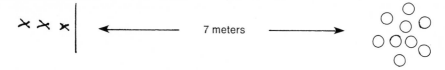

Fig. 16-12. Formation for ninepins.

cles. Have from 2 to 5 players line up behind a restraining line approximately 7 meters from the pins (Fig. 16-12). Player 1 rolls the ball toward the pins, then runs to the pins, counts the number knocked over, and sets all of them back up in their proper position. While player 1 is retrieving the ball and is returning to the line, player 2 rolls the other ball. Player 1 gives the ball to player 3 and goes to the end of the line. The winner is the player who knocked over the greatest number of pins (each counts 1 point) after all the players have had the same number of turns. (Vinton, 1970.)

If a set of bowling pins and a bowling ball are available, you may stimulate a meaningful discussion by comparing the original materials and rules to those of the modern game.

CONCEPT: Bicycles were introduced in the United States about a hundred years ago.

Level: Intermediate.

Subconcepts: (1) In this country they are primarily used for recreational riding and racing. (2) In Europe and many other countries they are a major form of transportation.

Materials: A bicycle for each child and the materials described in the following activities.

Activities: For recreational riding, assist the children in planning bicycle trips to points of interest in the community (e.g., historical sites, parks, the beach, a state recreational area). Discuss safety measures and alternate routes.

Cycling activities also provide an opportunity to discuss topics such as the following:

• How and why the bicycle was developed
• Why it is more widely used as a form of transportation in Europe than in the United States
• What bicycle courtesy is
• How bicycle riding contributes to the development of physical fitness
• What a person can see, hear, and experience when riding a bicycle, as compared to riding in a car

In racing, designate areas in which the children can participate in a variety of racing events, such as the following.

Dashes. Mark off distances ranging from 30 to 100 meters. Encourage each child to improve his time (speed) rather than emphasize winning and championships.

Marathons. Determine intervals of 1, 2, 5, and 10 kilometers where children can ride safely. Encourage them to gradually build up their endurance by riding greater distances. Let them race these distances.

Relays. Two types of relays can be used. One type involves team races of specified distances. The other uses obstacles or mazes. Following are examples of the first type.

1. File formation relay. Have the children line up as shown in Fig. 16-8, *B*. On the starting signal player 1 rides to the turning line, around the road cone, and back to the team and then touches the hand of rider 2. This is repeated until all the team members have had a turn.

2. Shuttle relay. The riders line up as shown in Fig. 16-8, *A*. On the starting signal rider 1 rides across the area between the two lines and touches the hand of rider 2. Rider 1 then goes to the end of 2's line while rider 2 rides across and touches rider 3's hand. Play continues until all are back in their starting position.

3. Rescue relay. Have the teams line up in the formation shown in Fig. 16-13. Rider 1 begins behind the starting line. On the starting signal, rider 1 rides to the turning line, turns around, and takes hold of rider 2's hand. They continue holding hands while riding back to the starting line. When they cross the line, they drop hands, and rider 2 rides back to the turning line to "rescue" rider 3. Play continues until all the team members have been rescued.

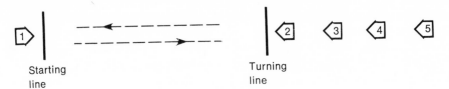

Starting
line

Turning
line

Fig. 16-13. Rescue relay.

Starting
line

Finish
line

Fig. 16-14. Baton relay.

4. Baton relay. This activity is the same as the track event involving passing the baton. A team consists of 4 members spaced along (or around) an area, as shown in Fig. 16-14. Rider 1 holds the baton in his right hand and rides up to the left side of rider 2, placing the baton in the latter's left hand. As rider 2 is riding toward rider 3, he transfers the baton to the right hand. The baton is passed in this way to each team member. Play continues until rider 4 rides across the finish line holding the baton.

Relays involving obstacles and mazes can be developed by using structures and areas on the school grounds. In open areas, road cones or painted plastic jugs can be arranged in challenging designs. The children can ride around these just for practice and fun, or they can compete by having their times clocked. The winner is the person who completes the course in the shortest time.

Contests

CONCEPT: The settlers made contests out of the tasks they had to perform in their work.

Level: Intermediate.
Materials: Wooden stakes and a small sledgehammer, logs and a crosscut saw, and a stopwatch.
Activities: Match the children according to size and strength. Have them compete as individuals and/or teams to see who can drive the stakes into the ground the quickest and which

2 children can saw the log the quickest. Discuss how teamwork is essential in sawing, how the settlers had to do everything by hand, and how physically fit they had to be to do all this hard work. Point out that it is necessary for you to time each participant, but in the old days each man had his own sledgehammer and saw, and so they could compete by heats.

CONCEPT: The pioneers used whatever was available as materials for their contests.

Level: Intermediate.
Materials: See specific activities.
Activities
Gunnysack race. Each child stands behind a starting line with both feet and legs inside a sack. On the starting signal the contestants jump to the finish line.

Three-legged race. Give each pair of children two strips of cloth. Instruct them to stand beside each other and tie one strip around their inside legs just above the ankles and the other around their thighs. Contestants stand behind a starting line. On the starting signal each pair races to the finish line. If they come untied, they are disqualified.

Hoop races. Each child is given a hoop and a stick. They compete by using the stick to rool the hoop over a goal line or around a series of obstacles. Discuss how the pioneers used barrel hoops for this contest.

Horseshoe pitching. If horseshoes are not available, you can substitute circles cut from large plastic lids. Since plastic is light, adjust the distance between the pegs.

Corncob relay. This activity is the same as a relay in which a baton is passed from one team member to another, except that corncobs are used in place of the baton.

Creek-jumping contest. Mark a creek on the floor or playground, as shown in Fig. 16-18. Have the children compete by taking off from a standing position and using a running start. A child who fails to clear the opposite bank is disqualified. Two or more trials may be given at each distance. The winner is the one who jumps the farthest.

Jump rope marathon. The contests consist of seeing who can jump the longest without missing. Separate contests can be held for hopping on the right foot only and the left foot only, jumping on both feet, using a rebound step, and using a rocker step.

Tug-of-war. Add interest to this age-old activity by telling the children how it was played by the Eskimos. It was played in the fall as a mock battle. The two teams were selected according to birth dates. All the children and adults with birthdays in the winter were on the team designated the Ptarmigans. (These white birds have natural snowshoes on their feet so they do not leave tracks in the snow for predators to follow.) The other team consists of persons born in the summer and is called the Ducks because ducks migrate in the winter. The Eskimos used a sealskin rope. They believed that if the Ducks won, they would have a mild winter, but if the Ptarmigans won, they would have a colder winter. The Indians of the Northwest also played the game in this way, but they did not name their teams after birds nor attach this type of significance to winning or losing. (Vinton, 1970.)

CONCEPT: Before pumps were invented, people had to carry all their water from a stream, river, or well.

Level: Intermediate.

Subconcepts: (1) On farms the house and barns were built near the water supply. (2) In some towns the water had to be carried from wells located in the center of the town.

Level: Intermediate.

Materials: A water bucket for each team. Fill the buckets half full of water if playing outside or half full of sand if playing inside.

Activities

Water bucket relay. Divide the class into relay teams and position them as shown in Fig. 16-15, *A*. Give player 1 on each team a bucket. On the starting signal, player 1 runs to player 2 and hands him the bucket. Player 1 then goes to the end of player 2's line while player 2 runs to and hands player 3 the bucket. Player 2 then goes to the end of player 3's line while player 3 runs to and hands player 4 the bucket. Play continues until the players are all back in their starting positions. The team that finishes first is declared the winner.

Variation: Line the teams up in file formation, as shown in Fig. 16-8, *B*. Give player 1 on each team one or two filled buckets. On the starting signal player 1 must run to the turning line, around the object on that line, and back to the team, handing the bucket (or buckets) to player 2, who repeats the task. The team that finishes first wins.

CONCEPTS: In the early days there were no fire fighters. When there was a fire people lined up to form a bucket brigade so that the water to put out the fire could be passed from the well, stream, or river to the burning building.

Level: Intermediate.

Materials: Water buckets filled to match the size and strength of the children.

Activities

Bucket brigade relays. Divide the class into teams and have them line up side by side, as shown in Fig. 16-16. Give the first player of each team a bucket containing water or sand. On the starting signal the bucket is handed from player to player up the line and back down again. The team finishing first wins.

Variation: Fill the buckets almost full of water. Give 1 point to the team that finishes first and 1 point to the team that has the most water in its bucket after each round. Repeat until a team reaches a specified number of points (e.g., 10).

CONCEPTS: The pony express carried the mail overland from St. Joseph, Missouri, to

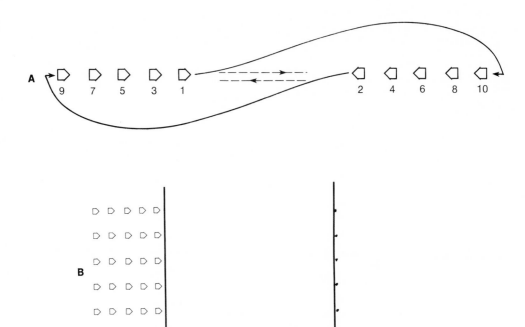

A

9   7   5   3   1   2   4   6   8   10

B

Starting line   Turning line

Fig. 16-15. A, Shuttle relay formation; **B,** file formation.

Fig. 16-16. Bucket brigade relay.

Sacramento, California, from 1860 to 1861. The horses were stationed along the route so that each rider rode several during his assignment, covering approximately 120 kilometers. (Encyclopaedia Britannica, 1960.)

Level: Intermediate.

Materials: A pouch or purse with a shoulder strap and road cones or other obstacles that can be used as station markers.

Activities

Pony express relay. Set up an obstacle course that simulates the pony express route (Fig. 16-17). Divide the class into teams consisting of no more than 5 members. Station the team members along the route, as shown in Fig. 16-10. On the starting signal the rider 1 runs to the first station, runs around the marker (symbolizing changing horses), and on to the second marker. He also runs around the second marker and on to the third, where he passes the pouch to rider 2. This procedure continues until the last rider has crossed the finish line. If there are only enough materials and space for one team to run at one time, their time can be clocked and the teams' times compared. If more space is available, it is desirable to set up multiple routes so that all the teams can run at one time.

Variation: Have a bicycle at each station.

The rider must get off of one and onto another at each station marker.

CONCEPTS: Forts were constructed to protect the settlers during attacks by hostile Indians. Sometimes these attacks occurred without warning, and the settlers had to run from their fields and houses in an attempt to reach safety within the fort.

Level: Intermediate.

Materials: A picture or diagram of a fort and the surrounding settlement.

Activity

Run, settlers, run! This game is an adaptation of the game "run, rabbit, run"! The class is divided into two groups. Approximately three fourths of the children are settlers and the other one fourth are Indians. A space at one end of the playing area is designated as the fort, and a space at the other end is the woods. The area in between is the settlement (Fig. 16-18). The Indians roam in the woods, and the settlers go about their work in the settlement. Suddenly you call out "Run, settlers, run!" This is the signal for the Indians to chase the settlers. Any settler that is tagged before reaching the fort becomes an Indian. The last settler caught is declared the captain of the fort and has the responsibility of calling out "Run, settlers, run" when the game is repeated.

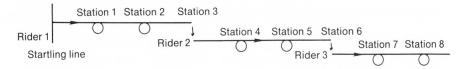

Fig. 16-17. Pony express relay.

Fig. 16-18. "Run, settlers, run!"

Folk dances

CONCEPT: Play-party games are simple folk dances.

Level: Beginning.

Subconcepts: (1) They were developed during the time when music and dancing were considered to be inventions of the devil. (2) When the pioneers' urge to dance could no longer be contained, they created these rhythmical games accompanied by their own singing. (3) Play-party games have a variety of themes expressing different aspects of the people's daily lives. For example, (a) ''Mulberry Bush'' depicts household tasks, (b) the paw paw is a fruit that grows in the central and southern part of the country, and (c) ''Bingo'' is a song about a dog.

Materials: The sheet music or a recording of each song's melody.*

Activities

''Mulberry Bush,'' World of Fun Record no. 2.
''Paw Paw Patch,'' Folkraft 1189.
''Shoo Fly,'' Folkraft 1102 or 1185.
''Skip to My Lou,'' Folkraft 1192.
''Polly Wolly Doodle,'' RCA LPM 1625.
''Oh Susannah,'' RCA LPM 1623.
''Captain Jinks,'' Hoctor LP 4001.
''Bingo,'' Hoctor LP 4001.
''Jump Jim Crow,'' RCA LPM 1625.
''Jingle Bells,'' Folkraft 1080.

CONCEPT: American round dances are patterned after eighteenth century European dances.

Level: Intermediate.

Subconcepts: (1) They are called round dances because the couples proceeded around the room in a circle. (2) American round dances portray the lively, vigorous movements associated with the pioneers who tamed the wilderness in the new land.

Materials: Recordings of musical accompaniments.

Activities

''Glow Worm,'' RCA LPM 1623.
''Pop Goes the Weasel,'' RCA LPM 1623 or

---

*A description of each of the play-party games listed here may be found in Vick and Cox (1970).

''Parachute Activities with Folk Dance Music,'' KEA 9090.
''Pattycake Polka,'' RCA LPM 1625 or Folkraft 1260.
''Teton Mountain Stomp,'' Folkraft 1482.
''Cotton-Eyed Joe,'' RCA LPM 1621.
''Jessie Polka,'' Folkraft 1071 or 1093.

CONCEPT: The third kind of American folk dances are those performed in lines, with the couples facing each other.

Level: Intermediate.

Subconcepts: (1) This formation is called a *long-ways set.* (2) These dances were brought to this country by the early settlers. (3) They were danced in all thirteen of the original colonies by people in all walks of life. (Harris, Pittman, and Waller, 1968.)

Materials: Recordings of the musical accompaniment.

Activities

''Virginia Reel,'' RCA LPM 1623.
''Bow Belinda,'' Folkraft 1189.
''Ten Pretty Girls,'' RCA LPM 1624.

CONCEPT: Square dances are the most widely known form of American folk dance.

Level: Intermediate.

Subconcepts: (1) Square dances are also called ''quadrilles'' because a set is formed by four couples. (2) Although the square dance is often considered to be uniquely American in origin, it did in fact originate in France. (Harris, Pittman, and Waller, 1968.) (3) There are two types of American square dance—New England Quadrille and Western Square Dance. (4) The traditional instruments used for accompaniment of square dance are the fiddle, banjo, guitar, accordian, and sometimes the piano. (5) A square dance has four parts:

a. The *introduction* involves movements such as bowing, swinging, clapping, balancing, and circling.
b. The *main figure* is the part of the dance from which the name is derived; for example, Bird in the Cage, Take a Little Peek, Texas Star, or Inside Arch, Outside Under.
c. The *trimmings,* also called breaks or fillers, are short chorus figures used between

the main figures of the dance; for example, Do-Si-Do, Star Through, Swing Opposite, and Allemande.

d. The *ending* conclude the dance; for example, honor and Promenade.

Materials: Recorded music.

Activities: The type of learning activities involving square dance are determined by your interest and previous experience, the available recordings, amount of time you have, and the purpose the dances are to serve.

If taught in a logical sequence, children can ordinarily master a number of dances in a short period of time. Record albums are available with and without calls. The RCA Victor series recorded by Richard Kraus and the *Honor Your Partner* series by Ed Durlacher both contain sequential step-by-step instructions. Durlacher's series also contains holiday square dances and square dances with calls but without oral instructions. Numerous other square dance recordings appropriate for elementary school are available from school record sources.

HOLIDAY CELEBRATIONS

Valentine's Day

CONCEPTS: Valentine's Day is celebrated in many countries. It is a special day for people to be thoughtful and kind to each other, and so it is a time for us to play and dance happily together.

Levels: Beginning and intermediate.
Materials: See specific activities.
Activities
Valentine relay. Divide the class into teams of no more than 6 members. Have them line up in relay line formation (Fig. 16-8, *B*). Give each team two red hearts cut from 9 × 12 inch construction paper. On the starting signal player 1 lays one heart on the floor and steps on it. Then he lays the other one down, steps on it, picks up the first heart, lays it down ahead of him, and steps on it. This procedure continues until he reaches the turning line, where he picks up both hearts, runs back to his team, and hands the hearts to player 2. Play continues until all the team members have had a turn. For variation, the paper may be cut into other shapes and used as a part of the celebration for other holidays, such as four-leaf clovers, Easter eggs, turkeys, Christmas decorations, or presents.

Valentine game. The children form a large circle (they may be standing, sitting on chairs, or sitting on the floor). One child is in the center of the circle and is the mail carrier. The mail carrier says "I have valentines for _____ and _____," naming 2 of the children in the circle. These 2 children must exchange places while the mail carrier attempts to get into one of their places. If successful, the child who does not have a space (or a seat) is the new mail carrier. For variation, the mail carrier may call out the names of several children. Also, the game may also be used at other holidays; such as the child in the center could be the Easter Bunny and call out "I have Easter eggs for _____ and _____." Or he could be Santa Claus and call out "I have presents for _____ and _____."

Valentine dances used at the intermediate level:

Valentine Hop
Sweetheart Schottische

St. Patrick's Day

CONCEPTS: St. Patrick's Day originated in Ireland. The tradition was brought to the United States by the Irish immigrants and has become a popular day throughout this country.

Levels: All.
Materials: See specific activities.
Activities
Shamrock race. Mark the outline of a large shamrock on the playground or lay ropes in this shape on the gym floor. Divide the class into teams consisting of no more than 5 members. Have each team line up in file formation at the bottom of the stem of their shamrock. On the starting signal player 1 runs around the outline of the shamrock and back to his team, where he touches the hand of player 2, who repeats the action. Play continues until all the team members have run.

Potato race. Divide the class into relay teams and have them line up in file formation. Give runner 1 in each line a tablespoon and potato. On the starting signal this runner must balance the potato on the spoon, hold it out in front of him, and run to the turning line and back. He then gives the spoon and potato to player 2, who repeats the action. A child who drops the potato must stop, pick it up, and place it back in the spoon. A child may not run while touching the potato with the free hand. The first team that finishes wins.

St. Patrick's Day dances used at the intermediate level:

Sham-Rock
St. Pat's Hop
Shamrock Polka
St. Patrick's Stomp

Easter

CONCEPTS: Like Christmas, Easter is celebrated all over the world. It is a joyous time. The games played on this holiday often involve Easter eggs and sometimes the Easter Bunny.

Levels: All.
Materials: See specific activities.
Activities

Easter egg relay. Divide the class into relay teams and place the teams in file formation, as shown in Fig. 16-8, *B*. On the starting signal, player 1 on each team runs to the turning line and picks up an Easter egg. He then runs back to the starting line and hands the egg to player 2, who runs to the turning line and puts the egg down. He then runs back to the starting line and touches the hand of player 3, who repeats the actions of player 1. The relay continues in this manner until player 5 runs across the starting line while holding the egg. The first team to finish wins.

Variations

1. Have the children jump like a rabbit rather than run. Shorten the distance between the lines.
2. Have them balance the egg in a tablespoon while running.

Easter Bunny relay. Divide the class into relay teams and have them line up in file formation (Fig. 16-8, *B.*) Each participant is required to jump to the turning line and back.

Jump the stick relay. Have relay teams line up so that each child is an arm's length behind the one in front of him. The first 2 in each line hold the ends of a wand (or a short rope) and stand facing their team. On the starting signal they bend over and move down the line of players. Each player must jump over the wand when the 2 reach the end of the line (see the illustration on p. 000). Player 1 stays there while player 2 runs back to the front of the line. Player 3 takes hold of one end of the wand, and the play is repeated. Play continues until player 1 is again at the head of the line.

Easter dances used at the intermediate level:

Bunnie Trail
Easter Frolic

The record and story "Little Duck" from the *Dance-a-Story* series, contains Easter themes appropriate for stimulating creative movement experiences with younger children. Older children enjoy "The Bunny Hop," available from Capital Records.

Halloween

CONCEPT: Halloween is celebrated in England, Ireland, and the United States.

Levels: All.
Subconcepts: (1) Halloween originated as a festival to celebrate the end of the summer, which was the end of the year in ancient Britain. (2) The people believed that as winter approached, the spirits of the dead visited their kinsmen, seeking warmth and good cheer. (*Encyclopaedia Britannica,* 1960.) (3) This is why skeletons, ghosts, witches, devils, and black cats are associated with Halloween.

Materials: See specific activities.
Activities

Devils and Witches (an adaptation of Brownies and Fairies). Divide the class in half and have them stand behind two goal lines (Fig. 16-19). One team is Witches and the other the Devils. Play begins by one team (e.g., the Witches) turning around so that their backs are toward the other team (the Devils). On a signal (such as beckoning with your hand), the Devils sneak across the space between the two teams and when they are within a few feet of the Witches, you call out "The Devils are coming!" This is the signal for the Witches to turn around and chase the Devils. Any devil tagged before he runs back across his goal line becomes a member of the Witches' team. Play is repeated with the Devils turning their backs and

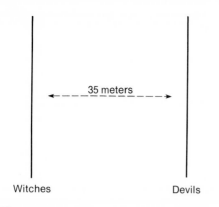

Fig. 16-19. Formation for Devils and Witches.

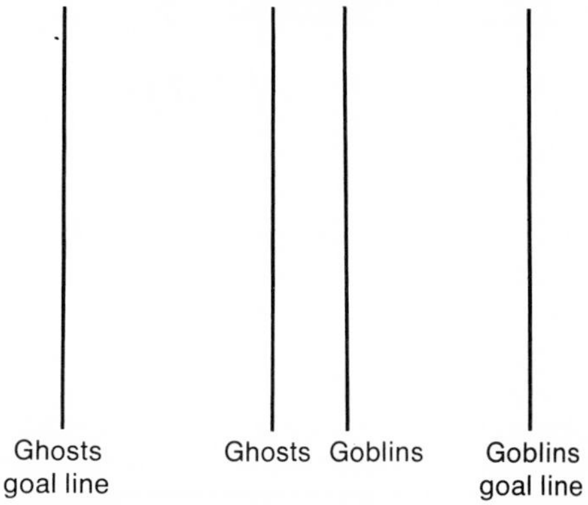

Ghosts
goal line
　　Ghosts Goblins
　　　　　Goblins
goal line

Fig. 16-20. Formation for Ghosts and Goblins.

the Witches sneaking up on them. Play continues as the teams alternate.

Ghosts and Goblins (an adaptation of Crows and Cranes). Divide the class into two teams and have them stand on two parallel lines about a meter apart (Fig. 16-20). Call out the name of either team. If you call "Ghosts," the Ghosts must run toward their goal line. The Goblins chase and attempt to tag them before they cross their goal line. Any ghost tagged becomes a member of the Goblins' team. Play continues by your calling out the name of either team. The team with the most players at the end of the playing period is declared the winner. Suspense is added by slowly pronouncing the "G" and then quickly calling out the name of a team.

*Halloween dances** used at the intermediate level:

Casper the Ghost
Halloween Swing
Spook Time
Halloween Hoedown

Veterans Day

CONCEPT: Veterans Day was originally called Armistice Day.

Level: Intermediate.

Subconcepts: Veterans Day was designated as a national holiday in Great Britain, France, and the United States to commemorate the end

of World War I. (2) After World War II it was redesignated as Veterans Day and specified as a day in which to honor the veterans of all wars.

Materials: Two flags made of two pieces of cloth of different colors, attached to the ends of two sticks.

Activities

Capture the flag. Divide the class into two teams, named by the color of their flag. The players are identified by wearing the same color as their flag (e.g., a red or blue scarf or headband). The playing area is marked off as shown in Fig. 16-21. Each team tries to capture their opponents' flag and prevent the capture of their own flag. If a player is tagged while in enemy territory, he must go to the prison. To "rescue" a prisoner, a teammate may go to the prison, take the prisoner's hand, then both run back to their home court. If either the rescuer or the prisoner is tagged while in enemy territory, both become prisoners. A rescuer may rescue only 1 prisoner at a time. All defenders of the flag must stay out of the area marked off around the flag. When a player captures the opponents' flag and carries it back over the center line to his home court, his team wins the game.

Variations: The game may be prolonged and contain an additional challenge if each team has several flags.

Discuss the following:

* The significance of the flag in war (this could be related to the writing of our national anthem)

---

*The description for all the holiday dances listed in this section may be found in Stuart, Gibson, and Jervey (1963).

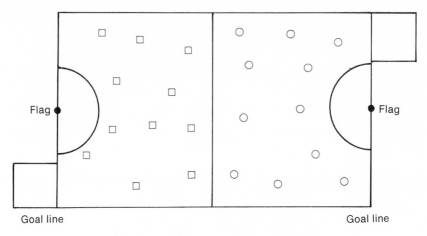

Flag

Goal line

Flag

Goal line

Fig. 16-21. Playing area for capture the flag.

- The elements of this game that resemble those of a battle
- How all the prisoners are freed and can return home when the war is over

Thanksgiving

CONCEPTS: Thanksgiving is the oldest holiday originating in the United States. It is a traditional harvest festival first celebrated in this country by the Plymouth Colony in 1621.

Levels: All.

Materials: See specific activities.

Activities: Thanksgiving is a good time to play stoolball (pp. 218 and 219) or town ball (p. 217), since both these games were played at Plymouth.

Catch the turkey's tail. Each child has a cloth band ("tail"), one end of which is tucked into the back waistband. When the music begins, the children move about the play area trying to grab someone's band (turkey tail), at the same time trying to prevent anyone from getting theirs (Fig. 16-22). A player (turkey) who loses his band (tail) is out of the game. Play continues until some child has acquired four turkey tails. This child is the winner. The tails are then returned to their owners and the game begins again.

Thanksgiving dances used at the intermediate level:

Pumpkin Square
Turkey Flag
Turkey Glide

The Virginia Reel is also an appropriate Thanksgiving dance, since it was used in the early colonies and is sometimes danced to the tune of "Turkey in the Straw."*

Christmas

CONCEPTS: Christmas is a time for giving and sharing. It is a time when people should play joyfully together.

Levels: All.

Materials: See specific activities.

Activities

Toy charades. Divide the class into groups containing from 2 to 5 children. Challenge each group to think of a toy that moves and ways they can move like that toy. Give the children time to practice, then have them perform as the rest of the class try to identify the toy. Older children may extend the game by putting the movements together to tell a story about these toys being under the Christmas tree.

Catch the candy cane. Divide the class into groups of 8 to 10 members. Have each group form a circle and count off so that each child has a number. Select 1 child to be in the center. Give this child a cane or a wand approximately a meter long. The child in the center holds the cane upright with one end touching the floor and calls out the number of one of the children in the circle, at the same time letting go of the

---

*The words and music for "Turkey in the Straw" are given in Bley (1960), pp. 72 and 73.

Fig. 16-22. Catch the turkey's tail.

cane. The child whose number is called must rush into the circle and catch the cane before it falls to the floor. If successful, the child who was in the center must try again. If the cane is not caught, the child who failed to catch it must stay in the center and call someone else's number. The child who first held the cane goes into the circle.

And then something exciting happened (classroom game). Read the children a Christmas poem or story while they are sitting in their seats. Tell them you are going to digress from the story occasionally and say "And then something exciting happened." When you say this, they are to all jump up and run to someone else's seat.

Variations

1. You can remove one seat and have one of the children read. This child can say the cue to move whenever he desires, and as the other children are exchanging seats, he

attempts to get into one. The child without a seat becomes the new reader.
2. Select a cue word in the poem or story, such as Santa, reindeer, snow, presents, or tree. Each time this cue word is read, the children must change seats.

Christmas dances used at the intermediate level:

Christmas Joy	Snowball Roll
Christmas Tree Spree	St. Nick's Glide
Holly Bells	Frosty Schottische
Holly Time	Jingle Bell Stomp
Santa's Schottische	Mistletoe Twist
Santa's Sleigh	Reindeer Rock

The record and story "The Toy Tree" from the *Dance-a-Story* series contain stimulating ideas and music for creative movement. They can be effectively used with children who have no previous creative dance experience, as well as with those who have.

Chapter 17

REGIONAL STUDIES

This chapter contains activities designed to stimulate an interest in people of other countries. The concepts convey comparisons and contrasts with the history and culture of the United States. The characteristics of the people are emphasized, as well as the factors that have influenced their behavior and their way of life.

The content has been divided into regions, with a focus on the countries having traditional games and dances appropriate for elementary school children. In some instances, activities have been created to provide active learning experiences. Most of these relate to the geography and to the occupations and products of the regions. An attempt has been made to retain the authentic flavor of the countries so that the children can sense and comprehend the essense of each different culture. As you direct their participation, it is suggested that you encourage them to try to imagine themselves in the time and place of the people being studied.

Learning activities

Mexico

CONCEPT: Mexico is a poor country because its industry has not been highly developed and because much of the country consists of mountains, deserts, and tropical marshes, which cannot be farmed.

Level: Intermediate.

Subconcept: The people of Mexico tend to live close to the land and make their living by farming or from crafts such as metal work, weaving, and making pottery.

Materials: A large outline map of Mexico traced in the dirt on the playground or layed out with ropes on blacktop, in the gym, or in a hallway; copies of the treasure map shown in Fig. 17-1 with a note at the bottom of each, instructing the team how to find their treasure; colored station markers placed at the proper locations on the play area; and the treasures listed, placed in brown paper bags and hidden where the appropriate team will find it by following their instructions:

- *Blue:* silver (any kind of silver-colored object resembling an article that is manufactured in Mexico)
- *Green:* corn (kernels of dry corn)
- *Red:* fruit (plastic fruit such as a banana or any kind of citrus fruit or melon)
- *Purple:* woven straw products (baskets, mats, a hat, a coaster, etc.)
- *Yellow:* pottery (a piece of red clay or painted pottery such as a flower pot)

Activities

Treasure hunt. Divide the class into five groups. Give each group a treasure map mounted on the color paper that identifies the team. Have each group locate the stations marked with their color (Fig. 17-1). Tell them they are to begin at this station and follow the arrows on their treasure map, traveling entirely around the country of Mexico until they return to the station where they began. On returning to their home station, they are to follow the instructions at the bottom of their map, telling them how to locate their treasure. The instructions written at the bottom of each map are for that specific team:

- *Blue:* Jump north into the mountains.
- *Green:* Jump south through the Yucatan Peninsula.
- *Red:* Jump east toward the ocean.
- *Purple:* Jump south down the peninsula.
- *Yellow:* Jump south along the coast.

When all the teams have found their treasure,

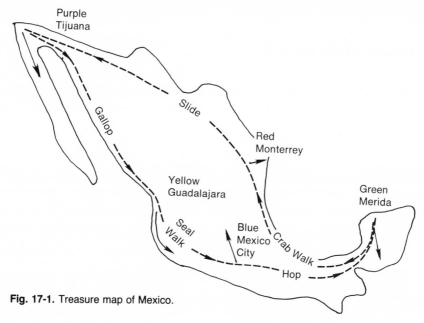

Fig. 17-1. Treasure map of Mexico.

have the class gather together and discuss the significance of each treasure.

Variations

1. Write some of the words on the treasure map in Spanish rather than in English. Some of the Spanish words that could be substituted follow:

Blue	Azul	Purple	Purpura
Green	Verde	Yellow	Amarillo
Red	Rojo		

The movements to be executed between the stations and to the treasures:

Seal Walk	Foco Andar
Hop	Brincar
Crab Walk	Cambaro Andar
Slide	Resbalar
Gallop	Galopar
Jump	Saltar

2. Add to the instructions the number of jumping steps the children must execute between their home station and the location of the treasure. Have them count out loud in Spanish as they execute each step:

One	Uno	Six	Seis
Two	Dos	Seven	Siete
Three	Tres	Eight	Ocho
Four	Cuatro	Nine	Nueve
Five	Cinco	Ten	Diez

■ ■ ■

Level: Intermediate.

Subconcepts: (1) The tendency of the Mexican people to be quiet and shy reflects their Indian heritage, but many of their dances are fast and exciting, portraying the influence of the Spaniards. (2) Dance is an important part of Mexican culture, each state having an official state dance.

Materials: Recordings of the dance music and written dance instructions:

"La Raspa," RCA LPM 1623
"La Cucaracha," RCA LPM 1621
"Mexican Hat Dance," Folkraft 1038

BRITISH ISLES

CONCEPT: The British Isles are divided into the countries of England, Scotland, Ireland, and Wales.

Level: Intermediate.

Subconcepts: (1) Ireland is a separate island. (2) The other three countries are located on the same body of land — Scotland occupies the northern portion and Wales is located to the west between England and the Irish Sea.

Materials: A large outline map of the British Isles drawn on the playground or formed by ropes on the floor (Fig. 17-2); objects, or pictures of objects, that signify something about each of the countries (e.g., plaid cloth or

Fig. 17-2. The British Isles.

Write the name of one major city in each of the four countries on cards (make one set of cards for each team). Examples of cities are Dublin, Glasgow, Cardiff, and London. Place each pile of cards (e.g., all Dublin cards) on the approximate location of the city. Play the game as previously described, except that the children run to the pile of cards instead of objects in the appropriate country, pick up a card, and carry it back to their team. You may make the activity more challenging by having more than one pile of cards in each country:

England	Scotland
London	Edinburgh
Plymouth	Glasgow
Liverpool	Aberdeen
Ireland	Wales
Dublin	Cardiff
Belfast	Swansea
Killarney	Bangor

England

CONCEPT: The game of hopscotch originated in England a long time ago.

Level: Beginning.

Subconcepts: (1) The children marked the diagrams for the game on the flat paved roads built by the Romans (Vinton, 1970). (2) A variety of diagrams and rules have evolved over the years. Examples of two diagrams are shown on p. 4.

Activities: Any hopschotch games.

CONCEPT: The English streets and roads formed natural boundaries for games.

Level: Beginning.

Subconcepts: (1) Tag games were popular pastimes because they required no materials and any number of children could play. (2) A variety of tag games could be created by just changing a few simple rules or rearranging the goal lines.

Materials: A large indoor or outdoor playing area where the children can run freely.

Activities: Following is an example of a tag game played by English children.

Chain tag (an adaptation of the English game relievo [Horrigan, 1929]). One player is selected as "It." All the other players scatter

woolen tweed for Scotland, cars or china for England, coal for Wales, fish or linen for Ireland). Place the objects on the area of the map representing that country. You will need a set of objects for each team.

Activities: Divide the class into groups containing 4 children and have them line up in file formation behind a starting line (Fig. 16-8, *B*). Tell the children you will call out the name of one of the countries in the British Isles and they must run to the map of that country, pick up one of the objects which represents that country, and run back to their team. Explain that you will call out the names of the different countries so that everyone will have a turn. When all the countries have been called and all the objects retrieved, discuss the significance of each object in relation to the geography, economy, and occupations of the country. Review the locations of the countries.

Variations

1. Make the activity a contest by awarding 1 point to the team that returns first to the starting line after retrieving the object. The team with the most points at the end wins the contest.

2. Rather than products, you may emphasize the locations of major cities in each country.

around the playing area. To begin, It attempts to tag any of the players. A player who is tagged joins hands with It, and together they try to tag others by using only the free hand. As each player is tagged, he joins hands with the one who tagged him. Only the two end persons are allowed to tag, and the line of players must remain unbroken. Play continues until all the players are tagged.

CONCEPT: Two types of English dances have been popular in the United States—song plays and country dances.

Level: Beginning — song plays.

Subconcept: The English song plays are simple dances accompanied by a song and so resemble the American play-party games.

Materials

"London Bridge Is Falling Down," Ickis, 1969, or Bley, 1960
"Pussy Cat, Pussy Cat," Hoctor HLP4026
"Jolly Is the Miller," Folkraft 1192B
"Round and Round the Village," RCA LPM 1625
"Oats, Peas, Beans, and Barley Grow," Folkraft 1182 and RCA 45

■ ■ ■

Level: Advanced—country dances.

Subconcepts: (1) The English country dances were performed at English festivals and on social occasions. (2) The basic steps of country dances are running, skipping, and sliding. (3) These dances are performed with traditional English dignity and precision.

Materials: Construction paper, pictures, and the following records:

"Ribbon Dance," RCA LPM 1621
"Gathering Peascods," RCA 1621
"Black Nag," Folkraft 1174
"Maypole Dance," RCA LPM 1621
"Circassian Circle," Folkraft 1247

Activities

Creative dance. The ever-popular English Christmas carol "Twelve Days of Christmas" as the theme for creative movement provides a novel means of studying British holiday customs. The song portrays the old English custom of a man showing his sweetheart how much he

loves her by giving her a present each day during the Christmas season.

Divide the class into twelve groups and give each group a piece of construction paper with a picture of one of the following:

• Partridge in a pear tree
• Two turtle doves
• Three French hens
• Four calling birds
• Five golden rings
• Six geese-a-laying
• Seven swans-a-swimming
• Eight maids-a-milking
• Nine ladies dancing
• Ten lords-a-leaping
• Eleven pipers piping
• Twelve drummers drumming

Instruct the groups to think about the kinds of movements that express the theme of their picture and convey the festive mood of their day. Challenge them to select the best movements and sequence so that they form a short dance. When the individual groups are prepared, bring all the groups together. Sing the song once without actions. Then have each group perform their dance. After each group has performed, discuss the significance of their movements. Ask each group to select one particular movement that portrays their theme. Have the class sing the song, with each group leading the entire class in their movement each time that part of the song is sung.

Scotland

CONCEPT: Scotland has many unique customs and traditions.

Level: Intermediate.

Subconcepts: (1) The mountains, forests, and seas make it a colorful country. (2) Another colorful aspect of Scotland is the plaid material. (3) Each original Scottish clan (family) is represented by a different color or design; on festive occasions the men wear kilts and a long shawl made from this material. (4) Their dances are accompanied by music played on a bagpipe.

Materials

"Highland Schottische," RCA LPM 1621
"Highland Fling," RCA LPM 1621

Ireland

CONCEPT: Large numbers of Irish people helped to settle and develop this country.

Subconcepts: The Irish are characteristically witty, fun loving, and hospitable. (2) Their customs and traditions have become a part of the American culture. (3) Our celebration of St. Patrick's Day is an example.

For *Irish games* see those described under St. Patrick's Day, pp. 227 and 228.

Irish dances used at the intermediate level:

"Irish Washerwoman," RCA LPM 1623
"Irish Jig," RCA LPM 1623
"Waves of Tory," RCA LPM 1623

SCANDINAVIA

CONCEPT: The Scandinavian countries are Norway, Sweden, and Denmark.

Level: Intermediate.

Subconcepts: (1) Norway and Sweden make up the Scandinavian Peninsula. Their land mass resembles twin curved fingers attached to the northern part of the European continent. (2) Denmark is also a peninsula; it is attached to Germany. (3) The countries have extensive sea coasts. (4) The terrain of Norway and Sweden is mountainous. (5) The games and dances of the countries are vigorous and spirited, which one would expect in a rugged countryside and cool climate. (6) The geography of the countries determines the major occupations and products; fishing, lumbering, and farming are the primary occupations.

Materials: Oval playing areas marked off to resemble maps of the three Scandinavian countries, markers, and hoops scattered inside these areas; the total number of hoops needed is one less than the number of couples in the class.

Activities: Have each child select a partner. Give each couple a name designating one of the principle occupations of one of the Scandinavian countries. Instruct each couple to go to the country they represent and stand inside a hoop marked with their occupation (Fig. 17-3). One extra couple is "It." They place themselves in an advantageous location and call out the name of the country and one or more of the occupations. For example, they might call out "Norwegian fisherman." All the couples in this cate-

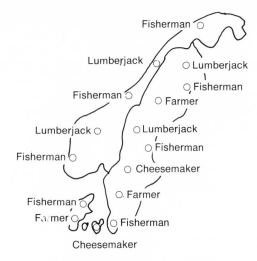

Fig. 17-3. The Scandinavian countries.

gory must exchange places while the couple that called out the names attempt to get in a hoop, leaving out another couple to be It.

Variations

1. Call out "All Danes" (or Norwegians or Swedes), in which case all the couples in Denmark must exchange places.
2. Call out "All fishermen (lumberjacks, farmers, or cheesemakers), requiring all the couples in this category to find a hoop in a different country.

Norway

CONCEPTS: Norway, "the land of the midnight sun," is an extremely mountainous country. The people are hospitable, fun-loving, and very active.

Level: Beginning.

Materials: A shoe or beanbag.

Activities: Children in Norway play games similar to those found in other parts of Europe. Examples of these are blind man's bluff, hop in paradise (similar to hopscotch), and hunt the slipper (Bancroft, 1909).

Hunt the slipper. This is an ancient Greek game in which the children sit in a circle with their knees bent and their feet flat on the floor. A shoe (or beanbag) is passed under the knees from one player to the next. Meanwhile, one of the children is sent to another part of the room. This child returns and attempts to locate the shoe. If successful, he exchanges places with the child who has the shoe.

Variation: Another version of the game has the child who is "It" stand in the center of the circle. A more active version has It chase the child with the slipper around the outside of the circle. If the child with the shoe is tagged, they exchange places.

Norwegian dances used at the intermediate level:

"Tri-La-La Ja Saa," RCA LPM 1622
"Norwegian Mountain March," RCA LPM 1622
   and Hoctor LP 4028

Sweden

CONCEPTS: Like their ancestors the Vikings, the Swedes are adventurous, active people. Their games and dances examplify the characteristics of friendliness and kindness, and although they are vigorous, there is no roughness.

Level: Beginning.
Materials: Playing area.
Activities

"Are you awake Mr. Bear?" (ICHPER, 1967). In this game, the playing area has a bear's den in one corner and a safe area, or home, in the corner diagonally opposite (Fig. 17-4). One child is selected to be the "bear," pretending to be asleep in his den. The rest of the children gather in their home. The children softly call out "Are you awake Mr. Bear?" as they sneak across the playing area. The children call out louder and louder as they get closer to the den, but the bear continues to snore away. Suddenly he jumps up and chases the children, attempting to tag as many as possible. The children are safe when they are within their home. All those tagged become bear cubs and must join the bear in his den and in the attempts to tag others.

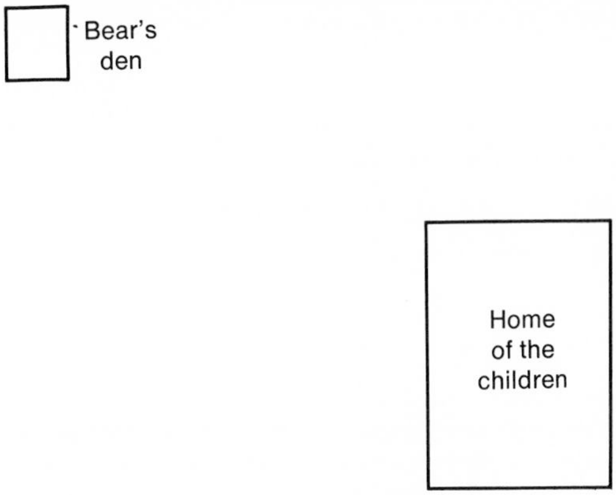

Swedish dances used at the *beginning* level: "I See You" and "How Do you Do, My Partner?" are easy Swedish dance games. Both may be accompanied by singing the song given in the instructions. Both are recorded on RCA LPM 1625. "I See You" is also available on Hoctor LP 4026. Another dance is "Carrousel," RCA LPM 1625.

Dances at the *intermediate* level:

Bear's den

Home of the children

Fig. 17-4. Are you awake Mr. Bear?

"Gustaf's Skoal," RCA LPM 1622, and Hoctor LP 4027
"Bleking," RCA LPM 1622

The polka is a common step in Swedish folk dances. This is the basic step of the following lively dances:

"Hopp Mor Annika," RCA LPM 1624
"Lott' Ist Tod," RCA LPM 1622
"Tantoli," RCA LPM 1621

Denmark

CONCEPTS: The Danes are hard working, friendly, pleasure-loving people. Their games and dances portray these characteristics as well as symbolizing factors that affect their occupations and way of life.

Level: Intermediate.
Materials: Hoops or circles drawn in the dirt.
Activities

The ocean is stormy (McEniry, 1969). Circles (hoops may be used) are placed on the floor around the room. The children pair off and each couple stands inside a circle, or home. There should be one less circle than there are couples (Fig. 17-5). These two children are "whales." Each couple standing in a circle decides what type of fish they will be. (The types of fish caught by Danish fishermen are cod, herring, mackerel, salmon, plaice, eel, and shellfish.) The "whales" walk around the room calling out the names of fish common to Denmark. When they call out the name of a cou-

Fig. 17-5. The ocean is stormy.

ple's fish, that couple leaves their circle and walks behind the "whales." After all the names have been called or whenever the "whales" cannot think of any more names, they call out "The ocean is stormy." This is the signal for all the players to run to a circle, but no fish can return to the same partner nor the same circle. The two children left without a home in a circle pair up and become the new whales.

Danish dances used at the beginning level:

"Dance of Greeting," RCA LPM 1625
"Shoemaker's Dance," RCA LPM 1624
"Nixie Polka (Nigarepolska)," RCA LPM 1625
"Seven Jumps," RCA LPM 1623
"The Crested Hen," RCA LPM 1624

CENTRAL EUROPE

CONCEPT: Europe is a small continent with a large population and well-developed industry, and so trains provide an efficient means of transporting goods and people.

Level: Intermediate.

Subconcepts: (1) There are many rivers and mountains in Europe. (2) Bridges had to be built and the railroads designed so that the trains could pass over or under the mountains.

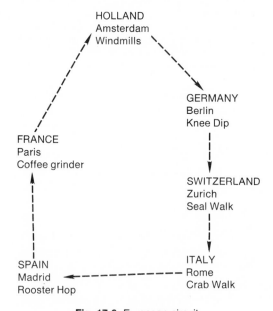

HOLLAND
Amsterdam
Windmills

GERMANY
Berlin
Knee Dip

FRANCE
Paris
Coffee grinder

SWITZERLAND
Zurich
Seal Walk

SPAIN
Madrid
Rooster Hop

ITALY
Rome
Crab Walk

Fig. 17-6. European circuit.

Materials: Station markers set up in the locations shown in Fig. 17-6, each marker stating the name of the country, the major city, and the stunt to be executed at that station.

Activities: Divide the class into six groups. Go over the concept and subconcepts and explain that each group is a train which will travel to each of the European countries in the circuit. Explain that they are to stand one behind the other and place their hands on the hips of the child in front of them. The child in the front of the line (the locomotive) puts his hands on his hips. They are to maintain this position while walking from one station to the next. Assign each group to one of the stations. Instruct them to execute the prescribed stunt as long as the music is playing and to move like a train to the next station when the music stops.

When they have completed the circuit, call the class together and discuss the significance of each stunt. The following concepts can be explained.

- Holland (Windmills): The windmill is used as a major source of power before electricity became readily available.
- Germany (Knee Dip): Formal calisthenics and exercises to develop strength are associated with Germany, since these have traditionally been emphasized in their physical education and military training.
- Switzerland (Seal Walk): This stunt executed on a low level is intended to illustrate the fact that the trains pass through many tunnels in this mountainous country.
- Italy (Crab Walk): Italy is a peninsula, and therefore fishing and gathering seafood are principal occupations.
- Spain (Rooster Hop): Cockfighting is a popular pastime in Spain.
- France (Coffee Grinder): Coffee is a popular beverage in France. People love to sit in the sidewalk cafes and visit as they drink coffee and eat pastries.

Germany

CONCEPTS: German people are characteristically active and industrious. The rich farmland and natural resources supply the materials they convert into quality products such as cars, textiles, chemicals, and plastics.

Level: Intermediate.

Subconcepts: (1) The games German children play are similar to those played by children in the United States. (2) They play hopscotch, tag games, and ball games.

Activities

Panther game (Diem, 1975). This is a tag game. One child who is the ''panther'' stands

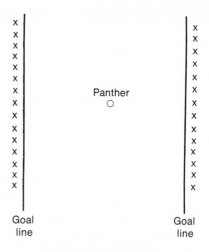

Fig. 17-7. Panther game.

in the center of the playing area. Half the class stands behind the goal line on one end and half behind the line on the other end (Fig. 17-7). The panther calls out, ''Who is afraid of the wild panther?'' The children answer ''Not me'' or ''No one'' and then run across the playing area. The panther attempts to tag them, and anyone caught joins him in the center. The game continues until everyone is tagged. The last child tagged is the panther when the game is played again.

■ ■ ■

Subconcept: German folk dance is active and joyful and frequently contains percussive movements such as clapping and stamping.

Materials

Beginning level:

''Kinderpolka (Children's Polka), RCA LPM 1625
''Eins Zwei Drei,'' Hoctor LP 4026

Intermediate level:

''Bummel Schottische,'' RCA LPM 1622
''Hansel and Gretal,'' RCA LPM 1624
''Come Let Us Be Joyful, RCA LPM 1622

Advanced level:

Dances for advanced students are available in the album *German Folk Dances,* FLP 5, a Foldraft record. This album contains fourteen selections, with instructions for each folk dance.

France

CONCEPTS: Unlike most other European countries, France has few well-known, traditional games or dances. The dances that were developed by the working class are short and playful, indicating that they were performed as leisure-time activities at the end of a long working day.

Level: Intermediate.

Activities

Exchange (French blind Man's bluff [Bancroft, 1909]). The players sit on chairs arranged in a circle. One child is "It" and stands in the center blindfolded. The children number off consecutively. The child in the center calls out two numbers. The children whose numbers were called must exchange places. As they are doing so, the player in the center attempts to tag one of them or sit in one of the vacant seats. If It is successful, the child tagged or the one without a seat becomes It.

French dances used at the beginning level:

"Gay Musician," RCA LPM 1625 or Hoctor LP 4026

"Chimes of Dunkirk," RCA LPM 1624 or Hoctor LP 4026

"Bridge of Avignon," RCA LPM 1625

Italy

CONCEPT: Italian games and dances are similar to those of other European countries and the United States.

Level: Intermediate.

Subconcepts: (1) Italian children play a variety of tag games and ball games. (2) Their dances have a relaxed, joyous quality and are sometimes accompanied by a tambourine. (3) The best-known Italian dance is the Tarantella.

Activities

Bocce. This Italian lawn bowling game is rapidly gaining in popularity in the United States. It may be played by 2 to 6 players. The instructions are included with the balls. The set of nine wooden balls are reasonably priced and are available through sporting goods dealers.

An *Italian dance* used at the intermediate level is "Sicilian Tarantella," RCA LPM 1621.

Holland (The Netherlands)

CONCEPT: Even though Holland is a small country, it has many interesting customs that have spread throughout the world.

Subconcepts: (1) The game of ninepins was brought to this country by the early Dutch settlers (pp. 220 and 221). (2) At the beginning of this century the Dutch developed korfball, a team sport similar to basketball. (3) Traditional Dutch dances contain steps that reflect the custom of wearing wooden shoes; the feet stay close to the floor, and the steps have a heavy quality.

A *Dutch dance* used at the intermediate level is "Dutch Couple Dance," RCA LPM 1620.

Switzerland

CONCEPT: Switzerland is a very mountainous country; the mountain slopes and the valleys provide excellent pasture lands and hay fields to sustain the chief agricultural enterprise—dairying.

Level: Intermediate.

Subconcepts: (1) The country is rich in folklore, much of it related to the mountains and the cows. (2) The heart of community life is the village; Weggis is an example of a folk dance named after a Swiss village. (3) Swiss games are similar to those played in other European countries and the United States.

Activities

Drei Mann Hoch (ICHPER, 1967). In the United States this game is called three deep. The children stand in a double circle facing the center (Fig. 17-8). A "runner" and a "chaser" stand in the center. The chaser attempts to tag the runner, who is safe if he stands in front of one of the couples. When this occurs, the player at the back of the three-deep group becomes the runner. If the chaser tags the runner, the two change roles.

Variations

1. The couples may stand side by side in a

Fig. 17-8. Three deep.

circle or in scattered formation. The runner may stand on either side of the couple, and the person on the other end of the group becomes the new runner.

2. The couples sit down facing each other. They hold hands to form a "house." The runner is safe when he jumps into the house. The player he has his back toward becomes the new runner.

A *Swiss dance* used at the intermediate level is "Weggis," Hoctor LP 4029.

Russia (U.S.S.R.)

CONCEPT: Physical activities play a major role in Russian culture.

Level: Intermediate.

Subconcepts: (1) The Russians are a very active people who enjoy music, dance, gymnastics, track and field, and games and sports. (2) Many of their games and dances symbolize occupations and historical facts.

Materials: A bell and a small box.

Activities

Ting-a-ling (Hunt, 1941). Moscow is known as the city of bells. This game is based on an extremely old Russian legend about the city.

A playing area is laid out as shown in Fig. 17-9. The square in the center is called the "steeple" and the child in the steeple is the "clapper." The clapper holds a small box containing a bell. One of the children standing on the large square is designated as the captain. Play begins by the clapper giving the captain the bell and then hiding his eyes while the captain hands one of the players the bell. The captain then leads the players around the square and along the diagonal lines. As the children are walking, the one with the bell rings it softly and passes it to another player. Each player rings the bell and passes it on while the clapper attempts to discover who has it. When he thinks he knows who is holding it, he claps his hands. This is the signal for all the children to circle the clapper. The player holding the bell drops it into the clapper's box and proceeds to run around inside the big square. The clapper tries to tag this player. If he succeeds, play stops. However, another player may grab the bell out of the box, and if this occurs, the clapper must chase the child with the bell. The one being chased may escape by passing the bell to another player. If the clapper is unable to tag anyone, the captain may give a signal for play to stop, in which case the child holding the bell is the clapper during the next game.

Russian dances used at the intermediate level:

"Troika," Hoctor LP 4027
"Koroboushka," Hoctor LP 4028

Greece

CONCEPT: The ancient Greeks believed that the complete life resulted from development of a sound mind in a sound body.

Level: Intermediate.

Subconcepts: (1) To reach this goal, they participated in a variety of physical activities, as well as studied music, poetry, and drama. (2) Games and dances were an important part of their festivals. (3) Games and contests became so popular with the Greeks that they started the Olympic Games. (4) The Greeks believed that honor rested in the games, not in the reward.

Materials: A playground ball.

Activities

Greek ball game (Horrigan, 1929). The players are divided into two teams and numbered off as shown in Fig. 17-10. A playground ball is placed in the center of the field. When the signal is given, the first player on each team rushes

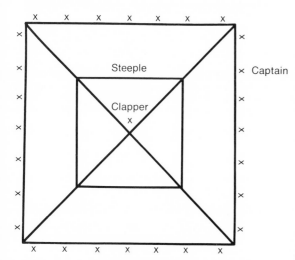

Fig. 17-9. Ting-a-ling.

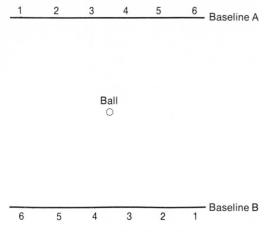

Fig. 17-10. Greek ball game.

to the center and attempts to get the ball. The one who gets it tries to throw it over the opponent's goal line. Play continues until one team is successful. A point is awarded each time the ball goes over the opponent's baseline. A game consists of 10 or 15 points. Each time a team scores, the players in the center go to the end of the line, and the 2 players with the next number go to the center when the signal is given.

■ ■ ■

Level: Intermediate.

Subconcepts: (1) Greek contests consisted of athletic events. (2) The ancient olympics were races, the broad jump, the discus throw, boxing, wrestling, and the pentathlon, which consisted of the combination of all these, plus boxing. Chariot races were also included in the olympics.

Materials: A rope approximately 5 meters long.

Activities: Track and field events appropriate for children may be used as Olympic events in the elementary schools. Recommended activities follow:

25-meter dash	Standing broad jump
50-meter dash	Long jump
150-meter dash	Triple jump (hop, step, and jump)
200-meter run	Frisbee throw
550-meter run-walk	Softball throw
220-meter relay	Wrestling with different body parts (pp. 213 and 214)

The children may also do imitation chariot races. In these races 2, 3, or 4 children pretend to be the horses by standing side by side, holding the middle of a long rope. Another child holds the ends of the rope and drives the team. Teams may compete in heats.

■ ■ ■

Level: Intermediate.

Subconcept: The most common form of folk dance in Greece is the group dance in which the dancers are in a line or a circle.

Materials

"Gaida Gidas," Hoctor HLP 4027
"Misirlou," RCA LPM 1620
"Tsamiko," RCA LPM 1620

AFRICA

CONCEPT: Africa is nearly four times the size of the United States.

Level: Intermediate.

Subconcepts: (1) Africa contains over fifty countries. (2) It is inhabited by hundreds of tribes who speak over 800 languages. (3) Although the continent is rich in natural resources, it is underdeveloped. The major reasons for this follow: (a) transportation and shipping difficult; no network of railroads or highways and few bays or harbors where shipping ports can be established; (b) power for fuel lacking (little coal or oil), sources for hydroelectric power abundant, but much of this potential located in the interior of the continent and not developed; (c) soil mediocre and sometimes poor, and farming methods primitive; (d) industry slow to develop; wealth derived from the resources of the continent not invested in developing the potential of the continent; (e) vast areas of the continent—desert, jungle, or mountains—not inhabitable.

Materials: A large outline map of Africa traced in the dirt of the playground or laid out with string or ropes on the floor; markers placed on the map to indicate where the stations are located (see the boldface names on Fig. 17-11; tumbling mats and pictures of the pyramids and the Sphinx placed at the Cairo station; climbing ropes or jump ropes at the Mount Kilimanjaro station; beanbags and a box, target, or waste-

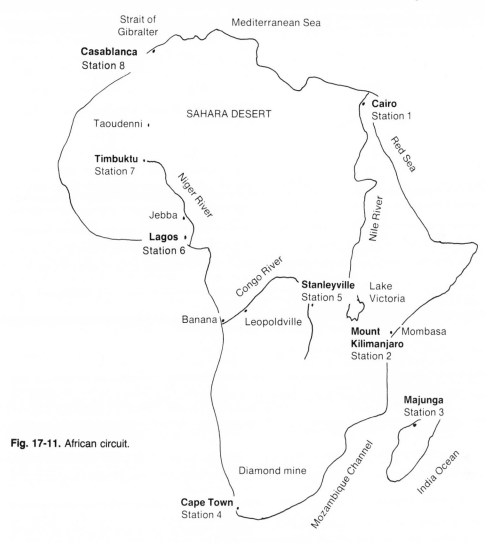

Fig. 17-11. African circuit.

basket at the Casablanca station; pictures of wild and domestic animals indigenous to Africa; pictures of passenger ships, riverboats, and African canoes; and a map and a copy of instructions for each group.

Activities

African safari. Divide the class into eight groups. Give each group a map and a set of instructions and assign them to begin at the station with their number. Instructions follow:

Station 1. Cairo

   a. Study the pictures of ancient Egypt. Build a pyramid with three levels (i.e., some children on a low level, lying down or on their hands and knees; some on a medium

level, bending at the waist or on their hands and feet; and some on a high level, standing up). Challenge the children to create a shape that resembles a pyramid or the Sphinx. Caution them not to arrange themselves so that any child must support the weight of any other child.

   b. Ride a riverboat up the Nile River to Lake Victoria. Join the natives as they paddle their canoes into the lake to fish. Ride the train to the foot of Mount Kilimanjaro.

Station 2. Mount Kilimanjaro

   a. If climbing ropes are available, have the children climb these to simulate climbing the mountain. If these are not available, have them jump rope to condition their legs and develop the endurance necessary in mountain climbing.

  b. Get back on the train and ride to the seaport of Mombasa on the coast of Kenya. Board a ship and sail to Majunga on the island of Malagasy (Madagascar).

Station 3. Majunga

  a. Do a Coffee Grinder, turning completely around twice with your right hand on the floor, then twice with your left hand on the floor.

  b. Return to the ship and sail through the Mozambique Channel, around the Cape of Good Hope to Cape Town, South Africa.

Station 4. Cape Town

  a. Do an Elephant Walk to the diamond mine. When you get there, make a diamond shape with your arms. Sit down and make a diamond shape with your legs. Form a diamond shape with a partner. Do an Elephant Walk back to Cape Town.

  b. Return to the ship and sail to Banana in the Congo. Go ashore and then ride a riverboat up the Congo River to Stanleyville.

Station 5. Stanleyville

  a. Do a Skin the Snake with your group. Practice until you can lie down and get up smoothly.

  b. Ride the riverboat back down the Congo River to Leopoldville. Board a plane and fly to Lagos, Nigeria.

Station 6. Lagos

  a. Do a Stork Stand. Stand on your right foot and hold it as long as possible; then stand on your left foot.

  b. Ride the train to Jebba. Ride a riverboat up the Niger River to Timbuktu (Tombouctou).

Station 7. Timbuktu

  a. Join a salt caravan and do a Camel Walk across the Sahara Desert to Taoudenni. The salt caravan stops here, so ride in a jeep across the remainder of the desert and the mountains, to Casablanca, Morocco.

Station 8. Casablanca

  a. Toss five beanbags into the target (box or wastebasket).

  b. Board a ship and sail through the Strait of Gibraltar and across the Mediterranean Sea to Cairo.

The activities at the stations can be adapted to fit the physical environment of your school. For example, if there is a horizontal ladder, jungle gym, or cargo net in your school, these could be used. Other ideas are given in the articles by Bockholt (1975) and Chamberlain and Ryan (1975).

When the children have completed their safari, discuss the significance of the activities they performed at the stations and relate these to other facts about the countries. The following points are examples of discussion topics.

Station 1

  a. Purpose of the ancient Egyptian pyramids and the Sphinx.

  b. Importance of the Nile River to the countries in this area.

  c. Why riverboats are frequently used as a means of transportation in Africa.

  d. Where Lake Victoria got its name and the fact that it is the second largest freshwater lake in the world. Only Lake Superior is larger.

  e. The extent and role of rail transportation in Africa.

Station 2

  a. Rope is made from sisal, one of the products of Kenya and Tanzania.

  b. Kilimanjaro is the highest mountain (19,340 feet) in Africa and is higher than any mountain in the United States outside of Alaska.

  c. Mombasa is Kenya's major seaport.

Station 3

  a. Agriculture is essential to the economy of Malagasy. In addition to coffee, they produce large quantities of rice, cocoa, cotton, vanilla, sugar cane, and spices.

  b. The island of Malagasy is about the size of the state of Texas and is located about 250 miles off the coast of Africa across the Mozambique Channel.

Station 4

  a. Mining is a major industry in the Republic of South Africa. In addition to diamonds, the area is rich in gold, silver, iron, and coal.

b. Many wild animals find a home in this country, but their number is decreasing because of the effects of civilization.

c. Because of its location, the ports of this country have been vital to the shipping industry for hundreds of years.

Station 5

a. The fine harbor at Banana has made it a major trading post ever since the sixteenth century.

b. Stanleyville is a thousand miles upriver from Leopoldville.

c. The jungles are the habitat of many animals, reptiles, and birds. Among these are monkeys, apes, lions, leopards, cheetahs, zebras, and hyenas. The most common snakes are pythons, cobras, and puff adders. Numerous types of birds are found here, among which are parrots, pelicans, crows, owls, and cuckoos.

Station 6

a. Nigeria is the home of hundreds of species of birds. Among these are storks, ostriches, parrots, and game birds such as geese and pigeons.

b. Lagos is the chief port of Nigeria. Freight trains bring cattle, peanuts, cotton, lumber, tin, coal, and other products to the harbors at Lagos and Harcourt, where they are exported. And, in turn, the ports of these two cities serve as receiving centers for imported goods.

c. In addition to cattle, the most common domestic animals in Nigeria are sheep and goats.

Station 7

a. The Sahara is the world's largest desert, stretching across Africa and occupying over one fourth of the continent's land area.

b. About two thirds of the Sahara's inhabitants live in the oases and make their living by farming. The principal crop is dates.

c. The camel caravans still transport salt across the desert, and in earlier times they also carried ivory.

Station 8

a. Farming is a principal occupation in Morocco. Cereals are the major crops. Other important crops are olives, figs, almonds, dates, and citrus fruits.

b. Casablanca is a major international port, serving to link West Africa, Europe, and the Americas.

CONCEPT: African children, like children everywhere, play with whatever natural materials they find.

Level: Intermediate.

Subconcepts: (1) Stones, seeds, and sticks are examples of natural materials that African children use. (2) They also play tag, hide and seek, and follow the leader, as well as wrestle and run races. (3) The games played in Africa today evidence the influence of the European countries that have politically and economically dominated the African countries. For example, soccer is now played in many parts of the continent, and the games that follow are similar to those played in other parts of the world.

Activities: Following are games played in Nigeria.*

Fire on the mountain. The children pair off and form two concentric circles with one partner standing behind the other (Fig. 17-12). The players sing, "There is a fire on the mountain!" This is the signal for the players on the outside

_____

*The games in this section were described to one of us (E.C.B.) by Ebenezer Oriaku, a student from Nigeria.

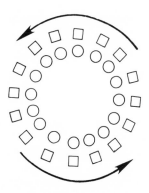

Fig. 17-12. Fire on the mountain.

of the circle to run in a counterclockwise direction. Suddenly, someone shouts, "The fire is out." This is the signal for all the runners to quickly return to their starting position behind their partner. The last person to get back in place and his partner are both out of the game. This couple must go to the center of the circle and remain there. Play continues until only one couple remains on the outside of the circle. When the game is repeated, the partners exchange places.

Head and tail. The players form three concentric circles, as shown in Fig. 17-13. Player 1 is the "head" and player 3 the "tail." Two people stand in the center; one is the "runner" and the other the "chaser." The chaser pursues the runner, attempting to tag him. If successful, they exchange roles. The runner may be safe by standing in front of the head or behind the tail of any group. If he stands in front of the head, the tail of that group becomes the runner; if he stands behind the tail, the head of that group becomes the runner.

CONCEPT: In their native dance the Africans speak with their bodies.

Level: Intermediate.

Subconcepts: (1) Their priests, warriors, hunters, and doctors are all dancers. (2) Some of their dances are based on occupations, and others convey legends and tribal histories. (3) Some tribes wear elaborate costumes, and others paint their bodies; some even wear masks, and some dance on stilts. (4) Anything capable of making a sound is used to accompany dances, including turtle shells, seeds, pebbles, sticks, gourds, harps, flutes, gongs, xylophones, and drums of all sizes. (Primus, 1958.)

Activities

Jog Trot (Doll and Nelson, 1965). This is a creative dance from the book *Rhythms Today*. The children are given a theme and respond to a drumbeat with interpretive movements. The theme is from a folk tale that describes how, during a drought, the lion shows the other animals how to dig a well. The lion begins digging; then by ones and twos other animals begin to appear. Soon there is a wide variety, each moving in his own way.

Uba. This, too, is a creative dance performed to the rhythm of a drumbeat. The movements symbolize physical strength. It consists of sharp, quick movements that demonstrate a buildup of energy from one body position to the next. This dance is also from *Rhythms Today* (Doll and Nelson, 1965).

Ibo. This dance is from Nigeria. It expresses the majesty and proud vigor of a people who refused to be subjected to slavery. It is included in *Ethnic Dances of Black People Around the World,* available from Education Activities, Inc., K9040.

Yon Va Lou. This is a sacred dance originating in Nigeria. It honors the god Damballa, whose symbol is a snake, and emphasizes movements of the shoulders and back. It, too, is included in *Ethnic Dances of Black People Around the World.*

African Heritage Dances (Educational Activities, Inc., AR 36). This album contains instructions for several folk dances of African origin, accompanied by exciting big-drum rhythms. The dances are performed without partners. Included in the album are the dances Ibo, Bongo, Bele Kawe, and Hallecord.

Singing Games of Ghana. (Educational Activities, Inc., MM 103.) This album contains songs from several tribes in Ghana. The music was recorded by native Ghanaians. The selections are designed to appeal to American school children.

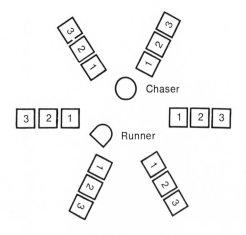

Fig. 17-13. Head and tail.

ASIA

Israel

CONCEPT: Israel is one of the oldest nations in the world and, at the same time, one of the youngest.

Level: Intermediate.

Subconcepts: (1) Ancient Israel survived under various conquerors until 135 A.D. (2) After hundreds of years, during the latter part of the eighteenth century, a few Jews began to return to Palestine. (3) Finally in 1948 the Jewish people had gathered in sufficient number to declare themselves a nation reborn. (4) Like our country, their Declaration of Independence resulted in a War of Independence, and although they fought against tremendous odds, they eventually won.

Materials: Nine beanbags and a playing area laid out as shown in Fig. 17-14 for each group of children.

Activities

Lighting the Menorah. In December the Jewish people celebrate Hanukkah, the Feast of Lights. The celebration lasts for 8 days. During this time certain candles are lit on the Menorah each day. The center candle is lit first and then it is used to light the others. The following activity has been created to enable the children to envision the sequence of events.

Show the children a Menorah or a picture of one. Explain the significance of the Feast of Lights. Show them how the center candle and one on the end of the Menorah are lit on the first day of Hanukkah. They burn down during the night and are replaced. The second day the center candle and two of those on the end are lit. This process is repeated until on the eighth day of Hanukkah the center candle and the other eight are all lit, thus making a total of forty-four candles lit during Hanukkah. Demonstrate the

Fig. 17-14. Lighting the Menorah.

activity and explain how it simulates lighting the candles during Hanukkah.

The children line up behind the starting line and number off 1 through 8. The first child is given two beanbags and the others are each given one. Player 1 walks to the center candle and places one of his beanbags on it, then he walks to the first candle and places his second beanbag on it. He then returns to the end of the line. Player 2 walks to the center candle, picks up the beanbag that is there and replaces it with hers. She then goes to the first candle and "lights" it by picking up the beanbag resting on it, replacing it with the beanbag obtained at the center candle. She goes to the second candle and lights it by placing on it the beanbag she picked up at the first candle. Player 3 repeats the process and finishes by lighting the third candle. Play continues until everyone has had a turn and all eight candles (plus the center candle) are lit.

Variations

1. If beanbags are not available, the children may light the candles by simply stooping down and touching the floor.
2. Make a circle at the top of each candle and mark an X on the shaft of the Menorah. Require the children to stand where X marks the spot and light their candles by tossing the beanbag into the circle at the top of the candle.

CONCEPT: The dances of the Jewish people originated as a form of prayer performed during ceremonies and festivals.

Level: Intermediate.

Subconcepts: (1) Jewish folk dance is characterized by smooth, fluid movements, with a lifting quality (Lidster and Tamburini, 1965). (2) The common formation of Jewish dances is a single circle with hands joined.

Materials

Mayim Mayim (Hoctor LP 4027). This popular Israeli line dance is also available on the album *Parachute Activities With Folk Dance Music* (Educational Activities Inc.) A simplified version is given on Hoctor album 4001.
"Hora," RCA LPM 1623 and Folkraft 1118
"Patch Tanz," Folkraft 1118
"Cherkassiya," RCA LPM 1623
"Kuma Echa," Folkraft 1478
"Debka," Folkraft 1478

THE ORIENT

CONCEPT: The oriental countries have extensive seacoasts.

Level: Intermediate.

Subconcepts: (1) Taiwan is an island. (2) The country of Japan consists of four major islands. (3) Korea is a peninsula divided into two countries, North Korea and South Korea. (4) The east and southeast coasts of mainland China are bordered by the sea. (5) The major form of transportation between these countries is by boat.

Materials: A large outline map of the countries listed (Fig. 17-15); the map may be traced in the dirt on the playground or layed out with ropes on the floor or a hard-surface area.

Activities: Divide the class into five groups and assign each group to one of the countries on the map. Each group must stand within the

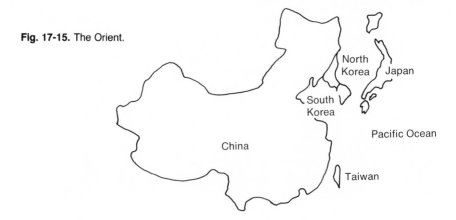

Fig. 17-15. The Orient.

boundaries of the asigned country. You stand beside the map (in the area of the Pacific Ocean). Have the children in each area call out the name of their country and point out its location. As soon as everyone is familiar with the names and locations, you call out, ''Boats sail between _____ and _____'' (e.g., ''Boats sail between Taiwan and South Korea''). The children standing in these two areas must exchange places by running from one country to the other. You rapidly call out different combinations of countries.

Variations

1. Have one of the children call out the countries.
2. Use only the map of Japan, having the children run between two of the islands when the names of these islands are called out.
3. Add other countries with seacoasts, such as Vietnam, Cambodia, Thailand, and the Philippines.
4. Make the activity into a contest. Assign only 1 child (or 2 children holding hands) to each country. Select another child to be ''It,'' who calls out the names of two countries and, while the children are exchanging places, attempts to get into one of the countries. The player who is left out then becomes It. That child may call out more than two countries or may say ''Boats sail everywhere,'' requiring all the children to exchange places.

CONCEPT: The oriental countries are densely populated, and the people live close together both in the cities and in the country.

Level: Intermediate.

Materials: A room that is empty except for some chairs next to the walls.

Activities: Have the children scatter around the room and find a space in which they can stand and move their body parts without touching anyone else (a personal space). Play some original music and instruct the children to move around the room through general space without imposing on anyone else's personal space. Tell them they must stay within the area prescribed by the chairs. While the children are moving, gradually move the chairs in toward the center of the room. When the space be-

comes too small and the children cannot freely move, stop the music and ask them to stand in the space and think about how it feels to be that crowded. Ask them to contrast the feelings associated with moving in a large space with moving in a small space. Relate their moving in the small space to the crowded living conditions in the oriental countries. Discuss how the oriental characteristics of being quiet, calm, meditative, and moving slowly while taking small steps are all consistent with the way people must live when their life space is so small.

Japan

CONCEPTS: The country of Japan consists of four main islands and many smaller islands. The names of the main islands are Honshu (hon-shoo, meaning original state or mainland), Hokkaido (ho-kid-o, meaning north sea land), Kyushu (qu-shoo, meaning nine states), and Shikoku (she-ko-koo, meaning four countries).

Level: Intermediate.

Materials: A large outline map of Japan's four islands laid out on the playground or on the floor of the playing area (Fig. 17-16) and a

Fig. 17-16. Islands of Japan.

sheet of paper inside each island with the name of the island written on it.

Activities

Relay. Divide the class into relay teams consisting of no more than 6 members. Tell the children you will call out the name of an island and the movement they are to execute to go there. Explain that they must continue to execute the specified movement until they are close enough to place one foot inside the designated island; then they may run back to their team. The child who returns to his team first is

Fig. 17-17. Janken. **A,** using the hands. **B,** using the legs.

awarded a point. The winning team is the one with the most points after each player has had a turn.

The movements that may be called out follow:

Hop to Kyushu
Jump to Shikoku
Crab Walk to Honshu
Run to Hokkaido

If there are more than 4 players on a team, repeat any of the movements until each player has had a turn.

CONCEPTS: A central characteristic of Japanese games is group cooperation. Because of the large number of students that must participate in small playing areas, most children's games are designed to permit participation of a large group.

Level: Intermediate.

Activities

*Janken.** This Japanese game is popular with American children. It is usually a contest between 2 children, but can be played by a small group. The players face each other with their right hands making a fist. The fists are raised and lowered three times in a rhythmic sequence as the players count, "1, 2, 3." Immediately after the count of 3, the players extend their hands simultaneously in one of three possible positions, as follows (Fig. 17-17, *A*):

Stone = hand clenched into fist
Scissors = hand with the index finger and middle finger outstretched
Paper = hand open with all fingers outstretched

The contest is decided in the following manner:

Stone beats scissors, since the scissors cannot cut the stone and the stone can break the scissors.
Paper beats stone, since paper covers or wraps up the stone.
Scissors beat paper, since scissors cut paper.

A game may consist of any predetermined number of points, such as 2 out of 3 or the first person to win ten times.

---

*The games and contests in this section were described to one of us (E.C.B.) by Dr. Hideo Suzuki.

Variations

1. Two players stand behind a starting line. They play janken, with the winner of each round moving toward a goal line according to the number of steps allocated to his position:

Scissors	One step
Stone	Two steps
Paper	Three steps

   The child reaching the goal line first is declared the winner. The number of steps awarded each position may be doubled if the size of the playing area permits.

2. Maketara negeru (escape if you are beaten). Each player stands behind a line facing his opponent. They play janken as previously described, with the winner pursuing the loser, attempting to tag him before he reaches the goal line on his side of the room. A point is awarded each time a player is tagged. This game can be played as a contest between 2 players or as a team game. If it is a team game, all the points for the players on each line are totaled at the end of the playing period.

3. The legs can be substituted for the hands in any of the contests already described. The players jump up and land in one of the following positions (Fig. 17-17, *B*):

Stone = legs together and arms forming a medium-sized circle
Scissors = forward stride with hands behind head
Paper = sideward stride with arms straight out to the side

Squirrel in the tree. This game is the same as the American game of squirrel in the tree, except that there are three types of signals to which the players must respond. Play begins with 2 players holding hands to form a "tree," and a third player, the "squirrel," standing between them. There are 1 or 2 squirrels without a tree. One of these squirrels may call out any of the signals, and the players are required to respond as follows:

Signal	*Action*
Squirrels	All the squirrels must run to a new tree while the homeless squirrels attempt to get inside a tree.

Signal	*Action*
Trees	All the trees run to find a new partner and form a tree around a squirrel. All the squirrels except those without a home stand still. The homeless squirrels attempt to find a partner and become trees.
Fire	Everyone runs, the trees attempting to find a new partner and the squirrels to find a new home. Squirrels without a tree or trees without a squirrel become "Its."

Omi gokko (escape from evil). This game resembles three deep. The players sit in rows containing 5 children. The rows are arranged like spokes in a wheel, with everyone facing the center. Two players stand in the center — the runner and the chaser (Fig. 17-18). The runner runs around the rows with the chaser in pursuit, attempting to tag him. If the chaser is successful, they exchange roles. The runner is safe when he stops at the back of a line. As he sits down, the player in the front of that line becomes the runner.

CONCEPT: Japanese dances often include interpretative pantomime of the songs that have been derived from the occupations of the people, their traditional folk tales, and their great love of nature.

Level: Intermediate.

Activities: A brief but comprehensive overview of Japanese dance is given by Bauer (1935). Her article includes instructions for several Japanese dances. These can either be used as described or adapted as the basis for creative rhythms.

Haiku provide effective themes for creative rhythms that express the characteristics of the Japanese. When the children become familiar with this form of poetry, their learning will be enhanced by writing their own Haiku. A sample lesson based on Haiku is given in Burton (1977).

The Wind Blew East (Doll and Nelson, 1965). The gentle, sustained movements of this improvised dance from *Rhythms Today* are adapted from traditional Japanese folk play. They include the nonlocomotor movements of swinging, bending, and stretching, as well as a shuffle walking step.

"*Sho Sho Shojoji* (Barlin and Barlin, 1970). This song from *Dance-a-Folk Song** is based on a legend about badgers who have magic powers. The children interpret the movements of the animals as they dance in the moonlight.

Tanko Bushi (Coal Miner's Dance). This dance pantomimes miners digging coal, throwing sacks over their shoulders, peering into the darkness of the mine, and pushing the heavy

*This book contains descriptions of ten original dances created to traditional folk songs from different countries. The dances are designed for children 4 to 8 years old and may be used in the classroom and for festivals and holidays. Accompanying the book are two records with music and children singing.

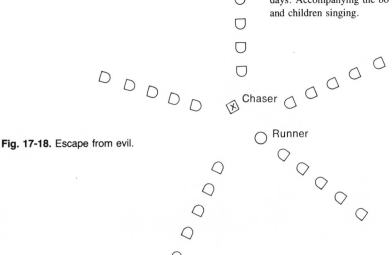

Fig. 17-18. Escape from evil.

carts. It is from the book *Rhythm Today* and is also included in "Honor Your Partner," available from Educational Activities, Inc., HYP 22.

China

CONCEPT: Some of the traditional games played by Chinese children down through the ages are similar to those children play in the United States.

Level: Intermediate.
Materials: A playing area.
Activities

Chinese Wall (Bancroft, 1909). The playing area is marked off as shown in Fig. 17-19. One child is chosen to be the "guard" who stands on the wall. The rest of the class members stand behind the goal line at one end of the playing area. When the guard says "Go," all the players must run across the playing area, attempting to get over the wall without being tagged. The guard must stay within the wall and tag as many players as possible. Each one he tags joins him inside the wall and assists in tagging as play continues. The last child caught is the guard when the game is repeated. The wall in this game represents the Great Wall of China. This symbolism is more evident if you show the children a picture of the wall.*

Chinese chicken (Bancroft, 1909). Divide the class into relay teams consisting of no more than 6 players. Have the children take off their

---

*An excellent illustration is given on Plate I facing p. 562 of volume 5 Encyclopaedia Britannica, vol. 5, 1960.

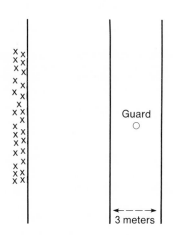

Fig. 17-19. Chinese Wall.

shoes and place them in a straight row 25 centimeters apart (Fig. 17-20). Play begins as player 1 in each group simulates the movements of a lame chicken by hopping over each shoe until he reaches the end of the row. He picks up the last shoe and hops back over the remaining shoes. Player 2 then repeats the action. Play continues until all the players have had a turn.
Variations
1. After each child has had a turn, each one hops a second time, replacing their shoe in the line. This results in all of the shoes being put back where they were when play began. The children can then move up one place in their line and repeat the game.
2. Make the activity into a contest by declaring the team that finished first the winner.
3. Substitute bean bags or wooden blocks for the children's shoes.
4. Vary the number of objects the children hop over.

CONCEPTS: Chinese dance is often happy and lively and movements are very expressive.

Level: Intermediate.
Materials: Sometimes their dances include acrobatics or the use of small props such as a fan, umbrella, stick, or pole.
Activities
Ribbon Dance. Printed music and instructions are given in the book *Rhythms Today* (Doll and Nelson, 1965). A kit that includes instructions, recorded music, and ribbon sticks is available from Educational Activities, Inc.
Chinese Friendship Dance. This dance from the album *Dances Around the World*, by Glass and Hallum, available from Educational Activities, Inc., AR 572, is done by children throughout the People's Republic of China. The main idea of the dance is to promote friendship by meeting different people. The music for the dance was recorded in China. The album includes easy-to-follow, step-by-step directions.

The Philippines

CONCEPT: As a people the Filipinos love singing, dancing, and feasting.

Level: Intermediate.
Subconcepts: (1) Filipino games and dances

Fig. 17-20. Chinese chicken.

reflect the influence of the Spanish occupation, which lasted for more than three centuries. (2) Their recreational activities are playful and convey a cheerful spirit.

Activities

Pasa at aso (cat and dog) (Reyes and Ramos, 1935). The children (''cats'') form a circle around a single player (''dog'') who is seated in the center. The dog is surrounded by several beanbags, (shoes or stones may be substituted). The dog must remain seated while the cats attempt to steal his bones (beanbags). The dog tries to catch the cats by tagging them with his hands or feet. If the dog tags a cat, they exchange places. If the cats get all the bones without any of them being caught, the bones are placed back in the center, and the game is repeated with the same dog. However, a new dog can be selected.

Filipino dances at the intermediate level:

Carinosa (RCA 1619). The basic step of this partner dance is walking. It begins with a ''saludo'' (salute), which is a typical beginning step in Philippine folk dance. This dance portrays the Spanish influence.

''Apat Apat'' is also from *Dances Around the World*.

''BA-O Dance'' (Philippine Coconut Shell Dance), Educational Activities, Inc.

''Tinikling,'' RCA LPM 1619; Educational Activities, Inc., KEA 9015 and 8095; or *Rhythms Today*.

SELECTED REFERENCES FOR PART FOUR

CHAPTER 14

Gerhardt, Lydia A.: Moving and knowing: the young child orients himself in space, Englewood Cliffs, N.J., 1973, Prentice-Hall, Inc.

Gilliom, Bonnie Cherp: Basic movement education for children: rationale and teaching units, Reading, Mass., 1970, Addison-Wesley Publishing Co., Inc.

CHAPTER 15

Burton, Elsie C.: The new physical education for elementary school children, Boston; 1977, Houghton Mifflin Co.

Gerhardt, Lydia A.: Moving and knowing: the young child orients himself in space, Englewood Cliffs, N.J., 1973, Prentice-Hall, Inc.

CHAPTER 16

Bley, Edgar S.: The best singing games for children of all ages, New York, 1960, Sterling Publishing Co., Inc.

Buttree, Julia M.: The rhythm of the redman, New York, 1930, A. S. Barnes and Co.

Doll, Edna, and Nelson, Mary J.: Rhythms today, Morristown, N.J., 1965, Silver Burdett Co.

Duggan, Anne Schley, Schlottman, Jeanette, and Rutledge, Abbie: Folk dances of the United States and Mexico, New York, 1948, A. S. Barnes & Co.

Encyclopaedia Britannica, Chicago, 1960, William Benton, Publishers.

Fait, Hollis F.: Physical education for the elementary school child, ed. 3, Philadelphia, 1976, W. B. Saunders Co.

Fletcher, Alice C.: Indian games and dances with native songs, New York, 1915, AMS Press.

Harris, Jane A., Pittman, Anne, and Waller, Marlys S.: Dance a while, ed. 4, Minneapolis, 1968, Burgess Publishing Co.

Hotsinde, Robert: Indian games and crafts, New York, 1957, William Morrow & Co., Inc., Publishers.

Joseph, Joan: Folk toys around the world, New York, 1972, Parents' Magazine Press.

Mason, Bernard S.: Dances and stories of the American Indian, New York, 1944, A. S. Barnes & Co.

Mason, Bernard S.: The book of Indian crafts and costumes, New York, 1946, The Ronald Press Co.

Salomon, Julian Harris: The book of Indian crafts and Indian lore, New York, 1928, Harper & Brothers.

Shafter, Mary Severance: American Indian and other folk dances for schools, pageants and playgrounds, New York, 1927, A. S. Barnes & Co.

Stuart, Frances R., Gibson, Virginia L., and Jervey, Ar-
den: Rhythmic activities, series IV, Minneapolis, 1963, Burgess Publishing Co.

Vick, Marie, and Cox, Rosann M.: A collection of dances for children, Minneapolis, 1970, Burgess Publishing Co.

Vinton, Iris: The folkways omnibus of children's games, Harrisburg, Pa., 1970, Stackpole Books.

CHAPTER 17

Bancroft, Jessie H.: Games for the playground, home, school and gymnasium, New York, 1909, The Macmillan Co.

Barlin, Anne, and Barlin, Paul: Dance-a-Folk Song, Los Angeles, 1974, Bowmar Publishing Corporation.

Bauer, Lucille: Japanese dances for children, Journal of Health and Physical Education 6:17-23, May, 1935.

Bockholt, Jack L.: Jungle time at Westwood School, Journal of Physical Education and Recreation 46:39, Oct., 1975.

Burton, Elsie C.: The new physical education for elementary school children, Boston, 1977, Houghton Mifflin Co.

Chamberlain, James R., and Ryan, Pat: Disney World in an open gym, Journal of Physical Education and Recreation 46:43-44, May, 1975.

Culin, Stewart: Games of the Orient: Korea, China, Japan, Rutland, Vt., 1958, Charles E. Tuttle Co., Inc.

Diem, Liselott: Kinder Sport Fidel, Frankfurt, 1975, Wilhelm Limpert Verlag.

Doll, Edna, and Nelson, Mary J.: Rhythms today, Morristown, N.J., 1965, Silver Burdett Co.

Douglas, Norman: London street games, London, Chatto & Windus, 1931; reissued in 1968 by Singing Tree Press, Detroit, Mich.

Duggan, Anne Schley, Schlottman, Jeanette, and Rutledge, Abbie: Folk dances of the British Isles, New York, 1948, A. S. Barnes & Co.

Duggan, Anne Schley, Schlottman, Jeanette, and Rutledge, Abbie: Folk dances of European countries, New York, 1948, A. S. Barnes & Co.

Duggan, Anne Schley, Schlottman, Jeanette, and Rutledge, Abbie: Folk dances of Scandinavia, New York, 1948, A. S. Barnes & Co.

Duggan, Anne Schley, Schlottman, Jeanette, and Rutledge, Abbie: Folk dances of the United States and Mexico, New York, 1948, A. S. Barnes & Co.

Encyclopaedia Judaica, vol. 7, Jerusalem, 1971, The Macmillan Co.

Harbin, Elvin Oscar: Games of many nations, Nashville, Tenn., 1954, Abingdon Press.

Horrigan, Olive K.: Creative activities in physical education: correlated and integrated games and dances from many countries, New York, 1929, A. S. Barnes & Co.

Hunt, Sarah Ethridge, and Cain, Ethel: Games the world around, New York, 1941, A. S. Barnes & Co.

Ickis, Marguerite: The book of games and entertainment the world over, New York, 1969, Dodd, Mead & Co.

International Council on Health, Physical Education, and Recreation: ICHPER book of worldwide games and dances, Washington, D.C., 1967, AAHPER Press.

Kraus, Richard G.: Folk dancing, New York, 1962, The Macmillan Co.

Lidster, Miriam and Tamburini, Dorothy H.: Folk dance progressions, Belmont, Calif., 1965, Wadsworth Publishing Co.

McEniry, Joan: Games for Girl Scouts, ed. 2, New York, 1969, Girl Scouts of the U.S.A.

Mudie, Jacqueline: The story of dancing, London, 1968, Purnell & Sons Ltd.

Primus, Pearl: Views of dance around the world: Africa, Dance Magazine **33:**42-49, 90-91, March, 1958.

Reyes, Francisca S., and Ramos, Petrona: Philippine folk dances and games. New York, 1935, Silver Burdett & Co.

The Universal Jewish Encyclopedia, vols. 1 and 4, New York, 1968, Universal Jewish Encyclopedia Co.

United States Committee for UNICEF: Hi Neighbor, New York, 1958, UNESCO.

PART FIVE

Music and art

Music, art, and movement share many common concepts.

Music, visual art, and movement are closely related art forms. Within the educational setting these curricular areas share the opportunity to assist children in developing self-awareness, creative expression, and the capacity to esthetically experience and appreciate their own beings and their environments.

Children can express only what they have experienced. Artistic experience involves multisensory perception. Children must perceive with all their senses; they must become aware of their inner and outer worlds by seeing, hearing, smelling, tasting, and feeling. Their awareness should be further enriched through inquiry into the nature of things and events. These experiences and processes furnish the raw material for concept formation and acquisition of the knowledges and understandings necessary to interpret sensory input and give it form. These factors are therefore general artistic abilities and should be developmental goals in each of the related arts.

Music, art, and movement also share common components. Line, accent, balance, harmony, intensity, and rhythm are essential aspects of all three art forms. These common concepts can serve as the connecting links between the related arts. Emphasis on the similarities in art form unifies and reinforces the children's learning experiences. This approach develops the ability to engage in relational thought, rather than the capacity to laboriously memorize fragmented facts.

In the following chapters, music and art activities are separated, and movement activities are utilized as the learning medium for both areas. However, it is suggested that as you work with the content, you should seek to emphasize the related concepts and, whenever possible, provide integrated learning experiences involving all three art forms.

Chapter 18

MUSIC

The approaches of Dalcrose, Kodaly, and Orff (Landis et al., 1972) have verified the interdependence of music and movement. The optimal development of the child's musical and motor capacities is dependent on rhythmical sensitivity and responsiveness. Yet this unified approach to teaching these subjects has not become a functional aspect of the curriculums in most schools. Physical education is still generally learned in the gym or on the playing field, using the game approach, and music is still generally learned in the music room and performed in the auditorium, with children sitting or standing. Rarely is the content of music and physical education combined to give the child a total rhythmical education involving the mind and the whole body.

To fully experience rhythm, the child must be *receptive* to a variety of rhythmical stimuli, *aware* of the elements of music, and *capable* of translating feelings and concepts into meaningful expressions. The full development of these capacities is possible only when the whole child is actively involved in the learning process because the child's moving body serves as a vital informational source and as his principal expressive instrument.

Skilled human movement is rhythmical and therefore there are many common elements in music and movement. These include dynamics, tempo, pitch, mood, shape, phrasing, and rhythmical structure. Movement activities provide an ideal medium in which children can analyze, relate, and express these elements. By attending to the lesson theme as they move in response to it, children internalize musical concepts. Thus the child's music education is based on real experiences, rather than on abstract concepts.

Children cannot fully use their bodies as rhythmical instruments until they have developed basic body awareness. Body awareness consists of developing a sensory awareness and a mental image of each body part as it functions in stillness and in motion. Several body awareness activities are described on pp. 280 and 281. Others may be found in the book references for this chapter. Many of the learning experiences provided at the beginning level of creative dance are designed to develop body and spatial awareness.

As soon as possible, children should be provided with opportunities to physically respond to a rhythmical beat. Actually, this ability is innate. Infants can be observed bobbing to the rhythm of water dripping, a motor running, or music playing. This response must be extended and refined or it will be lost in the everyday necessity for purely functional movement. Children have a natural rhythm. This should be discovered and utilized as the basis for rhythmical responses, rather than children being forced to submit to an externally imposed rhythmical pattern. Their awareness of rhythmical patterns should evolve from their learning to associate their own internal rhythm with sounds. Through their auditory and kinesthetic senses they can hear *and* feel changes in dynamics, tempo, phrasing, and rhythmical patterns. They should learn to identify these and organize them into musical compositions.

The higher level of mastery is the ability to create. This is where children's music and movement experiences should lead. They should be encouraged to use their knowledge and skills in a personally expressive manner, rather than simply imitating. It is neither possible nor necessary to cover the topic of creative rhythmical responses extensively in the present work, since entire volumes have been devoted to this subject, concerning which several of the dance books provide excellent material. The most inclusive is *Dance in Elementary Education* by Murray (1975). Murray's book and the AAHPER publication *Children's Dance* also contain comprehensive lists of suggested resources, including songbooks, recordings, and films.

The learning activities presented are arranged sequentially under specific subject headings. This format has been used because the divisions are logical and the learning activites are arranged in a progression. It is not intended, however, that you follow the exact order or content as stated. Rather, these activities are viewed as suggestions or ideas for lesson content. Some of the ways in which these activities might be used follow:

1. To be a part of the group music lesson
2. To introduce or review certain concepts
3. To provide essential physical activity periods within the school day
4. To personalize instruction by providing stimulating individual and small group activities
5. To transform abstract concepts into concrete concepts

Some of the activities are highly structured and could therefore be lifted from the text and superimposed on the children. This is not our intent, however. Rather, we intend that you modify and adapt the activities to fit your teaching methods and to meet the needs of the children. It is imperative that the creative aspect of the children's rhythmical experiences be preserved and enhanced. Your lesson content and teaching methods should stimulate participation in activities that enable children to experience the rhythmical response of their moving bodies. Their feeling states should be emphasized and their personally expressive responses encouraged. Every precaution should be taken to prevent the passive imitation of others or the listless performance of prescribed movements. Just ''going through the motions'' does not produce positive learning outcomes. This is the reason the preferred types of rhythmical accompaniment used in the early stages of learning are sounds created by the children and the beat of a drum. These sounds can be altered to match the rhythmical responses of the children, whereas recordings require that the children's responses conform to the structure of the music. Some music does, of course, permit individual interpretations and variations, and this kind of music can be appropriately employed. (The *Dance-a-Story* series contains this type of music. Other sources include some classical, ethnic, electronic, rock, and jazz compositions). When children have developed the ability and willingness to rhythmically respond to the array of sounds in the world around them, more highly structured content can be introduced. For instance, folk dancing is essential subject matter content, but emphasis should be placed on the feeling states associated with the children's rhythmical movement, rather than on perfect execution of the steps. The ultimate goal—to enable the child to be receptive, aware, and responsive—should guide your selection and application of the content that follows.

Learning activities

RHYTHM

Rhythm is a pattern of tension and relaxation. A person can become aware of rhythm by feeling this tension and relaxation in his body. The concept of rhythm can be readily understood when sound and silence are related to motion (tension) and stillness (relaxation). Children's initial rhythmical experiences should include activities designed to enhance their perception of the feelings associated with body tension and relaxation.

CONCEPT: When I move it feels different than when I am still.

Level: Beginning.

Subconcepts: (1) I can keep my body very still. (2) While I am still, my body can be tense or it can be relaxed. (3) I can move individual body parts and I can move my whole body.

Materials: None.

Activities

1. Have the children close their eyes and sit very still. Challenge them to think about how it feels to be perfectly still. Ask them to try to feel different body parts while keeping them very still.
2. ''Slowly wiggle your fingers. How does that

feel? Is there more feeling now? Hold them still again. What happens to the feeling? Make your hands into fists and squeeze them very tight. How does that feel? Does that help you feel your arms too?''

3. ''Put the palms of your hands together. How does that feel? Now rub them together. Does that feel different? Stop rubbing and press them together as hard as you can. Does that help you feel your arms? Hook your fingers together and try to pull your hands apart. How does that feel?''

4. Have the children concentrate on the feelings associated with stillness and motion in their feet and legs. Instruct them to alternate wiggling their toes, flexing and rotating their feet, and pressing their feet against the floor and against each other.

5. Tell the students to lie down on the floor. If there is not sufficient space for them to lie down, some of the following activities can be adapted to children sitting at their desks.

How does the floor feel? Is it hard or soft? Warm or cold? Slick or fuzzy?

Put the palms of your hands on the floor and rub them around. Can you feel more when you are rubbing? Turn your hands over and rub with the backs. Can you feel more with the palms or the backs of your hands?

Now I want you to press your body parts hard against the floor. Let's start with your heels. Now the backs of your legs, your seat, your back, your shoulders. Let the pressing travel down your arms to your fingertips. Now press your neck and the back of your head against the floor. Now all of your body. Press hard.

Let go and just be very still. Don't move, just lie there and think about how you feel and how this feeling is different from when you were pressing against the floor.

Now instead of pressing against the floor, we'll tighten the muscles in different body parts. Let's start at the top of our bodies this time. Can you make a hard frown? Frown with your mouth and your forehead. Can you make the frown go all the way down into your neck? Now let go and just let your face relax.

Now let's smile. Smile big with your whole face. Does smiling feel different than frowning? Can you feel the difference between smiling and relaxing your face?

This time, tighten the muscles of the back of your neck. Make them really tight so your head is pulled back. Relax the muscles on the back of your neck and tighten those on the front. Relax.

Tighten the muscles of your shoulders. Can you hunch your shoulders so high your neck seems to disappear? Relax. Tighten the muscles of your arms so hard that the tension travels down into your hands and makes a hard fist. Let go.

Now tighten all the muscles in the center of your body. Can you make the middle of your back touch the floor?

Tighten your legs. Make them so tight your heels press into the floor.

You have tightened your body parts, now let's tighten the whole body. Can you make all your body parts tense at the same time? Can you make them very tight? Let go! I want you to make them tight again, and this time think about how they feel. Let go! Think about how you feel now that you are relaxed.

6. Tell the children to stand up and find a big personal space. Explain that they have been moving in a very small space while lying down. Now you want then to feel the difference between movement and stillness in a larger space. ''Take one step forward and stop. We're going to do that again and this time I want you to think about how you feel when you are stepping. Ready, step. Do it with your eyes closed so you can really think about how it feels when you move.'' Let them take several steps. Then challenge them to think about how they feel when they are standing still and to contrast the feelings of moving and standing still. Have them move in different ways, concentrating on how these movements feel. Some examples follow:

Movements		*Stunts*
Run	Crawl	Log Roll
Jump	Skip	Seal Walk
Hop	Slide	Inch Worm

7. Have the children explore the contrasting feelings associated with movements that are weak and strong, soft and hard. Here are some of the activities you may include:

- Clapping the hands versus bringing them together slowly and softly
- Walking with light steps versus stamping
- Jumping and landing softly versus landing hard

Use of imagery

- Walking like a fairy versus walking like a giant
- Floating on a cloud versus falling off and landing on the ground
- Walking like a cat versus walking like an elephant
- Floating like a sea gull above the ocean on a still day versus flying like a sea gull into a hard wind
- Walking weightless in outer space versus walking with a heavy load on your head
- Tossing a balloon versus throwing a medicine ball
- Hopping like a happy bird versus walking like an angry gorilla

8. Have the children explore the contrasting feelings associated with moving fast versus slow. Challenge them as follows:

Walk slowly, then run.

Jump slowly, then jump as rapidly as possible.

Pretend you are a locomotive pulling a long train up a steep mountain, then coasting your bicycle down a hill.

Pretend you are a horse pulling a wagon, then a horse running a race.

Walk down the road on a hot day, then run to get out of a sudden rainstorm.

9. Challenge them to explore the contrasting feelings associated with executing slow, heavy movements versus fast, light movements. Challenge each child to think of an object or animal that moves heavy and slow or fast and light. Ask some of the students to demonstrate their object or animal and have the rest of the group guess what it is. Then discuss the characteristics that create this type of movement and the feeling states associated with it.

Beat

CONCEPT: The beat is a series of pulsations we can hear and feel.

Level: Beginning.

Subconcepts: (1) When we repeat the same sound or the same movement over and over, we can recognize the beat. (2) There is a steady beat, called the basic rhythm. (3) We can follow this beat by moving or making sounds.

Materials: A rubber ball or a jump rope and a drum.

Activities

1. Ask the children to make a sound like a horn. Select one child and tell him to make the sound over and over. As the child is saying "Beep, beep, beep, beep" or "Toot, toot, toot, toot," have the students respond by tapping one hand on their desks or on the floor so that they are tapping out the rhythmical pattern. Challenge them to think of others sounds they can make and ways they can move in response to these. Some possibilities follow:

Sounds

Swish, swish, swish, swish	Click tongue
	Snap fingers
Shhh, shhh, shhh, shhh	Ha-ha, ha-ha, ha-ha, ha-ha
Clang, clang, clang, clang	Bow-wow, bow-wow, bow-wow, bow-wow
Chuga, chuga, chuga, chuga	Gobble, gobble, gobble, gobble
Tap, tap, tap, tap	

Movements

Clap hands	Bend different body parts
Knock knuckles on floor	
Clap hand on thighs	Walk
Tap feet on floor	Run
Nod head	Jump
Shrug shoulders	Hop

All these examples result in an even rhythm in 4/4 meter (Fig. 18-4). Some of the children may automatically begin accenting alternate beats or the first beat of each measure. If they do, ask them to demonstrate for the group and use this as a technique for introducing the concept of accented beats.

2. Instruct the children to explore the rhythmical beat associated with their moving various objects; for example, have a child bounce a ball and the others move in response to the sound of the ball striking the floor. Or have 2 students hold the ends of a jump rope and swing it back and forth, challenging the others to move their arms or their bodies in the same way the rope is moving. This may be followed by asking the children to name other objects that move rhythmically and to imitate these movements; for example, a windshield wiper, the pendulum of a clock, a perculator, or a washing machine.

3. Have the children move in one of the ways described in no. 1 while you beat out the rhythm of their movements on a drum.

Tempo

CONCEPT: The beat may be slow or fast or in between.

Levels: Beginning and intermediate.

Subconcepts: (1) The speed of the beat is called its tempo. (2) Quick or fast sounds and movements have a fast tempo. (3) Slow sounds and movements have a slow tempo. (4) The tempo may change from slow to fast or from fast to slow. This change may be sudden or gradual.

Materials: None.

Activities

1. Select any of the sounds under no. 1 on p. 262 that lend themselves to being repeated slowly; for example, tapping, clicking the tongue, snapping the fingers, ha-ha, or bow-wow. Repeat this sound slowly, challenging the children to respond by clapping their hands on their thighs.
2. Continue to slowly repeat the sound stimulus but change the movement response to tapping the feet, nodding the head, or shrugging the shoulders.
3. Change the sound stimulus but continue with the same movement executed in no. 2.
4. Challenge the children to think of sounds that can be repeated slowly. Use these as stimuli for slow movements.
5. Instruct them to execute slow movements without rhythmical accompaniment, challenging them to discover their own rhythmical pattern.
6. Have the students walk, jump, and hop to a slow rhythmical beat.
7. Repeat nos. 1 through 6, substituting sounds and movements with a fast tempo.
8. Alternate fast and slow sounds and tell the children to respond with movements in the correct tempo.
9. Ask the children to respond to a slow beat. Gradually accelerate the speed, and when it has reached a very fast tempo, begin decelerating the tempo. Continue until the sounds and movements become so slow they stop.

10. Have the children work in partners, with one child making fast and slow rhythmical sounds and the other moving to these.
11. Tell them to make up a sequence of sounds and movements in which they alternate fast and slow movements.
12. Have them create a sequence in which the sounds and movements accelerate and decelerate.
13. Challenge the children to explore different dimensions of space while moving fast and slow. The following examples illustrate some of the possibilities:

Direction: Walk forward on the fast beat and backward on the slow beat.

Level: Move on a high level on the fast beat and a low level on the slow beat.

Size: Take small steps on the fast beat and large steps on the slow beat.

Pathway: Move along a straight line on the fast beat and a curved line on the slow beat.

Accent

CONCEPT: A beat that is emphasized by making it harder or stronger is called an accented beat.

Level: Beginning.

Subconcepts: (1) We can accent the beat by making a strong movement or a loud sound. (2) Accented beats are used to mark the beginning of a group of beats.

Materials: A drum.

Activities

1. Observe the children moving in the preceding learning activities. If you detect a child naturally accenting some of the beats, ask him to move in the same way for the class. Challenge the children to detect how some of this child's movements differ from some of his other movements. Ask one of the students to beat the drum, imitating the pattern that the moving child has developed. Discuss the concept of an accent beat being harder or heavier.
2. If none of the children has accented the beats, beat the drum in 4/4 meter, asking them to listen and determine if some of the beats are different. Then discuss the concept of an accented beat.
3. Challenge the children to explore ways of

accenting the beat with different body parts. (Percussive movements such as clapping and stamping are common responses.)

4. Have the children practice echo clapping. Then have them respond by walking rather than clapping, accenting the first beat of each measure.
5. Beat out a rhythmical pattern on the drum, challenging the children to walk the pattern, accenting the proper beats by stamping their feet.
6. Have them change the direction in which they are moving on each accented beat.
7. Vary the meter so that they accent alternate beats (2/4 meter), the first of 3 beats (3/4 meter), and the first of 4 beats (4/4 meter).
8. Have the children use their body parts in different ways as they move to accented and unaccepted beats. Examples follow:

   - Step on the whole foot on the accented beat and walk on tiptoe on the unaccented beats.
   - Make a strong movement with the hands or arms to accent the beat as they are walking.
   - Jump forward on the accented beat and jump in place on the unaccented beats.

Meter

CONCEPT: Beats are grouped together to form a unit called a measure.

Levels: Beginning and intermediate.

Subconcepts: (1) Measures are usually divided by an accented beat that occurs on the first note of each measure. (2) Measures contain notes. (3) Notes represent beats. (4) There are different kinds of notes, identified by how much time we give them; there are whole notes and all other notes are fractions of the whole.

Materials: A drum, enlarged illustrations of notes, beanbags, and cards with notes drawn on them (see also nos. 22 and 23).

Activities

1. Beat out several measures of 4/4 meter on the drum, accenting the first beat of each measure. Have the children count 1, 2, 3, 4, 1, 2, 3, 4, accenting the 1. Tell them to clap as they count. Review the concept that each group of 4 beats makes a measure.
2. Have the children walk, jump, or hop a certain number of measures.

3. Explain how music is written in notes and compare this to the way words are written with letters (Fig. 18-1).
4. Show the class an illustration of a whole note. Point out that its shape is curved. Have the children make their bodies into a whole note by curling into a tight ball facing the floor, as shown in Fig. 18-2, *A*).
5. Place 2 half notes under the whole note. Explain that 2 half notes equal 1 whole note. Relate this to the fact that all notes except the whole note are fractions. Challenge the children to create the shape of a half note, using their whole body (Fig. 18-2, *B*).
6. Place 4 quarter notes under the half note. Explain that 4 quarter notes equal 1 whole note or 2 half notes. Challenge the children to form the shape of a quarter note. (They must put their toe on the floor and flex their knee until the space between their thigh and lower leg is closed [Fig. 18-2, *C*]).
7. Place 8 eighth notes under the quarter notes. Explain that 8 eighth notes equal 1 whole note, 2 half notes, or 4 quarter notes. Challenge the children to form their body into the shape of an eighth note (Fig. 18-2, *D*).
8. Place 16 sixteenth notes under the eighth notes. Explain how the value of these relates to that of other notes. Have the children form sixteenth notes with their bodies, as shown in Fig. 18-2, *E*.
9. Instruct the class that the notes are different because they are given different amounts of time. The sound or the movement of a whole note lasts much longer than that of a quarter note. Illustrate this concept by clapping your hands on the first beat of a 4/4 meter measure and holding your hands together on counts 2, 3, and 4. Have the children clap with you. Repeat, using half note and eight note time values.
10. Tell the children to stand up. Repeat the activities in no. 9, substituting nonlocomotor movements such as bending or twisting instead of clapping.
11. Repeat the activities in no. 9, substituting the locomotor movements walking, jumping, or hopping.

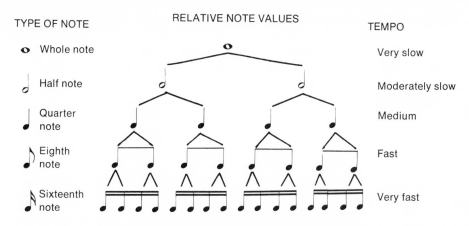

Fig. 18-1. Types and values of notes.

Fig. 18-2. Children forming notes with their bodies.

12. Have the children position themselves in the places of the notes shown in Fig. 18-3; that is, 1 child forms the shape of a whole note, 2 children form half notes, 4 children form quarter notes, and 8 children form eighth notes. Review the concepts concerning the relationship of each row to all the others and explain that each row is a measure.

13. Tell the children to stand up but retain their position and note identity. Tell them you

Fig. 18-3. Arrangement of different note values in measures that the children can imitate by using their bodies.

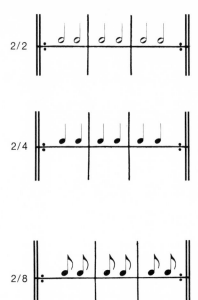

Fig. 18-4. Quadruple meter.

Fig. 18-5. Simple duple meter.

are going to count "1 and 2 and 3 and 4."
Instruct each child to bend at the waist on
the appropriate count and to hold that position until you finish counting. (For example, the whole note, first half note, first
quarter note, and first eighth note all bend
on the count of "1" and remain in that position. The second eighth note bends on
"and." The second quarter note and third
eighth note bend on the count of "2," etc.)
Let the children practice. When they have
mastered the procedure, instruct them to
unbend (stand up) on the appropriate count
of the second measure. Progress to having
them bend on odd-numbered measures and
stand up on even-numbered measures. Ask
them to change roles.

14. Instruct the children to develop a move-
    ment orchestra. Divide the class into three
    groups. Assign one group to be whole
    notes, another to be half notes, and the re-
    maining group to be quarter notes. Chal-
    lenge each group to think of a locomotor
    movement that is characteristic of their
    note value. For example, the movement
    of the whole note might be jumping for-
    ward, the half notes might take slow walk-
    ing steps, and the quarter notes might hop.
    Explain that you will beat out a rhythm
    consisting of 4 beats, and each group is to
    respond by moving on the appropriate beat.
    (That is, whole notes jump on the accented
    beat and hold their position on 2, 3, and 4.
    Half note step forward with the right foot
    on the accented beat and forward on the left
    foot on count 3. Quarter notes hop on each
    beat.) When the children have mastered
    the sequence, repeat it over and over. With
    more advanced students, add eighth notes
    doing running steps. A possible variation
    is moving like animals or objects.

15. Draw a diagram of a quadruple (4/4) meter
    that you have been using in the previous
    activities (Fig. 18-4). Explain how the
    notes are arranged within the measure and
    how the number and type of notes in the
    measure determine the meter. Show the

children how meter is written as a fraction
and explain that the top numeral indicates
the number of beats in the measure and the
bottom number specifies the type of note
that gets the beat. (That is, in 4/4 meter
there are 4 beats in a measure and quarter
notes each get 1 beat.)

16. Have the children echo clap simple duple
    meter in 2/2 time (Fig. 18-5) while they
    count it out loud. Then have them move to
    the different tempos by executing any of
    the following movements:

    • Bend and stretch different body parts
    • Twist and straighten arms, legs, or waist
    • Push and pull different body parts
    • Walk
    • Jump
    • Hop

17. Repeat no. 13, using triple meter (Fig.
    18-6).

18. Have the children explore the rhythmical
    patterns of their names, with the group
    clapping and then moving to the rhythm.
    Examples are shown in Fig. 18-7.

19. Select words with syllables that match
    duple and triple meter. Have the children
    execute movements as they repeat these

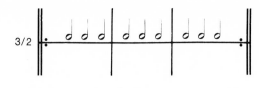

Fig. 18-6. Simple triple meter.

words in the correct rhythmical pattern (Fig. 18-8).

20. Use the rhythmical patterns of proverbs, slogans, or nursery rhymes, with the children creating simple movement sequences in response to the rhythm of the words (Fig. 18-9).

21. Divide the class into pairs. Give each pair of children a beanbag. Have them pretend the beanbag is a certain type of note in 4/4 meter. They toss the beanbag to each other, holding it while they count out the number of these notes that would be in the measure. For example, if the beanbag represents a quarter note, the child catching it would count 1, 2, 3, 4 and then toss it back to his partner, who would then count 1, 2, 3, 4. If the beanbag represents a half note, the children would slowly count 1, 2. When this activity is introduced, clap or beat out

Tom   Mar-y   Char-lie   Brown   Sus-an   Jen-kins   Tim-o-thy   Mar-tin

Fig. 18-7. Exploring the rhythmical patterns of names.

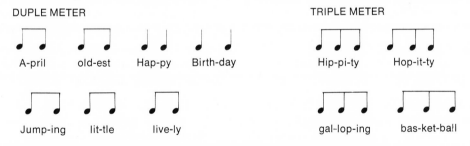

Fig. 18-8. Words with syllables that have duple or triple meter.

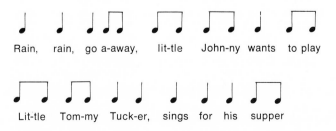

Fig. 18-9. Rhythmical patterns of proverbs, slogans, or nursery rhymes.

the notes as you count during the first few times the children catch the beanbag. When they are thoroughly familiar with the activity, they can call out the note value as they toss the beanbag to their partner.

22. Mark off lines on the floor to represent five measures (Fig. 18-10). Give each of 20 children a card with a quarter note drawn on it. Tell them they will be the note on their card and they are to place themselves in the measures to form 4/4 meter; that is, 4 of them will stand side by side in each measure. Demonstrate this. Have the children count the beat in their measure. Give 5 children cards with half notes drawn on them. Instruct these children to take the place of 2 of the quarter notes in each of the measures. Have the children count the beat again, with the half notes counted as 2 beats. Continue, substituting whole notes and eighth notes.

23. After the students are familiar with the concepts explored in no. 22, have them take turns drawing a card with a whole, half, or quarter note on it and then arranging themselves within the measures so that the count is correct. Change the meter to 2/4 and 3/4, challenging them to create the correct number of beats in each measure. Following is a concept on rests, which also can be printed on some of the cards and used in the measures in place of notes.

Rests

CONCEPT: There are places in music that indicate no sound. These spaces are called rests.

Level: Beginning.

Subconcepts: (1) There is both sound and silence in music. (2) We can move to the sound and remain still in the silence. (3) When music is written, the sound are notes, and the silences are rests.

Materials: A drum.

Activities

1. Explain to the children that the drum is going to talk to them. They are to move when the drum tells them to, and be still and quiet when the drum is still. Beat a rhythm on the drum and ask the children how they want to move. Select one of the responses and instruct all the children to move that way when they hear the drumbeat and to stop moving when the drum stops talking. Beat the drum, varying the duration of the intervals of sound and silence.

2. Select other ways of moving suggested by the children and have the group move in this manner on the drumbeat.

3. Beat the drum with heavy, emphatic beats and let the children move any way this makes them feel. Alternate periods of emphatic sound and complete silence.

4. Beat the drum with light, slow beats, challenging the children to respond to the sound versus silence.

5. Alternate intervals of heavy beats and silence, light beats and silence.

6. Introduce the concept of rests by reviewing the activities that involve responding to sound and silence. Explain that when they are still and quiet, they are in fact resting and that rests are written into music in place of notes.

7. Review the concept of 2/4 meter by beating out several measures containing quarter notes. Accent the first beat of each measure. Have the children move to the beat by gently clapping their hands on their thighs. When the group is responding confidently, tell them to clap their thighs on the accented beat and rest on the unaccented beat.

8. Repeat no. 7, substituting locomotor and nonlocomotor movements such as walking and jumping or bending and twisting.

| Measure 1 | Measure 2 | Measure 3 | Measure 4 | Measure 5 |

Fig. 18-10. Exploring the concept of measures.

9. Change to 3/4 meter, then to 4/4 meter.
10. Have the children rest on different beats within the measure:
    - Rest on the second beat of 3/4 meter.
    - Rest on the third beat of 4/4 meter.
    - Rest on the second and fourth beats of 4/4 meter.
    - Rest on the first beat of 2/4 meter.
    - Rest on the first and third beats of 3/4 meter.
    - Rest on the first, second, and fourth beats of 4/4 meter.
    - Vary the measures within a phrase so that rests occur on different beats in the different measures.
11. Show the children illustrations of the different rests (Fig. 18-11) and explain how these are written into the music. Have the children form the shape and position of rests. Examples follow:
    - For a whole rest have 2 children hold the ends of a jump rope and pull it tight so that it makes a straight line approximately 30 centimeters above the floor. Instruct a third child to lie down under the rope on his back, with the body tucked to resemble the shape of a whole rest. (See Fig. 18-12.)
    - For a half rest place a jump rope on the floor in a straight line, or use a line painted on the floor. Have 2 children position their bodies in a tucked position facing the rope. (See Fig. 18-13.)
    - For a quarter rest have 4 children form the shape of a quarter rest by supporting their weight on their knees and toes, keeping their bodies straight while they extend their arms upward and backward (Fig. 18-14).
    - For an eighth rest have 8 children stand along a rope or a straight line, facing the left end of the rope. Have each one clasp hands, hold the arms straight out in front of the body, and place the head down between the arms. (See Fig. 18-15.)
12. Have the children form measures of different meters, combining notes and rests. Have the children identify these, then have

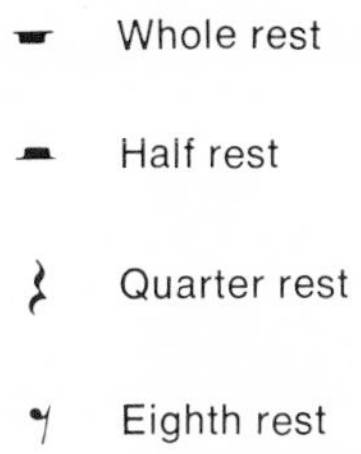

Fig. 18-11. Different kinds of rests.

Fig. 18-12. Whole rest.

Fig. 18-13. Half rests.

Fig. 18-14. Quarter rest.

Fig. 18-15. Eighth rest.

——— ——— ——— ——— ——— ———

Fig. 18-16. Rhythmical pattern of walking steps.

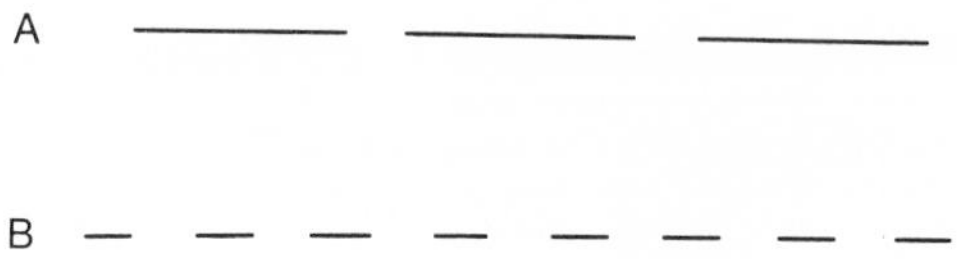

A ———————— ———————— ————————

B — — — — — — — —

Fig. 18-17. A, Rhythmical pattern of long, slow steps;
B, rhythmical pattern of small, quick steps.

——— — ———————— — ————————

Fig. 18-18. Rhythmical pattern of a long step, followed
by a short step; slow-fast sequence.

the notes move on the appropriate beat
while the rests remain still on their beat.

Even and uneven rhythms

CONCEPT: Some movements and sounds
have an even rhythm and some have an uneven
rhythm.

Level: Intermediate.

Subconcepts: (1) Movements such as walking, running, jumping, and hopping have an
even rhythm because each step takes the same
amount of time. (2) Skipping, sliding, and galloping have an uneven rhythm because the first
part of the step is slow and the second part is
fast.

Materials: A drum and a blackboard.

Activities

1. Have the students walk around the room,
   then begin beating the drum in the tempo of
   their steps. Substitute clapping for the
   drumbeat, then challenge the children to
   clap with you as they walk.

2. Challenge the children to illustrate the
   rhythmical pattern of their step by using
   lines (Fig. 18-16). Point out that the lines
   are all the same length, and so we say they
   are even and that walking has an even
   rhythm.

3. Tell the children you are going to beat the
   drum slowly and you want them to take
   giant steps. Ask them if their steps are long
   or short, then challenge them to illustrate
   these steps by using lines. (See Fig. 18-17,
   A.)

4. Explain to them that you are going to beat
   the drum fast and you want them to take
   small, quick steps. Challenge them to illustrate these by using lines. (See Fig.
   18-17, *B*.) Contrast the length of these lines
   with those drawn in no. 3.

5. Tell the children you are going to beat the
   drum differently this time—1 slow beat,
   then 1 fast beat. Demonstrate, repeating
   the slow-fast sequence. Instruct the class to
   step forward with their right foot, taking
   a long step on the slow beat; forward on
   their left foot, taking a short step on the fast
   beat; then repeat. Have the children illustrate this long-short sequence by using
   lines. (See Fig. 18-18.)

6. Compare the lines drawn in no. 5 with those in nos. 3 and 4. Explain that the rhythm in nos. 3 and 4 is even because all the lines in the sequence are the same length, whereas the rhythm in no. 5 is uneven because the lines are different lengths. Review the concept that the lines represent slow and fast steps.

7. Have the children gallop around the room. Beat out the rhythm of their steps.

8. Have the class sit down and listen to the rhythm you are beating; now tell them to walk. Challenge them to listen to the rhythm of their walking steps compared to that of their galloping and detect the difference. Challenge them to illustrate the rhythmical pattern of galloping by using lines. Point out that the rhythm of the gallop is uneven.

9. Have the children gallop again while attending to the rhythm of their steps and feeling the long-short pattern of the uneven rhythm.

10. Explain that skipping and sliding also have an uneven rhythm. Have the children move about the room skipping, then challenge them to illustrate the rhythmical pattern. Repeat, having them execute sliding steps.

11. Place note values above the lines of their rhythmical pattern so that they can see the relationship of the notes in the measure to the underlying beat of an uneven rhythm (Fig. 18-19).

12. Challenge the children to work in pairs, creating a short sequence of movements in an even rhythm. Specify that these must involve using the body parts in a way other than executing locomotor movements.

13. Ask them to change their movements from an even to an uneven rhythm.

14. Challenge the children to jump for four measures, then ship for four measures. Then challenge them to create a sequence in which they execute movements with an even rhythm in the first four measures and movements with an uneven rhythm in the last four.

PITCH

CONCEPT: Music has high sounds and low sounds.

Level: Beginning.

Subconcepts: (1) We can move to the pitch. (2) We reach high on high tones. (3) We move on a low level on low tones.

Materials: Instruments or records to produce high and low tones, balls and a parachute.

Activities: Create high and low tones, using a variety of verbal, percussive, recorded, and instrumental sounds. Challenge the children to respond to these as follows:

1. Have them reach high and low, extending the range of the tones and their movements as they become more familiar with the sounds. Include very high tones that require standing on tiptoe and stretching, as well as very low tones requiring the children to sit or lie down.

2. Have them "touch" the pitch by placing their hands at a level that corresponds to tones in the high, medium, and low range as well as points in between.

3. Repeat no. 2, using other body parts such as the elbows, head, feet, and knees.

4. Have the children toss or roll the ball to a partner. Instruct them to throw it in a high arc for high tones, a straight line for midrange, and roll it for low tones.

5. Let the children move the parachute on a level that corresponds to sounds differing in pitch. For example:

Low tones: Hold the parachute below the knees and twist it alternately to the left and to the right.

Mid-range tones: Hold the parachute at chest lev-

Fig. 18-19. Rhythmical pattern of uneven locomotor movements.

el and make ripples and waves by moving the arms up and down.

High tones: Make a mushroom with the parachute by raising it high overhead and then taking four steps toward the center.

6. Challenge the children to think of things that move on the levels that correspond to sounds with high and low pitch. Have them move the way these things make them feel, for example:

High tones: birds, giraffes, clouds, and tall trees waving in the breeze.

Low tones: Turtles, snakes, cats, and grass or grain waving in the breeze

7. Have the children respond to sounds that differ in both pitch and tempo. For example, in response to low, slow sounds they might crawl or crouch while moving slowly. On high, fast sounds they might run on tiptoe.

MELODY

CONCEPT: The melody is the theme of a musical composition, expressing the meaning or the mood of the music.

Level: Intermediate.

Subconcepts: (1) The melody is created by combining notes that have different pitches and different time values. (2) When the melody is written, the notes are placed on a staff according to the sound they make. (3) The notes that represent tones with a high pitch are placed higher on the staff, and those representing low tones are placed lower on the staff. (4) The notes are named with letters according to where they are located on the staff.

Materials: Jump ropes taped on the floor to form the five lines of the musical staff (or the staff may be formed by placing masking tape on the floor or by drawing lines in the dirt on the

Fig. 18-20. Walking down the lines of a staff.

playground), a piano, bells, and a xylophone (glockenspiel) or other type of melody instrument.

Activities

1. Have a child stand in each of the spaces on the staff. Tell them to face the right end of the staff, hold hands, and walk to the end of the staff. (See Fig. 18-20.)
2. When all the children have had a turn moving down the staff, have the groups start over. Point out how they remain on the same level as they move along the staff. Hum a tune that stays on the same level as the children move along the staff.
3. Instruct each group of children to line up one behind the other at the bottom of the staff. Tell them to jump into each of the spaces going up the scale. Repeat, going down. (See Fig. 18-21.)
4. Repeat no. 3, having the children step on each of the five lines as they move up and down the scale.
5. Have the children sit on the center line of the scale facing the right end. Review the concept of pitch. Tell them you are going to create sounds that have different pitches and they are to touch the toes of one foot to the place on the staff where they think the pitch would be located. Give examples of a high, mid-range, and low pitch and assist the students in locating them on the staff. Then give the children a variety of sounds, challenging them to locate the pitch.
6. Instruct groups of 9 children to stand on the lines and in the spaces of the staff, as shown in Fig. 18-22. Explain that they represent notes and that music is written by placing the notes on a staff.

7. Explain that the notes on the staff represent tones with different pitches; the notes at the top of the staff have a high pitch and those at the bottom a lower pitch. Demonstrate this by sounding in order the notes shown in Fig. 18-23. Identify the children standing on each line or space with the tone they represent by playing this tone. Instruct them to quickly bend and then straighten their knees so that their body bobs down and back up when their tone is sounded. When all the children (tones) have been identified, tell them you are going to play the tones in order, starting with the lowest one and ending with the highest. When their note is played, the students are to bob so that everyone can see the tones moving up the staff.
8. Repeat the activity in no. 7, starting with the tone at the top of the staff and moving down.
9. Put nos. 7 and 8 together so that the sounds move up and then down. Repeat.
10. Begin with tones located at different places on the staff, challenging the children to recognize their tone wherever it sounds.
11. Tell each child the name of the note he represents. Point out that the notes are in alphabetical order but they do not follow the whole alphabet. Rather, only seven letters—those from A through G—are used as names of notes. Explain that this makes identifying notes just by their name very confusing. To simplify this, one note has been designated the home tone. This note is C, and it is located one space below the bottom line on the staff. It is called middle C, and since it is not written on the staff, it has a line through it so that it can be easily recognized. Show the children a picture of middle C in its proper location be-

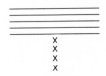

Fig. 18-21. Jumping up the scale.

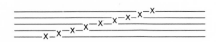

Fig. 18-22. Standing on the lines and spaces of the staff.

Fig. 18-23. Position of notes on the staff.

low the staff (Fig. 18-24). Have the top 3 children of each group of 9 standing on the staff (those representing D, E, and F) come down below the staff. Tell them you are going to change their identity so that the notes can begin with middle C. Position 1 of these children in the location of middle C at the beginning of each group. Give each of these children a wand to hold across their body to symbolize the line through the note. Explain that another note is located just below the bottom line of the staff, between middle C and E. Have 1 of the children stand in this position in each group. Identify these children as being the note D. Tell them that the 8 children now standing on the staff represent a musical scale. Sound the tones of middle C and D so that these children become familiar with the sound they represent. Then play the scale from bottom to top and top to bottom. Let the third child who moved down from the top of the staff act as the conductor.

12. Play the song "Do, Re, Mi," from *The Sound of Music,* challenging the children to respond by bobbing when their note is played. Explain that the sequence of sounds in a song is called the melody. Point out how the melody of "Do, Re, Mi," moves up the scale, with each note used in order. Select other songs or dance tunes and challenge the children to identify the melody and specify whether it moves up or down or stays level.

13. Review the concept of the notes being

C D E F G

Fig. 18-24. Location of middle C, as well as D, E, F, and G.

named according to their location on the staff. Have the children toss beanbags onto a staff laid out on the floor and challenge them to identify the name of the note on the line or in the space where the beanbags come to rest (see illustration on p. 257).

14. Have the children stand at the bottom of the staff laid out on the floor. Tell them you are going to call out the name of a note and they are to jump into the space or onto the line that is the home of that note.

15. Mark measure lines across the staff on the floor. Show the children an illustration of the melody of a song (a large poster is best). Give each child a card containing a note or a rest in the melody of the song. Have each child take the place of his note on the staff in the correct measure. Play the tune of the song on a rhythm instrument, instructing the children to bob down on their note.

16. Place large construction paper notes on the staff to create a melody such as that of the song "Ten Little Indians." Make each type of note a different color so that they can be more easily identified, for example:

D	Purple	A	Green
F	Yellow	B	Orange
G	Red		

Have the children sing the song, attending closely to the pitch and time values of the notes. Beat the rhythm on a drum so that the children can hear the difference between the quarter and eighth notes. Challenge them to step out the melody by walking on the notes laid out on the floor. Have them sing as they walk, since this will assist them in keeping in time with the music.

17. Make a poster illustrating the melody of the Maori chant "Koo-ee" (Fig. 18-25).

1 2 3   1 2 3 12   3 1 2 3   1 2 3   1 2 3 12   3   12 3
Ma Ko Way Ko Tay Oh Way Koo-ee Tah Na   Ma Ko Way Ko Tay Oh Way Koo-ee Tah Na

Fig. 18-25. Melody of Maori chant "Koo-ee."

Teach the children the song, then teach them the patterns of the Lummi sticks game. Have them sing the melody as they beat out the rhythm of the chant by executing the patterns of the game.

18. Have the children listen to different melodies and describe the way the music makes them feel (its mood). Encourage them to move to express these feelings. Select music that will stimulate them to explore the following kinds of movement possibilities:

large, expansive	jagged, sharp, angular
small, contracted	
high, reaching	curved, rounded
low, dejected	twisted, distorted
fast, quick, rapid	smooth, flowing, sustained
slow, gradual	
wide, spacious	sudden, percussive, staccato
narrow, restricted	

19. Play one or more of the following *Dance-a-Story* records from the series by Anne and Paul Barlin, challenging the children to identify the moods of the music and the movements that express these:

"Little Duck"
"Magic Mountain"
"Balloons"
"Brave Hunter"
"At the Beach"

20. Play folk music from different countries and challenge the children to describe the moods and themes of the various selections. Teach folk dances that have music and steps which reflect the moods of different cultures.

21. Have the children relate music and color. Select music with the following qualities:

bright, vigorous, lively, varying dynamics and pitch
dark, heavy, slow tempo with a low pitch
light, transparent, high pitch
pale, soft, high pitch

Challenge them to move the way the colors and the music make them feel. Discuss the contrast in these feeling states.

DYNAMICS

CONCEPT: Music has loud sounds and soft sounds.

Level: Beginning.

Subconcepts: (1) Whether sounds are loud or soft depends on the amount of energy, or force, used to create them. (2) Sounds may suddenly become louder or softer or they may gradually increase or decrease in volume.

Materials: A drum; the music and equipment suggested in nos. 8 and 10.

Activities

1. Have the children clap their hands softly, then loudly. Have them close their eyes as they clap softly, then loudly. Instruct them to feel and think about how much more energy they use when they are clapping loudly.

2. Have them stand up and tap one foot on the floor, then stamp it. Have them close their eyes and feel the difference in the energy and force. Also have them attend to the difference in the sound of tapping versus stamping.

3. Beat the drum softly and have the children move the way it makes them feel. Then beat it loudly and challenge them to respond to these sounds.

4. Combine tempo and intensity by challenging the children to respond to a slow, hard drumbeat; a fast, hard beat; a slow, soft beat; and a fast, soft beat.

5. Have them begin responding to a soft beat with one body part such as one hand and gradually add other body parts as the beat becomes louder, continuing until all of their body is actively involved.

6. Begin beating a strong, loud beat and challenge the children to respond with their whole body. Gradually decrease the volume as the children diminish the magnitude of their movements until the beat grows soft and fades away and their bodies are at rest.

7. Vary the tempo and the intensity of the beat, challenging the children to spontaneously respond to the variations.

8. Challenge the children to think of emotions and feelings that seem loud and hard and those that seem light and soft, for example:

Loud—surprise, anger, excitement
Soft—sorrow, shyness, contentment

Have them move to express these feeling states. Adding music assists in evoking more intense feeling as they move.

9. Discuss situations or objects associated with loudness and softness and let the children move like these things make them feel, for example:

- A balloon floating in the air
- A ball hitting the wall
- A sea gull soaring with wings outstretched
- An angry gorilla stamping through the jungle
- A kitten
- A tiger
- Snow falling
- Thunder and lightning
- The feel of flannel, velvet, or cotton
- The feel of sandpaper
- Coasting to a stop
- A screeching halt

10. Give each child one of the following:

rope	playground
wand	ball
rhythm	tin can and
sticks	stick

Challenge each one to explore the sounds they can create. Instruct them to make both loud and soft sounds. Have them share their sounds as the rest of the children move the way the sounds make them feel.

11. Discuss the contrasts between the way loud and soft sounds make them feel. Point out that loud is usually associated with tenseness and leads to fatigue, whereas softness leads to relaxation and restfulness.

FORM

CONCEPT: A phrase consists of two or more measures that express a single theme.

Level: Intermediate.

Subconcepts: (1) A musical phrase is like a sentence; they both express a single thought. (2) Some phrases (like some sentences) are very short, others are longer. (3) Several phrases may be joined together to create a song or a composition, just as sentences are joined together to form paragraphs and stories.

Materials: Recorded or piano music with distinct phrasing and jump ropes.

Activities

1. Have the children listen to music in which the phrases are distinctive. Challenge them to respond to the phrases by moving in different ways. For example, they could move their arms on the first phrase, their feet on the second phrase, their head on the third, and their shoulders on the fourth.

2. It may be easier for the children to recognize musical phrases if they can sing the words. Singing games such as "Peas Porridge Hot," "Oh Susannah," and "Climbing up the Mountain" (Rise Sugar Rise)* contain simple, distinct phrasing. Have the children sing and move to these, as described in no. 1.

3. Ask the children to clap the underlying beat of the song, accenting the first beat of each phrase. "Peas Porridge Hot" has a distinct underlying beat in 4/4 meter that is easy for them to follow.

4. Tell the children to walk, hop, jump, or skip to the music, changing directions on the first beat of each phrase.

5. Have them execute nonlocomotor movements such as bend and stretch or twist and turn, changing movements at the beginning of each phrase.

6. Have them execute a locomotor movement on one phrase and a nonlocomotor on the next phrase.

7. Point out the way phrases are often repeated in music. Show the children how the repetition may be exact or it may differ slightly. For example, in the song "Oh Susannah," the first phrase is repeated in the verses and then is repeated at the end of the chorus. In the song "Climbing up the Mountain," the first and third phrases are identical and the second phrase differs only in its pitch being one step lower. Select music in which at least one phrase is repeated. Have the children execute different movements to phrases that differ, and the same movements to phrases that are repeated. For example, if the children were moving to "Oh Susannah," they could

*These songs and the printed music for each may be found in Krause (1966).

walk forward on the two phrases of the verses and the last phrase of the chorus and could jump in place during the first phrase of the chorus. Accenting the first beat in each of the walking phrases by stamping the foot assists the children in attending to the phrasing. In "Climbing up the Mountain" the children could walk forward on the first and third phrases (since they are identical), walk backward on the second phrase (since it differs only slightly), and hop during the last phrase.

8. Divide the class into two groups. Have one group move to a phrase and the other group echo their movements.

9. While in two groups have one group sing a phrase and the second group move to the same phrase.

10. Have the divided group sing and move to the phrases of rounds such as "Three Blind Mice," "Row, Row, Row Your Boat," "Are You Sleeping" and "Kookaburra" and to songs that can be sung in parts such as "Ten Little Indians," "The Farmer in the Dell," and "Skip to My Lou."

11. Have the children sing jump rope jingles* and identify the phrasing. Then they may jump rope by turning the rope forward on one phrase and backward on the next phrase. They may also change steps at the beginning of each phrase, alternately executing (a) the basic two-foot jumping step with a rebound in between, (b) a hop over the rope with a rebound hop, and (c) a rocker step (one leg forward with a shift of weight from the back to the front foot as the rope passes under the feet and a shift to the back foot as the rope passes over the head).

12. Have the children work in partners, composing movement phrases in response to music. Encourage the children to think in terms of there being three parts to the phrase: a beginning in which the theme of the phrase is introduced, a middle in which the theme is expanded, and an end in which it is brought to a climax and a definite conclusion.

13. As the children gain experience and confidence, encourage them to create dance sequences by combining the phrases to express the themes of a complete musical composition.*

14. Teach folk dances, emphasizing the relationship of the dance figures to the musical phrasing.

---

*A variety of jingles may be found in Butler and Haley (1963) or Skolnik (1974).

*Detailed information on children creating dances may be found in Fleming (1976) and Part V of Murray (1975).

Chapter 19

ART

Movement activities provide a medium in which children may develop many of the aptitudes and abilities essential in artistic expression. Awareness, perception, feelings, and creativity are essential aspects of movement activities as well as the visual arts.

Movement activities have the potential to enhance awareness in three ways. First, they encourage children to be more open to experience. Their body movements are natural and sensorily satisfying. Therefore movement assists them in receiving and taking in more sensory information. Second, being actively involved assists children in more acutely attending to the stimulus source as well as increasing the intensity of their involvement in the learning medium. Third, movement is a holistic experience comprised of actions of body parts. This provides opportunity for children to observe detail and, at the same time, to perceive a meaningful whole.

The relationship between perception and movement is evident when one realizes that a child perceives all objects and spatial relationships in reference to his own body. To perceive these relationships, the child must be able to recognize and make connections between the factors involved. The child's body is the stable reference point that gives the external world proportions. Concepts relative to direction, size, distance, and level develop as children move their bodies in relation to objects and spaces. Children use their body positions to orient themselves in space. They also use stable body positions as reference points for locating and manipulating objects in space.

Feelings are inherent in the sensory experience of moving, and the child's body naturally serves as an expressive instrument for feeling states and emotions. Thus movement activities provide ideal laboratories for exploring how feeling states are evoked, why they need to be expressed, and how they can be expressed in constructive and satisfying ways.

Ideally, children's awareness, perceptions, and feelings find creative outlets. Movement and art experiences should enable children to conceive of the act of creating as an adventure with the inner self that leads to knowing through feeling. As this knowledge is being acquired, children should be encouraged to give their inner experiences outward expression in a variety of visual forms, including creative movement.

In addition to sharing common aptitudes, abilities, and processes, movement and art also share common concepts. In both mediums, children must use concepts relative to space, line, shape, form, color, and design and composition. Applying and reinforcing these concepts in movement activities as well as in art activities provides more pleasurable and meaningful learning experiences.

BODY AWARENESS

The activities in this section serve to review body part identification, as well as to enhance the children's awareness of their moving body.

SPATIAL AWARENESS

Humans live in space. Their bodies are physical objects that occupy space; as they move, they are physical objects moving through space. Also, at all times their bodies have a spatial relationship to all other objects and surfaces in the environment. These are the basic concepts children need to explore to become fully aware of their physical reality. This awareness is a prerequisite to the development of concepts relative to line, form, space, and design. The activities in this section are planned to assist children in becoming acutely aware of their physical being and its relationship to the spatial world around them.

DESIGN AND COMPOSITION

Because of the wide variety of learning activities relating to movement concepts, as well as variations in the kinds of materials available in a particular school and the differences in interests and backgrounds of teachers and students, the content of this section differs from that of previous sections. A sequence of learning activities is introduced. This is followed by lists of movement-related materials, themes, and art mediums. The learning activities suggest ways of combining these three factors. The content of the lists is designed to stimulate the imagination of both teacher and student so that they may create an endless variety of movement-related art activities. The learning level of these activities is dependent on which factors are selected, how they are combined, and the type of outcomes expected to result from the learning experiences.

Learning activities

Body awareness

CONCEPT: It feels different when I move my body parts in different ways.

Level: Beginning.

Subconcepts: (1) Touching feels different than rubbing or pressing. (2) Pressing feels different than clapping. (3) Bending feels different than stretching. (4) Stretching feels different than twisting. (5) Moving fast feels different than moving slow. (6) Sudden, forceful movements feel different than gradual, soft movements.

Materials: Recorded music to accompany the movements.

Activities: Tell the children you are going to play music and call out the names of different body parts. Instruct them to move different body parts in various ways. Some examples follow:

1. Ask the children to shake their hands (arms, shoulders, head, one foot, one leg).
2. Have the children move around the room. On a signal (such as stopping the music or a drumbeat) have them stop and point a certain body part toward you (i.e., if you say "Right foot," they point the right foot toward you and hold the position until you give the signal to begin moving again). Call out a number of different body parts.
3. Instruct the children to hide the body part when you give the signal (i.e., "Hide your elbows so I can't see them"). Call out different combinations of body parts such as hands and feet or right hand and right foot.
4. Tell the children to pretend they are puppets with strings tied to different body parts. Ask them to imagine the string is pulling them around the room. Tell them to move as long as the music is playing and to stop when it stops. Name a different body part each time the music stops. Examples are "The string is tied to your wrists—let your wrist lead you through space. Now it is tied to your ankle. That ankle must lead your movements—it takes you where you are going."
5. Have the children lie down and close their eyes. Ask them to press different body parts against the floor and think about how it feels. Start with the head and move down (i.e., head, neck, shoulders, arms, hands, back, seat, legs, heels). Then ask the students to contrast the feelings of pressing hard and soft body parts, i.e., head versus seat or elbows versus legs. If mats (or a carpeted surface) are available, tell the children to contrast the feelings associated with pressing body parts against this surface versus the bare floor.
6. Have the children lie down on mats or a carpeted floor. Instruct them to slowly lift the body part you name, and when you say "Drop" to let the body part fall to the floor. Call out several different body parts such as one hand, the other hand, one leg, the other leg, one shoulder, both arms, arms and legs.
7. Ask them to lift the body part, hold it as long as they can, and then to let it drop. (With older children discuss the fact that they are lifting and holding against the force of gravity.)
8. Give the children the experience that each body part comes alive until their whole body is fully alive. Have them begin by

making themselves as small as possible and remaining very still. Then one body part begins to stir and to move out into space. Other body parts follow, one by one, until their whole body is alive and moving through space.

9. Instruct the children to explore the feelings associated with touching, rubbing, and pressing different body parts. Have them contrast these feelings with clapping and slapping.

10. Have them contrast the feelings of bending and stretching different body parts. Contrast stretching and twisting.

11. Have them contrast the feelings of moving different body parts fast and slow.

12. Have them contrast the feelings of sudden, forceful movements versus gradual, soft movements.

Spatial awareness

CONCEPT: There are a number of different environmental directions:

right, left	close to, far away
front, back, beside	across, around, along
forward, away from	into, out of, through
forward, backward, sideward	over, under

Level: Beginning
Materials: Beanbags.
Activities:

1. Give each child a beanbag. Instruct them to find a personal space somewhere in the room and stand in that space. Challenge the children to respond to the following directions:

   Place the beanbag on the palm of your right (left) hand.
   Place it on your right shoulder.
   Put it on the floor in front (in back, beside) of you.
   Put it on a body part that is close to the floor.
   Put it on a body part that is far away from the floor.
   Put the beanbag on the floor beside your right foot. Move around it.
   Move the beanbag forward with your right elbow.
   Move it backward by using some other body part.

2. Place objects around the room and challenge the children to move in relation to them. For example:

   Move toward the chair.
   Move over the milk carton.
   Move under the pole supported by two chairs.
   Move along the line.

3. Take the children out on the playground. Challenge them to move all around the playground and to remember where they go.

Fig. 19-1. Using different body parts to move an object.

When they return to the schoolroom, draw an outline of the playground on the board and put in the objects located on the playground, such as the trees, fences, play equipment. Ask the children to recall how they moved in relation to these objects. Point to an object in the diagram and ask them to tell you which of the following ways they moved.

toward	around
away from	into
along (beside)	out of
across	through

4. Repeat the activity in no. 3 while playing follow the leader and calling out the name of the object and your relationship to it, for example:

We are moving toward the fence.
We are moving away from the school building.
We are moving around the softball field.
We are under the tree.
We are going into the school building.

5. Repeat no. 4, with the children executing certain movements, for example:

Run toward the fence.
Skip away from the building.
Slide along the sidewalk.
Jump around the jungle gym.

CONCEPT: Small movements take up little spaces and large movements fill big spaces.

Level: Beginning.
Materials: A drum.
Activities
1. Have the children make small and large movements with different body parts, for example:

Move just your fingers, making a small movement.
Now move your hands.
Add your arms, but keep it very small.
Now let's do the same thing with your toes, add your feet, let your legs join in.
Let your feet carry you through space, taking very small steps.

Repeat these activities using large movements.
2. Have the children hold hands to form a large

circle, then drop hands and face counterclockwise. Tell them they are to begin walking when you beat the drum, and each time you beat the drum, they are to take one step sideward toward the center of the circle. Have them move inward until the circle is small and they are walking very close together. Tell them to sit down. Discuss the size of their steps when the circle was large versus the size when the circle was small. Have them stand up and repeat the activity by moving outward. Discuss the feelings associated with moving in a large space, and contrast these with moving in a small space.
3. Challenge the children to think of animals that take small steps and others that take large steps. Let them imitate these movements.

CONCEPT: We can move on different levels and in different directions.

Level: Beginning.
Materials: None.
Activities
1. Have the children find a personal space. Challenge them to get their whole body as low as possible and to think about how it feels to be lying there, flat on the floor. Tell them to reach up with a body part, reaching as high as possible but still keeping their back on the floor. Tell them to use another body part to reach up. Repeat, using two or more body parts to reach upward.
2. Ask them to pick out a spot on the ceiling and try to touch it with their feet. Challenge them to stand up and try to touch that point. Have them reach toward it with different body parts.
3. Tell them to reach high with one body part and low with another, for example:

Reach high with your right hand and low with your left.
Reach high with your left hand and low with your right foot.
Reach high with your right knee and low with your right elbow.

4. Have the children move forward while keeping their body as low as possible and then backward while their body is high.

5. Challenge the children to think of things that move on high levels and things that move on low levels. Let them imitate the movements of the things they name.

6. Take the children outside on a sunny day and let them make shadow figures. Some of the concepts you can review follow:

Stand so your shadow is in front of you (behind you, beside you).
Make your shadow very big (small).
Make it tall (short).

Ask the children to work with a partner, exploring different dimensions. Progress to having them make shadows with contrasting dimensions (i.e., one big, the other small one tall, the other short). Challenge them to touch their partner's shadow figure with their shadow figure. Have them play shadow tag in partners, with one attempting to step on the other's shadow.

CONCEPTS: The shapes we can form with our bodies and body parts are as follows:

narrow	angular
wide	twisted
curved	

Level: Beginning.

Materials: Jump ropes, a piece of tubular stretch jersey, and posters illustrating stunts to be performed in no. 18.

Activities

1. Have the children lie down on the floor their arms overhead. Challenge them to stretch while making their body as long and narrow as possible.

2. Challenge them to make their body as wide as possible by moving their arms and legs to the side.

3. Challenge them to lie on their side, keeping their body long and narrow.

4. While lying on their side have them make a wide shape.

5. Challenge them to make their body as small as possible, then ask what shape their body has (their back is rounded or curved).

6. Have them sit up and form curved shapes with different body parts:

fingers	legs and feet
both arms	back

7. Challenge them to again make a very small shape with their whole body and to think about the shape of their arms and legs while

Fig. 19-2. Making shadow shapes.

they are in that position. (Their arms and legs are bent, forming angular shapes.)

8. Have the children stand up and form angular shapes with different body parts and combinations of body parts. Repeat these while lying down (Fig. 6-11).

9. Challenge them to form angular shapes with a partner.

10. Discuss the fact that it is easier for humans to make angular shapes than it is to make curved shapes because of the way they are made. (The joints form angles when they bend.)

11. Tell the children there is another kind of body shape. Have them stand and, without moving their feet, look at the wall behind them. Ask them what shape their body is making (twisted).

12. Challenge them to make twisted shapes with different body parts such as arms and hands, legs and feet, neck.

13. Review the subconcepts in this lesson concerning the relationship of body parts while they are forming different shapes. Emphasize the following facts:
    a. The body parts must be close together to form a narrow shape and far apart to for a wide one.
    b. The trunk of the body can be curved to form a rounded shape.
    c. Angular shapes have corners, and so most of our joints form angular shapes.
    d. A twisted shape is formed by having one body part face one direction and another body part face a different direction.

14. Give each child a jump rope. Challenge them to form a shape with the rope and then make their body into the same shape. (With *older* children introduce the concept of contrasting shapes and have them make a shape with the rope and an opposite shape with their bodies [i.e., the rope straight, their body angular; the rope curved, their body straight; the rope narrow, their body wide].)

15. Combine concepts of shape and environmental directions, for example:

Make a narrow shape while going through the door.

Make a wide shape while moving along the line. Make a twisted shape while going around the chair.

16. Have 1 child crawl into a piece of tubular-shaped stretch jersey. (You may use a piece about 1 meter long and let the child's head and feet stick out at the ends, or you may use a longer piece (about 1.25 meters) and have it cover the entire child.) Challenge the child to slowly reach out with different body parts, creating a variety of shapes. Have the children select a shape they particularly like and sketch it.

17. Have 2 children get inside the jersey tube. Challenge them to make different shapes on different levels. Instruct them to make symmetrical and asymmetrical shapes. Have them hold a particularly interesting shape. Have 2 other children form the same shape and hold it. Ask the children to describe the similarities of and differences between the shapes inside and outside the tube. Have them make sketches that portray the contrasting factors of the inside and outside shapes.

18. Set up a circuit similar to the one shown in Fig. 19-3. Divide the class into 5 groups and have each group go to one of the stations. Instruct the children to perform the stunt described on the marker at their station and then to sketch the shape of their body while they were performing the stunt. If they have trouble visualizing their body

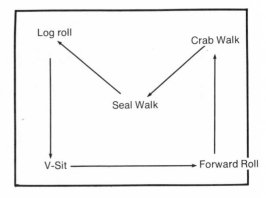

Fig. 19-3. Studying the shapes created by executing stunts.

position, suggest that one child act as a model for the group. Have each group rotate to all five stations. When everyone is finished, call the class together and discuss the various shapes.

Variation: With *older* students use stunts or exercises in which the body shape changes during execution. Examples of stunts that could be used follow:

Inch Worm	Jackknife
Windmill	Wring the Dishrag
Turk Stand	Chinese Getup

On the *intermediate* and *advanced levels,* children should solve movement problems. The following problems involve elements relating to body shapes:

1. Keep one foot on the floor while creating an angular shape with three body parts.
2. Make a wide shape with four body parts on the floor.
3. Make a twisted shape with three body parts on the floor.
4. With a partner make a curved shape that your partner can move under.
5. In partners, one make a wide shape on a low level, the other a narrow shape on a high level.
6. Challenge the children to think of objects and structures and to create their shapes. Examples are trees, bushes, a mug, a table, a house with windows and doors.

CONCEPT: As we move we create straight, angular, or curved pathways on the floor and in space.

Level: Beginning.
Materials: None.
Activities

1. Have the children walk along lines marked on the floor or sidewalk (jump ropes can be laid out on the floor, or chalk can be used to mark lines on some floors and on sidewalks). Point out that these lines form pathways they can follow and these pathways may be straight, angular, or circular (Fig. 19-4).
2. Name one type of pathway and have the children walk along imaginary lines. Name each of the other types and challenge them to create these.
3. Have the children find a partner. Blindfold one of them. The child who is not blindfolded leads the blindfolded child along a pathway. Challenge the blindfolded child to guess what type of pathway he is following. When the blindfolded child has experienced all these types of pathways, have the two exchange places.
4. Challenge the students to think of objects that follow a pathway; for example, cars on the road, a ball rolling on the floor, a train, a boat on a river, a baseball player running around the diamond. Challenge the children to identify the pathway of the object they name and to imitate its movements along its pathway.
5. Have the children hold hands and form a circle. Instruct them to skip around the circle. Challenge them to identify their pathway.
6. Have the children line up and follow the leader around the school building or the playground, then identify the pathways that the group followed.
7. Ask the children to sit on the floor. Explain how pathways on the floor are formed by the feet because the feet are moving over that surface. Point out that the rest of their body is creating a pathway in space. Illustrate this by having them use their hands to create straight, angular, and curved pathways in space.
8. Instruct the children to use other body parts

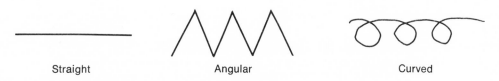

| Straight | Angular | Curved |

Fig. 19-4. Pathways may be straight, angular, or curved (circular).

Fig. 19-5. We can create different pathways in space by changing the shape of our bodies and the level on which we move.

Fig. 19-6. Spatial relationships of side by side and close together.

Fig. 19-7. Our bodies are symetrical.

to create pathways in space, for example, elbows, feet, knees, head.

9. Have them run, jump, and skip. Challenge them to describe how the pathway of their body through space differs when they execute these movements.

10. Tell them to move through space, creating different pathways by changing the shape of their body and the level on which they move (Fig. 19-5).

11. Have them work with a partner, exploring ways to create different pathways as they move through space together.

CONCEPT: The spatial relationships we can have to other objects are as follows:

face to face	close together
back to back	far apart
side by side	

Level: Beginning.
Materials: None.
Activities

1. Review the concept that the children's bodies are physical objects occupying space. Point out that all objects have a relationship to all other objects in space. Have them pair off and stand facing each other. Point out that they now have a face-to-face relationship with each other. Explain the other types of spatial relationships by having them stand as follows:

back to back	close together
side by side	far apart

2. Have them move around the room in pairs, executing different locomotor movements while maintaining one of the spatial relationships specified in no. 1.

3. On the *intermediate* and *advanced levels,* challenge them to develop movement sequences in which they move in different spatial relationships to their partner.

4. Point out that in addition to having a spatial relationship to their partner, they have a relationship to all other objects and surfaces in the room. Lead them in exploring these relationships, for example:

Stand facing the door.
Lie down with your back toward the floor.

Stand close to the wall.
Stand far away from the blackboard.
Stand beside your desk.

CONCEPTS: Symmetrical objects and movements are the same on both sides. Asymmetrical means not symmetrical: the two sides are not the same.

Level: Intermediate.
Materials: A string with a weight tied to one end.
Activities

1. Tell one of the children to stand in front of the group. Ask the students to name all the body parts that are pairs (i.e., all the parts where we have two just alike). Hold a string with a weight on the end in front of the child (Fig. 19-7). Point out how the body parts on the right and left sides of the string are just alike, are located in the same places, and have the same shape. Explain that the word symmetrical means the same on both sides, and so we say the body is a symmetrical object. Point out other objects in the room that are symmetrical, such as a chair, table, vase, lamp.

2. Have the child in front of the group raise his arms so that they are straight out to the side; then have him jump to a sideward stride position. Point out that these are symmetrical movements because the body parts on both sides of the body are doing the same thing. Have the class stand up and execute these movements. Add others, such as the arms straight forward and overhead, or forming a circle in front of the body.

3. Ask the children to put their right arm straight out to the side, leaving their left arm hanging down to their side. Ask them if this is a symmetrical movement. Ask them why it is not. Explain that there is a word for this type of movement; it is called asymmetrical, meaning not symmetrical.

4. Have the students swing one leg. Discuss the fact that this is an asymmetrical movement. Ask them to swing one arm diagonally back and forth in front of the body and point out that this is an asymmetrical movement.

5. Tell the children to jump and then hop. Dis-

Fig. 19-8. Ways a line may be varied.

cuss why jumping is symmetrical and hopping is asymmetrical.

6. Have them do the following stunts and then discuss why each is symmetrical or asymmetrical:

Symmetrical	Asymmetrical
Turk Stand	Windmill
Squat Jump	Coffee Grinder
V-Sit	Lame Dog Walk

7. Have them do forward and backward rolls and headstands. Discuss the fact that these must be symmetrical movements to be correctly done.

Line

CONCEPT: A line is a path made by a moving point. It can be varied by changings its:

width	direction
length	position
amount of curvature	texture

Level: Beginning.

Materials: Lines painted or taped on the floor and road cones or other types of markers.

Activities

1. Let us explore how your body parts can form different types of lines (Fig. 19-8).

Hold up one finger. Now hold up all four fingers. How did that change the line you created? (Changed its width.)

Hold up just your hand. Now hold up your forearm and your hand. Now hold up your whole arm and hand. How did these changes effect the line you created? (Changed its length.)

Hold your finger up very straight. Now bend it just a little. Bend it a little more. How are you changing the line? (Amount of curvature.) Now let's try that with your arm. Hold your arm straight out in front of you. Now bend your

wrist and elbow just a little bit. Now bend it a little more. See how the line formed by your arm becomes more curved?

Point to a spot on the ceiling directly above you. What is the direction of the line formed by your arm and hand? (Up.) Now point to the floor beside your foot. What direction is this? (Down.) Point to the wall directly in front of you. What direction is this? (Forward.) Point to the wall beside you. What is the direction of your arm line? (Sideward.) Point to the wall behind you. Name that direction. (Backward.) Point to a corner of the room where the walls and ceiling meet. Now what is the direction of your arm line? (Diagonal or diagonally upward.)

2. Now let us explore how your whole body can form different kinds of lines.

Stand up with your arms straight overhead so that your body forms a narrow line.

Slowly bend backward so that your body forms a curved line.

Make your body line as long as you can. Now make it as short as possible.

Arrange your body parts so that some part of you is a line in a forward direction and another part of you is a line going backward.

Make some body part into a diagonally upward line and another part into a diagonally downward line.

Lie down. Make a straight line with one leg and a diagonal line with the other.

When you were lying down, how did the position of your body line change?

3. Let us move through space, making different kinds of lines.

a. Have the children walk along a straight line painted on the floor, placing one foot directly in front of the other. (If there are no painted lines, masking tape can be put down, or jump ropes can be laid out

Fig. 19-9. Creating a straight and wide line by doing a seat walk.

in straight lines.) Ask the children to describe the line created by their footsteps. (Straight and narrow.)

b. Tell the children to do a seat walk along the line by pulling with their heels and scooting with their seats (Fig. 19-9). Ask them to describe the line this created. (Straight and wide.)

c. Put a chair or other obstacle at one end of the room. Challenge the children to run to the chair and back to place. Ask them to describe the line this created. (Changed direction.)

d. Set up road cones as shown in Fig. 19-10 and challenge the children to run around them. Ask them to describe the line their running steps created (Curved line that changed direction.)

e. Tell the students to jump and/or hop along a line. Challenge them to visualize the type of line created by these movements (Broken.)

4. Let us explore the kinds of lines a group of people can create.

a. Have the children stand shoulder to shoulder in a straight line, facing the same direction. Challenge them to describe the line they form. (Straight and narrow.)

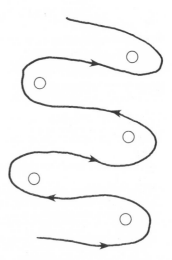

Fig. 19-10. Creating a curved line that changes directions.

b. Tell the children to turn so that they are standing in a straight line one behind the other, with their feet in a sideward stride position. Ask them to describe this line. (Straight and wide.)

c. Have them stand side by side and hold hands. Challenge them to move apart until their arms are stretched out straight. Ask them how this changed the line. (Became longer.)

d. Have the child on one end of the line walk around the room until he meets the child at the other end (Fig. 19-11). Ask him to describe this line, (Curved.)

e. Instruct the students to skip counter-clockwise in the circle, then turn around and skip clockwise. Ask them how this alters the line. (Curved line changes direction.)

f. Have them form a circle facing the center. Tell the children to walk toward the center of the circle until they are squeezed up very tight together. Ask them to look at the size of the circle. Then have them step backward until the circle is very large. Discuss how the size of the circle changed, and relate this to the length of the line comprising the circle.

g. Ask the children to lie down on their backs end to end so that they create a line that is long and narrow (Fig. 19-12).

h. Have them turn so they are lying side-ways, with their arms and legs extended sideward so their line is long and wide.

i. Tell them to make a narrow shape with their bodies and lie down very close to-gether so that their line is short and wide.

j. Challenge the students to describe how they changed the position of the line when they changed from standing to lying down. (From vertical to horizon-tal.)

k. Ask the children to form the line de-scribed in g. Then tell them to bend their knees. Discuss how this changes the texture of their line. (See Fig. 19-13.)

l. Have them turn over and lie face down, then change the texture of their line by bending their knees and stretching their arms overhead on the floor (Fig. 19-14).

m. Instruct the students to support their weight on their hands and knees. Dis-cuss how the texture of this line con-trasts with the lines created in k and l.

CONCEPT: Lines may be used to create repetition, opposition, and transition.

Level: Intermediate.

Subconcepts: (1) Repetition means the same kind of line is repeated. (2) Opposition means one line has a position opposite that of another. (3) Transition means a line leads from one line to another line that has an opposite position.

Materials: None.

Activities

1. Count the children off by twos. Have the "ones" assume the position shown in Fig. 19-12 and the "twos" assume the position in Fig. 19-13. Point out how the line thus formed in Fig. 19-15 by the ones is repeated and so is the line formed by the twos.

Fig. 19-11. Changing a straight "people" line into a curved line.

Fig. 19-12. Creating a long and narrow line.

Fig. 19-13. Changing the texture of the line.

Fig. 19-14. Changing the texture by changing the body positions.

Fig. 19-15. Exploring the concept of repetition.

Fig. 19-16. Repeating the line of every third person.

Fig. 19-17. Combining opposition and repetition. **A,** Assuming vertical and horizontal body positions. **B,** Being long and short.

2. Count the children off by threes. Have the "ones" lie as shown in Fig. 19-12, the "twos" as in Fig. 19-14, and have the "threes" assume the position described in no. 4m (Fig. 19-16). Point out how the lines are now repeated by every third person.

3. Have the children pair off and explore the concept of opposition. One partner forms one type of line with his body and the other forms the opposite type of line. These contrasting types of lines are as follows:

Length—short versus long
Width—wide versus narrow

Position—vertical versus horizontal
Amount of curvature—straight versus curved
Direction—forward versus backward
Texture—smooth versus bumpy

4. Instruct the children to explore ways of combining opposition and repetition. Achieve this by having two or more pairs of children join together and form one line. For example, one child can assume a vertical body position and another a horizontal position (Fig. 19-17, *A*). Or one may be long and the other short (Fig. 19-17, *B*), or one high and one low.

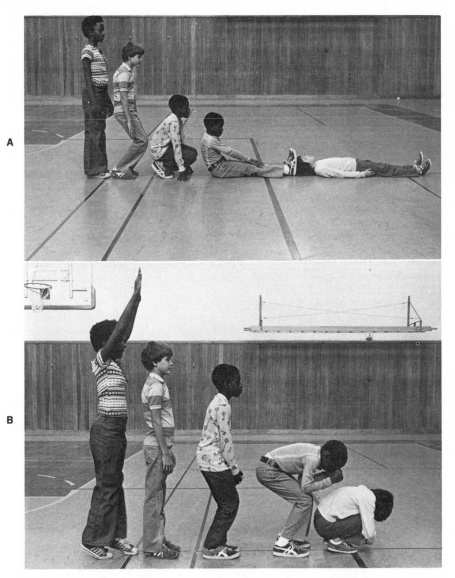

Fig. 19-18. Making a transition. **A,** From vertical to horizontal. **B,** From long to short.

5. Divide the class into groups containing 4 or 5 children. Challenge them to explore the concept of a line making a transition between two opposite lines. For example, the child on one end of the line is standing up and the child on the other end is lying down. The other 3 children assume the positions shown in Fig. 19-18, *A*; that is, they make a transition from a vertical to a horizontal position. Another example is shown in Fig. 19-18, *B;* the children make a transition between the opposites long and short.

CONCEPT: Different kinds of lines stimulate different feelings, and these feelings can be translated into movements that have different qualities, such as the following:

Vertical	Tall, long, stretchy
Horizontal	Quiet, calm
Diagonal	Sudden, dynamic
Broken	Staccato, jerky
Curved	Sustained, flowing
Wide	Strong, slow
Narrow	Sudden, fast

Level: Intermediate.
Materials: None.
Activities
1. Guide the children's exploration of the feeling states evoked by the different types of lines listed.
2. Have the children pair off. Challenge them to create a movement sequence in which the partners execute movements stimulated by contrasting lines. Require them to relate the movements so that one follows the other.
3. Challenge the students to have a nonverbal conversation in which partners communicate with movements stimulated by the same kind of lines. Then have them progress to conversing nonverbally by following their partner's statements with movements stimulated by a different type of line.
4. Have each pair develop a nonverbal line conversation that tells a story.

Shape

CONCEPT: When lines are connected they create shapes.

Level: Beginning.
Subconcepts: (1) We can connect lines to create shapes that are straight, angular, or curved. (2) We can alter the shape we create by moving the lines.
Materials: Road cones or other objects to be used as markers, beanbags, elastic or rubber bands cut from tractor inner tubes (see also materials needed for nos. 16 to 21).
Activities
1. Have the children hold hands and line up in two parallel lines facing each other. Then tell the children on both ends of both lines to move toward each other and hold hands. Challenge the children to make their lines curved. Discuss how this action changed their straight lines into a circle with a round shape.
2. Tell the children to count off consecutively around the circle. Divide the total number by 4. Have the children drop hands and square off with each of the groups forming one side of the square.
3. Instruct two of the adjacent sides of the square to stay where they are and the other two sides to form a straight line facing the angle of the remaining sides so that the group forms a triangle. Discuss how changing the lines changed the shape they created.
4. Set up road cones as shown in Fig. 19-19. Have the children run on a diagonal line

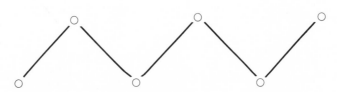

Fig. 19-19. Creating a zigzag shape by combining diagonal lines.

from one to the next. Ask them to describe the shape they created by combining diagonal lines.

5. Set up another row of road cones, as shown in Fig. 19-20. Have 2 children begin running at points *A* and *B* and continue to the end. Let the other children follow. Discuss how this action creates diamond shapes.

6. Have the children sit on the floor and draw imaginary shapes with their heels.

7. Have the children move a beanbag on the floor, creating different shapes. Challenge them to use body parts other than their hands to move the beanbag; for example, they might use their elbow, foot, or knee.

8. Set up a road cone at each end of the room. Challenge the children to move between these two points by the most direct route (a straight line) and by an indirect route. Compare the shape of their pathways in these two situations.

9. In the areas of the country where it snows, many of the activities in nos. 1 to 8 can be adapted to moving outdoors after a fresh snowfall. Also, building snow figures is an excellent way for the children to observe how their rolling the snowballs translates lines into a sphere and how the spheres become the form of a snow figures.

10. On sunny days the children can explore shadow shapes. Have them work in partners or groups of 3. One or 2 create shadow shapes and the other child describes them. The activity may be varied by having the child creating the shadow hold the position while the partner moves around it by running, hopping, skipping, or walking. Another variation consists of one child tracing his partner's shadow shape on a large sheet of paper.

11. Have the children work with a partner, combining their body lines to create a statue with a certain shape.

12. Tell them to create a stationary statute that begins moving while retaining its original shape.

13. Have child 1 make a shape and hold it while child 2 makes a shape that relates to that created by child 1. Continue adding children until approximately 10 students are forming a statue that creates a group shape.

14. Give each child a large rubber band cut from a tractor inner tube. Tell the children to hold and stretch the band with different body parts, creating different shapes.

15. Have the students experience and observe the different shapes created by their body lines when they are lying, sitting, standing, and running.

16. Instruct one partner to study the body shape of the other and make a model of this shape by using pipe cleaners.

17. Have the children make interesting body shapes and then make a picture of their shape by pasting soda straws on black paper.

18. Tell the children to create a shape with construction toys and then imitate this shape with their bodies.

19. Have the children create body shapes like those of natural objects such as shells, stones, leaves, trees, bushes, the moon, animals, and birds.

20. Ask them to create body shapes resembling commercially made objects such as a

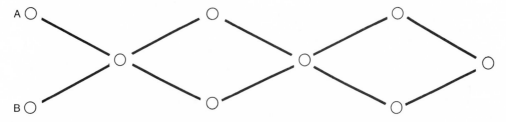

Fig. 19-20. Combining zigzag shapes to form diamond shapes.

wheel, telephone pole, chair, cup, railroad track, and highway signs.

21. Make a set of task cards cut in different geometrical shapes. Arrange teaching stations as shown in Fig. 19-21. The children move from station to station, performing the prescribed tasks at each one. Play music while the students are at the station. Instruct them to move on to the next station each time the music stops. (This creates a smooth flow of traffic and eliminates bunching up at any one station.) The following examples illustrate the types of tasks that can be printed on the cards.

Circle

a. Can you move around the large circle on the floor while doing the following?
   • Running
   • Skipping
   • Hopping
b. Can you move around the large circle on a low level?
c. Can you move around the circle taking very small steps? Very big steps?

d. Can you jump into one of the small circles and make your body into a curved shape on a low level? Jump into another small circle and make a twisted shape on a high level? Jump into one more circle and make a narrow shape on a low level?
e. Go to the mat. Make your body into a curved shape and do forward and backward rolls.
f. Can you return your circle task card to the large circle?

Square

a. Can you slide around the square?
b. Can you jump into the square from one side and out another side?
c. Can you leap diagonally across the square from one corner to the other?
d. Can you sit on one of the small squares and form a square with the following?
   • Your hands
   • Your arms
   • Three body parts
   • Your whole body
e. Can you do a Crab Walk while moving around the small squares?
f. Can you return your square task card to the large square?

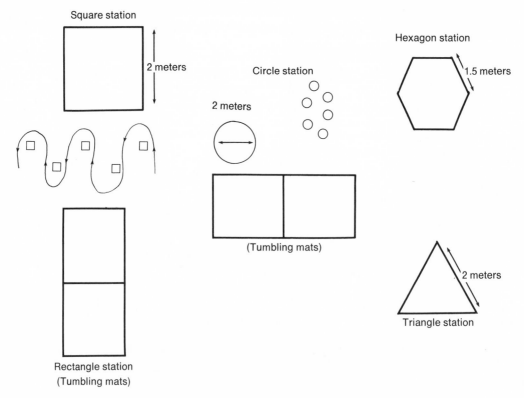

Fig. 19-21. Exploring the concepts of geometrical shapes in a circuit.

Rectangle

a. Can you hold your task card so that it is tall and skinny? Can you make this shape with your body? Can you hold the task card so that it is short and wide? Can you make a similar shape with your body?

b. Can you move around the rectangle formed by the mats by walking forward on a low level along the long side and backward on a high level along the short side?

c. Can you do a Log Roll from one end of the rectangle to the other end?

d. Can you sit in the rectangle and do a Turk Stand?

e. Can you see any other rectangles in the room? Are there any you can move through? Are there any you can move around?

f. Can you return your task care to the rectangle formed by the tumbling mats?

Triangle

a. Can you trace the shape of your card by moving your foot around the floor? Can you trace this shape with some other body part?

b. Can you form the shape of your card with the following?
   • Two body parts
   • Three body parts
   • Your whole body

c. Can you hop around the large triangle on the floor? Can you move around it on three body parts?

d. Can you move in a different direction along each side of the triangle?

e. Can you make a triangular shape with your body and sit in a balanced position while maintaining that shape?

f. Can you return your triangle task card to the large triangle?

Hexagon

a. Can you gallop around the large hexagon on the floor?

b. Can you dribble the playground ball around the outside of the hexagon?

c. Can you form a hexagon with your hands and arms?

d. Can you move around the hexagon, making your body into a different shape each time you come to an angle?

e. Can you form a hexagon with the rope? Can you hop into and out of your rope shape?

f. Can you return your hexagon task card inside the large hexagon?

Form

CONCEPT: The five basic forms are cube, sphere, cylinder, cone, and pyramid.

Level: Intermediate.

Materials: Pictures of the five basic forms and an object shaped like each of them.

Activities

1. Show the children pictures or models of the five basic forms (Fig. 19-22). Discuss the similarities and differences.

2. Divide the class into groups containing 4 children. Assign each group one of the basic forms and challenge them to create a group shape that resembles their form.

3. Challenge each group to think of an object shaped like their basic form and to describe the feeling states this object evokes. Have them move in a way that expresses these feeling states, for example:

Cube	Ice cube
Sphere	Playground ball
Cylinder	Tunnel
Cone	Pine cone
Pyramid	The Egyptian pyramids

Fig. 19-22. The five basic forms.

4. Instruct the children to experiment to find out how objects with each of the basic forms move when they are pushed. They can observe that the cube and pyramid fall over, whereas the sphere rolls. The cylinder and cone roll when placed on their side. However, the cylinder rolls in a straight line, but the cone rolls in a circular pathway.

Color

CONCEPT: We play with objects that differ in color.

Level: Beginning.

Materials: Different colored yarn balls or beanbags.

Activities: Have the children sit in a circle. Place different-colored yarn balls (or beanbags or nerf balls) in the center of the circle. Roll or toss one of the balls to one of the children, calling out the color of the ball as you toss it. The child calls out the color when he catches the ball. Then he passes it around the circle, and each child names the color as he receives the ball.

Variations

1. Repeat the previous activity, having one of the children go to the center, select a color, and toss that ball to a child in the circle.
2. Do not call out the color when you toss the ball. Rather, challenge the child who receives it to name its color and then toss it back to you.
3. If the child correctly identifies the color, he comes to the center, selects another color, and tosses that ball to one of the children.
4. When the child in the circle catches the ball, have all the children call out the name of its color.
5. After the children have called out the name of the color, have them all jump up and walk around in a circle counterclockwise, chanting the color name as they walk.

CONCEPT: There are three primary colors—red, yellow, and blue.

Level: Beginning.

Materials: Red, yellow, and blue yarn and construction paper.

Activities: Divide the class into three groups. Tie a piece of red yarn around the right wrists

of one group, yellow yarn around the right wrists of the second group, and blue yarn around the right wrists of the remaining group. Have the children scatter around the room. They walk around the room while you play music. When the music stops, call out the name of one primary color. Everyone with that color on his wrist sits down.

Two variations are that you call out two colors or call out "All primary colors."

Color chase. Have the children stand or sit in a circle. Go around the circle, giving each child the name of one of the primary colors. (If the children have difficulty remembering their color, you can give them a small piece of colored construction paper.) One child is chosen to be "It." Walking around the circle, It touches each child and names one of the primary colors. If he touches a child named the color he says, this child chases It around the circle, attempting to tag him. If It is tagged, he joins the circle, and the other person becomes It. A variation is that instead of attempting to tag, the 2 children run in opposite directions, racing to see who can get back to the empty space first. The person who loses becomes It.

CONCEPT: The secondary colors are orange, purple, and green.

Level: Beginning.

Materials: A poster and old clothing the color of each primary and secondary color.

Activities

1. Have the children scatter around the room. Review the names of the primary colors and name the secondary colors. Place posters around the room, as shown in Fig. 19-23. Have the children play follow the leader while moving from one color to another. The leader calls out the name of the color they are moving toward; for example, "We are walking to orange."

Variations

a. Have the leader call out different locomotor movements as follows:

Jump to purple.	Slide to orange.
Hop to blue.	Gallop to green.
Skip to yellow.	

b. Each time the children arrive at a color,

have them make a circle around it and move counterclockwise while chanting the name of the color and whether it is a primary or secondary color; for example, "Primary yellow" or "Secondary green."

2. Have the children identify the articles of clothing they are wearing that are either primary or secondary colors. Then tell them to move through space as you play music. When the music stops, you name a color and they must touch the article of clothing that color. The clothing may be their own or someone else's.

3. Divide the class into teams containing no more than 5 members. Have the teams line up in relay formation. Place in front of each team a pile of clothing containing articles that are the six primary and secondary colors (e.g., caps, gloves, socks, scarves, sweaters, shirts). Call out one color and have the child at the front of the line run to the pile and get the article of clothing that color. Variations are that the children put on the article of clothing before returning to their line or that the activity is made into a relay race.

CONCEPT: Secondary colors are formed by combining the primary colors.

Level: Intermediate.

Subconcepts: (1) Purple is created by combining red and blue. (2) Green is created by combining blue and yellow. (3) Orange is created by combining yellow and red.

Materials: Posters and cards the color of each primary and secondary color.

Activities

1. Place posters around the room, as shown in Fig. 19-24. The children follow the leader, moving from one primary color to another and then forming a circle around the secondary color that is created by combining those two primary colors. For example, they walk from blue to yellow, then make a circle around green.

Variations

a. Have the children skip around the secondary color.

b. Vary the locomotor movements the children execute between the colors; for example, "Hop between blue and red or jump from red to yellow and slide around orange."

c. Move the posters closer together so that the class as a whole can make a circle around the two primary colors and the secondary color they create. Then have the children execute one of the locomotor movements in a counterclockwise direc-

RED

Orange   Purple

YELLOW   BLUE

Green

Fig. 19-23. Primary and secondary colors.

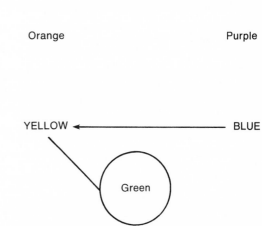

Fig. 19-24. Combining primary colors to form secondary colors.

tion around the three colors (i.e., ''Skip around blue, yellow, and green'' or ''Gallop around blue, purple, and yellow.''

2. At one end of the room place piles of cards (or circles) made from the primary colors. Divide the class into teams containing no more than 5 children. Have the teams line up in relay formation, facing the piles of cards. Call out one of the secondary colors. The first child in each line runs to the pile of cards and picks up the two primary colors that are combined to create the secondary color you named. Continue until each child has had a turn.

Variations

a. Place green, purple, and orange cards in the piles. Call out the names of two primary colors, requiring the children to retrieve the correct secondary color.
b. Place cards of all six primary and secondary colors in the piles. Call out either ''primary'' or ''secondary,'' requiring the children to retrieve any color in the category you name.
c. Print the names of different locomotor movements on the colored cards. Require the children to execute that movement while they are returning to their team.
d. Make the activity into a race.

CONCEPT: Different colors stimulate different feelings and we can express these feelings in the way we move.

Level: Intermediate.

Subconcepts: (1) Red, orange, and yellow are warm colors. (2) Blue, purple, and green are cool colors. (3) Pink, yellow, and white are light colors. (4) Brown and black are dark colors. (5) Bright colors and dull colors differ in intensity.

Materials: Samples of all the colors just listed.

Activities

1. Show the children the colors red, orange, and yellow. Talk about the fact that these are warm colors. Ask them to name objects that are these colors, such as the sun, a flame, or something that is ''red hot.'' Have them think about how they feel when they are warm and when they are hot. Have them show these feelings by moving their bodies. Challenge them to create a movement sequence that tells a story about being warm or being hot.

2. Show them the colors blue, purple, and green. Discuss the fact that these are cool colors because they are associated with things that make us feel cool, such as trees that make shade, grass, lakes or the ocean. Have the children think about how they feel when they sit in the shade or go swimming on a hot day. Have them move like these experiences make them feel.

3. Show the class the colors pink, yellow, and white. Ask them how these light colors make them feel. Then show them brown and black. Ask them to describe the contrasting feelings the light and dark colors evoke. Have them move to express light and dark colors. Have them create movement stories that express these feelings.

4. Show the children dull colors such as gray and brown. Have them describe the feelings these stimulate. Then show them bright colors such as orange and red. Discuss the fact that these colors differ in intensity. Have them move in response to colors with different intensities. Suggest that they create strong, expansive movements in response to high-intensity colors and low, heavy, slow movements in response to low-intensity colors.

Design and composition

CONCEPT: Designs are created by combining and organizing lines, colors, shapes, and textures.

Materials: Samples of designs in materials, paintings and photographs, yarn, beanbags and the equipment suggested in nos. 6e, 6f, 7, and 8.

Activities

1. Have the students use their bodies to reproduce designs in cloth, paintings, or photographs. Discuss the characteristics of the subjects they reproduce, such as the type of lines used, shapes they create, spacing, and focal point (Fig. 19-25).

2. Use different kinds of physical activities

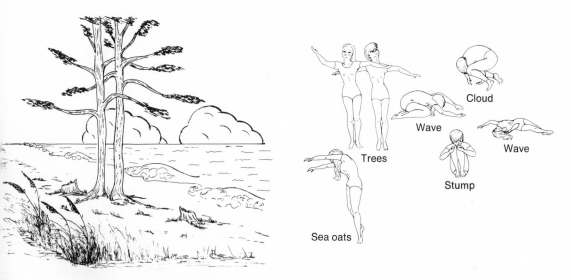

Fig. 19-25. Reproducing the design of a drawing by creating the shapes with the body.

as themes for pictures the children create. Examples are how they stand and move in games, or dances, or while executing specific skills or stunts. The children may create the pictures from memory or by using other children as models.

3. Have the students record in an art form the pathways created in space by their moving bodies. They may record either the floor patterns created by their feet or the spatial patterns created by their body or body parts.

4. Instruct the children to use their bodies to create lines and shapes that they observe in their environment. These may be either natural or commercially made and static or dynamic.

5. Challenge the children to create pieces of sculpture with their bodies. They can do this alone, in pairs, and in groups of 3 or more.

6. Have the children create pieces of sculpture by using their bodies in combination with various materials. Examples follow:

a. Give each child a piece of yarn (or elastic) approximately 2.5 meters long. Challenge them to create designs by moving their body lines and the yarn lines in different directions and on different levels while creating a variety of shapes.

b. Have 2 children tie their pieces of yarn together. Challenge them to explore ways of creating interesting designs with their bodies and the yarn.

c. Give a group of 5 children a ball of yarn (or a long piece of elastic). Have each child grasp the yarn at a different place and hold it in a way that creates an interesting design in combination with the other 4 children (Fig. 19-26).

d. Give the students beanbags and challenge them to arrange these in an interesting design. Then have them make a shape with their body and/or a piece of yarn that connects or relates to the beanbag design.

e. Give the group a cage ball or a tumbling mat. Challenge them to use this object as the focal point of their design, arranging their bodies around it to create a three-dimensional design.

f. Give them a pile of tires and challenge them to create a design or a piece of sculpture in which at least two of their body parts are touching at least two of the tires.

7. Challenge the children to create designs

Fig. 19-26. Creating a design with a piece of elastic.

Fig. 19-27. Creating a design with small equipment.

with the following combinations of equipment:

- Balls of various sizes, colors, and textures
- Hoops and wands
- Wands and jump ropes
- Balance beams and hoops
- Parallel bars and badminton net
- Jungle gym and jump ropes
- Wands, hoops, ball, and beanbags

8. Let the children arrange and build a playground structure. Encourage them to think

Fig. 19-28. A piece of sculpture that is a play environment.

of it as a piece of sculpture that is a play environment. Have them use a variety of materials and complete the project by painting designs on it (Fig. 19-28).

9. Let the children mount their movement drawings and paintings and them combine them into a book.

10. Let them paint a movement mural for the halls, gym, or classroom.

11. Show them a picture of a frieze, such as one that decorated the buildings of ancient Greece. Have them create a frieze portraying movement themes.

12. Have them make a mobile by using shapes or pictures depicting various movement activities (Fig. 19-29).

13. Have them sketch the design of play structures or equipment on the playground.

14. Let them make posters, costumes, or scenery to complement their study of other cultures such as the Indians, Greeks, Africans, Japanese, English.

Movement-related art materials. The following lists suggest numerous ways in which the child's moving body or objects associated with movement activities can be combined to provide child-centered learning experiences.

Art materials

Ropes, string, yarn,   Mats
  elastic, and streamers   Nets

Fig. 19-29. Movement mobile.

Art materials — cont'd

Balls of different sizes, shapes, colors, and textures
Beanbags
Hoops
Wands and hockey sticks
Tires
Inner tubes

Paddles, rackets, and bats
Portable gymnastic equipment
Parachute
Jungle gym
Playground designs and markings

Art mediums

Drawings
Paintings
Prints
Posters
Models
Sculptures

Murals
Friezes
Mobiles
Structures
Collages
Costumes and scenery

Art themes

Locomotor and nonlocomotor skills
Manipulative and basic sports skills
Movement activities such as games and dances
Swimming, gymnastics, and stunts

Lines formed by body parts and body actions
Shapes created by the body and by adding objects and equipment
Colors associated with movement activities and movement responses.

SELECTED REFERENCES FOR PART FIVE

CHAPTER 18
Recordings

The following list contains suggestions for recordings and compositions that can be used to stimulate children to actively explore various elements of music. In the first part of the list the names and addresses of the leading education record companies are given, followed by a description of the recordings suitable for the combined study of music and movement. The second part of the list contains suggestions for classical compositions and contemporary music containing movement themes.

EDUCATIONAL RECORD SOURCES

Bowmar Publishing Corporation, Order Department, P.O. Box 3623, Glendale, Calif. 91201.

The Bowmar Orchestral Library consists of three series, including lesson guides and theme charts emphasizing creative responses. The content ranges from *Fairy Tales in Music* in series 1 to *United States History in Music and Symphonies* in series 3.

The three records of ethnic dances include "Dances of Hawaii," "Mexican Folk Dances," and "Canadian Folk Dances." Each record is accompanied by a fully illustrated booklet giving directions for dances for grades 4 to 7.

The records in Bowmar's singing games and folk dance series contain a variety of favorite songs and dances.

Educational Activities, Inc., P.O. Box 392, Freeport, N.Y. 11520.

This company distrubutes the most complete line of new records developed for use in physical education. Some of these follow:

"Dances Around The World," no. AR 572. A new collection of ethnic folk dances for upper elementary grades.

"Soul Folk Dances," no. AR 573. A new approach to dance, using current rhythm, rhyme, and jargon.

"African Heritage Dances," no. AR 36. Dances performed without partners to the exciting rhythms of the big drums.

Authentic Afro-Rhythms," no. K 6060. Rhythms from Africa, Cuba, Haiti, Brazil, Trinidad, and Puerto Rico; manual gives historical background and suggestions for use.

"Ethnic Dances of Black People Around the World,"

no. K 9040. Teaches about the differences in black cultures through their rhythms and dance.

"Singing Games from Ghana," no. MM 103. Contains the music of several tribes recorded in Ghana.

"Rhythmic Parachute Play," no. KEA 6020. Music and narration for executing popular parachute routines.

"Parachute Activities With Folk Dance Music," no. KEA 9090. Folk dances modified for use with the parachute.

"Clap, Snap and Tap," no. AR 48. Music to stimulate an awareness of body parts and a basic rhythmical beat.

"Rhythm Stick Activities," no. AR 55. Contemporary music adapted for this purpose.

"Simplified Lummi Stick Activities," no. K 2015. Designed for primary grades; music from sources such as the *Wizard of Oz* and *Sesame Street* provides accompaniment for simple movement patterns.

"Contemporary Tinkling Activities," no. KEA 8095. Uses contemporary 4/4 meter music to extend the learning experiences of this popular dance.

Folkraft Records, 10 Fenwick St., Newark, N.J. 07114

Distributes an extensive line of folk and square dance albums and singles.

Folkways Records, 701 Seventh Ave., New York, N.Y. 10036

Distributes a variety of recordings for use with children.

Hoctor Dance Records, Inc., Waldwick, N.J. 07463

Distributes a variety of dance recordings.

Macdonald & Evans, Ltd. (Educational Recordings), 8 John St., London WCIN 2HY England.

Distributes a series of "Listen and Move" records developed especially for creative movement activities; includes percussion, voice, and piano accompaniment.

RCA Records, Educational Department, 1133 Avenue of the Americas, New York, N.Y. 10036

Distributes an excellent graded series entitled *The World of Folk Dances.* Also produce a series of square dance records, the *Dance-a-Story* series, the *Adventures in Music for Elementary Schools* series, and a variety of other quality recordings.

CLASSICAL MUSIC WITH MOVEMENT THEMES FOR CHILDREN

Beethoven: *Symphony No. 6* (third, fourth, fifth movements)
Berlioz: *Symphony Fantastique*
Bizet: *L'Arlesienne Suites 1 and 2* and *Children's Games*
Copeland: *Rodeo, Appalachian Spring,* and *Grand Canyon Suite*
Debussy: *Nocturne for Orchestra Fetes* and *Children's Corner Suite*
Dvorak: *New World Symphony*
Grieg: *Peer Gynt Suites 1 and 2*
Grofé: *Grand Canyon Suite*
Handel: *Water Music*
Haydn: *Symphony No. 94* (third movement)
Khachaturian: *Gayne Ballet Suite No. 1* (Saber Dance)
Liszt: *Hungarian Rhapsodies Nos. 1 to 7*
Moussorgsky: *Pictures of an Exhibition* and *Night on Bald Mountain*
Prokofiev: *Peter and the Wolf*
Ravel: *Bolero*
Rimsky-Korsakov: *Scheherazade*
Rossini: *Overture to Barber of Seville* and *Overture to William Tell*
Saint-Saëns: *Carnival of the Animals* and *Danse Macabre*
Schumann: *Traumerei*
Sibelius: *The Swan of Tuonela, Finlandia,* and *Valse Triste*
Strauss: *Emperer Waltz* and *Annen Polka*
Stravinsky: *Rites of Spring* and *Firebird Suite*
Tchaikowsky: *Nutcracker Suite* and *Sleeping Beauty*
Vivaldi: *The Seasons*
Wagner: *Ride of the Valkyries*

POPULAR MUSIC

"Talk to the Animals"
"Raindrops Keep Falling on My Head"
"Do, Re, Mi"
"My Favorite Things"
"Winter Wonderland"
"Twelve Days of Christmas"
"Zorba's Dance" (from the movie *Zorba the Greek*)
Contemporary music using the sitar, the moog synthesizer, and other electronic instruments.

Books

American Alliance for Health, Physical Education, and Recreation: Children's Dance, Washington, D.C., 1973, The Association.
Aronoff, Frances Webber: Music and young children, New York, 1969, Holt, Rhinehart & Winston, Inc.
Baylor, Byrd: Sometimes I dance mountains, New York, 1973, Charles Scribner's Sons.
Barlin, Anne, and Barlin, Paul: The art of learning through movement, Los Angeles, 1971, The Ward Ritchie Press.
Butler, Francelia, and Haley, Gail E.: The skip rope book, New York, 1963, The Dial Press, Inc.
Cherry, Clare: Creative movement for the developing child, rev. ed., Belmont, Calif., 1971, Fearon Publishers/Lear Siegler, Inc.

Dimondstein, Geraldine: Children dance in the classroom, New York, 1971, The Macmillan Co.
Doll, Edna, and Nelson, Mary Jarman: Rhythms today, Morristown, N.J., 1965, Silver Burdett Co.
Fleming, Gladys Andrews: Creative rhythmic movement: boys' and girls' dancing, ed. 2, Englewood Cliffs, N.J., 1976, Prentice-Hall, Inc.
Gates, Alice A.: A new look at movement—a dancer's view, Minneapolis, 1968, Burgess Publishing Co.
Harris, Jane A., Pittman, Anne, and Waler, Marlys S.: Dance a while, ed. 4, Minneapolis, 1968, Burgess Publishing Co.
Joyce, Mary: First steps in teaching creative dance, Palo Alto, Calif., 1973, National Press Books.
Keetman, Gunild: Elementaria: first acquaintances with Orff-Schulwerk, London, 1970. Scott & Co., LTD.
Kraus, Richard: Folk dancing, New York, 1962, The Macmillan Co.
Kraus, Richard: Folk and square dances and singing games for the elementary school, Englewood Cliffs, N.J., 1966, Prentice-Hall, Inc.
Laban, Rudolf: Modern educational dance, ed. 2, London, 1963, MacDonald & Evans, Ltd., Publishers.
Landis, Beth, and Carder, Polly: The eclectic curriculum in American music education: contributions of Dalcroze, Kodaly and Orff, Music Educators' National Conference, Washington, D.C., 1972.
Lidster, Miriam, and Tamburini, Dorothy: Folk dance progressions, Belmont, Calif., 1965, Wadsworth Publishing Co.
Monsour, Sally, Cohen, Marilyn C., and Lindell, Patricia E.: Rhythm in music and dance for children, Belmont, Calif., 1966, Wadsworth Publishing Co.
Murray, Ruth Lovel: Dance in elementary education, ed. 3, New York, 1975, Harper & Row, Publishers.
Nye, Robert E., and Nye, Vernice T.: Music in the elementary school: an activities approach to music methods and materials, ed. 3, Englewood Cliffs, N.J., 1970. Prentice-Hall, Inc.
Russell, Joan: Creative movement and dance for children, rev. ed., Boston, 1975 Plays Inc.
Saffran, Rosanna B.: Creative rhythms, New York, 1963, Holt, Rinehart & Winston, Inc.
Shaw, Lloyd: Cowboy dances, Caldwell, Idaho, 1949, The Caxton Printers, Ltd.
Skolnik, Pater L.: Jump rope, New York, 1974, Workman Publishing Co., Inc.
Stecher, Miriam, and McElheny, Hugh: Joy and learning through music and movement improvisations, New York, 1972, Macmillan Publishing Co.
Vick, Marie, and Cox, Rosann McLaughlin: A collection of dances for children, Minneapolis, 1970, Burges Publishing Co.
Wiener, Jack, and Lidstone, John: Creative movement for children: a dance program for the classroom, New York, 1969, Van Nostrand Rineholdt Co.
Wilt, Miriam E.: Creativity in the elementary school. New York, 1959, Appleton-Century-Crofts, Inc.
Winters, Shirley J.: Creative rhythmic movement for chil-

dren of elementary school age, Dubuque, Iowa, 1975, William C. Brown Co., Publishers.

Many of the major textbook publishers produce a series of graded music texts for elementary school children. These contain excellent songs and music activities. You should consult your local music supervisor or the music education department of a college or library to obtain information concerning the availability of these most useful reference materials.

CHAPTER 19

Gaitskell, Charles D., and Hurwitz, Al.: Children and their art: methods for the elementary school, ed. 3, New York, 1975, Harcourt Brace Jovanovich, Inc.

Linderman, Earl W., and Herberholz, Donald: Developing artistic and perceptual awareness, ed. 2, Dubuque, Iowa, 1969, William C. Brown Co.

Sanderson, Gretchen S.: Elementary teacher's art ideas desk book, West Nyack, N.Y., 1974, Parker Publishing Co., Inc.

Sawyer, John R., and deFrancesco, Italo L.: Elementary school art for classroom teachers, New York, 1971, Harper & Row, Publishers.

Wachowiak, Frank, and Ramsay, Theodore: Emphasis art: a qualitative art program for the elementary school. Scranton, 1971, Intext Educational Publishers.

STUNTS THAT CAN BE USED IN ACTIVE LEARNING SITUATIONS

When using stunts as a learning medium, their educational potential should be fully utilized. This infers that the children must be challenged to execute the stunts in a way that will correctly exercise their bodies. It also implies that the activity will promote development of body, spatial, and kinesthetic awareness. In the following descriptions of the stunts, the educational value of each is specified. Their contribution to the development in the psychomotor domain is given in parentheses, and the cognitive concepts are italicized. Children naturally enjoy stunts, and if the "fun" element is maintained, the children will be positively reinforced in the affective domain.

For the students to be a worthwhile educational experience, two factors should receive your special attention. The first consideration is that the stunt should be age appropriate. This is the reason certain stunts have been suggested for children on particular learning levels. Stunts that do not interest or challenge the children are not a worthwhile use of their school time. The second consideration is that the stunt should be executed correctly. The activity does not challenge the child or contribute to his physical development unless it is performed in the correct manner.

In some instances, variations of the stunts have been suggested to enable you to use these in other types of learning situations if you wish.

Alligator Walk (laterality)

Alligator Walk.

While lying *face down* on the floor, the children *pull* themselves *forward* by alternately *bending* the arm and leg on the right and then the left side of the body (unilateral movements).

Variations

1. Have the children move the right arm and left leg forward at the same time, then bend the left arm and right leg simultaneously (cross-lateral movements).
2. Have them move *backward* by using unilateral movements of the arms and legs.
3. Have them move *backward* by using cross-lateral movements.

Bear Walk (coordination)

Bear Walk.

With *hands* and *feet touching* the floor, the children move *forward* and *backward* by using unilateral and then cross-lateral movements.

Camel Walk (coordination)

Camel Walk.

The children *bend forward* from the *waist* and place *hands behind back,* making a *fist* with one hand and *holding* the fist with the other hand so that it looks like the hump on the camel's back. The children walk *slowly forward* and *backward, bobbing head* and *chest upward* and *downward* on each step.

Chinese Getup (coordination)

Chinese Getup.

The partners stand with *backs together* and *elbows hooked*. They *press against each other's* back as they slowly lower the body to a sitting position. They stand up by *pushing against their partner's back*. (Emphasize the need to keep their feet flat on the floor so that they have a *secure base of support*. When this stunt is reviewed with older children, discuss how *friction between the feet and the floor is essential for the force of the leg muscles to be transferred to the back rather than being absorbed by the sliding of the feet*).

Coffee Grinder (arm and shoulder strength)

Coffee Grinder.

The children place the right hand on the floor and assume a slanting body position, with their right side facing the floor. They keep arms and legs straight while they walk their feet around in a *circular pathway*.

Crab Walk (coordination and strengthening of abdominal muscles)

The *hands* and *feet support* the body weight, with the *back facing* the floor. The *body* must be kept *straight* as the children walk forward,

Crab Walk.

backward, and sideward. (The abdominal muscles must contract to hold the body in a straight position. Thus correctly executing this stunt assists in strengthening these muscles. When the hips are allowed to sag, the abdominal muscles relax, and the value of the stunt as a conditioning activity is lost.)

Variation: The children move forward and backward by using unilateral movements.

Dragon Walk (coordination)

Dragon Walk.

This stunt is the same as the bear walk, except that the head is tilted upward as far as possible.

Duck Walk (balance, coordination, and flexibility)

The children assume a squat position, with *knees apart*. The *hands* are placed *under* the *armpits* so that the arms form imaginary wings. This position is maintained while the feet swing *outward* and *forward* on each step and the wings flap *up* and *down*.

Duck Walk (variation).

Variation: An alternative position is to clasp both hands behind the seat and move them from side to side to imitate the movement of the duck's tail.

Egg Sit (balance)

The children sit on the floor with legs extended. They grasp their ankles and *rock backward until their body is in a balanced position.*
Variation: They let go of their ankles and hold the body in a balanced V-Sit position. (See the illustration on p. 313.)

Elephant Walk (coordination)

Elephant Walk.

The children *bend forward* from the waist, with arms hanging *downward* and *hands clasped together* to simulate the elephant's trunk. On each step the arms *swing* rhythmically from *side* to *side* as the children walk forward and then backward.

Forward Roll (coordination, flexibility, and agility)

Forward Roll.

The children assume a squat position, with hands on the mat just ahead (6 to 10 inches) of the toes. They form the body into a *curled shape,* with chin touching the chest. The body is kept *round like a ball* as the children *rock* forward and *roll* over and then roll forward to a sitting position.
Teaching suggestions:
1. Some children may need to cross their feet in midair to keep the legs flexed throughout the roll. However, as soon as possible they

should execute the roll with legs together so that they will be in a position to stand up and go into a series of rolls.
2. Emphasize landing on the base of the neck and the shoulders and keeping the back rounded as they roll. You may need to demonstrate how a ball rolls and point out that it rolls easily because it is round. This will give the children a concrete image to which they can relate their own movement.
3. If assistance is needed, kneel beside the child, placing one of your hands on the back of the neck and your other hand on the back of the thighs. As the child tips over, press down on the back of the neck and gently lift the legs.
4. On the intermediate level discuss the following movement principles:
   a. When the body is rolling forward, backward, or sideward, it *rotates around its center of gravity.*
   b. *As the center of gravity passes outside the base of support, the body is off balance,* and *if it is in a rounded shape, it will roll.*
   c. When rolling to a standing position, the body must roll forward far enough so that *the center of gravity is over the center of the base* (the feet).

Frog Jump (coordination)

Frog Jump.

The children assume a squat position, with arms *between* the knees and hands on the floor slightly *in front* of the feet. The child *pushes off* from the feet by *quickly* extending the legs and *lands on all fours.* (Point out the similarity between the Frog Jump and the Rabbit Jump described on p. 312. Discuss the fact that the Frog Jump is more difficult because *the body does not have a base of support during the suspension phase of the movement* and also because the child must coordinate the movement of the arms and legs so that the hands and feet *land on the floor at the same time*).

Inch (Measuring) Worm (coordination and flexibility)

Inch (Measuring) Worm.

The children assume a front-leaning position. They walk their feet forward, keeping the *legs straight* and *hands stationary*. They bring the feet as close as possible to the hands. They then *walk* the *hands forward* while the *feet* remain *stationary*.

Jack-in-the-Box (leg strength and endurance)

Jack-in-the-Box.

The children assume a squat position, with the *hands on the* floor outside their legs. They suddenly jump *straight up as high as possible*. They *land* on the *balls* of their feet and *flex* ankles, knees, and hips to return to the starting position.

Jackknife (coordination and flexibility)

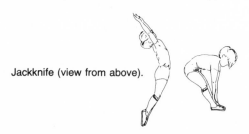

Jackknife (view from above).

The children lie down with their *side* on the floor and arms *stretched overhead*. They *arch* their body backward, moving the head, arms, and feet as far back as possible without flexing knees or elbows. Keeping arms and legs straight, they bring the head forward and flex the trunk and hips until their fingertips touch the lower legs. Then they open their body and return to an arched position. They continue alternately *opening* and *closing* the knife. Then they turn over and repeat on the other side.

Kangaroo Jump (balance)

Kangaroo Jump.

The children stand with *knees* slightly *bent* and *arms folded* over the *chest*. They *jump forward* and *upward,* landing on the balls of their feet and flexing hips, knees, and ankles.

Variation: From a squat position (balance and leg strength) the children jump forward and backward while maintaining the squat position and keeping the arms folded over the chest. Compare this Kangaroo Jump with the one just described and discuss the fact that it is more difficult to jump in a squat position because *it is harder to maintain balance* and because *the force for the jump must be exerted without the legs being fully extended.*

Knee Dip (balance and leg strength)

Knee Dip.

The children stand on a mat. They lift the right leg backward and grasp the right ankle with the left hand. They *flex* the left knee and *bend* downward until the right knee touches the mat. Then they *extend* the left leg and return to a standing position.

Lame Dog Walk (balance)

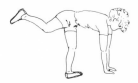

Lame Dog Walk.

The body weight is *supported* on the *hands* and *feet*. One leg is *lifted* from the floor and extended *upward* and *backward*. The children then walk forward on *both hands* and *one foot*.
Variations
1. The children walk backward.
2. The children elevate one hand and walk on *both feet* and *one hand*.

Log Roll (coordination and trunk strength)

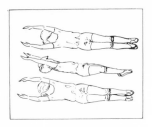

Log Roll.

The children lie on their back on one end of a mat, with arms overhead and body making a *narrow shape*. They turn their body over and over in a *sideward direction* by *twisting* the shoulders and hips in the direction they wish to turn and roll to the end of the mat and back.

One-Legged Squat (balance and leg strength)

One-Legged Squat.

The children stand on a mat with arms extended sideward. They lift one leg forward and upward while *flexing* the knee of the supporting leg. They squat as low as possible. Then they *extend* the supporting leg and return to a standing position.
Variation: The children cross their arms over chest while executing the stunt.

Rabbit Jump (coordination)

Rabbit Jump.

The children assume a squat position, with *hands* on the floor *between* the *knees*. They move *forward* by placing *both hands* in *front* of the body, then *pushing* off with *both feet* and bringing the feet *up* to the hands.
Variation: When the children have mastered the forward *jump,* the stunt may be varied by having them reverse the movements and *jump backward.*

Rooster Hop (dynamic balance)

Rooster Hop.

The children stand on one foot with hands placed under the armpits. They hop forward and backward in *straight, curved,* and *angular pathways.*
Variation: The children stand on the right foot with the left foot behind the body. They grasp the left foot with the right hand and hop while using the right arm to assist in maintaining balance.

Seal Walk (abdominal, arm, and shoulder strength)

Seal Walk.

The children assume a front-leaning position, with *feet together* and *toes pointing backward*. The hands are flat on the floor. They *walk* their *hands forward* while *dragging* their feet. The body should remain *straight* with the head *up*.

Skin the Snake (flexibility and coordination)

Skin the Snake.

A group of children (5 to 8) stand *one behind the other with their legs in a sideward stride position*. They bend over, reaching their right hand backward between their legs and their left hand forward to grasp the hands of the children in back and in front of them. On a signal the last child in the line lies down and the line moves backward over him. As each child reaches the end of the line he lies down. This continues until all the children are lying down. Then the last one to lie down stands up and walks forward, straddling the line. As he moves forward, he pulls up the next child, and this continues until everyone is in the starting position.

Squat Jump (leg strength and endurance)

Squat Jump.

From a standing position, the children crouch down and place the palms of both hands on the floor. They quickly extend the legs while raising the arms, springing into the air, and keeping the legs straight. Their feet should be 4 inches off the floor at the top of the jump. They flex knees, hips, and ankles when landing and return to the starting position.

Stork Stand (balance)

The children stand on *one foot* in a balanced position.

Stork Stand (variations).

Variations
1. The children *fold arms* over the *chest*.
2. The children place the *sole* of the free *foot* against the *calf* of the supporting leg.

Turk Stand (balance and coordination)

Turk Stand.

The children sit cross-legged with arms folded over the chest. They incline their body forward so that the *center of gravity is over the feet*. They thrust the body upward by extending the legs. They *keep the head and chest in a forward position to maintain balance while rising*.

V Sit (balance)

V-Sit (variation of Egg Sit).

This is a variation of the Egg Sit on p. 310.

Wicket Walk (coordination and flexibility)

Wicket Walk.

The children *bend forward* and *grasp* the legs just *above* the ankles. While maintaining this position they walk forward and backward, taking short steps. (When this stunt is used with older children, they should grasp their ankles and walk without bending their knees.)

Windmill (flexibility)

Windmill.

The children stand in a sideward stride position with arms straight out to the side. They twist at the waist while bending over to touch the right hand to the left toe. Repeat to the opposite side. The knees should not be bent.

Wring the Dishrag (coordination and flexibility)

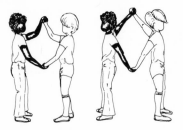

Wring the Dish Rag.

Partners *face each other* with *both hands joined*. Thye *lift one pair* of clasped hands and walk *under* the raised arms while turning *back to back*. They raise the other pair of arms and walk under, returning to a *face-to-face* position.

INDEX

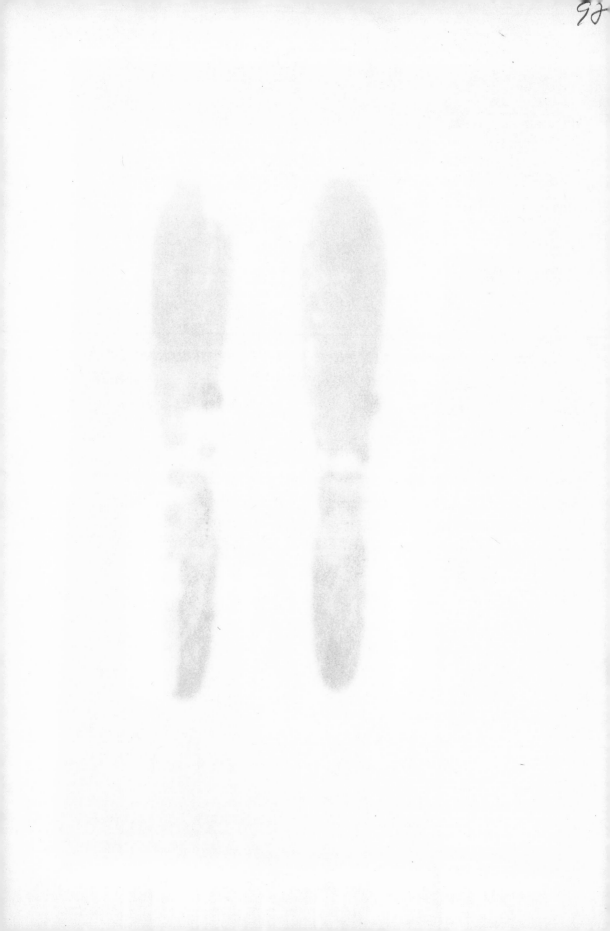